*The Victoria Cross
at Sea*

The Victoria Cross at Sea

John Winton

LONDON
MICHAEL JOSEPH

First published in Great Britain by
Michael Joseph Limited
52 Bedford Square
London WC1B 3EF
1978

ISBN 0 7181 1701 8

Typeset by Granada Graphics Ltd., and
printed and bound by Redwood Burn,
Trowbridge and Esher

Contents

Edward Unwin COMMANDER HMS *River Clyde*, Gallipoli 25.4.1915

George Leslie Drewry MIDSHIPMAN RNR HMS *River Clyde* Gallipoli 25.4.1915

Wilfred St Aubyn Malleson MIDSHIPMAN HMS *River Clyde* Gallipoli 25.4.1915

William Charles Williams ABLE SEAMAN HMS *River Clyde* Gallipoli 25.4.1915

George McKenzie Samson SEAMAN RNR HMS *River Clyde* Gallipoli 25.4.1915

Arthur Walderne St Clair Tisdall SUB-LIEUTENANT RNVR *Anson Battalion RN Division* Gallipoli 25.4.1915

Walter Richard Parker LANCE-CORPORAL RMLI Gallipoli 30.4-1.5.1915

Edward Courtney Boyle LIEUTENANT COMMANDER HMS/M E.14 Dardanelles 27.4-18.5.1915

Martin Eric Nasmith LIEUTENANT COMMANDER HMS/M E.11 Dardanelles 19.5.1915

Reginald Alexander John Warneford FLIGHT SUB-LIEUTENANT No.1 Sq. RNAS Belgium 16.6.1915

Frederick Daniel Parslow LIEUTENANT RNR HMT *Anglo Californian* Atlantic 4.7.1915

Edgar Christopher Cookson LIEUTENANT COMMANDER HMS *Comet* Kut-el-Amara 28.9.1915

Richard Bell Davies SQUADRON COMMANDER No. 3 Sq. RNAS Bulgaria 19.11.1915

Humphrey Osbaldeston Brooke Firman LIEUTENANT ss *Julnar* Kut-el-Amara 24.4.1916

Charles Henry Cowley LIEUTENANT COMMANDER RNVR ss *Julnar* Kut-el-Amara 24.4.1916

Edward Barry Stewart Bingham COMMANDER HMS *Nestor* Jutland 31.5.1916

John Travers Cornwell BOY 1ST CLASS HMS *Chester* Jutland 31.5.1916

Loftus William Jones COMMANDER HMS *Shark* Jutland 31.5.1916

Francis John William Harvey MAJOR RMLI HMS *Lion* Jutland 31.5.1916

Gordon Campbell COMMANDER HMS *Q.5* Atlantic 17.2.1917

Ronald Niel Stuart LIEUTENANT RNR HMS *Pargust* Atlantic 7.6.1917

William Williams SEAMAN RNR HMS *Pargust* Atlantic 7.6.1917

Charles George Bonner LIEUTENANT RNR HMS *Dunraven* Atlantic 8.8.1917

Ernest Herbert Pitcher PETTY OFFICER HMS *Dunraven* Atlantic 8.8.1917

Archibald Bisset Smith LIEUTENANT RNR ss *Otaki* Atlantic 10.3.1917

Frederick William Lumsden MAJOR RMA France 3.4.1917

William Edward Sanders LIEUTENANT RNR HMS *Prize* Atlantic 30.4.1917

Joseph Watt SKIPPER RNR HM Drifter *Gowan Lea* Otranto Straits 15.5.1917

Thomas Crisp SKIPPER RNR HM Smack *Nelson* North Sea 14.8.1917

John Henry Carless ORDINARY SEAMAN HMS *Caledon* Heligoland 17.11.1917

Geoffrey Saxton White LIEUTENANT COMMANDER HMS/M E.14 Dardanelles 28.1.1918

Alfred Francis Blakeney Carpenter COMMANDER HMS *Vindictive* Zeebrugge 23.4.1918

Norman Augustus Finch SERGEANT RMA HMS *Vindictive* Zeebrugge 23.4.1918

Arthur Leyland Harrison LIEUTENANT COMMANDER HMS *Vindictive* Zeebrugge 23.4.1918

Edward Bamford CAPTAIN RMLI HMS *Vindictive* Zeebrugge 23.4.1918

Albert Edward McKenzie ABLE SEAMAN HMS *Vindictive* Zeebrugge 23.4.1918

George Nicholson Bradford LIEUTENANT COMMANDER HMS *Iris II* Zeebrugge 23.4.1918

Richard Douglas Sandford LIEUTENANT HMS/M C.3 Zeebrugge 23.4.1918

Percy Thompson Dean LIEUTENANT RNVR HM *Motor Launch 282* Zeebrugge 23.4.1918

Victor Alexander Charles Crutchley LIEUTENANT HMS *Vindictive* Ostend 9/10.5.1918

Geoffrey Heneage Drummond LIEUTENANT COMMANDER RNVR HM *Motor Launch 254* Ostend 9/10.5.1918

Roland Richard Louis Bourke LIEUTENANT COMMANDER RNVR HM *Motor Launch 276* Ostend 9/10.5.1918

Name	Rank	Unit/Ship	Location	Date
Harold Auten	LIEUTENANT RNR	HMS *Stock Force*	English Channel	30.7.1918
Daniel Marcus William Beak	COMMANDER RNVR	*Drake Battalion* RN Division	France	21.8.-4.9.1918
George Prowse	CHIEF PETTY OFFICER RNVR	*Drake Battalion* RN Division	France	2.9.1918
Augustine Willington Shelton Agar	LIEUTENANT	HM CMB 4	Kronstadt	16-17.6.1919
Claude Congreve Dobson	COMMANDER	HM CMB 31	Kronstadt	18.8.1919
Gordon Charles Steele	LIEUTENANT	HM CMB 88	Kronstadt	18.8.1919
Gerard Broadmead Roope	LIEUTENANT COMMANDER	HMS *Glowworm*	Norwegian Sea	8.4.1940
Bernard Armitage Warburton Warburton-Lee	CAPTAIN	HMS *Hardy*	Narvik	10.4.1940
Richard Been Stannard	LIEUTENANT RNR	HMS *Arab*	Namsos	28.4.-2.5.1940
Jack Foreman Mantle	LEADING SEAMAN	HMS *Foylebank*	Portland	4.7.1940
Edward Stephen Fogarty Fegen	CAPTAIN	HMS *Jervis Bay*	Atlantic	5.11.1940
Kenneth Campbell	FLYING OFFICER RAFVR	22 Squadron Coastal Command	Brest	6.4.1941
Alfred Edward Sephton	PETTY OFFICER	HMS *Coventry*	Crete	18.5.1941
Malcolm David Wanklyn	LIEUTENANT COMMANDER	HM/M *Upholder*	Mediterranean	24.5.1941
Eugene Esmonde	LIEUTENANT COMMANDER	825 Squadron Fleet Air Arm	Dover Straits	12.2.1942 " "
Thomas Wilkinson	LIEUTENANT RNR	HMS *Li Wo*	Java Sea	14.2.1942
Peter Scawen Watkinson Roberts	LIEUTENANT	HM/M *Thrasher*	Mediterranean	16.2.1942
Thomas William Gould	PETTY OFFICER	HM/M *Thrasher*	Mediterranean	16.2.1942
Robert Edward Dudley Ryder	COMMANDER	HM MGB 314	St Nazaire	27.3.42
Stephen Halden Beattie	LIEUTENANT COMMANDER	HMS *Campbeltown*	St Nazaire	27.3.1942
William Alfred Savage	ABLE SEAMAN	HM MGB 314	St Nazaire	27.3.1942
Anthony Cecil Capel Miers	COMMANDER	HM/M *Torbay*	Corfu Roads	4.3.1942
Frederick Thornton Peters	CAPTAIN	HMS *Walney*	Oran Harbour	8.11.1942
Robert St Vincent Sherbrooke	CAPTAIN	HMS *Onslow*	Barents Sea	31.12.1942
John Wallace Linton	COMMANDER	HM/M *Turbulent*	Mediterranean	4/5.1943
Lloyd Allan Trigg	FLYING OFFICER RNZAF	200 Squadron Air HQ West Africa	Atlantic	11.8.1943 " " "
Donald Cameron	LIEUTENANT RNR	HMS/MX.7	Kaafjord	22.9.1943
Basil Charles Godfrey Place	LIEUTENANT	HMS/MX.6	Kaafjord	22.9.1943
David Ernest Hornell	FLIGHT LIEUTENANT	RCAF No. 162 Sq. Coast Command	Atlantic	25.6.1944 "
John Alexander Cruickshank	FLYING OFFICER RAFVR	210 Squadron Coastal Command	Arctic	17.7.1944 "
Thomas Peck Hunter	CORPORAL	43 Commando	Italy	2.4.1945 " " "
Ian Edward Fraser	LIEUTENANT RNR	HMS/MXE.3	Johore Straits	31.7.1945
James Joseph Magennis	LEADING SEAMAN	HMS/MXE.3	Johore Straits	31.7.1945
Robert Hampton Gray	LIEUTENANT RCNVR	1841 Squadron Fleet Air Arm	Japan	9.8.1945 " "

Naval VCs 18!

List of Illustrations

10

Preface

Most of this book is true. Some of it is very probably true, and part of it is possibly myth. The Victoria Cross is still so emotive, romantic and controversial a subject that it is often difficult to separate fact from fiction. The Victoria Cross still arouses fierce national, county, local and family pride, generates frantic newspaper correspondence, sets regiment against regiment, unit against unit. Everybody is an expert on the Victoria Cross. Everybody has met a winner, or is related to, or has served with, or lived next door to, a winner, or has been to a school, won a prize, drunk beer in a pub, named after a winner. In such a heated atmosphere, hearsay can quickly become received fact, speculation can become tradition, and gossip become gospel. An unchecked newspaper cutting, with wholly imaginary information, can become accepted research material for generations afterwards. The awards themselves depended in the first place upon eyewitness accounts, notoriously subjective sources, especially when clouded by the fog of war. Some citations, especially the earlier ones, are so laconic as to be almost meaningless. No citation can be taken as entirely reliable, and one at least (Halliday's) was actually challenged later by the winner himself! Any writer on the Victoria Cross has ultimately to strike his own balance of truth.

The Victoria Cross was Queen Victoria's own idea. She realised, as the preamble to the original Royal Warrant of 29th January 1856 stated, that there was no way of 'adequately rewarding the individual gallant services either of officers of the lower grades in Our naval and military service, or of warrant and petty officers, seaman and marines in Our navy, and non-commissioned officers and soldiers in Our army.' In other words, from its inception the Victoria Cross was a medal for everyman. All persons were on a perfectly equal footing – 'neither rank, nor long service, nor wounds, nor any other circumstance or condition whatsoever, save the merit of conspicuous bravery' would qualify a man for the VC. It was not an Order of Chivalry like the Garter or the Bath. It was open to any officer or man who served the Queen in the presence of the enemy and then performed some signal act of valour or devotion to his country. The Queen desired that the medal should be 'highly prized and eagerly sought after'.

Victoria took a keen interest in every aspect of the Cross and personally supervised the design, the wording, the size and the material of which it was made. On 5th January 1856, a communication from Windsor Castle to the then Secretary of State for War said: "The Queen returns the drawings for the "Victoria Cross".

She has marked the one she approves of with an X; she thinks, however, that it might be a trifle smaller. The motto would be better "For Valour" than "For the Brave", as this would lead to the inference that only those are deemed brave who have got the Victoria Cross.'

The design the Queen chose was a cross patté, very similar to and often called a Maltese Cross, measuring 1⅖ inches square, attached by a 'V' to a bar on which is a sprig of laurel. Obverse, a Royal Crown surmounted by a lion with a scroll underneath bearing the words 'For Valour'. Reverse, plain, with an indented circle in the centre, with the date or dates of the act of valour inscribed in it. The name of the winner is engraved along the back of the bar.

The cross itself was not of silver or gold, or encrusted with precious stones, but intrinsically almost worthless, being cast in bronze cut from the cascables (the round pieces at the end of the barrels) of Russian cannons captured at Sebastopol in the Crimean War. The medals, traditionally always made by the same firm, Hancocks, hung on ribbon 1½ inches wide, red for Army winners, blue for the Navy. When the RAF became a separate organisation on 1st April 1918 it was realised there was no really suitable colour for RAF VCs, and, as the two colours had always been somewhat unnecessary, it was decided by King George V that thenceforth all VCs would have the red ribbon. The last naval VC to have a blue ribbon was Prowse (gazetted on 30th October 1918) and the first to have a red ribbon was Beak (gazetted 15th November 1918). When the ribbon only was worn on a tunic, a miniature cross was set in its centre. For a bar, a second miniature cross was worn. No naval VC has won a Bar.

VC winners, except those of commissioned rank, received a pension of £10 a year, with £5 extra for a Bar. This sum remained unchanged for over a century until 1959, when Mr Harold Macmillan, replying to a question from Sir John Smyth VC, MP, announced that all VC winners, of whatever rank or rating, would receive a pension of £100 a year, tax free.

The first awards, made retrospective to cover the Russian War just ended, appeared in the London Gazette of 24th February 1857. There were 85 names in that first list, 27 of them from the Navy and the Marines. The Queen herself held the first Investiture of VCs, in Hyde Park on Friday, 26th June 1857. Of the 62 VCs invested that day, Commanders Raby, Bythesea and Burgoyne, Lieutenants Lucas and Hewett, Warrant Officers Mr Robarts, Mr Kellaway, and Mr Cooper, and Trewavas, Reeves, Curtis and Ingouville, represented the Navy. Lieutenant Dare and Bombardier Wilkinson represented the Marines. The Admiralty sent off the VCs for those naval winners serving abroad so that they could be invested on their foreign stations.

A total of 1,352 VCs have been awarded, including three Bars, to date. Of those, 124 are described in this book. They include all the

Royal and Commonwealth Navy and Marine VCs won on sea, land or in the air, with four Coastal Command VCs.

The first act of gallantry to win a VC was by Mate Lucas, of HMS *Hecla*, in the Baltic on 21st June 1854. The first man to be gazetted was Buckley, because his name was the first alphabetically of the naval officers, who came first because they were in the Senior Service. Likewise, the first man ever to wear a VC was Commander Raby, the senior officer of the Senior Service present at the Hyde Park Investiture. The first VC awarded to a member of the lower deck was won by William Johnstone, who was not a seaman but a stoker and almost certainly not a British citizen, being very probably one of the many Scandinavians recruited into Napier's under-manned Baltic Fleet. His VC was, presumably, sent abroad.

The youngest naval VC was Boy Cornwell, who was sixteen and a half at the Battle of Jutland. But he was not the youngest VC: Hospital Apprentice Arthur Fitzgibbon, of the Indian Medical Establishment, was born on 13th May 1845 and won his VC at the Taku Forts, China, on 21st August 1860, aged fifteen years and three months. However, the Navy has several very young VC winners, such as Midshipmen Mayo and Boyes (both seventeen) and Guy and Malleson (eighteen) when they won their VCs. The oldest naval VC winner was Lieutenant Frederick Parslow RNR, who was born on 14th April 1856 and was in his sixtieth year when he won his posthumous VC in 1915. Captain Peters was fifty-three, Unwin was fifty-one.

The first naval VC of the First World War, though not the first to be gazetted, was won by Commander Ritchie of HMS *Goliath* on 29th November 1914. The first to be gazetted was won by Lieutenant Holbrook, of B.11, on 13th December 1914. Similarly, the first naval VC of the Second World War, though not the first to be gazetted, was won by Lieutenant-Commander Roope of HMS *Glowworm* in action against the *Hipper* on 8th April 1940. The first naval VC to be gazetted was won by Captain Warburton-Lee of HMS *Hardy* at Narvik on 10th April. Captain William Peel, of the Naval Brigade, won his VC for three separate acts of gallantry in the Crimea in 1854 and 1855. Lieutenant Hewett and Midshipman Daniel (another seventeen-year-old) each won their VCs for two separate acts in the Crimea. But none of these awards is considered as a VC and Bar. The first Marine VC was won by Corporal John Prettyjohn of the RMLI, in the Crimea.

After the original Royal Warrant of January 1856 successive Warrants over the years gradually extended the scope of VC awards. In 1859 'Non-Military Persons who, as Volunteers, have borne arms against the mutineers, both at Lucknow and elsewhere, during the late operations in India' were made eligible; in 1867, local forces in New Zealand; in 1881, 'officers and men of Our Auxiliary and Reserve Forces (Naval and Military)'; in 1911, officers, NCOs and

13

men of the Indian Army; and on 22nd May 1920, when Winston Churchill was Secretary of State for War, a major restatement of the VC terms was pronounced, confirming previous warrants and extending eligibility to nursing sisters, and civilians of either sex. Officers of the Mercantile Marine, such as Parslow and Bisset Smith, had been given Honorary RNR rank posthumously, but the 1920 Warrant regularised the position, extending the award to the Merchant Navy. It also, somewhat belatedly, officially recognised the change of ribbon colour..

In 1902, King Edward VII permitted VCs to be delivered to *representatives* of officers and men who had fallen in the war against the Boers. This put posthumous awards on an official basis for the first time. The Hon. Lieutenant Frederick Roberts, son of Lord Roberts VC, had been mortally wounded retaking the guns at Colenso but was afterwards awarded a VC. On several occasions VCs were awarded to men who had died between the act and the award, or to men who had been promised a VC and had then been killed.

The precise definition of 'posthumous' is always open to debate. It is now generally taken to mean an award to a man who was killed in the performance of the act for which he won his VC. The first posthumous naval VC was awarded to Able Seaman W.C. Williams, of the *River Clyde*, at Gallipoli. Latterly, the number of posthumous naval VCs has greatly increased. In the Second World War, for example, eight out of the first ten awards were posthumous, and Wanklyn, the ninth, did not long survive.

Section Fifteen of the original Warrant of 1856 laid down that any VC winner convicted of treason, cowardice, felony or any infamous crime, should forfeit his VC. The first man to suffer that penalty, and the only naval VC ever to forfeit his medal, was Midshipman Daniel, who forfeited his VC on 4th September 1861. His story reads like a Victorian morality play. Although forfeiture is still theoretically possible under Warrant, King George V expressed his distaste for the practice so strongly in 1920 that it is now extremely unlikely to occur. A Victoria Cross is, after all, an award for valour, not a Sunday School prize or a hire-purchase credit rating.

Section Thirteen of the original Warrant authorised a squadron, a ship's company, or a detached body of seamen and marines, not under fifty in number, *when all of them are deemed equally brave and distinguished*, to award VCs by selection: the officers to choose one officer, the petty officers one petty officer, and the seamen or marines two of their number. In 1917, when the Q-ship HMS *Pargust* was awarded a VC, the officers chose Stuart, the First Lieutenant, and the sailors chose Seaman Williams, the gunlayer. Similarly, in another Q-ship, *Dunraven*, Petty Officer Pitcher was selected for the VC, although the VC awarded to Bonner, the First Lieutenant in that ship, was not an elected one. After the Zeebrugge raid in April 1918, Captain Carpenter, Captain Bamford RMLI, Sergeant Finch RMA and Able Seaman McKenzie were all elected to receive their VCs. Those men who took part in the ballot, but who were not successful, later had the fact that their names were in the Zeebrugge VC ballot entered on their official documents. There were no more elected naval or marine VCs after Zeebrugge but in 1942, after a very similar raid on St Nazaire, Lieutenant-Commander Beattie of HMS *Campbeltown* was gazetted for his VC 'in recognition not only of his own valour but also of the unnamed officers and men of a very gallant ship's company, many of whom have not returned'. In the same raid, Able Seaman Savage of MGB 314 was gazetted for his own gallantry and devotion to duty 'but also of the valour shown by many others unnamed, in Motor Launches, Motor Gun Boats and Motor Torpedo Boats who gallantly carried out their duty in entirely exposed positions against enemy fire at close range'. These two citations were, arguably, variations on the old practice of award by ballot.

No naval father and son have both won the VC. Lieutenant Frederick Parslow RNR won the VC and his son, also Frederick, won the DSC in the same action. Skipper Tom Crisp won the VC and his son, also Tom, won a DSM in the same action. Lieutenant-Commander Bradford, of *Iris II*, won a posthumous VC at Zeebrugge, and his brother Lieutenant-Colonel Bradford of the Durham Light Infantry also won a posthumous VC in France in October 1916. (Their mother put obituary notices for them, and her two other sons who also distinguished themselves in battle, in *The Times* every year until her own death in 1951.)

When the Victoria Cross was first instituted, it and the Conspicuous Gallantry Medal, also first instituted in the Crimean War, were the only awards open to the junior officer, warrant officer, sailor or marine, whilst today there is a wide variety of decorations: the VC, DSO, DSC, CGM, DSM, as well as the George Cross and George Medal, and various life-saving medals. Undoubtedly, a proportion of nineteenth-century VC winners would today have been awarded some other medal. There was no major fleet-against-fleet action after Navarino in 1827 and the majority of naval nineteenth-century VCs were won on land. (Chicken won his on horseback, Arthur Knyvet Wilson in hand-to-hand combat against the Sudanese.) A VC won afloat was a rarity - only six before the First World War. In the twentieth century the picture changed completely and it was VCs ashore that became rare.

The VC has also become harder to win. The spontaneous movements of such as Lucas and Harding, in disposing of a live shell, although extremely brave actions in the circumstances, hardly compare with the sustained courage of Sherbrooke in the Barents Sea, or of Place and Cameron in their venture against the *Tirpitz*, or of Wanklyn, Miers and Linton in the submarine campaign of the

Mediterranean. Certain times and places – Lucknow in 1857, the Dardanelles in 1915; certain commanders, such as Beatty; certain raids, such as Zeebrugge and St Nazaire; and certain weapons, such as X-craft submarines, were particularly fortunate for VCs. To act early in a war rather than late was generally more fruitful; one was more likely to win a VC for shooting down the first Zeppelin than the thirty-first. Many VCs were won in an almost traditional (for the Navy and the Marines) penetration of a fortified enemy position: Sebastopol by Sheppard in 1855, Dar-es-Salaam by Ritchie in 1914; the Dardanelles by Holbrook, Boyle and Nasmith in 1915; Corfu Roads by Miers, Oran by Peters, in 1942; Narvik by Warburton-Lee in 1940; Kronstadt by Agar in 1919; Kaafjord by Cameron and Place in 1943; Johore Straits by Fraser and Magennis in 1945. The typically nineteenth-century exploit of rescuing a fallen comrade from the clutches of the enemy – Raby, Taylor and Curtis before the Redan at Sebastopol in June 1855, Hinckley in China in 1862, Odgers in New Zealand in 1860, Mitchell also in New Zealand in 1864 – was replaced in the twentieth century by the self-sacrificing immolation of a whole ship in a hopeless but gallant manner – Roope and *Glowworm*, Cookson and *Comet*, Firman and Cowley in *Julnar*, at Kut, Fegen and *Jervis Bay*, Wilkinson in *Li Wo*.

Many more VCs were awarded to officers, for obvious reasons. An officer had more control over his own destiny, could decide how and for how long his ship was in action, could make up his mind, so to speak, whether or not to be brave, whereas the sailor was carried willy-nilly into action and had to wait on circumstances. Thus, of the four Jutland VCs, three went to officers, of whom two were commanding officers. Of the fourteen submarine VCs, eleven were awarded to submarine captains. All the Fleet Air Arm and Coastal Command VCs were won by officers who were also pilots, or captains of their aircraft.

Such men as Wilson, Salmon, Commerell, Robinson, Miers and Place rose to high rank in the Service. Fraser marketed his VC and his talents as a frogman and became a successful businessman. But a Victoria Cross was no guarantee at all of success later in life. Sullivan and Trewavas committed suicide, as did Boyes after being court-martialled and dismissed the Service for what seems now a boyish escapade – climbing in over a dockyard gate late at night. Boyes went to New Zealand, as Daniel did after his disgrace and died of delirium tremens.

VC winners were as subject to the vicissitudes of life and death as any other men. Boyle, after surviving the dangers of submarine warfare in the Dardanelles and living into his eighties, was knocked down by a lorry crossing the road in Sunningdale, Berkshire and died of his injuries. Cowley was captured by the Turks and almost certainly executed. Lucas left his medals in a train and the VC worn by him was a replica. Mitchell had his VC stolen and, to have his photograph taken, made one out of cardboard. Samson, on his way to a public reception in his home town, was presented by a stranger with a white feather. Tisdall was a published poet. Magennis sold his VC to pay his debts. Ryder was impersonated. Guy became a chicken farmer, and Dobson a librarian in Kent.

VCs came from every kind of family background and from all parts of the United Kingdom and the Commonwealth. Trewavas was a Cornishman, Cruickshank an Aberdonian. Hall was a coloured man, the son of a freed slave, Ingouville a Channel Islander, Seeley an American citizen from New England, Gould a Jew, Johnstone probably a Swede.

It is always tempting, but seldom rewarding, to search for common links between holders of the VC. Do they have some common characteristic? Could you tell a VC by looking at him, before or after his award? It is true that some VCs, such as Peters and Esmonde, had already distinguished themselves in action, winning DSOs or DSCs, and their bearing and general professional conduct made them men to watch. But many thousands of other similar men did not go on to win a VC. It is also true that a surprising number of VCs were superb athletes (all the Zeebrugge winners, for example) and came from large families: Savage was one of a family of twenty-two, Sandford was a seventh son, and Commander Campbell of the Mystery ships called his autobiography *Number Thirteen* because he was the thirteenth in a family of sixteen. Many VCs came from naval and military family backgrounds. Their fathers, grandfathers and great-grandfathers had also served, and in families with such a long tradition of service to the Crown it could be expected that, sooner or later, the man, the moment and the medal would all come together. But, equally, hundreds of thousands of superb athletes, men from large families, and with impeccable naval and military lineage did not win the VC, and some of them indeed behaved with incompetence or cowardice under stress. Clearly, a Victoria Cross, like lightning, could strike anywhere.

Possibly, behaviour under stress is the only common asset shared by all holders of the Victoria Cross. The best description of this temperamental phenomenon, and the best epitaph on a VC, was written by a surgeon RN to *The Times* on 8th December 1915. He was writing, some months before the VC was actually gazetted, about Sub-Lieutenant Tisdall RNVR, who won his VC for gallantry during the terrible carnage at V Beach, Gallipoli, on 25th April 1915. 'I have seen and experienced many things since April 25th,' the surgeon wrote,

...and I have learnt, above all, that true courage is born when a man conquers fear by the power of his will. I do not believe in the man who has never experienced fear. The

17

courageous man is he who can best control his fear. The first thing that Tisdall said laughing to me was, 'I was never in such a funk in my life', and I believed him, for all honest men possess this sense of fear. He, however, possessed more power of self-control, perhaps, than any of us, and his conduct during our stay on V Beach was an inspiration to all of us.

For this book I have made use of some of the papers accumulated by my late mother, Mrs Margaret Pratt, who did research for a book on holders of the VC for many years but who died before starting to write it. I am grateful to Wing-Commander F.J. Carroll and to Miss Rose E. B. Coombs, of the Imperial War Museum, for general discussion on the Victoria Cross and its history, and for help with obtaining pictures. A bibliography on the VC, and the various actions and campaigns in which it was won, is included in this book, but students are recommended also to consult the Ranken material and the extensive files compiled by Canon Lummis MC, over many years - now at the Imperial War Museum. Wherever possible, details of books, articles, tapes and other sources especially relevant to one VC winner, or to a group of winners, are included at the end of their section.

JOHN WINTON

Charles Davis Lucas:
The Baltic, 1854

The earliest act of bravery to win a Victoria Cross was carried out by Charles Davis Lucas, a twenty-year-old Mate (what would now be called a Midshipman) serving in the 6-gun steam paddle sloop HMS *Hecla* with the Baltic Fleet, under Admiral Sir Charles Napier, in the summer of 1854. Napier was a highly popular admiral but he and his fleet had come under public and parliamentary criticism for lack of success against the enemy. The Russians were content to stay in harbour, sheltering inside their coastal fortresses, one of which was at Bomarsund, in the Åland Islands, guarding the entrance to the Gulf of Bothnia.

Although it was not normally good tactics for ships to attack heavily defended shore forts, the Navy had to find targets where they could, and on 21st June Captain W.H. Hall, commanding the *Hecla*, led his ship and the two 16-gun paddle-steamers *Odin* and *Valorous* through the narrow channel to Bomarsund. The ships were fired on by riflemen and artillery from the shore and the main fort batteries also opened fire, somewhat prematurely, betraying their position. All three ships anchored at about nine o'clock that evening (it was midsummer and light in those latitudes until nearly midnight) and began an intermittent but spirited bombardment which lasted until one o'clock the next morning, but without (as it later transpired) doing much lasting damage. Hall was later commended by the King of Sweden but criticised by the Admiralty for using so much ammunition.

At the height of the bombardment, a live shell from an enemy battery landed on *Hecla's* upper-deck, with its fuse still hissing. All hands were ordered to fling themselves flat on the deck, but Lucas, with what Hall called in a letter to Napier next day 'great coolness and presence of mind', ran forward, picked up the shell and tossed it overboard. It exploded with a tremendous roar before it hit the water. Some minor damage was done to the ship's side and two men were slightly hurt but, thanks to Lucas, nobody was killed or seriously wounded. He was immediately promoted to Acting Lieutenant for his bravery, and the Admiralty later confirmed the promotion on Napier's strongest recommendation. Lucas's Cross was gazetted in the first list of 24th February 1857, and he was present at the first Investiture to receive his Cross from Queen Victoria in Hyde Park on 26th June that year.

Lucas was born on 19th February 1834 at Drumargole, Co. Armagh, in Ulster, the son of Davis Lucas, of Clontibert and Drumargole, a member of the Lucas-Scudamore family, formerly of Castleshane, Co. Monaghan. He joined the Navy in 1848 and served in HMS *Vanguard*, then as a Mate in HMS *Fox* in the Burma War of 1852-3, playing a part in the successful captures of Rangoon, Pegu,

Dalla and Prome. He was a Lieutenant in *Dauntless*, and among his other ships were *Calcutta*, *Powerful*, *Cressy*, *Edinburgh*, *Liffey* and *Indus*. He was promoted Commander on 19th February 1862 and Captain on 25th October 1867. He retired from the Navy on 1st October 1873 and was promoted Rear-Admiral on the retired list on 1st June 1885.

In 1879 he married Frances Russell Hall, the daughter of his old Captain (by then Admiral Sir William Hutcheson Hall KCB, FRS) and of the Hon. Hilare Caroline Byng, daughter of Vice-Admiral Lord Torrington, the 6th Viscount (and of the same family as Admiral Byng, shot for cowardice in 1757). They had three daughters. Lucas lived at Great Culverden, near Tunbridge Wells, and at 48 Phillimore Gardens, Kensington. He was JP for Kent and for Argyllshire. He died on 7th August 1914 at Great Culverden, in his eighty-first year, and was buried at Mereworth, near Maidstone.

John Bythesea and William Johnstone:
The Baltic, 1854

The Navy had no regular terms of service nor formal means of recruiting when the Crimean War broke out, and Napier had great difficulty in manning his Baltic Fleet. At one point the First Lord advised him to try and 'pick up' some Norwegians, and in June 1854 the paddle-steamer *Porcupine* actually went to Stockholm to enlist Swedes who wanted to join. One of them could well have been the first man on the lower-deck to win the Victoria Cross. William Johnstone, the first bluejacket VC, was not a seaman but a stoker, and he was almost certainly not a British national.

The exploit which won Victoria Crosses for Lieutenant John Bythesea and Stoker William Johnstone reads like something from a boys' adventure story. On 7th August 1854, Captain Hastings Yelverton, commanding the 47-gun screw frigate HMS *Arrogant*, paid a formal call on Admiral Napier. He came back saying that the Admiral had told him that important despatches from the Czar were being landed at Wardo Island and forwarded to Bomarsund. The Admiral was surprised that nobody had sufficient enterprise to 'stop this kind of thing'.

Lieutenant Bythesea was officer on watch on deck and when relieved he went down to the ship's office to ask whether anybody on board spoke Swedish. He was told that Johnstone was a native of the country. Bythesea proposed that he and Johnstone land and intercept the Czar's despatches. Yelverton protested that two men were not enough, but he was persuaded that a larger party would attract unwelcome attention.

Bythesea and Johnstone rowed themselves ashore to a small, remote bay on Wardo Island on 9th August. At a near-by farm they were well received by the farmer, whose horses had recently been commandeered by the Russians and who was anxious to assist in any way he could. He said that the despatches were so valuable that the Russians had repaired nine miles of road to make their passage easier. While the farmer and his daughter sheltered them, on one occasion concealing them from a Russian search-party by dressing them as local peasants, Bythesea and Johnstone spent two nights reconnoitring the coastline in a small boat, returning before dawn.

On 12th August the farmer said that the despatches were due, and that night Bythesea and Johnstone hid in ambush beside the road - Bythesea being so close that a Russian actually brushed his sleeve. When the military escort turned back and the five Russians carrying the mails came on by themselves, Bythesea and Johnstone jumped out into the road and challenged them with their pistols (although Mrs Bythesea said much later that only her husband had a pistol, Johnstone being unarmed). Two of the carriers dropped their mail-bags and ran. The other three surrendered, believing themselves to be surrounded by a large force, and were taken down to their own boat, where Bythesea made them row back to *Arrogant*. Just as the party embarked, a Russian patrol came down the road, looking for the mails, but having seen nothing they went away singing, apparently to report that all was well. Both VCs were gazetted in the first list of 24th February 1857.

Not much is known of Johnstone. There was no Stoker William Johnstone in the muster list of *Arrogant* or of any other ship in the Baltic fleet. A Stoker William Johnston was awarded a Baltic Medal and a Crimean medal with Sebastopol and Azov clasps for service in *Wrangler*. There was a Leading Stoker John Johnstone serving in *Arrogant*, who was born in Hanover, Germany. His age was given as thirty-two, he had seven years' service at the time, and one good conduct badge. Possibly he was Bythesea's companion. His name may even have been Johannsen, and anglicised by the ship's clerk. Johnstone was serving abroad at the time of the first Investiture and his medal was sent to the Admiralty for presentation overseas, but there is no record of when, where, or by whom.

Bythesea was present to receive his Cross from the Queen. He had a long naval career, but met with mixed fortunes. He was born on 15th June 1827, the fifth and youngest son of the Reverend George Bythesea, rector and patron of Freshford, Somerset, and he was educated at Grosvenor College, Bath. His elder brothers all served in the Army, but John broke the family tradition and joined the Navy as a First Class Volunteer in 1841. He was promoted Lieutenant on 12th June 1849 and joined *Arrogant* in 1850, rejoining her when she paid off and recommissioned in September 1852. He was noted in the ship's subscription book as having given ten shillings towards the dependants of those drowned in the troopship

Birkenhead. After his VC exploit, Bythesea was appointed Lieutenant in command of the 3-gun *Locust* in the Baltic fleet and was promoted Commander in May 1856.

In March 1858 Bythesea was appointed Captain of the screw steam sloop *Cruizer* on the SE America Station, but when war broke out in China, *Cruizer* served under Admiral Hope and Lord Elgin in operations on the Yangtse, the Peiho forts and Nankin in 1859-60. He was promoted Captain on 15th May 1861 and appointed a member of the Commission to enquire into the state of the defences of Canada. He was invalided home from his next command, the sloop *Archer*, in February 1864. From 1865 to 1867 he was Naval Attaché in Washington. His next command, in May 1867, was the frigate *Phoebe* and he commanded her in the Flying Squadron which went round the world under Admiral Sir Geoffrey Hornby in 1869-70. He paid off *Phoebe* in 1870 and the following year was appointed Captain of the battleship *Lord Clyde*, in the Mediterranean.

The *Lord Clyde* was an awkward ship and accident-prone. Though powered by steam, she believed she was really a pure sailing vessel. In March 1872 the *Lord Clyde* went to the assistance of a steamer aground on the island of Pantelleria, west of Malta, and went hard aground herself, having to be towed off some days later by her sister ship *Lord Warden*. Bythesea and his navigating officer were both court-martialled, dismissed from their ship and severely reprimanded, and never employed at sea again. In November 1874 and for the next six years, Bythesea was Consulting Naval Officer to the Indian Government and was largely responsible for restructuring the Indian Navy. He retired from the Navy on 5th August 1877, and was promoted Rear-Admiral on the retired list. He was awarded the CB in 1877 and CIE the following year.

Bythesea married in 1874, at the fairly advanced age of forty-seven, Fanny Belinda, daughter of Colonel G.N. Prior. They had no children. They lived at 22 Ashburn Place, South Kensington, London SW, where the admiral died on 18th May 1906. He was buried on the 23rd of that month in the cemetery of Bath Abbey. Petty officers from *Victory* formed a guard of honour at his funeral, and his hat, sword and belt were laid on the coffin. He left the surprisingly large estate of £65,853.10s to his widow, who died in August 1926. A memorial to John Bythesea and his four brothers was erected in the church at Freshford.

William Peel:
The Crimea, 1854-5

Captain Sir William Peel VC, KCB was one of the most remarkable men ever to serve in the Navy. He actually won his Victoria Cross three times over, in three separate acts of gallantry during the

22

Crimean War. But for his premature death from smallpox at the age of thirty-three, he would have reached the highest ranks in the Service.

Soon after the Allied landing in the Crimea and the battle of the Alma in September 1854, the British C-in-C, Lord Raglan, asked for the assistance of the Navy. On 1st October, over a thousand bluejackets and officers, with over a thousand marines from the fleet, began to disembark with their guns and equipment at Balaclava. Amongst them were sailors and heavy guns from the 28-gun frigate *Diamond*, under Peel their captain. By the 7th the Naval Brigade had constructed and manned two gun batteries facing Sebastopol, mounting 32-pounder, 68-pounder and Lancaster guns from the ships, dragging them by hand up the hillsides from the harbour. The naval guns took part in the great bombardment of Sebastopol which began on 17th October. The next day, the horses drawing the ammunition wagon for the *Diamond's* Battery refused to face the heavy Russian fire. Volunteers went to clear the wagon and bring up the ammunition. Before the powder could be stowed in the magazine a 42-pounder Russian shell with its fuse burning fell in the middle of the powder-cases and the volunteers unloading them. Hearing the shout of alarm, Peel sprang to the shell, clasped it against his chest and carried it thus until he could throw it over the parapet. The shell burst almost as soon as it left Peel's hands but fortunately nobody was injured.

On 5th November, during the Battle of Inkerman, the Duke of Cambridge with some of his staff and about a hundred men were grouped round the colours of the Grenadier Guards in a place called the Sandbag Battery, which was an emplacement some thirty feet wide with embrasures for two guns. Unknown to them, their retreat had been cut off by the enemy, and two more Russian battalions were advancing from their left. Peel saw what was happening through his field-glasses and made his way in the smoke and mist to warn the Duke's party (one of the Army officers noticed that Peel was wearing 'a tall glazed hat' and was accompanied by his ADC, Midshipman Daniel, riding a pony). Thanks to Peel's warning the Guardsmen made an orderly retreat.

On 18th June 1855, the anniversary of the Battle of Waterloo, the British and French attempted to take by storm the massive fortress of the Redan at Sebastopol. The attacks were not properly co-ordinated, and the Redan was very strongly defended. The attackers, amongst whom there were many of the Naval Brigade with scaling ladders, had to run some way across open ground under heavy fire. There were many casualties amongst the bluejackets, and Peel, who had led the first scaling party to the very foot of the Redan wall, was himself hit and severely wounded in the arm. He was led back, half fainting with loss of blood, by Daniel who, according to Midshipman Evelyn Wood of *Queen*, also Peel's ADC, was the only one of seven naval officers in the assault unwounded. Peel won the Victoria Cross and also recommended both his young midshipmen for the medal but only Daniel was awarded it (Evelyn Wood's VC was won later during the Indian Mutiny, when he had transferred to the Army).

William Peel born on 2nd November 1824 at Great Stanhope Street, Mayfair, the fourth child and third son of Prime Minister Sir Robert Peel and Julia Peel, youngest daughter of Sir John Floyd. According to his father, William decided to join the Navy at the age of three. He went to the Reverend Mr Faithfull's school at Hatfield and then to Harrow (1837-8) before joining the Navy as a Volunteer First Class on 7th April 1838. His first ship was the line of battleship *Princess Charlotte* (104 guns), flagship of Admiral Sir Robert Stopford in the Mediterranean, and he served in her during the Syrian War at the capture of Acre in November 1840. (When he returned he brought home three orange trees for his mother, who was a keen gardener.)

After some time in the royal yacht *William and Mary*, Peel joined *Cambrian* (36 guns), under Captain Henry Chads and served in the China War of 1840-2. He came home in October 1843 and in November went to the gunnery school at HMS *Excellent*, where he passed all his examinations in such a short time (five months, when the normal was fourteen at least) and with such brilliance that Sir Robert Hastings, Captain of *Excellent*, and Sir Charles Napier both publicly commented upon his success. He received his commission as Lieutenant on 13th May 1844, only a week after he passed his last examination, and his father, who was then Prime Minister, felt obliged to assure the House that he had used no influence at all on his son's behalf.

At that period junior officers often signed themselves on to the books of ships so as not to lose time and seniority, and Peel is recorded as being in several ships in 1844 when he was in fact in London enjoying some social life and studying gunnery at Woolwich. He was however in the government steam yacht *Black Eagle* which brought Czar Nicholas on a state visit. Finally he was appointed to *Thalia* (42 guns) on the Pacific Station and went out in the flagship *Collingwood* as a supernumerary. When the *America* (50 guns) was sent north to investigate unrest between American and Canadian settlers in the Oregon Territory, Peel went with her and, with a marine officer and officials of the Hudson Bay Co., carried out the survey to determine the dispute. Peel was sent home early via Mexico to report on the situation.

After two temporary appointments, the steam sloop *Devastation* and the *Constance* (50 guns), Peel was promoted Commander on 27th June 1846, at the age of twenty-one. He was given command of the 12-gun sloop *Daring* on the North American and West Indian Station, where he served under Admiral Sir Francis Austen (Jane's brother) and in February 1848, after British residents in Nicaragua had been molested and their property damaged, took part in a punitive expedition up the San Juan river. *Daring* paid off in October 1848 and Peel was promoted Captain on 10th January 1849. At twenty-five he was the youngest post-captain in the Navy, but because of the political situation (his father was no longer in power) he was then told he could expect some years on half pay.

In January 1850, Peel applied unsuccessfully to be included in the expedition to search for Sir John Franklin. He went to Africa, with the object of examining and bettering the condition of the Negroes. With his Arabic teacher Joseph Churi he set off in August 1851 but, after they had both fallen ill, they returned prematurely. Peel published an account of his experience, *A Ride in the Nubian Desert* in June 1852. His father had died in July 1850 and left him about £25,000 with which he bought a somewhat neglected estate at Sandy in Bedfordshire, where he brought land under cultivation, laid out gardens and walks, and repaired and enlarged the existing house.

After he was wounded at the Redan in June 1855 Peel was sent to the Therapia Hospital, but his wound would not heal and he was invalided home, arriving in August. In September he was given a civic reception by the town of Tamworth, where his brother was MP. That autumn the people of Potton in Bedfordshire asked Peel if he would build a railway to connect their town to the main line at Sandy. The line was opened in June 1857 and the engine named *Shannon* after Peel's ship by his mother. The engine was on display at Didcot GWR station for many years.

Shannon was a new and experimental steam frigate of 51 guns, commissioned in the autumn of 1856, but due to various setbacks she did not sail for the China Station until March 1857. She was at sea in home waters when the first VCs were gazetted, including Peel's in February. *Shannon* was at Singapore when the news of the Indian Mutiny arrived in June 1857. Lord Elgin and his staff embarked in her and sailed for Hong Kong, where they took on detachments of the Marines and the 90th Regiment and arrived at Calcutta in August. Peel at once formed a Naval Brigade of nearly 400 officers and men and ten 8-inch heavy guns from *Shannon*, taking them up the river by steamer to Allahabad.

Under Peel's leadership, the Naval Brigade served with great distinction during the Indian Mutiny. Peel's Jacks, as they were called, were devoted to him. They marched, and fought, and marched again, handling their heavy guns like light field pieces, and enduring heat, short rations, disease and fatigue with courage and humour. Peel was always resourceful and cool under any pressure - on one occasion, while his guns were bombarding, restraining Army officers from going forward with the words, 'One more broadside, please, gentlemen', a remark which, smacking as it did of the sea, amused the army officers very much. He invented a form of armoured vehicle known as 'Peel's rocket cars', and even found time to survey and report on Allahabad's drainage system and make recommendations (none of which were carried out).

Peel had been awarded a CB for his services in the Crimea in July 1855 and in January 1858 he was made KCB, and an ADC to the Queen. During the second relief of Lucknow in March, Peel was badly wounded by a musket-ball in the thigh. The ball had to be cut out of the opposite side of his leg. He was fit enough to travel to Cawnpore, refusing the carriage which had been prepared for him and insisting on going in a *dhoolie* cart like one of his bluejackets. He arrived on 17th April and three days later, while at the house of the Reverend Thomas Moore, he fell sick of fever which the doctors diagnosed as smallpox. Despite the devoted nursing of Mrs Moore he died on 27th April, just after midnight, and was buried at 8 am the same day. There were so few troops in Cawnpore at the time that Mr Moore had difficulty in forming a burial party. Eventually, he recorded, only himself and John Bishop, Peel's steward, followed 'him whom all England will mourn'. W.H. Russell of *The Times* wrote of Peel: 'The greatness of our loss we shall in all probability never know.' A statue in white marble, subscribed for by the Army and carved by Theed, was erected to Peel's memory in the Eden Gardens, Calcutta, to 'commemorate him who was the noblest volunteer of this or any age, who was successful because he was really great and who, dying early, left a reputation without spot, the best inheritance he could leave to his country'. Peel never married and left his estate to his mother for her life and then to his youngest brother, Arthur.

William Nathan Wrighte Hewett:
The Crimea, 1854

On 26th October 1854, the day after the Charge of the Light Brigade at Balaclava, some 4,000 Russians attacked the British right flank before Sebastopol and were decisively routed by the Second Division under Sir de Lacy Evans. During the action the Russians threatened the Right Lancaster Battery which was manned by the Naval Brigade and commanded at that time by Acting Mate William Hewett, of HMS *Beagle*. Through a misunderstanding, an order was passed as from Captain Lushington (who was near by) to Hewett to spike his gun and retreat. Hewett disregarded the order, saying according to Lushington's report 'that such an order never came from Captain Lushington, and he would not do so till it did'. According to Evelyn Wood, Hewett used much stronger language, he shouted: 'Retire? Retire be *damned! Fire!*.'

The nearest Russians were by this time advancing up through the Careenage Ravine and were within 300 yards of Hewett's position and keeping up heavy rifle-fire. He slewed his gun round to the left so that its muzzle was against the parapet and blew the earthworks away with the next round. With a clear arc of fire, he poured a destructive rain of grapeshot upon the Russians who had begun to retreat. Hewett's gun pursued them as they fell back with solid 68-lb shot fired with what Lushington called 'fatal precision'. The soldiers suffered seventy-one casualties during the attack, but the sailors had none. The Russians left the near-by hillside strewn with bodies. For this, and again for his bravery during the battle of Inkerman on 5th November, Lushington mentioned Hewett in his despatches. Hewett's Victoria Cross was gazetted in the first list and he was the fifth man to receive his medal from the Queen's hands at the first Investiture.

William, known as 'Bully', Hewett was promoted Lieutenant and his rank back-dated to the day of his exploit. He was then serving in the 4-gun steam sloop *Beagle*, having landed on 4th October to join the Naval Brigade (and was mustered on the books of *Diamond* from that date). 'Bully' Hewett went on to a distinguished naval career. He was a solid, dependable, conscientious, very competent officer who rose high in the Victorian Navy. He took his chances, went wherever the exigencies of the Service demanded, served faithfully, lived respected and died regretted.

He was born in Brighton on 12th August 1834, the son of William Wrighte Hewett of Berkeley Square, surgeon and physician to William IV. He joined the Navy as a First Class Volunteer on 26th March 1847, aged thirteen, served as a midshipman in the Burmese War in 1851 and was present at the capture of Pegu. He also saw service in China in 1853. He appears to have been slightly wounded in the trenches because he was transferred from *Diamond* to *Wasp* for medical treatment for a couple of days in November. On the 18th of that month he was appointed Acting Lieutenant and Captain of *Beagle* (his confirmation in the rank had to wait until he had passed the necessary examinations, and it was then back-dated) and commanded her in several actions in the Sea of Azov, the Straits of Kertch, off Marienpol and in Maratch Bay, being mentioned again in despatches, before bringing *Beagle* home via Patras and Malta to Portsmouth in 1856.

At Patras, Bully Hewett met his wife-to-be, for in May 1857 he married Jane Emily Blackadder, daughter of Mr J. Wood, late Consul at Patras (they had six children, two of the sons following their father into the Navy). The same year he was confirmed as Lieutenant and appointed to the Royal Yacht *Victoria and Albert*, and was promoted Commander on 13th September 1858. Bully Hewett's career reads like a paradigm of typical Victoria naval names, ships and places: *Viper* in West Africa in 1859, *Rinaldo* in the North

27

American and West Indies in 1861, promotion to Captain on 24th November 1862, *Basilisk* in China in 1865-9, in China again in *Ocean* as Flag Captain in 1870-2, the ironclad *Devastation* in 1873, Commodore and C-in-C West African Station for the Ashanti War 1873-4, the capture of Coomassie, a KCB in March 1874, *Achilles* in the Mediterranean and Sea of Marmara in 1877, promoted Rear-Admiral March 1878, a KCSI in 1882, C-in-C East Indies in *Euryalus* in 1882-5, head of naval operations in the war in Egypt in 1884, mission to King John of Abyssinia in April, promotion to Vice-Admiral, July 1884, C-in-C of the Channel Squadron in 1886, flew his flag in *Northumberland* at the head of the Review line at Spithead, 1887, and, finally, retirement because of ill health in April 1888.

He was a blunt, forthright man who said what he thought and sometimes offended. His Commander in *Ocean* was 'Jackie' Fisher, later Lord Fisher, who wrote that Hewett: 'does try me very much at times. I don't think he means it, but he has the most ungovernable temper.' However, both had their deserts when *Ocean* paid off and the Admiral Superintendent wrote that *Ocean* fulfilled 'the conditions entitling her to be called a British man-of-war in its most comprehensive manner'.

Bully kept his bluff manner and 'naval officer's French' to the end. At a very crowded dance on board his flagship *Northumberland*, he caused something of a sensation amongst the married ladies by urging, *'si tous les dames ancientes voulez* [sic] *aller sur le poop'*.

He died at Haslar Naval Hospital on 13th May 1888, less than a month after retiring. He was buried at Highland Road Cemetery, Portsmouth, and his funeral was a great naval ceremonial occasion, in spite of the heavy rain which fell throughout. The Queen, the Duke of Edinburgh and the Board of Admiralty were represented and among those present were Admirals of the Fleet Sir Henry Keppel and Sir Geoffrey Phipps Hornby, and Admiral Sir John Commerell VC. Bully left a personal estate of £2,765 15s 1d to his widow, who died on 21st September 1910 and was buried with her husband. Two naval sons are also buried in the same grave.

Edward St John Daniel:
The Crimea, 1854-5

Edward St John Daniel's story was a personal tragedy, of a young man whose naval career began with the brightest hopes and highest courage and ended in dismissal with dishonour. He won his Victoria Cross three times over, and forfeited it in disgrace.

He was born at Clifton, near Bristol, of a well-known West Country family on 17th January 1837. He was a good-looking boy, with his fair complexion, light hair and wide-set hazel eyes, when he joined *Victory* as a naval cadet just before his fourteenth birthday in January 1851. He soon saw active service under Captain Granville Loch in the frigate *Winchester* at Pegu and Prome in the Second Burma War in 1852. It was in the swamps and jungles of Burma that he suffered the untreated insect bites and lacerations which led to the chronic leg ulcers which afflicted him for most of his life. As a Midshipman he joined *Diamond* under Captain Peel when she commissioned in 1853, went with Peel to the Crimea and landed with him with the Naval Brigade, becoming one of his two ADCs (the other being Evelyn Wood, of *Queen*).

Daniel was Peel's devoted shadow. He was one of the volunteers who brought up the ammunition wagon under a destructive fire on 18th October, when Peel won his VC. He was by Peel's side at Inkerman throughout that long and dangerous day and everybody remarked on the 'heroic boy' riding on a pony. When Peel was wounded on the glacis of the Redan on 18th June 1855, it was Daniel who tied a tourniquet on his arm and brought him back while exposed to a very heavy Russian fire. For his gallantry on these three occasions Daniel was awarded the Victoria Cross in the first list of 24th February 1857.

When *Diamond* paid off in February 1857, Daniel went with Peel to commission *Shannon* for the East Indies and again landed with him in the Naval Brigade during the Indian Mutiny. After long service and many hardships endured together, Daniel was Peel's most trusted officer and was sent to Cawnpore on a special mission on 16th October 1857, after the Naval Brigade had come up the Ganges to Allahabad.

There were some who were jealous of Daniel. Edmund Verney, Mate in *Shannon's* Naval Brigade, wrote to his father Sir Harry Verney in February 1857, when there was apparently some doubt whether Daniel would sail in *Shannon* after all, that 'I shall be very glad if he does not come out with us, because if he comes, the Captain would be sure to give him any little bit of duty that might end in promotion.' Three days later, Verney was writing that 'Daniel greatly distinguished himself in the Crimean without doubt but I expect is too well aware of it himself.' Verney even hazarded a guess at why Daniel was sent alone on that special mission to Cawnpore: because 'it is whispered that the Captain was very glad of an opportunity of sending him away, because twice already he has come under his notice, when he had drunk too freely.' Again, in June 1858, Verney described 'our midshipman Daniel' as 'such a drunkard that none of us would mess with him'.

Drinking too freely was to blight Daniel's career. Possibly Peel had been a father-figure to him and Peel's death of smallpox in April 1858 deprived him of the psychological support and encouragement he needed so desperately. For a time, things still went well for Daniel. On 13th July 1858, at Gyah in Bengal, *Shannon's* Naval

Brigade held a special parade, while Captain Frances Marten, Peel's successor in command of *Shannon*, formally invested Daniel with his Victoria Cross. In September 1859, Daniel was promoted Lieutenant and appointed to *Mars*. On 24th April 1860, he shook hands with the Queen, who was 'much impressed by him', at a Levée in St James's Palace.

But the shadows were already closing around Daniel. On 24th May 1860, when he was an additional lieutenant in the steam sloop *Wasp*, he was severely reprimanded and 'his conduct was to be reported upon in six months' for being twice absent without leave. On the night of 9th June, when the ship was in the English Channel, he failed to turn out for his middle watch, and was found in his cabin 'in a state of torpor'. He was court-martialled on board *Impregnable* at Devonport on 16th, when he pleaded guilty to the charge of drunkenness, but, in extenuation, told the court of his experiences in the Crimean winter and in the heat and dust of the climate in India. He produced testimonials from past captains and showed the court his Victoria Cross and his other medals (which certainly were an impressive collection: the Indian General Service Medal with Pegu clasp, the Crimea Medal with Sebastopol and Inkerman clasps, the Turkish and Sardinian Crimean medals, the Legion of Honour, the Turkish Order of The Medjidie, 5th Class, and the Mutiny medal with Relief of Lucknow and Lucknow clasps). The court was duly impressed and taking into consideration his gallantry before the enemy, sentenced Daniel 'only to dismissal from the *Wasp*, and to have his named placed at the bottom of the list of lieutenants for the period of two years'. Drunkenness was a very common offence in the Victorian Navy, among officers as well as men, and the use of the word *only* suggests that Daniel was known as a hardened offender and, but for his VC, would have suffered much worse. As he had only been a Lieutenant for some nine months, Daniel had only a little way to fall down the list.

But he was soon to fall much further. After a time on half-pay he was appointed Lieutenant to the steam vessel *Victor Emanuel*, in the Mediterranean, in January 1861. On 21st June he was placed under arrest for what his Captain described in a letter to the Admiral as 'taking indecent liberties with four of the Subordinate Officers'. On 26th the ship proceeded under steam to join Rear-Admiral Dacres at Corfu, where Daniel would clearly have to face another court martial. This time, he could not endure it. At about 10 pm on the night of 27th, the Master at Arms found that he was missing from the ship. A Sergeant RMA and ship's Corporal were sent ashore to arrest him but they could not find him. So, on the 28th, Daniel was formally marked RUN (i.e. a deserter) on the ship's books (normally a man was not so marked for a fortnight or more after disappearing, so it must have been assumed at once that Daniel was not coming back).

30

On 4th September 1861, the Queen, who had awarded Daniel his Cross and shaken his hand, issued a Royal Warrant which made Daniel the first man to have his name erased from the VC Roll:

Whereas it hath been reported unto us that EDWARD ST JOHN DANIEL late a Lieutenant in Our Navy, upon whom we have conferred the decoration of the Victoria Cross, has been accused of a disgraceful offence, and having evaded enquiry by desertion from Our Service, his name has been removed from the list of officers of Our Navy - Know ye therefore, that we are pleased to command and declare that the said Edward St John Daniel shall no longer be entitled to have his name enrolled in the Registry of persons on whom we have conferred the said decoration, but shall be and he is hereby adjudged and declared to be henceforth removed and degraded from all and singular rights, privileges and advantages appertaining thereunto.

By failing to surrender to his trial, Daniel had undoubtedly saved the Navy some embarrassment. The trial of a VC hero of the Crimea, one of the renowned Captain Peel's young men, on charges of indecent conduct and desertion would have caused a major public scandal. No wonder some relieved Admiralty official noted on the Admiralty Minute, 'No reference to the matter (i.e. the erasure) in the papers'. One can still hear the corporate sigh of relief from Whitehall.

As far as the Navy was concerned Daniel was a dead man, but he was by no means dead in fact. In late 1863 he was living in Melbourne, Australia, and when the New Zealand Colonial Government recruited an infantry battalion in Victoria for service in the Maori wars, Daniel enlisted on 18th January 1864. He gave his own name, his age as twenty-seven, (his birthday had been the day before), his occupation as 'Baker', and he enrolled for three years' service.

As Private E. St J. Daniel, No 428, of No.5 Company of his battalion of the Taranaki Military Settlers, Daniel arrived at New Plymouth in the Province of Taranaki, North Island, New Zealand, in the ship Gresham on 15th February 1864. His drinking habits were still causing trouble for he was 'confined to intensive labour' between the 8th and 15th of August 1864 and again from 30th August to 13th September.

Daniel took part in several operations and skirmishes in South Taranaki until the Military Settlers were disbanded in May 1867. As part of their payment, the Settlers were given grants of land on discharge. Daniel's number was 67/682 but obviously he could not settle as a farmer for he soon sold his land rights and enlisted again. It seems that only the restraints of a uniformed existence stood between him and the degeneration of his private life. On 26th November 1867 he was sworn in as Constable No.154 in No.2 Division, New Zealand Armed Constabulary Field Force, at Patea, South Taranaki.

In March 1868, there were serious disturbances fomented by the Fenians amongst the predominantly Irish mining community in the West Canterbury goldfields of South Island. Lieutenant-Colonel T. McDonnell, and about sixty members of No.2 Division, including Lance-Corporal Daniel, were despatched to Hokitika, a busy port and mining town, the centre of the disturbance. Daniel had 'been ailing for some time' and was admitted to Hokitika Hospital on 16th May 1868, where he died on the 20th. He was given a military funeral with proper honours and his obituary in the *West Coast Times* said that he 'was much respected by his comrades, and certainly, on this mournful occasion, everything was done that lay in their power to testify their regard for their lost friend and comrade'. He was buried in No.851 Grave in Block 27 of Hokitika Municipal Cemetery where, in 1971, the grave was reported as overgrown and unmarked. His death certificate gave the cause of death as delirium tremens.

J. Bryant Haigh, 'The Disgraced VC (Edward St John Daniel, 1837-1868)', *Bulletin of the Military Historical Society*, Vol. XXII, No. 86, November 1971.

James Gorman, Thomas Reeves and
Mark Scholefield:
Inkerman, 5th November 1854

At Inkerman the Russians made a determined effort to seize the commanding heights of land above Sebastopol. They failed, after a day of heavy fighting, which Russell of *The Times* described as 'a series of dreadful deeds of daring, of sanguinary hand-to-hand fights, of despairing rallies, of desperate assaults - in glens and valleys, in brushwood glades and remote dells'. The action began in darkness and continued in fog, thick mist and drizzling rain, when visibility was seldom more than a few yards. In conditions where commanding officers could see nothing, individual parties of soldiers and sailors were left to fight for themselves. There were 600 of the Naval Brigade in the field at Inkerman and as many more manning the gun batteries.

In the Right Lancaster Battery (where Hewett won his VC) the soldiers suffered many casualties under a fierce Russian attack. Five

Above left: Rear-Admiral Charles Lucas, who as a twenty-year-old Mate won the first VC, in 1854 (photo by Fradelle & Young).

Above right: John Bythesea (Photo by Maull & Fox, London)

Below: William Peel and his 'Jacks' at Lucknow ('Recollections of a Winter Campaign in India' by Captain O.J. Jones, 1859)

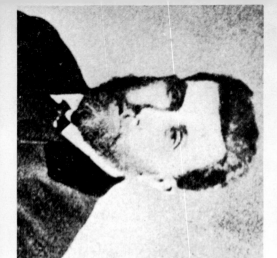

Above left: 'Gallant Act of Commander W
N. Hewett before Sebastopol' (Illustrat
London News, 13 July 1861)
Top: Hugh Burgoyne (Photo by Ma
& Fox, London)
Centre left: John Sullivan
Bottom left: Henry Cooper
Above: Henry Curtis (all from The Histo
of the Victoria Cross by Philip A. Wilkins)

sailors of the Naval Brigade were also in the battery and, as one of them said, they 'wouldn't trust any Ivan getting within bayonet range of the British wounded'. The five mounted the defence work *banquette* and kept up a 'rapid repulsing fire'. Wounded soldiers, lying in the trench below them, reloaded rifles for them and passed them up, until eventually the Russians 'fell back and gave no more trouble'. Two of the sailors were killed by the withering enemy fire which constantly swept the top of the parapet, but the remaining three, James Gorman, Thomas Reeves and Mark Scholefield, all seamen from HMS *Albion*, survived to be mentioned in Lushington's despatches and, in due course, gazetted for the Victoria Cross.

James Gorman was born James Devereux and changed his name to join the Navy, which suggests that he ran away to sea against his family's wishes. He joined in July 1850, giving his age as eighteen and his birthplace as London. He was described as having a ruddy complexion, blue eyes and light brown hair, and he had a vaccination mark. His height was five foot two inches when he joined, but he had grown to five foot five when he left. *Albion* was his first ship and he served in her for six years, joining as a Boy First Class in July 1850 and leaving as an Able Seaman in January 1856.

At the time of the first Investiture, Gorman was serving in *Elk* on the China Station and his medal was sent out there for presentation. He took part in operations in the Canton river in 1857 and was awarded the China Medal with Canton clasp. He was paid off from *Elk* at Sheerness in August 1860, and does not appear to have served in the Navy again. He resumed his name of Devereux and became a carpenter and journeyman turner. His VC pension of £10 was paid to him, at the usual rate of £2 10s a quarter, until his death in St Saviour's, Southwark, London, of 'chronic bronchitis and exhaustion' on 27th December 1889. His death certificate recorded that he was a holder of the Victoria Cross. His age at death was given as sixty-nine which would make his birthdate 1820, not 1832, an unexplainable discrepancy. He is supposed to have had two sons and three daughters. One son, F Devereux, witnessed the death certificate.

Thomas Reeves was the only one of the three to receive his Cross from the Queen at the first Investiture in Hyde Park in June 1857. He was born in Portsmouth in 1828 and gave his former trade as baker, although he must have only been an apprentice because he joined *Victory*, aged seventeen and a half, in August 1846. He was an Ordinary Seaman when he joined *Albion* in September 1850 and he was one of the ship's Yeomen of Signals when he won his VC. Later, he became a gunner's mate and was Captain of the Foretop when *Albion* paid off in January 1856. He had one good-conduct badge in August 1853, and he volunteered for ten years' continuous service in April 1856. He went to *Excellent* for a gunnery course, during which time he got married. He never served his full engagement because he was discharged in June 1860, although aged only thirty-two, for 'age and infirmity', on a pension of £25 a year. He died, wracked with the consumption from which he had suffered for the previous three years, in August 1862, at Portsea. He was buried in Portsea Island General Cemetery (which is now an open space called Mile End Gardens).

Mark Scholefield was born in Middlesex in April 1828 and his naval career was similar to Gorman's. He joined as a Boy Second Class in 1846 and served in *Tortoise*, the guardship at Ascension Island. He joined *Albion* as an Ordinary Seaman in October 1850 and was later Coxswain of the barge. He was five foot eight inches tall, with fair hair, hazel-brown eyes, and a crown tattooed on his left hand. After paying off from *Albion* in January 1856, he went out to China in the *Acorn* sloop and was present at the bombardment and capture of Canton in December 1857, gaining the medal. He was a quartermaster and petty officer when he died at sea in *Acorn* in February 1858. His only estate was his back pay, which came to less than £100.

At that time there were no posthumous awards of the Victoria Cross. The two other sailors who were killed in the action got no mention and no medal. Their names were not recorded and they themselves are now forgotten.

John Prettyjohn:
Inkerman, 5th November 1854

For the Marines from the fleet attached to the Light Infantry Division near the Lancaster Battery, Inkerman was a day of darkness, smoke and confusion, of unexplained firing heard in front and to the rear, of orders to advance and counter-orders to stay and hold their position. At one point the Marines came under accurate fire from a Russian frigate they supposed was in Sebastopol harbour, and from Russian snipers hidden in caves. One platoon, under Sergeant Richards and Corporal Prettyjohn, Royal Marine Light Infantry, of HMS *Bellerophon*, moved out to clear the caves. In doing so, they exhausted almost all their ammunition, and then discovered fresh parties of Russians creeping up the hillside towards them in single file. According to one marine who was there, Corporal Prettyjohn, 'a muscular West Countryman', at once said, 'Well, lads, we are just in for a warming, and it will be every man for himself in a few minutes. Look alive, my hearties, and collect all the stones handy, and pile them on the ridge in front of you. When I grip the front man you let go the biggest stones upon those fellows behind.'

When the first Russian appeared on the level ground in front of them, Prettyjohn seized him in a wrestler's grasp, 'gave him a West Country buttock' and threw him down the slope. The other Russians were knocked over by a shower of stones. 'We gave them a parting volley and retired out of sight to load; they made off and left us, although there was sufficient to have eaten us up.' Corporal Prettyjohn was awarded the Victoria Cross but Sergeant Richards apparently got nothing. Another NCO, Colour Sergeant Jordan, got the newly-instituted Medal for Distinguished Conduct in the field, and a pension of £20 per annum.

John Prettyjohn was born at Dean Prior, Ashburton, Devon on 11th June 1823, and joined the Marines at Stonehouse Barracks, Plymouth, on 10th June 1844, giving his occupation as labourer. He served in *Assistance* in China in 1858 and was in the Marine Battalion at the taking of Canton. He was discharged on pension as a Colour Sergeant after twenty-one years' service on 11th June 1865. He lived for some time at East Stonehouse, Plymouth, and was married in 1856. He had two daughters, one of whom lived to be ninety-five, dying in 1960. Prettyjohn himself died, and was buried, in Manchester on 20th January 1887.

John Sullivan:
The Crimea, April 1855

The seamen gunners of the Naval Brigade won another Crimean Victoria Cross in the spring of 1855. The winner was Boatswain's Mate John Sullivan, of HMS *Rodney*. Like a high proportion of *Rodney's* ship's company at the time, Sullivan was an Irishman, born in Bantry, Co. Cork on 10th April 1830. When he joined the Navy as a Boy Second Class in November 1846, aged sixteen and a half, he was described as being five foot eight inches tall, with a ruddy complexion, dark hair and dark blue eyes. He was as near a professional seaman as it was possible to be in his era: he joined *Rodney* as an Ordinary Seaman in March 1852, was rated Able Seaman that June, Leading Seaman in November 1853, and Captain of the Mizzen-top in February 1854. He had signed on for seven years' continuous service on 24th July 1853 and had quite evidently chosen the Navy as his permanent career.

As captain of one of *Terrible's* 68-pounder gun's crews, Sullivan had already distinguished himself in action. His gun had been credited with making the first serious breach in the walls of the great Malakoff redoubt, and also with blowing up an important magazine at the start of the siege of Sebastopol. He and his crew were transferred to No.5 Greenhill Battery where, on 10th April 1855, a volunteer was called for to go forward of the battery and place a flagstaff on a mound in front of the battery, to act as an aiming-point for some troublesome Russian guns which were concealed from the direct view of the sailors' battery.

As Captain of the gun, Sullivan considered that it was his duty to go. Although he was in plain sight of the enemy and under constant heavy rifle-fire when he reached the mound, Sullivan took his time, coolly looking both ways to make sure that he was on a straight line between the naval guns and the target. Reassured that he was, he calmly scraped a hole with his hands, planted the flag-staff and collected stones and earth to bank it up securely. The Russian snipers had seen him and bullets could be heard whistling around him, but he gave his flagstaff a final shake to test its firmness before scrambling back to shelter. His bravery was observed by Commander Kennedy, in command of the battery, who reported that Sullivan's 'gallantry was always conspicuous.' He was mentioned in Lord Lyons' despatches and gazetted for the Victoria Cross in the first list of 24th February 1857.

Sullivan was serving abroad at the time of the first Investiture and his VC was sent to *Prometheus*, where he was serving on the West Coast of Africa, for presentation. Besides the VC, Sullivan also held the Crimean medal with Inkerman and Sebastopol clasps, the Turkish Crimean medal, the Sardinian medal *Al Valore*, the French Légion d'honneur, the Royal Humane Society's silver medal, and the Conspicuous Gallantry Medal, which had been instituted by Order in Council in August 1855. It was originally sanctioned for the Crimean War, and only ten were awarded in 1855.

Sullivan served in the Navy for over thirty-seven years, for the last ten of them as the well-known Boatswain of Portsmouth Dockyard, before retiring as Chief Boatswain's Mate of the *Asia* in April 1884, on a pension of £150 a year. On retirement he went home to Ireland, where his end was clouded with sadness. He bought a smallholding of 44 acres, near Kinsale, Co. Cork. At some time in 1884 he began to complain of headaches. On the 28th of that month he suffered another headache and went out into the garden. He was found lying there later in the day, having cut his own throat with a sailor's knife. His death certificate recorded that he died of 'Haemorrhage from wound in throat suicide about half an hour'.

Cecil William Buckley, Hugh Talbot Burgoyne, John Robarts and Henry Cooper:
Sea of Azov, May and June 1855

In May 1855 a strong expedition of some 15,000 infantry and 56 ships - frigates, light draught steamers, gun and rocket boats, later augmented by twenty line-of-battleship launches armed with 24-pounder howitzers and rockets - was sent eastwards across the Black Sea to seize the Straits of Kertsch and to operate in the Sea of Azov beyond them. The Russians blew up their forts and retreated from the Straits so that the objectives were captured without the loss of a man. A steam flotilla under Captain Lyons (the C-in-C's son) went through the Straits and within a week had sunk four steamers of war and 246 merchant vessels of various kinds, captured corn, flour and powder magazines to the value of £50,000 and seized over 17,000 tons of coal.

The Azov operations encountered no seaborne opposition at all, and the actions therefore took the form of daring ventures by small parties, much like the Commando raids of a later age, to destroy enemy *matériel* ashore. On 29th May 1855, Lieutenant Buckley of HMS *Miranda*, Lieutenant Burgoyne of HMS *Swallow* and Gunner Robarts of HMS *Ardent* volunteered to land on a beach near the town of Genitchi, at a point where they were out of covering gunshot range of the ships offshore and where they knew the Russian Army were in strength. They met considerable enemy opposition from infantry and snipers, but set fire to corn stores, ammunition dumps and destroyed enemy equipment before embarking again, narrowly escaping from a party of Cossacks who all but cut off their retreat. On the night of 3rd June, Buckley landed again, this time with Boatswain Henry Cooper, also of *Miranda*, in a four-oared gig manned by volunteers, at the town of Taganrog in the north-east corner of the Sea of Azov, which was actually under bombardment by the Allied squadron at the time. The town was garrisoned by some 3,000 Russian troops but Buckley and Cooper landed at several places, whenever they saw a likely target, to fire government buildings and stores and destroy equipment and arms before embarking again, under fire themselves for most of the time. These quick and unexpected raids which the raiders seemed to be able to mount where and whenever they pleased, had a depressing effect on the enemy out of all proportion to the damage done. The Russians learned once again that there was no substitute for the speed, strength and flexibility of sea-power.

Buckley seized his golden moments during the Russian War. Like the careers of so many VCs, his later service did not match his exploits in the Sea of Azov. He was born on 7th October 1830 and joined the Navy in 1843. He served as a Midshipman in *Tweed* and *Cormorant* on the south-east coast of America and was commended, with others, for his part in an attack on a Brazilian fort at the mouth of the River Paranagua in July 1850. He passed for Mate in 1851 and served in *Daedalus* and *Royal George*. He was promoted Lieutenant on 11th January 1854 and joined the 14-gun steam corvette *Miranda* the following month. He was at the assault and capture of Kola, capital of Russian Lapland, in the White Sea in 1854. After his VC exploits, he was mentioned again for his service in boats at Taganrog in June, before being given command of the 6-gun steam sloop *Snake* in July. In her he was mentioned in despatches once again for his part in operations in the Straits of Kertsch.

Buckley was promoted Commander on 27th February 1856 and took command of *Merlin* on the West Coast of Africa and Cape of Good Hope Station in May 1857. He later commanded *Forte* and *Persian* before being promoted Captain on 15th April 1862. He then commanded *Pylades* in the Pacific from 1867 to 1871, having somewhat mixed fortunes in her. In December 1869 he was censured by the Board of Admiralty for neglecting gunnery practice. In June 1870 he was censured again for the tone of a letter he wrote to the Board and was removed from being senior officer at Rio to the West Indies so as to be under the eye of an Admiral there. But in January 1871 he was commended for the state of *Pylades* on her arrival at Bermuda 'after too long a time at sea'. Finally, he was given command of the battleship *Valiant*, a drill ship lying in the Shannon for the Fleet Reserve men in the Southern Irish coastguard, in December 1871, but fell sick and was admitted to Stonehouse Hospital, Plymouth, in September 1872. He retired from the Navy on 18th October and went on forty-two days' leave. He went to Funchal, Madeira, where he died on 7th December 1872.

Buckley married Catherine Senhouse Falcon, daughter of Henry Falcon, Esquire, of Doynton House, Doynton, in Gloucestershire, at the Parish Church, Doynton, on 30th August 1865. They had two children, a daughter Cecil Isabel, and a son, Percy Falcon. At his death Buckley's will referred to him as 'late of Calcott, Somerset'.

Hugh Talbot Burgoyne came of an illustrious family. He was the grandson of General Burgoyne, who surrendered the English forces at Saratoga in 1777, and the son of Field-Marshal Sir John Fox Burgoyne, Royal Engineers, Constable of the Tower and an influential figure in the counsels of the army in the Crimea. Hugh Burgoyne was born in Dublin on 19th July 1833 and entered the Navy as a cadet in 1847. He had a normal Service career in his early years, in *Inconstant*, *Thetis*, *Penguin and Impregnable*, passing his examinations and being promoted Mate on 18th January 1853 and Lieutenant on 11th January 1854. He was appointed to *Boscawen*, and then became senior Lieutenant in the 8-gun steam sloop *Swallow* in the Black Sea fleet. Apart from his VC exploit at Genitchi, he was several times commended in despatches for actions in the Sea of Azov. He was given command of the 4-gun *Wrangler* in June 1856,

38

promoted Commander on 10th July and on the 16th took part in the successful Allied attack on the fort and batteries at Petrovski.

In January 1857, Burgoyne began a successful commission in the line of battleship *Ganges* in the Pacific. In March 1858 he was commended for the assistance he gave in extinguishing a large fire in Valparaiso, and when she paid off in May 1861 *Ganges* was reported 'in a high state of discipline'. After promotion to Captain on 15th May 1861, he went to China in 1863 as second-in-command of the Anglo-Chinese Flotilla under Captain Sherard Osborn and served on the Naval Commission in China. When Osborn fell out with the Chinese government and resigned, the Chinese offered Burgoyne a generous salary to take the appointment, but he refused and the Flotilla was disbanded. From 1865 to 1867, Burgoyne commanded the small ironclad turret-ship *Wyvern* and then served in *Constance* on the North American and West Indies Station, running the blockade during the American Civil War. In 1864 he married Evelyn Laura Walker at Kensington.

Hugh Burgoyne's last command was the controversial ironclad turret-ship *Captain*, which was completed for sea by Cammell Lairds of Birkenhead early in 1870 after a long and bitter argument concerning ship design between Edward Reed, Chief Constructor of the Navy, and Captain Cowper Coles, *Captain's* designer (who served in the Crimean War and was unlucky not to get the VC himself). *Captain's* draught was much deeper than expected when she was completed, and she carried very much more top hamper than originally planned, and there were many who thought her unseaworthy. But Burgoyne said he was confident and at first it seemed he was right. But shortly after midnight on 7th September 1870, when *Captain* was in company with the fleet off Finisterre, a sudden squall overturned her and she sank.

Burgoyne himself was on deck at the end, wearing an old pair of trousers, a cap and a pilot-cloth jacket (suggesting he had been wakened and dressed in a hurry), giving orders to the watch on deck to let go main and fore topsail halliards and sheets, to strip sail off the ship and help her come upright. Afterwards he was seen clinging to an upturned pinnace by Gunner James May, one of the few survivors. 'My God, May'; he said, 'I never thought we were coming to this.' A launch with more survivors in it drifted near and Burgoyne urged his men to try and reach it. Some did, but Burgoyne himself did not follow them. May and the seventeen men who survived reached the Spanish shore next day. Burgoyne and the 471 men who drowned with him (including Cowper Coles himself) are commemorated by a plaque in St Paul's Cathedral.

Gunner John Robarts was born in Cornwall in 1820 and gave his former trade as miner. He joined *Wellesley* as a Boy and was awarded the China Medal in her in 1842. He went to *Excellent* for the gunnery course in 1846-7, joined *Ardent* as Gunner in 1851 and served in her until 1856, when he went back to *Excellent*. He married Annie Emma Victoria Butts at Chelsea in September 1861 and they had three sons, one of whom was born in February 1864 when Robarts was serving in *Asia*. He retired from the Navy in April 1873 and died of heart disease at Providence House, his residence at Park Lane, Southsea, on 17th October 1888, aged sixty-eight. In his will he spelled his name 'Roberts' although it was 'Robarts' on his V.C. He left a life interest in his estate to his wife Annie, and then equally to his three sons John, Thomas and William. With a touch of asperity, fitting an old parade-ground gunner, he directed that 'should there be any dispute over this will the one making it shall forfeit his interest therein'.

Henry Cooper, who was born in 1825 and joined the Navy as a Boy Second Class when he was fifteen, followed the sound of the guns for the whole of his adventurous Service career and he always seemed to be present whenever anything exciting or dangerous was happening. Whilst serving in *Philomel* on the west coast of Africa in 1848 he was one of a boarding party who seized a pirate-slaver, although their boat was riddled with grapeshot by the time they got on board the prize. One man was killed and nineteen were injured, but the slaver was taken and her crew of sixty made prisoner. When he was Boatswain of *Miranda*, leaving Plymouth for the Black Sea and saluting the Port Admiral, there was an explosion at the saluting gun which tore off a seaman's hands and blew him over the side. Cooper jumped in after him and kept him afloat until they were both rescued. In 1854, Cooper served in the White Sea and was at the capture and destruction of the town and forts of Kola, the capital of Russian Finland. He also took part in the attack on the fort of Arabat in the Sea of Azov on 28th May 1855, when the thirty guns of the fort were captured and the magazine blown up. The next day Cooper was one of the boats' crews in an expedition under Lieutenant Mackenzie and helped to set fire to some seventy Russian vessels and the corn stores at Genitchi, at the entrance to the Putrid Sea, where the enemy had six cannon and 200 men, in addition to a battalion of infantry and some Cossacks. This was the same expedition for which Buckley, Burgoyne and Robarts won the V.C, but Cooper was not gazetted. On 3rd June, at Taganrog, for which he did win a V.C, Cooper landed with Buckley and repeatedly fired stores and government buildings; by 3 pm in the afternoon, grain, planks, tar, vessels building on the stocks, the Customs House and other government buildings were all ablaze. On 17th June 1855, when *Miranda* was hit by guns of the Sebastopol forts, Captain Lyons was mortally wounded and died a week later. It was Henry Cooper who caught him up and carried him below out of range of the Russian guns. Again, as Boatswain of the *Miranda*, Cooper took charge of the ship's boats during an attack on the fortress at Kertsch, on the Straits, and he was the first man to take the British flag ashore and set it flying.

At some time he married Margery (née Searl) and they had seven children, six girls and a boy. When Henry Cooper retired from the Navy he went to live at Torpoint, in Cornwall, just across the river from Devonport. He died there at his house, 8 Wellington Street, on 15th July 1893, aged sixty-eight. He was buried in the churchyard at Antony, Cornwall, with the inscription on his stone, 'Lord all pitying, Jesu blest, Grant him thine eternal rest.'

Burgoyne, Robarts and Cooper were all present at the first VC Investiture in Hyde Park in June 1857 to receive their Victoria Crosses from the Queen.

Thomas Wilkinson:
The Crimea, June 1855

Some Victoria Cross citations read rather baldly now, obviously failing to capture even the essence of the atmosphere which surrounded the performance of an heroic act. Bombardier Thomas Wilkinson, Royal Marine Artillery, of HMS *Britannia*, won his Victoria Cross for 'gallant conduct in the advanced batteries, 5th June, 1855, in placing sand-bags to repair the work under a galling fire; his name having been sent up on the occasion, as worthy of special notice, by the Commanding Officer of the Artillery of the Right Attack'.

In April and May 1855, both sides hammered away at each other in the lines before Sebastopol. By the beginning of June the Russian fire had been so heavy that it had demolished most of the earthworks in some of the more forward Allied positions. Bombardier Wilkinson, who arrived with a party of marine volunteers for the trenches on 5th June, went up on to the parapet and, calling for sandbags to be handed up to him, rebuilt the works as the sandbags were passed up. It took him some time, as he went from place to place, setting the sandbags in position and making fresh embrasures for the guns' barrels. Eventually the enemy, and his mates all along the near-by trenches, noticed what Wilkinson was doing. The former fired, whilst the latter replied with volley on volley of cheering. Wilkinson was commended by Colonel Wesley, Deputy Adjutant General, Royal Marines, and gazetted for the Victoria Cross in the first list of 24th February 1857.

Thomas Wilkinson was born at Marygate, York, in 1831 and joined the Royal Marines at York on 23rd November 1850, aged nineteen and a half. He was discharged 'invalided' from the Marines on 12th October 1859, at the early age of twenty-eight, and afterwards became a Sergeant Instructor in the Auxiliary Forces. He married and went to live in York, where he was manager of Mr

Rymer's sand yard in North Street, York, on 22nd September 1887, aged fifty-five, after a long and severe illness which his death certificate described as hypertrophy of spleen, exhaustion and diarrhoea.

Henry James Raby, John Taylor and Henry Curtis: *Sebastopol, 18th June 1855*

The great combined British and French assault on the fortress of the Redan at Sebastopol on the morning of 18th June 1855 (the anniversary of the Battle of Waterloo) ended in utter failure. The assaulting forces, who included many bluejackets from the Naval Brigade carrying scaling ladders, had to cross too great an expanse of open, unprotected ground to reach the Redan, and the walls themselves were too great a physical obstacle to be mounted by men exposed to such fire. But, as so often in British military history, a gloomy tactical situation was brightened by acts of superb individual bravery. Besides Peel and Daniel, whose feats at the wall were cited in their VC awards, the Naval Brigade won three more Victoria Crosses, and but for sickness might have won a fourth.

Only one man, a bluejacket called Michael Hardy, actually penetrated the inner glacis of the Redan, but was killed. The survivors had to fall back and the ground in front of the Allied trenches was soon strewn with wounded, dead and dying. One soldier of the 57th (Middlesex) Regiment could be seen from the sailors' trenches, sitting up and calling for help. At once, Lieutenant Henry Raby, of HMS *Wasp*, who had himself been second-in-command of a scaling party, Lieutenant Henry D'Aeth, First Lieutenant of HMS *Sidon*, Captain of the Forecastle John Taylor of HMS *London* and Boatswain's Mate Henry Curtis of HMS *Rodney*, left the shelter of their battery works and ran forward a distance of some seventy yards across open ground towards the salient of the Redan to help the wounded man. He had been shot in both legs and could not help himself, so the four of them had to carry him. All four bore charmed lives - Curtis was supposed actually to have had a shot pass between his legs without hitting him - although the enemy's fire was intense, and none of them was hurt. They all reached the safety of the trenches with the soldier. Raby, Taylor and Curtis were mentioned in Captain Lushington's despatches and were gazetted for the Victoria Cross in the first list of 24th February 1857. The unfortunate D'Aeth contracted cholera and died of it on 7th August, after an illness lasting only a few hours.

Henry James Raby was clearly a man of very robust health with the constitution of a stout ox. He landed with the Naval Brigade on 23rd October 1854 and served in the trenches until 16th September 1855 (the whole Naval Brigade re-embarked on the 19th). He was at Inkerman and at the Redan, and in a score of lesser fights, and as 'a good and zealous officer' he was rightly promoted Commander on 29th September 1855 for his services in the trenches. Besides the VC he also held the French Légion d'honneur, the Order of Medjidie 5th Class, the Turkish and Sardinian Crimean medals, and the Crimean Medal with bars for Inkerman and Sebastopol. As the senior officer present of the Senior Service, Raby was the first man actually to be invested with his Cross by the Queen at the first Investiture in Hyde Park on 26th June 1857 (although Lucas's remains the first act, *in time*, to win the VC).

Henry Raby was born in Boulogne on 26th September 1827, the son of Arthur Tournour Raby, of Llanelly, Carmarthenshire, a member of a well-known family of industrialists in South Wales, who did much to open up Llanelly's industry in the earlier part of the nineteenth century (a street in the town is named after them). Henry went to Sherborne School in Dorset, and joined the Navy as Volunteer First Class on 8th March 1842, aged fourteen. His first ship was HMS *Monarch*. He gave a hand in removing and embarking the Xanthian marbles for the British Museum in 1842. He was promoted Mate on 7th March 1848 and Lieutenant on 15th January 1850. He served in *Wasp* on the West Coast of Africa before the war, and, when war broke out, in operations along the Circassian coast in support of the Turkish Army. After the war he commanded *Medusa* and *Alecto* on the West Coast of Africa. Noted as a 'very active officer with considerable knowledge of affairs on the coast of Africa', Raby was mentioned repeatedly in despatches for actions against slaving on the coast. In April 1861 he was wounded while commanding the boats of the Squadron in the capture and destruction of the slaving fort at Porto Novo and he was later officially thanked by the Foreign Office for negotiating a treaty with the chiefs of the Old Calabar River. Promoted Captain on 24th November 1862, Raby commanded *Adventure* on the China Station from 1868-71, was awarded the CB in 1875, and retired from the Navy on 27th September 1877, being promoted Rear-Admiral on the retired list on 21st March the following year.

On 9th December 1863 Captain Raby married Judith, daughter of Colonel Forster of Holt Manor, Troubridge, at Bradford in Wiltshire. They had three sons, one of whom died aged nine at Honfleur in France, one was a Captain of Royal Artillery, and the third followed his father into the Navy. In his retirement the Admiral lived at 8 Clarence Parade, Southsea, and took an active interest in local charitable affairs, including the Royal Sailors' Home at Portsea, and in schools and homes for orphans and for the blind. He died at home in his eightieth year, on 13th February 1907. After a full military funeral he was buried in Highland Road Cemetery, Portsmouth.

John Taylor was born in January or February 1822, in the parish of St Philip and St Jacob, Bristol, and later made his home in London. He joined the Navy at the age of nineteen, his first ship being *Cornwallis*. He joined her as an Ordinary Seaman in October 1841 and won the medal for service in China in her. Later he served in *Eagle*, as an Able Seaman, from 1845 to 1848 and then in *Hastings*, getting another medal for service in Pegu, Burma. He left *Hastings* as Captain of the Forecastle in May 1853 and joined *London*, serving in her throughout the Crimean campaign until 1856, being drafted ashore with the Naval Brigade in October 1854. He was marked 'R' i.e. RUN, as a deserter, from *London* from 17th August to 18th October 1853. He was described then as having a fresh complexion, grey eyes, brown hair, and as being five foot nine inches tall, with a crucifix and the initials JTMT tattooed on his right arm, and a tree on his left.

He was drafted to *Nightingale* in 1856 and shortly afterwards discharged. His health seems to have been permanently damaged by his service in the Crimea. He went to live in Woolwich, where he was a supernumerary Boatswain in the *Fisgard* flagship. He died in the Royal Marine Infirmary of bronchitis, and 'pulmonary congestion' on 25th February 1857, aged thirty-five. He had just heard, a few hours earlier, that he had been gazetted for the Victoria Cross, the first awards being published the day before. On 2nd March a notice appeared in *Jackson's Woolwich Journal and Army and Navy Gazette* that the

. . . deceased was much esteemed by the officers in the Dockyard, and by those who knew him, and although covered with honours, so unassuming was his character, that he could scarcely be prevailed upon to wear them. He had medals for the Kaffir and Murna wars, the Sebastopol medal with every clasp, the medals of the French Légion d'honneur and for meritorious conduct. Unfortunately this brave man has left a wife and family unprovided for.

He was buried in a common grave at Woolwich. Taylor's widow, Elizabeth, wrote to the Admiralty in March, asking if she could be present at the Victoria Cross Investiture in Hyde Park. Her letter was passed to the War Office, and it was revealing of how sailors' dependants were treated by officialdom in those days that the Secretary of State for War, Lord Panmure, replied to Mrs Taylor on 25th June that 'It would not be necessary for you to come to London as you suppose in connection with the ceremony to take place tomorrow, the 26th instant'. Taylor's Cross was sent to her through the post in July.

Henry Curtis was born in Romsey, Hampshire, in 1822, the son of a carpenter. He joined *Victory* as a Boy in June 1841. In August 1851, after ten years' service, he became a coastguard but was, in his own phrase, 'picked up' (i.e. conscripted) for *Rodney* in November. He was one of the very few good seamen in a crew which Midshipman (later Admiral) Kennedy, who joined the ship in December, described as 'picked up anyhow - long-shore loafers, jailbirds and such like, with a sprinkling of good seamen amongst them'. Curtis left *Rodney* when she paid off in January 1856 and after service in *Ringdove* he rejoined the Coast Guard Service in November. In the meantime, on 7th February 1856 (clearly when he still had *Rodney* paying-off money in his pocket) he married Maria Morley, a brewer's daughter, described on the marriage lines as 'a minor', at Alverstoke, near Gosport, in Hampshire. From March 1858 until his final discharge from the Navy in November 1864, Curtis served in the line-of-battleship *Marlborough*, flagship in the Mediterranean of Vice-Admiral Sir Fanshawe Martin, and known as 'the smartest ship in the Service'. Lord Charles Beresford joined her as a cadet in March 1861 when she was lying at St Helens in the Isle of Wight. It was his first ship and many years later he remembered Curtis as 'the great big boatswain's mate' who said to another sailor when he saw fifteen-year-old Beresford, 'Mate, 'ere's another orficer kim aboard' jist in toime; but, pore little beggar! - he ain't long fur this world.' When Curtis later got a berth as quartermaster on a cross-Channel steamer sailing from Southampton, Beresford recognised him, touched his old instructor on the shoulder and cordially shook hands with him. Henry Curtis died in Portsea of 'Podagra (gout) and Chronic Bright's Uraemia' on 23rd November 1896.

Joseph Trewavas:
Sea of Azov, July 1855

One of the most important strategic objectives of the Sea of Azov operations was a very large floating pontoon bridge which the Russians had built across the Genitchi Strait to connect the town of Genitchi to the Spit of Arabat. If that bridge were destroyed, the Russian's main supply route to the south would be cut, and the reinforcement troops and supply carts carrying food, stores and ammunition for the Russian army at Sebastopol would have to travel an extra 120 miles overland across country where roads hardly existed.

The task of destroying the bridge was given to a squadron of gunboats, including the light draught, 4-gun, screw steamer *Beagle*, commanded by Lieutenant Bully Hewett, himself a VC. The straits were so shallow that *Beagle* could not approach the bridge, so Hewett led a party himself to attack the bridge by night, but they were discovered and driven off. A second attack was made in *Beagle*'s boats by day and they too were driven off.

Although the Russian garrison was now thoroughly alarmed and on the alert, another attempt was made on 3rd July 1855, in *Beagle's* four-oared gig, commanded by Gunner John Hayles, and a small paddle-box steamer armed with one gun, under Midshipman Martin Tracy, of *Vesuvius*. After only one round, the gun forced its securing bolts and could not be fired again but when Hayles reported this to Hewett he was told to go on regardless. They were to cut the bridge, or risk court martial. As one sailor in the expedition, Joseph Trewavas, later put it, 'We did not like the job but we might as well be killed by Russian bullets as have the forebrace block as an awning' (i.e. be hanged from the fore yard-arm).

As the boats approached the pontoons, the crews could see the nearest shore lined with Russian troops. There were riflemen lying hidden behind a long bank of coal. Every window in every house in Arabat had its marksmen, ready to fire. When the gig ground against the bridge, Joseph Trewavas leaped out with an axe and began to hew away at the hawsers holding the pontoons together.

As soon as the Russians realised what was happening, they opened a tremendous fire upon the boats and especially upon Trewavas himself, some of the nearest riflemen from a range of less than eighty yards. Trewavas, still hacking steadily at the hawsers, seemed to bear a charmed life, but the little paddle-boat was riddled with bullets so many times that her crew had to bale furiously to keep her afloat. An officer in *Vesuvius* later said they were soon baling as much blood as water. At last, the strands gave way and the two severed ends of the pontoons began to drift apart. Trewavas was hit in the right shoulder as he got back into the gig. The crew gave a cheer, backed away and made their escape, covered by Tracy in the paddle-boat and supported by *Beagle's* own guns in action against the town. As Trewavas himself said, "by coolness and pulling for dear life and by the Russians' shocking aim, we got back, the boat being completely riddled and up to the thwarts in water.' In his report Hewett gave great credit to John Hayles, the Gunner, for 'his activity and zeal' and to Mr Tracy for the effective covering fire he kept up. Mr Hayles spoke 'in the highest possible terms of the boat's crews especially of Joseph Trewavas, Ordinary Seaman, lent from *Agamemnon*, who cut the hawsers'. Trewavas was awarded the VC in the first list of 24th February 1857 and was present at the first Investiture in Hyde Park. He was also awarded the Conspicuous Gallantry Medal.

As his surname suggests, Trewavas was a Cornishman. He was born in Mousehole on 14th December 1835 and went to the National School in the Parish of Paul. He gave no previous trade on his service papers, but he was almost certainly a fisherman until he volunteered for the Navy and joined the line-of-battleship *Agamemnon* on 15th October 1853. He landed with the Naval Brigade on 23rd October 1854, served in the trenches at Sebastopol and at the battle of Inkerman. He was lent to *Beagle* for the operations in the Sea of Azov from 25th May 1855 until he returned to *Agamemnon* on 18th November. He joined *Gladiator* on

46

4th June and was discharged from her when she paid off on 22nd May 1857.

Trewavas's next ship was *Pelorus*, which had an eventful commission in the East Indies. Trewavas himself was one of the Naval Brigade the ship landed in Burma during the Indian Mutiny, and when the ship went to New Zealand for action in the Maori Wars of 1860 he was probably, as he claimed, one of the landing party *Pelorus* sent ashore, although his name is not in the ship's medal entitlement roll. Trewavas never signed on for continuous service but by the time he was discharged to *Victory* to be paid off on 10th December 1862 he had served nearly ten years. He was described on the books of *Pelorus* as five foot six inches in height, with a ruddy complexion grey eyes, brown hair, 'no marks, wound in right shoulder, vaccinated, single, no trade, rank Able Seaman'.

Trewavas went home to Cornwall, to Penzance, where he became a respected member of the fishing community, with his own fishing lugger *Agamemnon*, No. PZ 17. In 1866 he married Margaret Harry, and they had a son, Joseph, and two daughters, Margaret and Elizabeth. He became a member of the Penzance Board of Guardians. When the compilers of *Who's Who* asked about his hobbies he said he had none, because it took him all his time to earn a living.

Trewavas's life ended in tragedy. He was stricken with paralysis which, after so active a life, depressed him. On 19th July 1905, he tried to cut his own throat by sawing at it with a cheeseknife. He died the next day, of the shock and haemorrhage of his throat wound, at Dumbarton House, his home in Mousehole. The coroner's verdict was that he committed suicide whilst of unsound mind.

George Dare Dowell and George Henry Ingouville:
Viborg, The Baltic, July 1855

In the summer of 1855 another great Anglo-French fleet, which eventually had a strength of over 100 warships mounting more than 2,500 guns, operated in the Baltic under Admiral Dundas. Like Napier's ships in the same waters the year before, Dundas's fleet was able to operate in almost complete freedom, blockading every fort and harbour in the Gulfs of Bothnia and Finland, denying the enemy the coastwise traffic by seizing or burning coastal shipping, and mounting small-ship actions against individual fortresses, until the major two-day bombardment and assault on the citadel of Sveaborg in August 1855.

On 13th July 1855, the boats of *Arrogant*, *Magicienne* and *Ruby* were in action against Russian boats and shore batteries at the fort of Viborg in the Gulf of Finland. At the height of the action, a direct hit from a

47

Russian shell severely damaged *Arrogant's* second cutter, killing Midshipman George Story who was in command, detonating the powder on board, and wounding many of the crew. Half swamped, with most of the oars smashed, and the crew incapacitated, the cutter began to drift inshore under the enemy guns. Although he had been wounded in the arm, one of the boat's crew, Captain of the Mast George Ingouville, slipped over the side, swam round to the boat's bows, took hold of the painter and tried to tow the cutter out to sea.

In spite of his efforts, Ingouville would almost certainly have been drowned or killed by the enemy's intense fire and the boat and its crew lost but for Lieutenant George Dare Dowell, Royal Marine Artillery, of *Magicienne*. Dowell was standing on *Ruby's* upper deck, waiting for his own boat to be reloaded with a fresh supply of rockets, when he saw what had happened to *Arrogant's* cutter and her crew. Calling for three volunteers, Dowell manned *Ruby's* quarter-boat, taking the stroke oar himself, and pulled out to the stricken cutter. While the Russians ashore and in their boats redoubled their fire, Dowell rescued three of *Arrogant's* men and brought them safely back to *Ruby*. That might have been enough for any man in the face of such sustained fire but Dowell went out a second time, pulled Ingouville from the water, took on board the rest of the cutter's crew, and began to tow the boat out of gun range. Towards the end, even the Russians are said to have stopped firing and joined in the cheering. Dowell and Ingouville were both awarded the Victoria Cross in the first list of 24th February 1857 and were both present in Hyde Park at the first Investiture.

The rescue of *Arrogant's* cutter was only one incident in a busy summer for Lieutenant Dowell. He had seen action the year before, in May, when *Magicienne* engaged Russian batteries at Hangor Head. In June 1855, *Magicienne* took part in the destruction of forts and barracks shelling Russian encampments and destroying thirty enemy vessels in the Bay of Werolax. In July, *Magicienne's* sailors were in action again, landing at Lovisa and firing government stores, shelling Cossack encampments and destroying their barracks. A week after the incident at Viborg, Dowell was mentioned in despatches for an engagement with shore batteries at Frederickshaven and, the following month, he was in *Magicienne* at the great fleet bombardment of the fortress of Sveaborg.

George Dare Dowell was born in Chichester on 15th February 1831, the son of George Dowell, Paymaster RN. He went to the Royal Naval School at New Cross, London SE, and he entered the Marines as a Second Lieutenant on 26th July 1848, joining the Royal Marine Artillery in June 1849. He was promoted Lieutenant on 6th October 1851, appointed to the paddle steam sloop *Magicienne* (16 guns) on 29th November 1852, and served in her until December 1855. He was promoted Captain on 22nd September 1859, Major on 17th September

1861 and went on half pay on 12th May 1865, being promoted Brevet Lieutenant-Colonel on half pay on 23rd April 1872. He served for a time as Inspector of Musketry, and as Adjutant of the Devon Artillery Militia. He retired on 29th January 1889.

While still a Captain, George Dowell married Mary, daughter of Robert Mansel, at Alverstoke, Hampshire, on 12th April 1860. They had nine children - five sons and four daughters. At some time the family appear to have emigrated to New Zealand, for Colonel Dowell died at The Haven, Remuera, Auckland on 3rd August 1910, and was buried at the Purewa Cemetery on the 5th of that month.

George Henry Ingouville was the first man from the Channel Islands to win the Victoria Cross. He was baptised on 7th October 1826, at St Saviour, Jersey, a member of an old Norman family who had lived in Jersey since the fifteenth century. He was probably the eldest son of Pierre and Eliza Maria Ingouville who lived in La Motte Street, St Helier. The first Naval record of him was when he joined *Trafalgar* as an Able Seaman on 7th July 1851. He joined the paddle steamer *Sampson* from *Trafalgar* on 17th April 1854 and left her for *Arrogant* as Captain of the Mast (a senior and responsible petty officer) on 31st January 1855. He was discharged from *Arrogant* to *Victory* on 26th February 1857 and from *Victory* to the Coast Guard Service as a Bosun at Langston Harbour, Sussex, on 25th April. He had signed for seven years' continuous service on 1st April 1855 but his later career was marred by spells of imprisonment for desertion in June and August 1858. He next appears as an Able Seaman in *Marlborough* in 1859-61 and in *Challenger* as Able Seaman, Coxswain of the Cutter, Bosun's Mate and finally as Able Seaman again in 1861-2. The incriminating word RUN, showing that he had been a deserter, was officially removed from his Service Certificate on 7th January 1863. On 4th April 1861, he married Mary Anne Le Rossignol, aged fifteen, daughter of Matthew Le Rossignol (deceased), Master Mariner, at the Roman Catholic Chapel, Bristol Road, Brighton. He appears to have served as a merchant seaman after leaving the Navy. The VC Pension Register makes no mention of desertion but gives a date for his decease, 13th January 1869, though no place of death. Family tradition has it that George Ingouville 'drowned in a very shallow place when going abroad'.

John Sheppard:
Sebastopol Harbour, The Crimea, 1855

The midget submarine crews, the charioteers, the 'cockleshell heroes' and all the special boat parties of the Second World War had a common ancestor in John Sheppard, Boatswain's Mate, who won the last bluejacket's VC at Sebastopol. On 23rd June 1855, Captain

The Hon. Henry Keppel, commanding the screw line-of-battleship *St Jean D'Acre* (101 guns), off Sebastopol, noted in his diary, 'Preparation by Quartermaster John Shepherd (the spelling varies) to destroy, alone, a Russian three-decker'.

Sheppard's plan was basically the same as the Elizabethan fireships' had been and the midget submarines' were to be in the Second World War - to penetrate an enemy harbour and destroy his shipping by fire or explosives. Early in the war the Russians had sunk six line-of-battleships across Sebastopol entrance to block the harbour, but there were still other ships as worthwhile targets further up harbour. Sheppard planned to paddle into Sebastopol by night, fix an explosive to the hull of a Russian warship, leaving it with a time-fuse, and then escape.

Sheppard was forty when he won his VC and he might have been thought a little too old for messing about in small boats in enemy harbours at dead of night. But he was an unusual man, a handyman, who could knit, sew and embroider, and once re-paired Captain Peel's jacket with 'invisible' mending. He could carve wood or bone, and play upon a home-made flute. He was a born inventor and he had designed what Keppel called 'a light iron case a foot long by eighteen inches, with a loop at each end. The case to be fitted with a Bickford's fuse, which burns under water. A sort of canvas duck punt was to be fitted to exactly hold the case amidships. The after part was to hold one sitter, who could easily steer with a canoe paddle without noise.' In this, Sheppard would paddle silently up to a Russian man-of-war, fix his explosive charge to her side, and paddle away again.

Keppel thought this 'simple enough' and when he took Sheppard to see the C-in-C, Admiral Lyons 'was amused and approved, leaving the time for the experiment to me'. But first Sheppard had to convince the sceptics in the fleet, which he did conclusively against HMS *London*. Sheppard said he would come unseen on a particular night and chalk the ship's name on her side just above the water-line. Double sentries were posted in *London* that night and the officers themselves kept special watch. But, in the morning, daylight showed the letters, just as Sheppard had promised.

Sheppard made his first attempt on the dark night, specially chosen, of 15/16th July 1855. Keppel and his coxswain went with him, guided to a place by the harbour shore, which was very close to the Russians, 'only separated by a spur of land covered by thick scrub and bush', 'At half past twelve the punt left the rough slips and was immediately lost to sight, nor was there the slightest sound.' The canoe floated only three inches above the water, and on such a night must have been virtually invisible.

Sheppard has left no account of his exploit, but Keppel has described how they waited for three hours, within range of Russian sentries, until there were signs of dawn in the sky but no sign of

Sheppard. Keppel was getting anxious, because if Sheppard were caught 'he would be shot as a spy'. However, an hour after they got back to camp they were all delighted to hear of Sheppard's safe return.

The plucky had pulled past and between a number of Russian steamers and was within 400 yards of the three-deckers, when a whole string of Russian boats pushed off from the western shore to convey troops across. For an hour he lay in his little punt hoping for an opening to pass through. Daylight came and he had not time to return the distance to where we were; he therefore struck at once for Careening Bay, one side of which he knew was in the possession of the French.

Apparently, a new plan of night attacks and bombardment by the British had made the Russians change their troop convoy routes across the bay, and so presented Sheppard with an unexpected obstacle. He made a second attempt from the French side of Careening Bay on 16th August, but could report no more success on that occasion either. However, both Keppel and Lyons mentioned Sheppard in their despatches and he was gazetted for the Victoria Cross in the first list of 24th February 1857.

Besides the Victoria Cross, Sheppard had the Conspicuous Gallantry Medal, the French Légion d'honneur, the Baltic Medal, the Crimea Medal with the Sebastopol clasp, the Turkish Crimean medal and the Sardinian Medal, *Al Valore Militari*. He also had the China Medal with the Canton 1857 clasp, won in *Highflyer*, which he joined in 1856 and where he was serving when the first VCs were invested by the Queen in Hyde Park on 26th June 1857. Sheppard's Cross was sent out to *Highflyer* and he was invested by his Captain, C.F.A. Shadwell, on board.

John Sheppard was a professional seaman, who spent his whole working life in the Navy or the Coast Guard Service. There is no record of when he joined the Navy but he was an Ordinary Seaman when he joined the *Fantome* frigate on 16th October 1840; he left her as Captain of the Forecastle on paying off on 20th October 1843. He spent the next ten years, from 7th November 1843, as a Coast Guard boatman, until 23rd October 1853 when he was 'lifted' (i.e. conscripted) for *St Jean D'Acre*, joining her as a Boatswain's Mate on the 25th. He later signed for continuous service, when he was described as of ruddy complexion, with grey eyes, brown hair, and as being five foot ten inches in height, vaccinated and married: his will gave his wife's name as Mary.

When he came home in *Highflyer* in 1861 he went as an instructor to the boys' training ship *Illustrious* in Portsmouth. He retired from the Service, as a Boatswain First Class, on 17th May 1870. In retirement he went to live in Hull. He had been born at Kingston-upon-Hull on 22nd September 1817, and his will, dated 1866, described him as 'late of Barrow in Co. Lincoln'. But he died at the other end of England, in Padstow, Cornwall, on 17th December 1884, when he possibly was on a visit to friends or relatives. His tombstone in Padstow Churchyard, which spells his name Sheppard, says that he died at John Harris's house in Padstow. His death certificate, which spells his name Shephard and is witnessed by John Harris, gives the cause of death as hypertrophy of the liver and erysipelas (inflammation, or 'St Anthony's fire') of the head. Both tombstone and death certificate record that he was a VC. Probate for his will was granted to a son, George, a Customs Officer.

Joseph Kellaway:
Sea of Azov, 31st August 1855

The first naval VC to become a prisoner-of-war was Boatswain Third Class Joseph Kellaway, of the paddle steam gunboat HMS *Wrangler* (6 guns), who was captured whilst taking part in one of the innumerable 'commando-type' raids carried out by the men of the Black Sea fleet during the summer of 1855 to cut Russian lines of communication and to destroy buildings, stores and equipment along the shores of the Sea of Azov. *Wrangler*, under Lieutenant Hugh Burgoyne (*qv*) was particularly active in these operations, and in a joint action on 31st August *Wrangler* and *Vesuvius* put boats' crews ashore at Marionpol to burn supply depots, while the paddle gunboats *Weser* and *Cracker* destroyed a bridge and government buildings at Arabat. That day Kellaway, Mr Odevaine the Mate, and three seamen from *Wrangler* landed in daylight near Marionpol to burn some boats, fishing stations and haystacks which were on the opposite bank of a small lake. They had nearly reached their objective when they were fired on by about fifty Russian riflemen, lying in ambush, who had slipped round behind Kellaway's party and cut off their retreat. One sailor was captured at once, but Kellaway, Odevaine and the other two seemed to be making good their escape when Odevaine slipped and fell headlong. Kellaway was sure he had been hit and wounded and came back to help him, although by that time the enemy had almost caught up with them. Because of the delay, Kellaway and Odevaine were surrounded and had to surrender after a very gallant but somewhat hopeless resistance. Burgoyne had been watching the whole incident through his telescope from *Wrangler's* upper deck and later wrote that 'I was myself an observer of the zeal, gallantry and self-devotion that characterised Mr Kellaway's conduct.' He was mentioned in Lord Lyons's despatches and awarded the Victoria Cross in the first list of 24th February 1857. He was present in Hyde Park for the first Investiture.

Kellaway and the others were not in captivity long. They were released by the Russians at Odessa on 20th October, being exchanged for two Russian officers and the wife and child of one of them. Boats put out from the shore and from the ship *Colombo* and the exchange was made at sea.

Kellaway was born in Kingston, Dorset, on 1st September 1824, and joined the Navy as a Boy in 1841. He served in *Cornwallis* in China in 1842 and in *Thalia*. He went as an Able Seaman to a gunnery course at *Excellent* in 1846, was rated Boatswain's Mate in 1848 and Boatswain Third Class in 1852. He joined *Wrangler* from *Tartarus* on 18th July 1854 and left her on 8th June 1856 to go to *Firebrand* as part complement Petty Officer of Rear-Admiral Stuart. He was promoted Chief Boatswain on 28th May 1868 and became Boatswain of Chatham Dockyard on 1st September 1870. On 9th December 1853, he married Hannah (née Cleverly) in Portsea and they had one daughter, Hannah Phoebe, who was born at their house in Trafalgar Place, Portsea, on 29th May 1857. Later, Kellaway lived in Luton Road, Chatham, dying there on 2nd October 1880 of 'Aneurism of ascending Aorta 3½ years and asphyxia', aged fifty-four. He was buried in grave space No.579, Section N, of Maidstone Road Cemetery, Chatham, where his wife and daughter, who both died in April 1890, are also buried with him.

George Fiott Day:
Sea of Azov, September 1855

Captain George Fiott Day VC, CB, RN was one of the most decorated officers in the Navy's history. His photograph shows him wearing three orders and nine medals, spaced across his uniform chest. The sight of this glittering array is supposed to have prompted the Prince of Wales (later Edward VII) to suggest in about 1870 that medals should be gathered neatly together on one bar.

Day's naval career was a particularly strenuous one, but it does show the kind of service demanded of the Victorian naval officer. He was hardly ever on shore, but went from one arduous and even dangerous sea appointment to another. He was born on 20th June 1819, the fourth son of the thirteen children of Mr and Mrs Charles Day, of Spear Hall, Beavis Hill, Southampton. He went to the Royal Naval School in Portsmouth and joined the Navy in August 1833, aged fourteen, as a Volunteer First Class. His naval adventures began at once, because his first ship, HMS *Challenger*, was wrecked at Molquilla on the coast of Patagonia on 19th May 1835. The coast there was barren desert but the crew successfully got ashore and maintained themselves for six weeks until they were rescued by *Blonde* on 6th July. As a Midshipman he served under Henry Keppel

53

in the brig *Childers* in 1836 during the Carlist War in Spain and later on the West Coast of Africa. In *Racer*, Day took five men in an open boat to capture a slaving schooner armed with an 18-pounder pivot gun a complement of thirty men. She was found to have a cargo of 230 slaves.

Day passed his examinations for Mate at Portsmouth on 10th November 1838 and as Mate of the *Benbow* (Captain Houston Stewart) he commanded the barge in the assault by the ship's boats on the town of Tortosa, on the coast of Syria, on 25th September 1840. He served in *Benbow* during the bombardment and capture of the great fortress of St Jean d'Acre in November, for which he received the Naval General Service Medal with St Jean d'Acre clasp and the Turkish St Jean d'Acre medal. He was promoted Lieutenant on 13th December 1845 and appointed to *Bittern* on the West African station. After a time on half-pay he went to *Excellent* for a gunnery course in 1847, passing out as a qualified gunnery officer on 3rd August 1848.

Day had campaign medals for the war in Burma in 1851 and for the Kaffir War in South Africa in 1853. On 12th November 1852 he was appointed Lieutenant in command of the paddle steamer *Locust* (3 guns) for the South American Station. He won official commendations for his service on the Plate and Paraguaya rivers during hostilities between the Argentine and Uruguay, and received the official thanks of the Admiralty for his running track-chart of the River Plate, the first ever prepared. *Locust* was also the first steam man-of-war to visit Asuncion Island. In 1854 *Locust* was sent to the Baltic under Napier, where Day won another medal at the capture of Bomarsund, *Locust* herself seizing two large troop-boats full of Russian soldiers.

In February 1855, Day was appointed to the command of another gunboat, *Recruit*, and in company with the 6-gun paddle sloop *Weser* sailed for the Black Sea. *Weser* ran aground on a rock at the entrance to the Dardanelles, but Day in *Recruit* successfully refloated her and towed her to Constantinople, lashed head-to-stern with *Recruit*, and with nineteen holes in her hull.

In 1855, *Recruit* took part in the expedition to force the Straits of Kertsch in May and in the attack on the fort of Arabat. In September she was cruising off the Genitchi Strait in company with other gunboats under Captain Sherard Osborn. Genitchi, on the north bank of the strait, was garrisoned by some 20,000 Russian troops. The south shore was defended by several guard-houses, with four gunboats moored near by, artillery, and several squadrons of mounted Cossacks. Day considered that if the Spit of Arabat could be properly reconnoitred, an attack might be mounted on the southern defences. A French officer, Captain Allemand of the steamer *Mouette*, had taken a party of about twenty ashore on the same errand a few days earlier. He and several of his men had been killed. Day thought that he travelled best who travelled alone. He took bearings of the masts of the Russian gunboats from *Recruit* and on the fine but very dark night of 16/17th September had himself rowed ashore in *Recruit*'s smallest boat by two sailors whom he told to lie off and wait for his hail. He had with him a pocket compass and, according to an account published in the 1860s, he also had some matches, a pair of 'double glasses', a revolver, and, in case he were arrested and wanted to prove he was not a spy, his lieutenant's commission in his pocket.

Day waded ashore at a point on the Spit of Arabat, a wilderness of sand and reeds and the home of thousands of marsh birds which he had to be careful not to disturb. He covered some four or five miles of swamp, sometimes having to wade thigh-deep, but got up to within 200 yards of the Russian positions. He saw that the gunboats were undermanned and lightly defended and seemed open to attack. At about two o'clock in the morning, after several hours ashore, he reached the beach, hailed his boat and was taken off.

Renewed enemy activity prevented any action next day, but on the 19th Day was back on shore. But this time the night was much colder and windier. He lost his way and blundered amongst the Russian outposts. He was alarmed to be fired on by Russian sentries (as he thought: they were actually firing to prove they were awake). He found the Russian gunboats fully manned and on the alert and decided that an attack was out of the question. It took him much longer to reach the point where the boat had dropped him and he could see no sign of it. He actually fired his pistol out to sea to attract their attention. Finally, numb with cold, drenched to the skin and almost exhausted he lay down among the reeds, where Mr W.H. Parker and a boat's crew from *Recruit* found him, more dead than alive and almost frozen stiff, the next morning. They had pulled inshore, afraid to find that their Captain was either dead or taken by the Russians. When he asked why they had not come in the night before, they said they had thought his shot was fired by the enemy. They fancied they saw him at one point, but did not approach the shore because, after all, he had said he would swim out to them (which was true). It took Day some forty-eight hours in bed to recover from his exertions but he was rewarded by a Victoria Cross in the first list of 24th February 1857. He was also awarded the French Légion d'honneur, the Turkish Order of the Medjidie 5th Class, the Crimean medal with Sea of Azov clasp, and the Turkish Crimean medal.

Day was promoted Commander on 19th November 1855 and given command of the steam sloop *Firefly* (4 guns) for service on the West African Station. They left on 26th May 1857 so Day was not able to attend the first Investiture in Hyde Park on 26th June. After *Firefly*, Day commanded the steam sloop *Sphinx* (6 guns) on the China

Station and gained yet another medal for actions against the Taku Forts and in the Canton River in 1859-61. He was promoted Captain on 20th August 1861 but ill-health prevented him taking any active service again and he retired on 14th February 1867. He was made a CB in May 1875.

In October 1858, Commander Day married Mary, daughter of James Ruddell Todd, MP for Honiton, Devon, in Kensington, London, and they had one daughter. In 1875, Captain Day and his wife and daughter went to live at 18 Claremont Crescent, Weston-super-Mare, where in December 1876 Day's health finally broke down. After lying paralysed in bed for six days, he died on 18th December.

Captain Day was buried in the local cemetery and his funeral was a great local occasion. It was attended by between two- and three thousand people, and many local tradesmen put up their shutters for the day as a mark of respect.

John Edmund Commerell and William Thomas Rickard: *Putrid Sea, October 1855*

The last Victoria Crosses for 'commando-type' raids by men of the Black Sea Fleet against Russian buildings and stores along the shore of the Azov and Putrid Seas were awarded to Commander John Commerell and Quartermaster William Rickard, of the steam gunboat HMS *Weser* (6 guns). Commander Commerell, *Weser's* Mate Mr Lillingston, and three seamen - Rickard, Milestone and Hoskins - rowed ashore in one of *Weser's* boats at about 2.30 am on the morning of 11th October 1855. They landed on the Spit of Arabat, hauled their boat out of the water and dragged it across dry land, which was about 200 or 300 yards wide at that point, and launched it again on the Sivash, or Putrid, Sea on the other side. They rowed across and reached the inland shore at about 4.30 am. While Mr Lillingston and Hoskins stayed behind in charge of the boat, Commerell led the other two inland. They walked for about two miles, using a hand compass to check their direction, and then waited for daybreak. As visibility improved with the dawn, they were able to see their objective, which was a fodder store containing about 400 tons of corn about a mile away, with a large red building beside it, close to the Cossack guard station and signal post. Commerell and his party waded through two canals, neck-deep in water, and set fire to the fodder stores. The red building would not ignite and the Cossacks came streaming out of their guard post while Commerell was still trying to light it. They saw the raiders and gave chase, but in the confusion Commerell had managed to gain about a mile start. Pursued by the Cossacks the three men ran down to the nearest canal, waded across it and set off for the second canal. The pursuit was so hot that Milestone became exhausted and begged to be left behind, but the other two removed his boots, swam with him across the second canal, and half-carried him, half ran with him, down to the boat. Assisted by Lillingston and Hoskins, who gave covering fire from the boat, the three managed to escape and embarked in time. The Cossacks were only sixty yards away when the boat pushed out from the shore and Commerell actually killed the nearest horseman with his pistol. Later, the look-outs watching from *Weser*'s masthead reported that the fodder store had burned to the ground. Commerell and Rickard were both awarded the Victoria Cross in the first list of 24th February 1857, but neither of them was present at the first Investiture.

John Edmund Commerell went on to a long and most distinguished career of public service, becoming an Admiral of the Fleet, MP for Southampton, a Lord of the Admiralty, GCB, and an ADC and Groom in Waiting to the Queen. Unlike almost all other VCs, he did not retire at a lower rank, or succumb to wounds or illness, but served on and reached the top of his profession. He died only a few months after the Queen herself and his naval service of over fifty-seven years covered the greater part of her reign, so that the ships he served in, the battles he fought in, the appointments he held, the orders and decorations and honours he won, are in their own way a concise history of the Victorian Navy.

He was born at Park Street, Grosvenor Square, London on 13th January 1829, the son of John William Commerell, of Strood Park, Horsham, Sussex. He went to Clifton and to the Royal Naval School before joining the Navy as Volunteer First Class on the 8th March 1842. He served in *Cornwallis* in China but had his first real experience of close action in the boats of the steam frigate *Firebrand*, under Captain (later Admiral Sir James) Hope, in the Paraná River, South America, in November 1845. He passed for Mate on 16th May 1848 and was commissioned Lieutenant on 28th December. As a lieutenant, on 13th October 1853, Commerell married Matilda Maria, fourth daughter of Joseph Busby of St Croix, West Indies. Dame Commerell died in London, at a very great age, in June 1930.

Commerell commanded the gunboat *Vulture* (6 guns) in the Baltic under Napier from 15th February 1854 until he was promoted Commander on 20th February 1855 and appointed in command of *Weser*. In April he sailed in *Weser* for the Black Sea, but on the 25th she caught fire, struck a rock and had to be beached at the entrance to the Dardanelles. *Weser* was eventually refloated and towed to Constantinople with the assistance of Commander George Day, himself a VC, in *Recruit*. He left *Weser* after the surrender of the Kinburn Forts in 1856 and went on to command *Snake* in the Mediterranean. He was unable to attend the VC Investiture in June 1857 because he was already on his way to China to command the steam vessel *Fury* (6 guns), and greatly distinguished himself whilst leading a division of seamen against the Taku Forts on 25th June. The attack was beaten off with the considerable loss (for those minor Victorian wars) of 64 officers and men killed and 252 wounded. But Commerell's part was praised, publicly and professionally; he was mentioned in despatches, and received an illuminated address of thanks from both Houses of Parliament. He was promoted Captain, and took command of the paddle-steamer *Magicienne* on the China Station on 18th July 1859.

Commerell generally managed to do something of note or interest in his commissions. In 1865 he commanded the new 'cupola' ironclad *Scorpion*, so called because of the cupola shape of her gun batteries. The following year he commanded the steam vessel *Terrible* (21 guns) and assisted in the laying of the Transatlantic cable, for which he was awarded a Civil CB. In December 1869, while commanding the ironclad turret ship *Monarch*, he took the body of the American philanthropist George Peabody across the Atlantic for burial in the United States. In 1871 he was Commodore and Senior Officer on the West Coast of Africa and took an active part in the Ashanti War; but in August 1873, while reconnoitring the Prah River, he was dangerously wounded by a musket-ball in the lungs and had to be invalided home. In 1874 the war was prosecuted and successfully ended by another VC, Commodore Bully Hewett. As ADC, on St George's Day 1874, Commerell attended the Queen when she inspected the Naval Brigade at the Royal Clarence Victualling Yard, Gosport.

Commerell was promoted Rear-Admiral on 12th November 1876 and the following year flew his flag in the five-masted ironclad *Agincourt* as Second-in-Command of the Mediterranean Fleet under Admiral Sir Geoffrey Phipps Hornby. It was a time of hostilities between Russia and Turkey, and Hornby kept his fleet as a stabilising influence at the eastern end of the Mediterranean and in the Dardanelles for over two years. Hornby, himself regarded as the finest seaman of his day, thought very highly of Commerell. When Hornby was knighted in 1878, he wrote to his wife that 'It will give me no pleasure to be called "Sir Geoffrey"; but I certainly am pleased and proud to know that the best men in the service - I mean such as Commerell, Hewett, Salmon, Baird & c.- are glad to serve under me.' A few days later, when Commerell (who had himself been made KCB on 31st March 1874, four years *before* his Admiral) was nearly drowned in a sailing accident, Hornby commented, 'The country would indeed have suffered a grievous loss if Commerell had been drowned the other day.'

As the last years of the nineteenth century ran out, honours and promotions were showered on Commerell: a Lord of the Admiralty in 1879; Vice-Admiral on 19th January 1881: in November, C-in-C of the North American and West Indies Station; Member of

Parliament from 1885 to 1888; full Admiral, 12th April 1886; a GCB at the Queen's Golden Jubilee in 1887; C-in-C Portsmouth in 1888 and the Navy's host for the Kaiser's visit and naval review in 1889 (the Kaiser was prevented by protocol from giving Commerell a decoration so gave him instead a beautifully jewelled sword); 1891, Groom in Waiting to the Queen; 14th February 1892, Admiral of the Fleet; and, finally, retirement on 13th January 1899.

The Admiral died at his home, 45 Rutland Gate, Hyde Park, London on 21st May 1901, and was buried in Folkestone. Representatives of the King, the Kaiser, the Duke of Cornwall, the Duke of Connaught, Prince Henry of Battenberg and many naval officers, serving and retired, attended the memorial service at All Saints, Ennismore Gardens, London SW.

William Thomas Rickard was born at Stoke Damerel, Devonport, on 10th February 1828. His naval career was very typical of his time. He joined in 1845 as a Boy Second Class, went to the West African Station in *Britomart* in 1847 and was wounded in the right foot so that he had to be invalided home. He joined the frigate *Arethusa* (50 guns) in February 1850 as an Able Seaman and served in her throughout the first year of the Crimean War, until he joined *Weser* as Quartermaster on 25th February 1855. He won his VC on Commerell's personal recommendation, who wrote: 'I must bring to your notice the excellent conduct of the small party who accompanied me, more especially that of William Rickard, Quartermaster, who, though much fatigued himself, remained to assist the other seaman who from exhaustion had fallen in the mud and was unable to extricate himself.'

Rickard served on in *Weser* after Commerell left and was very probably invested with his Victoria Cross on board by Commerell's successor, Commander Johnstone, sometime in 1857. Rickard must have celebrated his medal too enthusiastically because he forfeited on 26th December the good-conduct badge he had been awarded that July, and ended 1857 as an Able Seaman again. However, he regained his rate in July 1858 and was a Quartermaster when he was paid off to the *Impregnable* in Devonport in June 1859. His last ship was the screw liner *Donegal* as Captain of the Forecastle; he then joined the Coast Guard Service as boatman, chief boatman and latterly as Chief Officer of Coast Guards, retiring sometime in the 1870s.

In June 1860, Rickard married Rebecca Whitingham, of Kingsbridge, and they had two sons and a daughter. In retirement, Rickard was boatman to the Ryde Rowing Club in the Isle of Wight and he and his family lived first at the club's boathouse and then at Arethusa Cottage, Smallbrook, Ryde. Besides the VC, Rickard had the Conspicuous Gallantry Medal, the Légion d'honneur, the Crimean medal with clasps for Sebastopol, Inkerman and the Sea of Azov, and the Turkish Crimean medal. He had his VC pension of £10 a year, paid at £2 10s a quarter, and from September 1888 he also had £25 a year from the Greenwich Hospital Pension for Coast Guard Chief Officers, which became available to him through a death vacancy of another officer. He died on 21st February 1905, in the Royal Infirmary, Ryde.

George Milestone, the sailor whom Rickard rescued, was a much younger man, born in December 1834. He also came from Stoke Damerel, Devonport, and served with Richard in *Arethusa, Weser* and *Impregnable*. It is quite likely that Rickard took a fatherly interest in the young man from his own home village. Milestone was married, and he signed for ten years' continuous service in July 1855. He did not win the Victoria Cross and nothing more is known of him.

Commerell and Milestone shared in the same adventure. One of them became an Admiral, and walked with kings, queens and emperors. The other returned into oblivion.

Nowell Salmon and John Harrison:
Lucknow, November 1857

When the news of the outbreak of the Indian Mutiny reached Singapore in July 1857, the 50-gun steam frigate *Shannon* (Captain William Peel CB) was on her way to take part in the Second China War and the 21-gun steam corvette *Pearl* (Captain E.F. Sotheby) was serving on the Pacific Station. Both ships were diverted and sailed with troop reinforcements to Calcutta, where they arrived in August. The army in India was short of trained infantry and especially of heavy artillery. Naval Brigades were landed with ships' guns and sent inland to assist the army, the *Shannon's* up the Ganges to Cawnpore and Lucknow, the *Pearl's* up the Gogra River to North-West Bengal.

'Peel's Jacks', as they were called, were superb campaigners, able to march, fight, live off the land, handle guns and horses with equal ease, and soon won a fearsome reputation amongst the sepoys, who firmly believed that the Jacks were all four foot high by five foot wide from snout to tail, carried 9-pounder guns over their heads, and ate human flesh as much as they could, salting down the rest for future consumption.

On 16th November 1857 the Naval Brigade, which then consisted of about 200 sailors and marines, with six 24-pounder guns, two 8-inch howitzers, and two rocket tubes mounted on bullock-drawn carts known as 'hackeries', all under the command of Peel himself, were in action in Lucknow town, bombarding a massive fortress, a domed mosque surrounded by a thick masonry wall with loopholes cut for musket fire, known as the Shah Nujeff.
Although Peel led his guns up to within a few feet of the Shah

Nujeff wall and, as the British force commander Sir Colin Campbell said in his despatches, 'behaved very much as if he had been laying *Shannon* alongside an enemy's frigate', the Shah Nujeff resisted the attacks, and musket fire from the walls caused casualties amongst the sailors. Peel called for volunteers to climb a tree near the Shah Nujeff wall, to spot the enemy's positions and dislodge mutineers who were tossing grenades down amongst the guns' crews. Three men, Lieutenant Nowell Salmon, Boatswain's Mate John Harrison and Able Seaman Richard Southwell, responded. Southwell was killed and Salmon was hit by a musket-ball in the thigh, but they succeeded in dislodging what Salmon himself called 'the ruffians who were throwing grenades'. Salmon regarded his injury as 'a slight flesh wound, with not the slightest danger attached to it', and, as he wrote later to his mother, 'I have been promised the Victoria Cross, and for that I would have taken two wounds of the same sort.' Peel did indeed recommend Salmon, with Harrison, for the Victoria Cross, and both awards were in the *London Gazette* of 24th December 1858. Salmon received his medal, as a Commander, from Queen Victoria at Buckingham Palace on 8th June 1859. Harrison was invested by the Queen in the quadrangle of Windsor Castle on 4th January 1860. There were no posthumous VC awards at the time, so Richard Southwell received nothing and is now forgotten.

Nowell Salmon went on to a very long and very distinguished naval career, eventually retiring as 'Father of the Navy' after more than half a century of service. He was born on 20th February 1835 at the Vicarge, Swarraton, Hampshire only son of the Reverend Henry Salmon, rector of the parish, and Emily, daughter of Vice-Admiral Nowell, of Iffley, Oxford. He went to Marlborough College, and joined the Navy as a Volunteer First Class in May 1847, aged twelve. He served as a midshipman in the 38-gun frigate *Thetis* on the South American Station from 1851 to 1853, was promoted Mate in March 1854 and served in the Baltic in the 91-gun screw line-of-battleship *James Watt*, gaining the Baltic Medal. After promotion to Lieutenant on 5th January 1856, he joined *Shannon* as Junior Lieutenant in May.

Nowell Salmon was promoted Commander on 22nd March 1856, aged only twenty-one, and his first important independent command *was* the 11-gun steam corvette *Icarus* on the Mediterranean and West Indies Stations from 1859 to 1861. In August 1860, off the coast of Central America, Salmon captured the notorious American 'filibuster' William Walker and his remaining supporters. Walker had once actually set up his own government of Nicaragua but was then on the run from Honduras government forces. Salmon assured Walker and his followers that he was surrendering to British forces, but then turned his captives over to the Hondurenos. Described at the time as 'a young and pompous Commander', Salmon would listen to no arguments, even when reminded of his promise.

61

However, he did obtain pardons for all but Walker and his faithful lieutenant, Colonel Rudler. These two were sentenced to death by court martial on 11th September and shot the next day. Salmon received a gold medal from the Central American states.

Salmon was promoted Captain on 12th December 1863, aged twenty-eight, and commanded *Defence* in the West Indies, *Valiant* as guardship in the River Shannon, and in 1878 *Swiftsure* in the Mediterranean under Admiral Sir Geoffrey Phipps Hornby, who thought very highly of him, listing him with Hewett, Commerell and others, amongst the best men in the Navy. On 11th January 1866, at Upwey, Dorset, he married Emily Augusta, daughter of Erasmus Saunders, of Westbrook, and they had one son and a daughter.

For the last twenty-five years of his naval career, Nowell Salmon rose steadily, almost inexorably, through the ranks of the service. He was made ADC to the Queen in 1874, resigning the appointment when he was promoted Rear-Admiral on 2nd August 1879. He was C-in-C Cape of Good Hope 1882-5 and was promoted Vice-Admiral on 1st July 1885. C-in-C of China Station 1888-91, he was promoted Admiral on 10th September 1891. He was made a CB in 1876, KCB for the Queen's Golden Jubilee in 1887 and GCB for the Diamond Jubilee in 1897. As C-in-C Portsmouth from 1894 to 1897, he commanded the Diamond Jubilee Review in 1897, flying his flag in *Renown*. There were 65 British warships on view, drawn up in six lines, all from the Home Station; not one had been taken from service overseas. Nowell Salmon was promoted Admiral of the Fleet on 18th January 1899 and retired from the active list in 1905. He lived in retirement at Curdridge Grange, Botley, Hampshire and died on 14th February 1912 at 44 Clarence Parade, Southsea.

John Harrison was an Irishman, born at Castleborough, Co. Wexford on 24th January 1832, son of John Harrison, an estate carpenter, and Elizabeth. He was baptised at St Peters, Killigny, Clonroche, Co. Wexford on 29th January. He joined the Navy as a Boy Second Class, on 2nd February 1850. His first ship was *Prometheus*, in which he was rated Ordinary Seaman, and he joined the line-of-battleship *Agamemnon* on 1st February 1853. He served in her throughout the Crimean War, and left her as Leading Seaman and Coxswain of the pinnace in July 1856. His next and final ship was *Shannon*, which he joined on commissioning in October 1856. He was rated Boatswain's Mate and Petty Officer on 27th June 1858 (so he was actually a leading seaman when he won his VC) and was discharged from the Navy on 13th January 1859. With a letter of recommendation from Lieutenant Young VC, under whose immediate command he had been at the Shah Nujeff, he obtained a post with the Customs and Excise. He had been wounded during the relief of Lucknow and his health later in life was not good. He made several visits to the Naval Hospital for treatment for malaria, contracted during his service in the East. From notes in his diaries and two Bibles, still in the possession of his family, he appears to have been a deeply religious man and a firm Protestant. In his later years he lived at 5 Stafford Place, Westminster, London SW1. He died on 27th December 1865 and was buried at Brompton Cemetery, West London, on 29th. He never married.

Thomas James Young and William Hall:
Lucknow, November 1857

The relief of the British Residency in Lucknow on 17th November 1857 was one of the most famous incidents of the Indian Mutiny. Amongst the relieving force which fought their way street by street through Lucknow was a Naval Brigade from the 50-gun steam frigate *Shannon*, led by Captain William Peel CB.

On 16th November, the Naval Brigade, consisting of about 200 sailors and marines, advanced upon a high walled enclosure made of thick masonry, which was some 120 yards square and very strongly defended by the mutineers, known as the Secunderabagh. Naval guns and the Royal Artillery bombarded the place for an hour and a half before a breach was made and the fortress was stormed and taken, more than 2,000 mutineers being killed inside. The day was now well on, and it was four o'clock in the afternoon before the Naval Brigade, with the same six 24-pounder ship's guns and some mortars, arrived in front of their next objective. This was an even more formidable fortress, the domed mosque, surrounded by a masonry wall cut with loopholes for muskets, called the Shah Nujeff.

Under the immediate command of Lieutenant Thomas Young, *Shannon's* Gunnery Officer, the sailors ran their guns up so close to the Shah Nujeff wall that their muzzles almost touched the brickwork, and when they fired, the guns and their crews were completely hidden in smoke and brick dust. The guns' crews kept up a steady fire in spite of a hail of musket-balls and grenades from the defenders on the walls above. Able Seaman William Hall, a member of one gun's crew, said later that 'After firing each round we ran the gun forward until finally the crew were in danger of being hit by splinters of brick and stone torn from the wall by the round shot. Lieutenant Young moved from gun to gun, giving calm encouragement.' When Hall was left the sole survivor of his crew, all the rest being killed or wounded, Young took the last gunner's place and helped Hall load and serve the gun.

Three hours' hard pounding seemed to do very little damage to the Shah Nujeff. Sergeant John Paton, of the 93rd Highlanders, reconnoitred for himself round a corner of the bastion wall, found a small gap, and went in. The mutineers had all retreated and in a few minutes, the Shah Nujeff had been captured. Next day the naval guns were in action again, against a building called the Mess House, which was stormed and taken that afternoon. Troops went on to reach and relieve the Residency, which was still holding out, having been very ably defended by Sir James Outram. On Peel's recommendation, Young and Hall both received the Victoria Cross (as did Sergeant John Paton of the 93rd) and were gazetted together on 1st February 1859.

Young received his Cross from the Queen's hands at a special Investiture in the quadrangle of Buckingham Palace on 8th June 1859 (at the same time as Nowell Salmon) and added the medal to his Crimean Medal with Azov clasp, his Turkish Crimean medal, his Order of Medjidie 5th Class and his Indian Mutiny medal with Relief of Lucknow clasp. He had taken his chances and had had an adventurous and successful career. But his later days were undistinguished. He died, an obscure Captain on half pay, in a foreign land. Young was born in 1827 and very probably joined the Navy as a Cadet in the early 1840s. He was promoted Mate on 7th December 1848 and after a gunnery course at *Excellent* in 1850, became a Lieutenant on 11th April 1851. He was appointed a Junior Gunnery Lieutenant in the 90-gun screw liner *Agamemnon* on commissioning in September 1852, and served in her throughout the Crimean War. In June and July 1855 he took part in the expeditions into the Sea of Azov and was mentioned in despatches for his gallantry in the boats during attacks at Taganrog and Marienpol. He left *Agamemnon* on paying off in July 1856, and in September was appointed to *Shannon* as Gunnery Lieutenant on commissioning. Young was promoted Commander on 23rd June 1858, with his promotion specially back-dated to 22nd March 1858. On 28th October 1859 he was appointed Inspecting Commander of Coast Guard at Kingston, Devon, and while in this appointment he married Louisa Mary Boyes at the Parish Church, Paddington, on 10th January 1860. (Louisa was the sister of Midshipman Duncan Gordon Boyes, who won a VC in HMS *Euryalus* in Japan in 1864.) They had two daughters, Laura Mary and Georgina Victoria.

Young's next command was *Gibraltar*, in which he was cautioned by the Board for grounding her in a heavy squall at Piraeus in May 1865. Despite this mishap he was promoted Captain on 11th April 1866, but placed on half pay. His wife was living at 20 Manchester Street, Manchester Square, London, but Young himself died at Caen in Normandy, where he had presumably gone on holiday or perhaps to convalesce. He died on 20th March 1869, aged forty-two, and was buried in the Protestant Cemetery in the Rue du Magasin à Poudre. It was appropriate that a hero of the Indian Mutiny should be buried in a road named after a powder magazine, but a century later his grave was in a state of disrepair.

William Hall was the first coloured man to win the Victoria Cross. His father was an African negro, one of a cargo of slaves freed by the British frigate *Leopard* and taken to Nova Scotia during

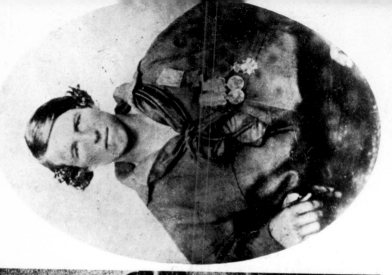

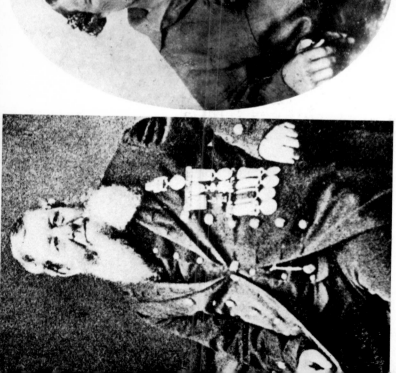

ve right: Joseph Trewavas (Author's Collection)
ve left: John Sheppard (Photo by Walker, Hull)

w left: George Fiott Day (Photo by Chaffin, Taunton)
w centre: John Commerell (Photo by John Hawke, Plymouth)
w right: William Rickard (Photo by Hughes & Mullins, Ryde)

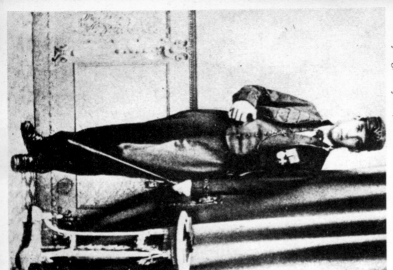

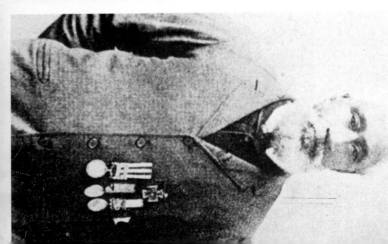

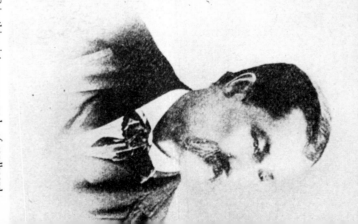

Above left: Samuel Mitchell, who lost his medal. The VC in this picture was made of cardboard (Photo by Tait, Hokitike).

Above right: William Seeley, the first American citizen to win a VC (Photo by Kivlan, Leominster, Massachusetts)

Below left: Arthur Mayo (From *Our Bit* by Charles Herbert Mayo, printed for private circulation by J.C. and A.T. Sawtell, Sherborne, Dorset, 1920)

Below right: William Hall, who in 1857 became the first coloured man to win the VC (Photo by E. Ayling, Croydon).

the war of 1812. The story goes that his father was cared for by a family called Hall, and eventually took their name, a frequent custom. For a time he is supposed to have worked for Sir Samuel Cunard as gardener and handyman, before moving to Horton's Bluff, where he farmed a smallholding and where William Hall was born on 28th April 1827. William Hall first went to sea at the age of seventeen and spent six or seven years as a deckhand in various ships before joining the Royal Navy, supposedly at Liverpool. His first record in the Navy was as Ordinary Seaman joining the line-of-battleship *Rodney* in February 1852. He served in her throughout the Crimean War and was awarded the Crimean Medal

After being paid off to *Victory* in Portsmouth after the end of *Rodney's* commission in January 1856, Hall deserted. His name was marked in the ship's books as 'R' (Run) to show that he was a deserter, on 12th March 1856. He forfeited all previous time, medals, prize money, bounty, uniform and personal effects left on board. However, he rejoined the Navy and was an Able Seaman again when he joined *Shannon*, soon after commissioning, in October that year. Whatever his misdemeanours, Hall was clearly an expert seaman: in *Shannon* he rose to be Leading Seaman (1st February 1858), and to Captain of the Mast and Captain of the Foretop (July 1858). His next ship, from June 1859 to June 1862, was the screw line-of-battleship *Donegal*. He was presented with his Victoria Cross at a special parade of officers and men on board *Donegal* by Rear-Admiral Charles Talbot, C-in-C at Cork, at Queenstown, Ireland, on 28th October 1859.

Hall was serving in *Canopus* in February 1866 when there was some controversy about his date of birth. He wished to sign for ten years' continuous service and stated that he was born on 28th April 1827. But his original service certificate gave his date of birth as 28th April 1821, making him over forty years old, and ineligible to sign for continuous service. The matter was referred to the Admiralty, who decreed that his birthdate was in 1828, and so in his next ship *Bellerophon*, at Lisbon in February 1869, Hall signed for continuous service, the engagement being back-dated to 1866. Hall finished his career as a Quartermaster and Petty Officer in *Peterel* and left the Navy in June 1876, and at once returned to his native Nova Scotia in July. He farmed a smallholding, like his father, at Avonport, and lived quietly with his two unmarried sisters (giving the compilers of a biographical dictionary the information that his chief recreation was 'shooting crows'). He died at his home on 25th August 1904 and was buried in near-by Brooklyn. The cemetery was abandoned and the grave fell into disrepair. However, the Hampshire County Branch of the Canadian Legion disinterred his remains in 1945 and reburied them on the lawn of Hantsport Baptist Church. A memorial cairn was erected and dedicated over the grave in 1947.

Arthur Mayo:
Dacca, November 1857

The Indian Navy, which evolved out of the old Honourable East India Company's Marine, also provided Naval Brigades during the Indian Mutiny, although their exploits had nothing like the publicity given to *Shannon* and *Pearl*. Serving with one detachment of the Indian Naval Brigade was Arthur Mayo, a young Englishman who had first come out to India as a Midshipman RN in *Wellesley* in 1855 and later transferred to the Indian Navy. In the summer of 1857 he was serving in the steam paddle frigate *Punjaub*, whose officers and men made up part of No.4 Detachment of the Naval Brigade that landed in Calcutta in June, and immediately went up-country for service in suppressing the mutiny in Eastern Bengal.

By November the Detachment were in Dacca, where the 73rd Native Infantry Regiment and elements of the Bengal Artillery were openly mutinous and had to be disarmed. Early on the 22nd, 5 officers and 85 men of the Brigade, under *Punjaub*'s First Lieutenant, Lieutenant T.E. Lewis, stormed and captured the Treasury, where thousands of rupees were stored, and went on to the Lall Bagh, a large enclosure in the town, formerly the palace garden of the rulers of Eastern Bengal.

When they got inside the Lall Bagh, the sailors found the sepoys already drawn up for battle in front of their magazine, with two 6-pounder guns in their midst. A domed mosque in the centre, a hospital, numerous buildings and a barracks on top of a hill, had all loopholes knocked in their brickwork and were heavily defended by armed men. The total strength of the mutineers was between 300 and 400 men. When the sailors deployed into line the sepoys opened fire with canister and muskets, but fired too high. The sailors replied with one volley and then charged uphill, broke down the barrack doors with musket butts and stormed inside. In a desperate hand-to-hand struggle, many sepoys were bayoneted to death. With the barracks secure, the sailors repeatedly charged downhill to take the remaining sepoys in the flank. For the last charge, Midshipman Mayo placed himself some twenty yards in front of his men and led the way, with a great cheer, to capture the 6-pounder guns.

Mayo served with the Naval Brigade until January 1860, having distinguished himself once again and been mentioned in despatches in February 1859, when he took part in an expedition with native infantry and artillery into the Abor Hills. Though wounded in the hand by a poisoned arrow, he led a storming party across a bridge to take a native stockade. His Victoria Cross was gazetted on 25th February 1862.

Mayo was only seventeen years old when he won his VC, one of the youngest naval winners. He was born in St Giles, Oxford, on

18th May 1840, the fifth son of Herbert Mayo FGS and Sarah Harman. He went to Berkhamstead School in 1847 and joined the Navy in 1854. His father was once an infantry cadet in the East India Company, and his elder brother John served in the 38th Foot at Sebastopol and at the Relief of Lucknow. Mayo's Victoria Cross was first sent out to India but was either returned or lost, and was sent out again to his mother's home at Theobald's, Waltham Cross, Hertfordshire. He was finally presented with his VC by the Prince of Wales on 22nd June 1864, when he was an undergraduate at Oxford. He had been invalided home in 1860 and in November 1862, when the Indian Navy had ceased to exist, he was finally pensioned.

Shortly after graduating, on 18th July 1865, he married Ellen Baker at Oxford; they had six children, two daughters and four sons. He was ordained Deacon by Bishop Hamilton of Salisbury in February 1866 and served as Curate at St Peter's, Plymouth, until October 1867. He was received into the Roman Catholic Church on 5th November. Subsequently, he resided for many years at St Mary's, Torquay, lived in Malta from 1892 to 1901, and finally settled in Boscombe, Hampshire. He died suddenly while entertaining friends at his home on his eightieth birthday, 18th May 1920, and was buried in Boscombe Cemetery.

Edward Robinson:
Lucknow, March 1858

In November 1857, guns of *Shannon*'s Naval Brigade joined in a three-day bombardment of the Kaiserbagh fortress in Lucknow, to cover the evacuation of European women, children and wounded, and stores, from the Residency. The naval guns and rocket tubes kept up their fire to the last moment and everybody was safely brought out during the night of 22nd/23rd November. But though the Residency had been relieved, the city of Lucknow was not finally captured by Sir Colin Campbell until March 1858, when some 400 officers and men of the Naval Brigade took part in the final assault which began on 2nd March. Sailors assisted in the building of a bridge to cross the Gumti river on 6th/7th, and the naval guns bombarded the strongpoints of the Martinière on the 9th and the Begum Cotee on the 11th.

By 13th March, the Naval Brigade were occupying earth defence works in the grounds of the Begum Cotee, with troops defending near-by houses and gardens. After several exchanges with sepoys in the houses opposite, a house immediately on the sailors' left was set on fire. Some skirmishers in front had to fall back on the sailors' lines, and the naval guns at once opened fire on the sepoys

Edward Robinson was born in Portsea and joined *Victory* as a Boy Second Class on 11th August 1852, when he was thirteen years old. He joined *Shannon* on commissioning in September 1856 and she appears to have been his last ship. After being invalided from the Navy in September 1858 he spent ten years until 1868 in the Coast Guard Service, and was then for the next ten years employed in the Naval Reserve office. He married Ann Goldsack at Dover in September 1865, and they had eight children. In 1893, through the friendly interest of the Duke of Edinburgh, Robinson became lodge-keeper in the Home Park at Windsor. It was a job specially kept for old sailors and soldiers of good character and brought with it a house and a small garden. For the last three years of his life he suffered from throat cancer, and died of it at his house, Albert Bridge Lodge, Old Windsor, on 2nd October 1896, aged fifty-seven. He was buried in Old Windsor Cemetery and the mourners included his five sons.

George Bell Chicken:
Suhejnee, Bengal, September 1858

George Chicken's was the only naval VC to be won on horseback. Strictly, he was not in the Navy at all at the time, but a civilian - a Volunteer serving with the Indian Naval Brigade. He was appointed into the Service on 31st July 1858, as Acting Master, borne on the books of HMS *Calcutta*. After a few months at Fort William he joined No.3 Detachment of the Naval Brigade, serving in the rough broken country and jungles of Jagdispur in Bengal against the mutineers under the brothers Kunwar and Amar Singh.

On 27th September 1858, George Chicken attached himself to a mixed party of 54 troopers of the 3rd Sikh Irregular Cavalry and 68 men of Rattray's mounted police, under Lieutenant Charles George Baker of the Bengal Police, in an attack on a force of about 700 mutineers encamped at a village called Suhejnee, near Peroo, in Bengal. Apparently, Chicken had openly announced his determination to win a Victoria Cross and he behaved with conspicuous gallantry during the charge that day. The mutineers were routed

advancing towards them. During the action, some sandbags on top of the earthworks were set alight. Able Seaman Edward Robinson jumped up and extinguished the fires in some of the bags and threw others clear, where they could do no damage. The nearest sepoys were now within fifty yards' range and Robinson came under very heavy musket fire. He was hit in the shoulder and knocked unconscious back into the trenches, where his mates on the guns' crew dragged him to safety. He was recommended for the Victoria Cross by Captain William Peel, and was gazetted on 24th December 1858.

and were soon in flight, pursued by Chicken and the others. Chicken quickly forged ahead, driving his horse recklessly across river nullahs and through sugar canes and thick jungle. When he caught up with a party of about twenty armed mutineers he was quite alone. Chicken at once charged them and killed five with his sword, but was then set upon by the rest, knocked off his horse and badly wounded. He would certainly have been killed had not four native troopers of the 1st Bengal Police and the 3rd Sikh Irregulars galloped up and rescued him. On receiving the despatches of Colonel Turner, in overall command of the cavalry column, Sir Colin Campbell (later Lord Clyde) recommended both Baker and Chicken for the Victoria Cross, and both duly received it.

Chicken returned to Calcutta in November 1859, and the following March was given command of HM Schooner *Emily* (2 guns). On 13th December 1858, Queen Victoria had signed a Royal Warrant 'to declare that Non-Military persons who as volunteers have borne arms against mutineers, both at Lucknow and elsewhere, during the late operations in India shall be considered eligible to receive the Decoration of the Victoria Cross'. Under the terms of this Warrant, Chicken's Victoria Cross was gazetted on 27th April, 1860. But, ironically, it is possible that George Chicken never heard of the award he had tried so hard to win, for in May his schooner *Emily* was lost with all hands in a violent squall off Sandheads, in the Bay of Bengal. The War Office posted the medal to his father, George Chicken, a master mariner, of Shadwell, London E., on 4th March 1862.

William Odgers:
Waireka, North Island, New Zealand, March 1860

Early in 1860 another Naval Brigade was in action against the Maoris in New Zealand. The cause of the dispute, as in the earlier Maori war of 1845-7, was the ownership of land. There was a general uprising amongst the Maoris, who began to wage skilful guerrilla warfare against the white settlers and the forces of the Crown making good use of their local knowledge, and operating from forts, or *pahs*, which they held for as long as they needed, before slipping away to safety somewhere else. By February 1860 the city of Auckland was in a near panic and the settlers of Taranaki province, on the west coast of North Island, had abandoned their possessions and retreated to New Plymouth, on the coast, whilst the Maoris inland burned their houses and plundered their settlements.

There was therefore great joy and relief at New Plymouth when the steamer *Adelaide* arrived on 1st March with troops of the 65th (Yorks and Lancs) Regiment accompanied by the 13-gun steam sloop

Niger (Captain Peter Cracroft RN). After nearly a month of operations, a party of settlers and volunteers were cut off by the Maoris at a fortified place called Omata, a few miles south of New Plymouth. There were reports that settlers' wives and children had been massacred. A force of some 300 officers and men of the 65th, with militia, volunteers, *Niger's* First Lieutenant, William Blake, 2 officers and 25 seamen, landed on 28th March and went inland.

At about 1 pm an alarm signal from the town showed that the relieving force themselves needed assistance. Two surf-boats came out to *Niger* and embarked Captain Cracroft, 6 officers, 32 blue-jackets and 10 marines, with a 24lb rocket tube. The party formed up on the jetty, put their rocket tube and ammunition in a bullock cart, and with a further 250 men of the 65th and some volunteers set off for Omata. (About 50 stokers and boys were left to look after *Niger*, however, there was no seaborne danger at all.)

They arrived at about 5 pm and found one volunteer dead and two more and Lieutenant Blake badly wounded. About a mile away, on a hill called Waireka, there was a large fortified *pah* with three Maori battle flags flying from it. Although an order had been given to retire, Cracroft led his men towards the *pah*, saying, according to one account, 'My lads, there are three flags flying in defiance of the Queen and our men. Ten pounds to the man that hauls the big flag down.' The sailors went on another half a mile on the Omata road, until they could hear Maoris firing at the 65th in a near-by gulley. They stopped and fired five or six rockets at about 700 yards' range

...and then stepped on easy like as it was getting quite dark. When we got to about sixty yards from the *pah*, the rascals saw us and began cheering so we gave out cheers and in we went amongst them, cutting and popping away quite lively, killed as many as we could see, tore down the flags, and then as we could not see friends from foes, we fell in and marched off in the best order we could.

Because of the suddenness of the dusk attack, the bluejackets had only four casualties.

The man who captured the largest flag was the Captain's Coxswain, Leading Seaman William Odgers who, with Captain of the Foretop Roger Glanville, Able Seaman William Older and Marine William Clarke, was recommended for the Victoria Cross. Cracroft recommended them all, but if they could not all get it, he specially mentioned Odgers 'being the most daring'. Odgers was gazetted on 3rd August 1860 and received his Cross at a special ceremony at Mount Wise, Devonport, from the C-in-C Plymouth, Admiral Houston Stewart, on 23rd July 1862.

Blake was promoted Commander for his bravery and Odgers was offered warrant rank, but he is supposed to have refused it, preferring to remain a petty officer as he had then become. There was a feeling in the Navy that a warrant was not worth Odger's while, and he should have been offered a commission (especially as Colour Sergeant McKenna VC of the 65th was commissioned for gallantry in New Zealand in September 1863). Although theoretically possible, no man from the lower deck was commissioned for gallantry between the Crimean and the Second Boer War.

Odgers's service certificate described him as being five foot seven and a half inches tall, with a dark complexion, black hair and grey eyes. He was a Cornishman, born in Falmouth on 14th February 1834, the son of a steward in the Packet Service. He joined the Navy in August 1852, aged eighteen, and served in the steam sloop *Vulture* in the Baltic and in the Black Sea. He joined *Niger* when she commissioned for the Far East in June 1856, and served during the China War. He was rated Leading Seaman in November 1857. He entered the Coast Guard Service as a boatman in March 1863 and served at Fowey, St George and St Mawes, finishing as a Quartermaster. Though he had signed on to complete his time for pension in January 1864, he left the Navy 'discharged unfit' in 1868 and took a pub, the Union Inn, at Saltash in Cornwall. He married twice, having a son by his first wife Ann (née May), who died in February 1865 when she was thirty-five, and a son and a daughter by his second wife Jane (previously Stoddon, formerly Dunsford). He died at the Union Inn on 20th December 1873, his age being given as forty. He was described as a 'Pensioner from the Royal Navy VC' and the cause of death was given as 'Phthisis with haemoptisis' (consumption with frequent spitting of blood). Jane Odgers died in 1901.

Letter from a young officer in the *Niger*, *United Service Gazette*, 16th June 1860. Despatches from Commodore Loring, *United Service Gazette*, 4th August 1860

George Hinckley:
Fung Wha, China, October 1862

It is curious how the careers of Victoria Cross winners sometimes crossed. In 1862 Captain George Fiott Day, who won a VC in the Sea of Azov in September 1855, was commanding the 6-gun steam paddle sloop *Sphinx* in the Far East when one of his ship's company, Able Seaman George Hinckley, won a Victoria Cross in an incident during the now forgotten campaign to suppress the Taiping Rebellion in China.

Hinckley was one of a Naval Brigade from *Sphinx*, who landed on 8th October 1862 and joined a much larger force consisting of some

3,000 men of the Imperial Chinese Army who had been commanded by the late American General Ward (who had died of wounds the previous month), 500 men of a French-Chinese force under Lieutenant Le Breton of the French Navy, and Naval Brigades from *Sphinx*, *Encounter* and the gunboats *Flamer* and *Hardy*.

Sphinx's bluejackets marched for some thirty miles overnight to attack the fortified town of Fung Wha, about ten miles below Shanghai. Carrying three days' rations of biscuit and salt pork, the sailors travelled over appalling roads and through incessant rain until, as they said, 'the only dry thing about us was our ammunition - seventy rounds of ball in our pouches'. They camped in the rain and took breakfast, of biscuit and a tot of rum, at four o'clock in the morning of 9th October. By eight o'clock they were with the main force in front of the gates of Fung Wha. Attacks by Ward's force in front of the town had met with heavy losses, and when the sailors went forward with some Chinese to force the main gate they found it blocked, and they themselves had to retreat under a hail of musket-balls, stinkpots, gingals, slugs, nails and great jagged lumps of iron fired from the loopholes in the walls above them. The ground in front of the gate was soon strewn with dead and dying. Mr Croker, assistant master of *Sphinx*, and Captain Bruman, of Ward's force, were both badly wounded and lay out in the open. Meanwhile the bluejackets, retiring under cover, could hear the ground in front of them being raked with hundreds of slugs and shots. Getting permission, Hinckley ran out, lifted Mr Croker in his arms, threw him face downwards over his shoulder and ran for the shelter of a joss-house 150 yards away. When he came back to his place, Hinckley volunteered again, ran out a second time and carried Mr Bruman to safety. He was quite rightly awarded the Victoria Cross and gazetted on 6th February 1863. He received his Cross from the C-in-C Plymouth, Admiral Houston Stewart, at a ceremony at Mount Wise, Devonport, on 7th July 1863, but lost the medal while attending a funeral in November and had to replace it, at a cost of twenty-four shillings.

Hinckley was born in Liverpool on 22nd June 1819, the son of a butcher. The first naval record of him seems to be when he joined the convict transport *Tortoise* at Hobart, Tasmania, for the passage home, on 22nd February 1842; this was unusual because most sailors on that station at that time exerted themselves to desert rather than enlist. He served in several ships before joining *Sphinx* in May 1860, where his career was somewhat chequered. He was rated second class for conduct in January 1862, discharged to Hong Kong prison for twenty-eight days in May, and won the VC in October. He was rated Leading Seaman in January 1863 and Quartermaster in July. He was discharged to shore as a pensioner in June 1867.

On 9th July 1865, at the Parish Church of Stoke Damerel, Devon, George Hinckley married Jane Oliver, a farmer's daughter, and they had at least one daughter, Jane Frances, born in Garden Street, Moricetown, Devonport, on 2nd July 1866. Hinckley, then calling himself George Oliver Hinckley, signed the birth certificate with his 'mark' of a cross. He lived in Devonport for the remainder of his life and died at 44 North Street, Plymouth, on 31st December 1904, aged eighty-five. His death certificate recorded that he was a holder of the Victoria Cross. He was buried in Ford Park. Jane Hinckley died at 35 Kent Road, Ford, on 13th July 1917, aged eighty-eight.

Samuel Mitchell:
Gate Pah, Te Papa, New Zealand, April 1864

The Maori Wars flared up several times in the early and mid-1860s and Naval Brigades took part in several actions, the last serious engagement being in April 1864, at Tauranga on the Bay of Plenty, on the west coast of North Island. On 26th April, a force of nearly 1,300 men under General Sir Duncan Cameron, and a Naval Brigade of over 400 officers and men of the Waikato Flotilla under Commodore William Wiseman of *Curacoa* (21 guns), landed at the Mission Station in Tauranga to attack a strongly fortified Maori position, known as the Gate Pah, at Pukehinahina, about three miles from a village called Te Papa.

The sailors set up a battery of three Armstrong guns from *Esk* in a position about 700 yards from the Gate Pah during the night of 27th/28th April and when it was light enough to see next morning, the naval guns and the 24-pounders of the Royal Artillery opened a bombardment to batter away at the nearest corner of the pah. At about 4 o'clock in the afternoon, a storming party of 80 sailors and 70 marines under Commander Edward Hay of the 17-gun steam sloop *Harrier*, and 150 soldiers of the 43rd Light Infantry (Oxfordshire and Buckinghamshire Regiment) ran to within 100 yards of the pah, where they paused under cover of a small hill to regain their breath. When ordered to advance again, the party dashed up the hill and over the walls of the pah and succeeded in establishing themselves inside.

But then things began to go wrong. The Maoris were securely entrenched in well-camouflaged positions, and the interior of the pah was like a maze, with many hiding places and passages. The Maori fire was heavy and accurate, and all the officers were either killed or wounded. When Hay was wounded he ordered his Coxswain, Captain of the Foretop Samuel Mitchell, to leave him and go to safety. Mitchell refused and carried Hay out of the pah on his back. Meanwhile some of the Maoris who had rushed out of the back of the pah had come back to face the attackers. Leaderless, and

73

subjected to heavy fire which had caused several casualties, the storming party wavered, and then fell back. At that moment reinforcements from the Naval Brigade and from the 68th Regiment arrived at the pah, to find the attackers retreating in confusion. The reinforcements also turned about and the whole force retired in a disorder which was close to a rout. Guns were brought up for a bombardment next day, but at 5.30 the next morning A.B. John Colenutt of *Harrier* entered the pah alone and found it deserted. The Maoris had evacuated it during the night. Hay died of his wounds the next day and there were some disagreeable accusations of cowardice against the Naval Brigade in the local press (which so incensed sailors from *Esk* that on their next visit to Auckland they were only restrained from dismantling the newspaper office by a personal apology from the editor). Amongst other awards for gallantry, Samuel Mitchell was awarded the Victoria Cross, on Commodore Wiseman's recommendation, and his citation appeared in the *London Gazette* of 26th July 1864. He received his Cross from the Governor of New South Wales at a ceremony attended by a crowd of more than 10,000 people at The Domain in Sydney on 24th September 1864. Afterwards he was borne shoulder-high through the streets of the city.

Samuel Mitchell was born at Apsley, Woburn, Bedfordshire, on 8th September 1841, the son of a labourer. He joined the Navy as a Boy Second Class in *Crocodile*, in August 1857. He did the gunnery course at *Excellent* in 1859 and joined *Harrier* on commissioning at Portsmouth in August 1860. He left her as Bosun's Mate on paying off in March 1865. On discharge from the Navy in May 1866 he went back to New Zealand, hoping to make his fortune in the West Coast gold rush. He lost his sea-chest, with all his gear including his Victoria Cross, in Sydney. The Cross turned up again many years later and was bought back by the family in 1928. Samuel Mitchell settled down as a farmer at Hokitika in South Island. He married Agnes (née Ross) in 1869 and they had ten children - seven daughters and three sons - all born in New Zealand. He was drowned in the Mikonui River, about twenty miles from Hokitika, on 16th March 1894. By coincidence, his body was found by a Mr Green who had served in *Eclipse* and had taken part in the attack on the Gate Pah. His grave stands on a hillside, about a hundred feet above the main road, near the town of Ross.

Duncan Gordon Boyes, Thomas Pride and William Henry Harrison Seeley:
Shimonoseki, Japan, September 1864

Whilst some Naval Brigades were fighting against the Maoris, others were in action in Japan, where the coming of western civilisation had caused as great a cultural, religious and racial shock as it had in New Zealand. A long period of tension, during which Europeans were attacked and sometimes murdered, came to a climax with the closing of the Shimonoseki Straits (at the western end of the Inland Sea) in the autumn of 1864 by the local Japanese Samurai chieftains, or *daimios*. Ships attempting to pass through the Straits were fired on and turned back.

An international squadron of British, French, Dutch (and one American) ships under Vice-Admiral Kuper, flying his flag in the 51-gun screw frigate *Euryalus*, bombarded and silenced the Japanese batteries on 5th September 1864. The next day the ships landed marines and bluejackets to spike and dismount the Japanese guns, and to dismantle their platforms and blow up ammunition. That afternoon, when the work of demolition was almost finished, the Naval Brigade at No.5 Battery were suddenly attacked by a strong force of Japanese who had gathered in a valley behind the battery. While marines advanced up one side of the valley, Captain Alexander, Flag Captain in *Euryalus*, led the sailors up the other. They were met by hot fire from the parapet of a ditch in front of the battery and from the top of an 8-foot wall protecting the palisade. 7 seamen were killed and another 26 were wounded. Captain Alexander was hit by a musket-ball in the ankle. But according to the account by Commander John Moresby, of *Argus*, 'Our men never checked, and rushing on, swarmed over the wall and won the stockade, the enemy disappearing into the bush.'

The Queen's colour was carried into action with the leading company that day by Midshipman Duncan Gordon Boyes of *Euryalus*, who kept the flag flying in spite of a fierce fire which killed one of his colour sergeants at his feet and badly wounded the other, Thomas Pride, Captain of *Euryalus*'s After Guard. Boyes and Pride were only prevented from going further forward by Captain Alexander's direct order. The standard Boyes carried was afterwards found to have six musket-ball holes torn in it. Ordinary Seaman William Seeley, also from *Euryalus*, distinguished himself that day by carrying out what his citation called a daring reconnaissance and then, though wounded, taking part in the final assault on the Battery. Boyes, Pride and Seeley were all awarded the Victoria Cross, and all three were gazetted on 21st April 1865.

When *Euryalus* returned to England in 1865, the Queen issued a special command that the VCs for Boyes, Pride and Seeley should be presented 'in such a public and formal manner as might be considered best adapted to evince Her Majesty's sense of the noble daring displayed by the officers and seamen concerned before the enemy'. The presentation was made by the C-in-C Portsmouth, Admiral Sir Michael Seymour, on Southsea Common, on Friday, 22nd September 1865. Officers, petty officers, seamen and marines who had already won the VC were assembled to right and left of the

Admiral, to witness the presentations. Captains, commanders and officers of the fleet attended in full dress uniform, with seamen and marines of Her Majesty's ships in port and at Spithead and marines from Fort Cumberland - the petty officers and seamen in blue jackets, white trousers and black straw hats, the Royal Marine Artillery and Light Infantry in parade dress uniform. Two battalions of the Naval Brigade, from *Excellent*, *Terrible*, *Recruit*, *Scorpion* and *Royal Sovereign*, paraded under Captain Astley Cooper Key, with a battery of field pieces from *Excellent* and the officers and entire ship's company of HMS *Euryalus*. So many thousands of people had gathered on the Common that the marines, acting as traffic policemen, had great difficulty in clearing a way for the Naval Brigades to march on and for the Admiral to arrive in his carriage. After the medals had been presented, *Victory* fired a gun salute, and officers and men doffed caps and gave three cheers.

Boyes was born in Cheltenham on 5th November 1846, the son of John Boyes. His sister Louisa Mary married Thomas Young, *Shannon's* Gunnery Lieutenant, who won a VC at Lucknow. Boyes went to Cheltenham College and then to North Grove House Academy to be prepared to enter the Navy. He was only seventeen when he won his VC, and *Euryalus* was his first ship. He left her when she paid off on the day after the presentation of the VCs. It had been the high point of his life. The rest was short and sad.

On 9th February 1867, when he was serving in *Cadmus* on the North American Station, Boyes and another Midshipman, Marcus McCausland, were court-martialled for disobedience of the C-in-C's Standing Order by breaking into the Naval Yard at Bermuda after 11 pm, after they had previously been refused admittance by the Warder at the main gate because they did not have a pass. Both admitted the offence and pleaded guilty. Both were sentenced to be dismissed from the service. It seems an astonishingly harsh punishment for what on paper was merely the aftermath of a midshipmen's run ashore, but obviously there was more to the story than appears.

Boyes suffered from fits of depression and, for his health's sake, went out to New Zealand where his elder brothers had a sheep station at Kawarau Falls in Otago Province. But he had a nervous breakdown and took his own life, on 26th January 1869 at Dunedin. His death certificate gives the cause of death as delirium tremens. He was buried in the Southern Cemetery at Dunedin, in supposedly 'Viking' fashion, with a stone at his head and his feet. The grave fell into disrepair. In 1954 the Dunedin Returned Services Association disinterred Boyes's remains and reburied them in the servicemen's section of the Andersons Bay Cemetery.

Thomas Pride was a Dorset man, born at Oldbridge, near Wareham, Dorset, on 29th March 1835. He joined the Navy on 17th February 1854 and was one of the first young men to undergo a seaman's training in HMS *Illustrious* at Portsmouth, under Captain

Robert Harris; *Illustrious* was the first proper boys' training ship in the Royal Navy. After his wound at Shimonoseki he was invalided to the hospital ship *Melville* in Hong Kong in January 1865 and subsequently discharged from the Navy in January 1866. He had married a Dorset girl, Mary Eliza Croombes, at St Mary's, Wareham, in 1861 and when he left the Navy he went back to Dorset, becoming keeper of the Waterloo Tollgate at Longfleet, near Poole. He died at Parkstone, Dorset, on 16th July 1893, and was buried at All Saints, Branksome.

William Henry Harrison Seeley was born at Topsham, Maine, on 1st May 1840 and was the first American citizen to win the Victoria Cross. At the time, American nationals were forbidden to enlist in the British Services and, ironically, had Seeley set foot on the American ship in the squadron off Shimonoseki he would have been liable to arrest. His first record in the Navy was when he joined *Imperieuse*, flagship on the China Station, on 17th July 1860. Possibly he joined from a merchant ship on the China coast. He transferred from her to *Euryalus* when she relieved *Imperieuse* on 17th November 1862. He was discharged from *Euryalus* on paying off, and went back to the United States. His VC pension and his naval pension, amounting to £22 10s. a quarter, were paid to him through the British Consul in Boston. He married and very probably had at least one son and a daughter. He died of a cerebral haemorrhage at 26 Barrows Street, Dedham, Massachusetts, on 1st October 1914. His death certificate gives his precise age as '74 years, 4 months, 11 days', from which his birthdate can be computed, and described him as a widower. He was buried in the Evergreen Cemetery, Stoughton, Massachusetts.

Israel Harding:
Alexandria, July 1882

On 11th July 1882 a British fleet went into action for the first time since the Crimean War. All that summer the eastern Mediterranean had been in its usual state of political tension. Arabi Pasha, a brigadier in the Egyptian army, seized effective power in Egypt. The country was financially almost bankrupt. There were violent anti-foreigner riots ashore in Alexandria. Europeans were evacuated. An ultimatum was issued to Arabi Pasha to disarm his guns along the shore at Alexandria. The ultimatum was ignored and expired at 5 am. Thus, at one minute to seven on a fine sunny morning, with a flat calm sea, eight ironclads of the Mediterranean fleet under the C-in-C, Admiral Sir Beauchamp Seymour, opened fire against the shore batteries at Alexandria.

The bombardment of the forts went on for most of the day, until all Arabi's guns were silenced and several magazines had been blown up. But the battle was by no means one-sided. The forts could bring to bear almost as many modern heavy guns as the ships, and every ship except two suffered damage and casualties. Six men were killed and twenty-seven wounded. The leading battleship, *Alexandra*, bore the brunt of the Egyptian fire. She was hit more than sixty times and her hull was penetrated in twenty-four places above the armoured plate. One man was killed and three wounded. There was considerable damage to the upper deck, and to officers' cabins, the ship's boats and standing and running rigging.

One ten-inch shell penetrated the ship's side, passed through the torpedo-lieutenant's cabin, struck the coaming of the engine-room hatch and rolled along the deck among the sailors there, who screamed 'A shell! A shell!' Hearing the alarm, the ship's Gunner, Mr Israel Harding, dashed up from below and, in his own words, 'as quick as thought I just picked up that shell, and flung it into a tub full of water; it was heavy, hot and grimy. It is dreadful to think what would have happened had the shell exploded. Close at hand was the hatchway leading to the magazine, which at that moment contained *twenty-five tons* of gunpowder.' For this quick thinking and brave action, which saved many lives, Mr Harding was recommended for the Victoria Cross by Admiral Seymour and gazetted on 15th September 1882. He was presented with his Cross by the C-in-C (who had by then become Lord Alcester) at Malta on 14th October.

Israel Harding was born to the sea, the son of a Queen's Pilot and the grandson of a King's Pilot, in Portsmouth on 21st October 1833. He went to the Bethel School, Bath Square, Portsmouth, and was taught navigation until he was fourteen years old. He first went to sea with his father in the steam vessel *Echo*, and joined the Navy as an Ordinary Seaman in 1849. He served in *Arrogant* from 1849 to 1852 and then went to do a gunnery course at *Excellent*. Harding served as a gunner's mate in the line-of-battleship *Cressy* during the Baltic War and was on board her for the bombardment of Sveaborg in 1855. He was rated Captain of the Foretop in *Cressy*, and on one occasion saved a sailor's life by jumping overboard and rescuing him from drowning. In 1871 he served in *Gladiator* on the South American station and was in charge of a party landed to fight a fire in the military arsenal in Rio de Janeiro. For this he was awarded a Brazilian order. Harding also served in the Ashanti War in 1878, in *Victor Emanuel*. He retired from the Navy as Chief Gunner in 1885, but returned to the colours at the outbreak of the Great War. He served in minesweepers, although he was over eighty, and broke his left leg when a mine exploded under his ship.

Israel Harding married twice, having a son by his first marriage and four daughters by Emma Annette Nunn, daughter of an Inspector in the Storekeepers' Department in Woolwich Dockyard, marrying her at the Parish Church in Woolwich on 10th November 1873. He died on 22nd May 1917, when he was visiting his daughter at Silkstead House, Billingshurst, Sussex. His body was taken back to Portsmouth, where he had lived at 84 St Augustine Road, Southsea, and he was given a funeral with full military honours on 26th May. He was buried in Highland Road Cemetery, Portsmouth.

Arthur Knyvet Wilson:
El Teb, Sudan, February 1884

'Tug' Wilson won his Victoria Cross by being in the right place at the right time. But, as he himself wrote in a letter the same day, 'I had no business to be there, but as I had nothing to do here, and the place where the battle was expected to, and actually did, take place was within walking distance, I thought I would walk out at daylight this morning in time to march out with the troops.' The place of the battle was El Teb in the Sudan, about eleven miles inland from the Red Sea. Two years earlier, the tribesmen of the Sudan had revolted under the Mahdi and the rebellion spread to the Red Sea littoral, where a slave dealer called Osman Digna had been created Emir.

At first the tribesmen had some success. They annihilated Hicks Pasha's force around Khartoum and on 4th February 1884, in an earlier battle at El Teb, had completely routed Baker Pasha's forces. A battalion of marines was sent out from home, regiments on their way to and from India were diverted, and marine detachments from ships of the Mediterranean Fleet were despatched to Port Said in the torpedo depot ship *Hecla*, commanded by Captain Wilson. An expeditionary force of some 4,000 men was assembled under Major General Sir Gerald Graham to deal with Osman Digna. Wilson was nominally on the staff of Rear-Admiral William Hewett VC, in overall command of naval forces, and *Hecla* had contributed 2 officers, 25 sailors and a Gardner machine gun to the Naval Brigade, but, as Wilson said, 'I had nothing to do with that and simply went as a spectator'.

On 29th February 1884, Graham's force advanced towards El Teb, in the form of the traditional British square, with the Naval Brigade and their machine guns at the two leading corners. The Arabs opened fire with two Krupps guns they had captured from Baker, and the guns of the Royal Artillery replied from within the square. As the square advanced towards the Arab position, general firing broke out. Several of the Naval Brigade were hit, including Lieutenant Royds of *Carysfort*, who was badly wounded through the body. Wilson took his place.

When they were about twenty or thirty yards from the Arab battery, some men of the 65th Regiment broke ranks and ran forward into the battery, thinking it was empty. They soon came back pursued by about twenty Arab spearmen. 'One fellow got in close to me,' Wilson wrote, 'and made a dig with his spear at the soldier on my left. He failed to reach him, and left his whole side exposed, so that I had a cool prod at him. He seemed to be beastly hard, and my sword broke against his ribs.' Wilson himself was slashed on the head by an Arab swordsman, but his pith helmet took the brunt and the blade only cut the skin. However, blood poured down over his face and beard and Wilson attributed his VC to his appearance: 'If only I could have got a basin of water and washed my face I should have escaped notoriety.' His exploit was noticed by Brigadier Redvers Buller, and he was duly recommended and gazetted for the Victoria Cross, on 20th May 1884. His Cross was presented to him by Admiral Sir Geoffrey Phipps Hornby, accompanied by HRH The Duke of Edinburgh, and witnessed by representative companies from *Hecla*, ships of the Channel Fleet, Royal Marines and the Royal Fusiliers, and thousands of spectators, at a special ceremony on Southsea Common on 6th June. Wilson noted in his diary for that day: '6th June. Docked ship. Received the VC.'

Arthur Wilson was a considerable figure in the Navy, one of the most important personalities in the Service during the late-Victorian and Edwardian eras. Like all naval Wilsons, he was called 'Tug', but the sailors also called him 'Ard 'Eart'. He was a stern man, somewhat forbidding, an exacting task-master, who knew his own profession surpassingly well and had a short way with those who failed him. He had an interesting and an eventful career, seeming to be wherever there was some action, and involved whenever there was some technical innovation. He became the foremost naval expert of his day on torpedoes. He never married. The service was his mistress, and he loved and served the Navy above all else, forsaking all others.

Arthur Knyvet Wilson was born on 4th March 1842, at Swaffham, Norfolk, the third son and third child (of five) of Rear-Admiral George Knyvet Wilson. He had several naval officers amongst his grandparents, uncles and cousins and his family were related to Henry Keppel - and to Lord Nelson. He went to Eton for two years and then sat the examination for the Navy on 11th June 1855. He passed and joined *Victory* as Naval Cadet on 29th June 1855. His first ship was the screw line-of-battleship *Algiers* (90 guns) and he served in her during the Crimean War, at Sebastopol, and at the bombardment of the Kinburn forts in October 1855. When *Algiers* went to Malta to refit, Wilson joined his father, who was Captain of *Rodney*, but after only a week was transferred to *Colossus* under Captain Keppel, on her way back to the Crimea. At Balaclava, young Wilson was sent ashore to look for a dog lost by an army officer. When he got back, *Colossus* had sailed for England. Wilson came back in another ship.

His next ship was the frigate *Raleigh*, again under Keppel, bound for the China Station. But on 15th March 1857 *Raleigh* struck a submerged rock and became a total loss. Her officers and ship's company were landed safely and Wilson joined the flagship *Calcutta*. He served her in the expedition to Canton and in the taking of the Peiho Forts. So, although only a Midshipman, Wilson had campaign medals for the Crimea and for China.

After passing his professional examinations, Wilson was promoted Lieutenant, with seniority back-dated to 11th December 1861. After service in the paddle steam frigate *Gladiator*, he went to *Excellent* to qualify as a Gunnery Lieutenant in April 1866. The Japanese government had asked for the British government's assistance in setting up their first training establishment for officers. Wilson was one of a small party of officers and senior ratings that went out to Japan in 1867 and set up a new school in Tokyo. The first class of sixty-three boys began their training on 1st January 1868 but political troubles forced the school to close and by December Wilson was back in England. However, in later years, no Japanese naval officer ever failed to pay his respects to Wilson as one of his Navy's earliest instructors.

From training Japanese naval officers Wilson went straight to the Royal Navy cadet training ship *Britannia* as First Lieutenant, where he tightened the already strict discipline of the establishment by introducing an 'Habitual Offenders List'.

In May 1870 when he was at *Excellent*, Wilson was chosen to be a member of a committee to investigate the possibilities of the new invention of the torpedo by Mr Robert Whitehouse. After extensive trials in the Medway, when the torpedoes were fired from a specially-constructed tube in the iron paddle-wheel sloop *Oberon*, the committee recommended that 'any maritime nation failing to provide itself with submarine locomotive torpedoes would be neglecting a source of power both for offence and defence'. Wilson was Gunnery Lieutenant in the ironclad *Caledonia*, and First Lieutenant of the frigate *Narcissus*, before being promoted Commander on 18th September 1873. He was then appointed executive officer of a new type of frigate, built of iron sheathed with wood, also called *Raleigh*, under Captain George Tryon.

On 26th April 1876, the torpedo school *Vernon*, in Portsmouth, became independent of *Excellent* and Wilson was her Commander and Executive Officer under Captain Arthur. He was promoted Captain on 20th April 1880 and ordered to bring up to date the *Torpedo Manual*, incorporating all his torpedo experience of the previous four years. On 25th March 1881 he was appointed in command of *Hecla*, a merchant ship bought off the building stocks by the Admiralty and converted into a torpedo depot ship (and, by coincidence, having the same name as the ship on which Lucas won his VC). Wilson took *Hecla* to Fiume, where Whitehead had his torpedo factory, to see the latest torpedoes and tubes for discharging them, before the Arab War broke out and the series of events began which led to his Victoria Cross.

Wilson was captain of the battleship *Sans Pareil*, second in line behind *Camperdown*, on 23rd June 1893 when, on the orders of Tryon, now an Admiral, she and *Victoria* turned inwards and collided. Tryon himself and 365 officers and men were lost. It was, as Wilson later said, 'apparently an act of madness' but Wilson was almost certainly right in his belief that Tryon had 'in an extra-ordinarily stupid bungle' mixed up the radius with the diameter of the ship's turning circles, and such was the confidence that Tryon inspired that everybody followed his orders.

Wilson had an extremely inventive mind and over the years devised such things as a truck semaphore for better long-distance signalling in the fleet, a device called a 'Pioneer' which enabled torpedoes to cut their way through protective nets, and an improved form of submerged torpedo tube. He was not a good committee man and was apt to be impatient with opposition. In his later career as a Sea Lord he was famous for his reaction to the coming of the sub-marine, which he instinctively recognised as a threat to the big ships he believed in. He failed to recognise the submarine as the best vehicle ever designed for delivering his beloved torpedoes, and he called it 'a damned un-English weapon' and recommended that submarine crews, when captured, should be hung as pirates.

Wilson succeeded his brother as 3rd Baronet in 1919. He died at Beech Cottage, Swaffham, Norfolk, on 25th May 1921.

Admiral Sir Edward E. Bradford KCB, CVO, *Life of Admiral of the Fleet Sir Arthur Knyvet Wilson Bart., VC, GCB, OM, GCVO* (London: John Murray, 1923.)

William Job Maillard:
Candia, Crete, September 1898

Surgeon Maillard was the first and only naval medical officer to win the Victoria Cross and he won it in what was technically peacetime, not in action against a declared enemy of the Crown but against an armed mob, in circumstances which today would perhaps be called 'confrontation'.

In January 1897, after two centuries of Moslem oppression, the Christians in the Mediterranean island of Crete, aided by Greek soldiers and encouraged by the Greek government, rose in rebellion against the Turks. The great powers - Great Britain, France, Russia, Italy, Germany and Austria - sent warships to restore some semblance of order. The Christians held the countryside whilst the Turks, aided by irregular mobs of Bashi Bazouks, held the towns. No permanent political solution could be found whilst the Turks remained. Austria and Germany withdrew, leaving Great Britain, Russia, France and Italy each to maintain order in one of four districts of the island.

In the British zone was the town of Candia, on the north coast, where by September 1898 the garrison had been reduced to one regiment, the Highland Light Infantry. A decision of a council of four admirals - British, Italian, French and Russian - to collect a part of the export customs duties aroused intense local indignation and when, on 6th September, Colonel Reid of the HLI attempted to install a new collector of taxes in Candia, the mob rose. They massacred some 500 Christians in the town and besieged about 130 of the HLI in the Customs House (the rest of the regiment, about 400 men, being spread throughout the British zone). The mob of several thousand began to inflict casualties on the Customs House garrison, which appealed for help to the only warship present, the British torpedo gunboat *Hazard* (Lieutenant Vaughan Lewes) lying in the roads off Candia.

Hazard sent two parties of about fifty men ashore but when, at about 2.15 in the afternoon, a message was received for medical help, Surgeon Maillard, Lieutenant Lewes, and the captain's steward, who was a volunteer, were rowed ashore by a crew of five in the Captain's gig. As they reached the harbour, the Bashis met them with a storm of fire. The eight men left the boat and ran for the cover of the Customs House, but two of them were killed and three wounded. Maillard had actually reached shelter when he saw one of the wounded, Ordinary Seaman Arthur Stroud, fall down in the boat. Maillard ran back through what his citation called 'a perfect deluge of bullets' and tried to help Stroud up. But the boat was drifting off, and made an unstable platform to stand on. Maillard was forced to leave the man, who was almost dead, and return to his place. His clothes were riddled with bullet holes, but he himself was quite unhurt. His VC was listed in the *London Gazette* on 2nd December 1898, and he was presented with his Cross by the Queen at Windsor Castle on the 15th of that month.

Afterwards, Maillard said that he should have been reprimanded instead of decorated because he was the only qualified medical man present to treat the wounded and should not have risked himself (and, indeed, he had to deal singlehandedly with about seventy HLI casualties on board *Hazard* that night of the 6/7th), but he was really intensely proud of being the first naval surgeon to win the Victoria Cross, and, he said, he could not resist running forward when he saw Stroud had been hit.

He was born on 10th March 1863 at Banwell, near Axbridge in Somerset, the son of Daniel Galland Maillard, a Wesleyan minister, and Elizabeth Dawkins. He went to Dunheved College, Launceston, and to Kingswood School, Bath, before going to Guy's Hospital from 1882 to 1889 to study medicine. He qualified as MRCS and LRCP, and his work won the Gold Medal for Medicine. He joined the Navy on

22nd August 1889 and studied for, and got, his MD whilst serving in the Navy. He served in the boys' training ship *Ganges*, the battleship *Iron Duke*, the cruiser *Blake*, and the gunnery training school *Excellent*, before joining *Hazard* in 1897. He was specially promoted to Staff Surgeon on 2nd June 1899. After *Daedalus*, an RNVR depot ship at Bristol (where he was remembered long afterwards as 'a very charming officer with a liking for gin'), his last ship was the cruiser *Archer*. He retired from the Navy because of ill health in 1902 and died in Bournemouth of brain disorder, possibly a brain tumour, on 10th September 1903. He was buried in Wimborne Cemetery in Dorset.

Maillard was devotedly nursed through his last illness by his wife, Maria Edith Beresford, a trained nurse, whom he married in British Honduras in 1893. Mrs Maillard was herself the holder of the Royal Red Cross Medal. They had no children. Edith Maillard died in Wimbledon, London SW, on 3rd August 1940.

The Maillards were related to the Drakes, a famous family name of the West Country. One branch of the family are supposed to have settled in Guernsey, where the French speakers could not get their tongues round 'Drake' so used the French equivalent *mallard*, corrupted to Maillard.

Relics, medals and pictures of William Job Maillard are preserved at the Royal Naval Hospital at Haslar, Hampshire.

Lewis Stratford Tollemache Halliday:
Peking, China, June 1900

In the summer of 1900 a long-felt Chinese resentment against the economic (and physical) presence of foreigners - the 'Hairy Ones' - broke into an open rebellion against law and order, largely conducted by a nationalist political group known as the 'Fists of Righteous Harmony': the Boxers. The Boxers had the moral approval of the old Empress and her Manchu ministers and the tactical assistance of Imperial Chinese troops, so that towards the end of May 1900 the situation in Peking had deteriorated to the point where Sir Claude Macdonald, the British Ambassador, telegraphed to the British naval C-in-C, Sir Edward Seymour, requesting that guards should be sent to protect the international legations in Peking.

The guards disembarked from their ships at Taku, on the mouth of the Peiho River, the nearest point to Peking, on 29th May and went to Peking by train, arriving to take over their posts on the 31st. Amongst them was Captain Lewis Halliday RMLI, of the cruiser *Orlando*, with fifty men of the Royal Marine Light Infantry. Like the Red Guards of the 1960s, the Boxers had no named leaders or recognised direction. They swirled around the northern provinces of China like some elemental force of nature, growing stronger and more confident with every outrage. On 24th June they attacked the west wall of the British Legation in Peking, setting fire to the stables and occupying some buildings near by. The fire was put out with great difficulty by the defenders, but the Boxers immediately opened a very rapid and accurate fire at close quarters. It was decided that they must be ejected from the buildings they had occupied.

A hole was knocked in the Legation wall and through it dashed Captain Halliday at the head of twenty men of the RMLI. In a desperate hand-to-hand struggle the Boxers were driven off, but Halliday received a terrible wound, which smashed his left shoulder-bone and tore away part of his lung, from a shot fired only a few feet away from him. Despite his pain and injuries, Halliday shot three Boxers and then, unable to go any further, ordered his men to go on without him. He made his own way back to the hospital, refusing assistance, because he did not want to divert even one of his men from the job of pursuing the Boxers.

These were the details of his exploit given in Halliday's VC citation in the *London Gazette* of 1st January 1901, but years later he challenged them. He said he had led a party of *six*, not twenty men. It was Captain Strouts, Royal Marines, who had cleared a hole in the wall and led out the party of twenty men. He *had* asked for assistance back to the hospital. He had killed *four* not three Boxers and then his pistol misfired:

I went down a narrow alley and ran into a group of five Boxers armed with rifles. The first fired without bringing his rifle to the present. I shot him and three others. The fifth ran away. I told the men to carry on. I got back unaided to the wall. I was helped through the hole and Dr Poole helped me to the hospital. Strouts then took out twenty or thirty men and pulled down the small building and cleared the field of fire. I think Strouts was killed before the final draft (of the VC citation) was made.

Halliday was presented with his Cross by King Edward VII at St James's Palace on 25th July 1901.

Lewis Stratford Tollemache Halliday was born on 14th May 1870 at Medstead, Hampshire, the elder son of Lieutenant-Colonel Stratford Charles Halliday RA. His family had a record of service in the Marine Corps going back to Brevet Major F.A. Halliday who joined in February 1830. Lewis Halliday went to Elizabeth College, Guernsey, and joined the RM Academy as a 2nd Lieutenant RMLI on 1st September 1889. He was promoted Lieutenant on 1st July 1890, Captain on 31st January 1898, Brevet Major on 12th September 1900, and full Major on 2nd April 1908. He commanded the Marine detachment in *Empress of India* in 1904, passed the Staff Course examination in 1906 and from 1908 to 1911 commanded a company of gentlemen cadets at the RMC, Sandhurst. In 1912 he was on the staff of

85

the Naval War College. During the Great War, he served as a Staff Officer with the Army in Malta in 1914, and in England and France 1915-16. In 1917 he went to the Admiralty as Assistant Director of Plans. He was promoted Brevet Lieutenant-Colonel on 2nd April 1915, Lieutenant-Colonel on 14th June 1915, Colonel on 1st October 1920, Colonel Commandant on 1st January 1923, Major-General on 11th December 1925 and Lieutenant-General on 16th June 1927. He was Adjutant-General, Royal Marines, from October 1927 to 1930. He retired at his own request in 1931.

Halliday's first wife was Florence Clara (née Budgen), oldest daughter of Brigadier-General W. Budgen. They married in April 1908. They had one son. His wife died in 1909 and in 1916 he married again, Violet (née Blake), daughter of Major Victor Blake, and they had one son and one daughter. The son, Francis Andrew Tollemache, also served in the Marines from 1937 to 1961, retiring as a Major. In retirement General Sir Lewis Halliday lived near Dorking, and in Kingsbridge, Devon. He was a tireless writer of letters to the newspapers, chiefly *The Daily Telegraph*, and was Honorary Colonel Commandant of the Royal Marines from September 1930 until May 1940. He attended various military functions connected with the Victoria Cross and when he died at Dorking General Hospital on 9th March 1966, in his ninety-sixth year, he was the longest surviving winner of the VC.

Basil John Douglas Guy:
Tientsin, China, July 1900

'My Midshipman has got the Victoria Cross. Isn't it splendid?' wrote David Beatty to Mrs Ethel Tree. 'I am perfectly delighted, but hope it won't spoil him.' The Midshipman was Mr Guy, of the battleship *Barfleur*, whose Commander and Executive Officer was David Beatty during the Boxer Rising. After the first outbreaks in May 1900, an international squadron of British, American, Japanese, Russian, French, Italian, Austrian and German warships anchored at the Taku bar, the entrance to the Peiho river, the nearest point to the capital, Peking. After some indecision amongst the admirals as to which of them should command, an allied force under the British C-in-C, Admiral Sir Edward Seymour, landed on 10th June to go by train up to Peking. But the line had been torn up beyond Tientsin and the force had to return to an arsenal at Hsi-Ku some miles north of Tientsin, where they were quickly cut off by hordes of Boxers and Imperial Chinese troops. Eventually a relief force which included sailors and marines from *Barfleur* under Beatty, relieved Hsi-Ku and the whole force returned to Tientsin. There, a mixed force of about 2,400 British, Russians, Japanese, French and Americans were

86

surrounded by about 15,000 Chinese troops armed with modern weapons. After some weeks' hectic defence of the settlement, with its vital railway station, it was decided on 12th July to attack the native quarter and forts across the river at daylight the next morning.

What happened is best described in the letter Beatty (who recommended Guy for the VC) wrote to Seymour and which later became largely the official citation in the *London Gazette* of 1st January 1901:

It was on the morning of the 13th, whilst we were advancing to the attack on the city of Tientsin, during which we had to cross amongst others a space of 150 yards quite open within 600 yards of the city walls, and on which was concentrated a greater portion of the fire from the city wall, and in consequence was literally swept with bullets, as was testified by the number of casualties that took place there, it being lined with the dead of several nationalities, we losing six casualties out of a very much reduced company, being barely thirty strong.

Among those who fell was one Able Seaman J. McCarthy, shot about 50 yards short of cover. Mr Guy stopped with him and, after seeing what the injury was, attempted to lift him up and carry him in, but was not strong enough so replaced him on the ground, and with his handkerchief and that of the man bound him up, and after making him as comfortable as possible ran in to get a door and assistance to carry him in, the stretchers being in use at the rear. While all this was taking place, the remainder of the company had passed on under cover, and the entire fire from the city wall was concentrated on Mr Guy and McCarthy; and observing that this state of affairs lasted fully five minutes, it was by a miracle alone that he hadn't been killed.

Shortly after Mr Guy had got in under cover, the stretchers came on; and again Mr Guy dashed out and assisted in placing McCarthy on the stretcher; and taking my corner of the stretcher, as I only having one arm was handicapped and delayed matters somewhat, he assisted in carrying the man in, who unfortunately was struck a second time and killed while so doing.

One handle of that stretcher was taken by Major E.V. Luke RM of *Barfleur* who later reported, in commending Guy, that the 'ground around him was absolutely ploughed up' with bullets. According to Guy himself, whose 'boyhood hero' Beatty was, Beatty told him to 'Get to hell out of it!' when he tried to relieve him of the stretcher's weight. Certainly, Beatty's casual revelation that he himself was there at the stretcher, suggests that he might have got the VC himself. 'We all took our cue from him,' Guy wrote of Beatty, 'he was always so cool and collected and absolutely fearless.' There

87

were those who thought that Beatty, Luke, Guy and Beatty's messenger, Ordinary Seaman Ernest Whibley (who took the fourth handle and got a CGM), *all* deserved the VC. Guy was surprised:

I had no idea that I had done anything special, or even been recommended or mentioned, till one night months later I was walking up and down the quarter-deck, when I heard my name read out by a signalman who was taking in a signal giving the names of promotions, decorations, etc. of those mentioned in the *Gazette* for the affair.

Barfleur arrived back in Devonport at one o'clock in the morning on New Year's Day, 1902. Guy was presented with his Cross by King Edward VII at the RN Barracks, Devonport, on 8th March 1902.

Guy's family background was clerical rather than naval or military. He was born on 9th May 1882 at Bishop Auckland, Co. Durham, where his father was a curate, son of Canon Douglas Guy who was later Vicar of Sedbergh, Yorkshire and Christ Church, Harrogate, and Honorary Canon of Ripon, and Mary, daughter of the Reverend Henry Owen from Queen's County, Ireland, then Vicar of Trusthorpe, Lincolnshire. Guy went to Aysgarth School, Yorkshire, Llandaff Cathedral School (where his uncle the Reverend Ernest Owen was headmaster) and then to HMS *Britannia*. He passed out as a Naval Cadet on 15th May 1898 and was appointed as Midshipman to *Barfleur* in the Far East on 15th July; he went out by P & O steamer but due to ship movements did not actually join *Barfleur* until December.

He was promoted Sub-Lieutenant on 15th January 1902 and served in the torpedo-boat destroyers *Lightning*, *Porcupine* and *Zephyr*. As a Lieutenant, promoted on 15th July 1903, he was in the cruiser *Leviathan* in the Mediterranean and commanded the torpedo-boat destroyers *Otter* and *Handy* on the China Station. He was in the cruiser *Natal* when she escorted King George V and Queen Mary to India for the 1911 Great Durbar, and he was First Lieutenant of the cruiser *Blanche* in 1913. In the Great War he commanded the sloop *Ceanothus*, (launched on 9th September 1917 by his wife) and the Q-ship *Werribee* (alias *Wonganella*).

In *Wonganella* Guy won a DSO for a gallant action in the Mediterranean on 11th March 1917. Picking up distress signals from the SS *Springwell*, which had been attacked by the German U-38, he closed her to help when the U-boat surfaced. Having first steered away, to lure his enemy after him, he hoisted the White Ensign and steamed towards the U-boat, opening fire with his 4-inch gun as he did so. Although the U-boat's gunfire damaged *Wonganella*, she was forced to dive. Guy's skilful ship-handling avoided a subsequent torpedo attack.

Guy was promoted Commander on 30th June 1918, but his naval

career ended in anti-climax. He was divisional officer of the Coast Guard at Torquay and for a time was maintenance commander on the staff of C-in-C Nore. He retired in 1923 and, after an Army vocational training course at Catterick in pig-farming, bought and renovated a sixteenth-century farmhouse at Pirbright in Surrey. Soon he turned to poultry and ran a modern chicken farm. He was chairman of Southern Counties Poultry Society Ltd in 1933. From 1937 to 1940 he served on the International Commission for Non-Intervention in the Spanish Civil War.

On 8th August 1917, at his father's church in Harrogate, Guy married Elizabeth Mary Arnold, daughter of William Sayles Arnold of Doncaster and Harrogate. They had two daughters. Guy was recalled for service in the Second World War, and died at St Thomas's Hospital, London, on 29th December 1956 in his seventy-fifth year.

Henry Peel Ritchie:
Dar-es-Salaam, November 1914

The first naval VC of the Great War (though not the first to be gazetted) was won in Dar-es-Salaam, which means 'Abode of Peace', the capital of German East Africa.

By the end of October 1914 the German raiding cruiser *Königsberg* had been rounded up and trapped in the Rufiji river delta, on the east coast of Africa. Amongst the warships in support of the cruisers who had chased *Königsberg* was the old pre-Dreadnought battleship *Goliath*, whose second-in-command, Commander Henry Peel Ritchie, was given the independent command of *Duplex*, an old German cable ship converted into an armed auxiliary vessel. In November, Ritchie went to Dar-es-Salaam, where a number of German ships had been keeping *Königsberg* supplied, barricaded as she was some miles inland. While *Goliath* and the old protected cruiser *Fox* remained outside, Ritchie made his preparations to enter the harbour.

Duplex's engines were unreliable, so a Maxim gun and extra deck protection were fitted to *Goliath's* steam pinnace, which Ritchie himself drove into Dar-es-Salaam on 28th November, accompanied by Lieutenant Paterson, *Goliath's* Torpedo Officer, in an ex-German tug called *Helmuth*, and Lieutenant E. Corson, of *Fox*, in *Fox's* steam cutter.

The harbour seemed as peaceful as its name. There were no warships, no sign of hostilities, and two white flags flew as tokens of truce from the harbour signal station flagstaffs. The Governor of Dar-es-Salaam had already agreed that any German ships found in the harbour would be British prizes of war, and could be destroyed or immobilised. While Paterson boarded the *Feldmarschall* to lay demolition charges and Surgeon Lieutenant Holtom, of *Goliath*, inspected the bona fides of a hospital ship called *Tabora*, Ritchie himself boarded the *König*. She was almost deserted. The few people on board were told to get into her boats, and the ship was demobilised by charges exploded under the low-pressure cylinders of her engines.

The next ship, *Kaiser Wilhelm II*, was also deserted. According to Petty Officer T.J. Clark, the pinnace coxswain, Ritchie's suspicions were aroused by a clip of three Mauser bullets with their pointed ends sawn off, lying on the deck and showing that someone had been preparing small arms for action. Ritchie had never been at ease in the eerie quietness and emptiness of that harbour, and as a precaution had two steel lighters lashed one on either side of the pinnace.

It was as well he did, for they soon heard small arms fire from the main harbour. In spite of the white flags, the Germans were firing on *Fox's* steam cutter. At once, Ritchie headed *Goliath's* pinnace out into the harbour, making for the entrance. A storm of fire burst upon them, the Germans firing shells and bullets from huts by the water's edge, from houses in the city, from wooded groves and hills above, even from a cemetery. Without the steel lighters, the pinnace must have been lost. As it was, Clark was hit and Ritchie took over the wheel but he, too, was hit eight times in twenty minutes - on the forehead, in the left hand, twice in the left arm, in his right arm and hip; finally, two bullets through his right leg laid him low and he fainted from loss of blood. Clark, roughly bandaged, took over the wheel from Able Seaman George Upton, and brought the pinnace back alongside *Goliath* with her decks literally running blood. In retaliation, *Goliath* opened fire with her main 12-inch guns and flattened the Governor's house.

The stoker of *Fox's* steam cutter was mortally wounded, steam pressure fell and the cutter slowed down. Lieutenant Corson clambered forward under fire, took the shovel from the dying man and stoked up pressure again. He received the DSC, Clark the Conspicuous Gallantry Medal, and Upton the Distinguished Service Medal. Ritchie's VC was gazetted on 10th April 1915 and he received his Cross from King George V on 25th November 1916. He was taken to Zanzibar Hospital, where he stayed for six weeks, and returned to duty in May 1915. Upton was lost when *Goliath* was torpedoed and sunk in the Dardanelles, also in May 1915. Paterson and Holtom were made prisoners-of-war (when Holtom was repatriated he revealed that the 'hospital ship' *Tabora* had indeed been a fake).

Ritchie was a Scot, born on 29th January 1876 at 1 Melville Gardens, Edinburgh, the son of Dr Robert Peel Ritchie and Mary (née Anderson). He went to George Watson's Boy's College, Edinburgh, and joined HMS *Britannia* as a Naval Cadet on 15th

January 1890, qualifying as a Gunnery Officer before being promoted Lieutenant on 30th June 1898. He was, incidentally, Army and Navy lightweight boxing champion in 1900. On 31st March 1902, at St Cuthbert's Edinburgh, he married Christiana Lillias Jardine, only daughter of James Aikman, a wine merchant, and they had two daughters.

Ritchie retired in 1917 and was promoted Captain on the retired list on 29th January 1924. He lived in Edinburgh, at Craig Royston House, dying there suddenly on 9th December 1958, in his eighty-third year.

From Dartmouth to the Dardanelles: A Midshipman's Log, edited by His Mother (London: Heinemann, 1916.)
Petty Officer T.J. Clark CGM, 'How Peel Ritchie Won his VC in the "Abode of Peace"', *Sunday Graphic and Sunday News,* 2nd June 1935.

Norman Douglas Holbrook:
The Dardanelles, December 1914

The first naval VC to be awarded in the Great War was also the first won by a submariner. The winner was a young lieutenant, twenty-six years old, in his first command. His boat was old, small, and obsolete. His target was an even more elderly Turkish battleship, built in 1874. But the exploit had a tremendous moral and tactical effect, thrilling all who heard about it, and, more important for the war, showing what a daringly handled submarine could do against a defended enemy position.

When Turkey entered the war on Germany's side on 30th October 1914, British ships based on Tenedos kept a watch on the western end of the Dardanelles. Amongst them were the submarines B.9, B.10 and B.11, and three French submarines. Spurred on by a French suggestion, the British decided to attempt a submerged penetration of the Straits. The Dardanelles was a formidable proposition: besides the natural hazards of a narrow channel, sometimes only two miles across, shoals and shallows, and a westerly current running between two and five knots, there were known Turkish minefields, batteries of guns, howitzers and even torpedo tubes on the shore, with patrols by day and searchlights by night.

Holbrook's B.11 was built at Vickers in 1905. She had a crew of two officers and fifteen ratings, and was armed with two 18-inch torpedoes in bow tubes. She had recently had a new battery fitted, giving her a top underwater speed of about six knots - but only for about two hours, after which the battery would be exhausted. Her practical underwater speed was much less. B.11 reached the

Dardanelles before dawn on Friday, 13th December and dived about a mile off Cape Helles at the western end. Shortly afterwards, a severe vibration on the hull forced Holbrook to surface again. A metal guard which he had had fitted to ward off mine cables from the starboard after hydroplane had twisted into a hook, much more likely to catch a mine cable than deflect it. It had to be jettisoned, by men working waist-deep in water in the half-light of dawn. After four hours submerged at eighty feet (so as to avoid mines which were believed to be moored about fifteen to twenty feet deep) B.11 came to periscope depth about ten miles from the western entrance, and about two miles short of The Narrows. Through the periscope Holbrook could see a large two-funnelled warship moored in Sari Sighlar Bay on the Asiatic side. She was the 10,000-ton battleship *Messudiyeh*. Holbrook fired his starboard torpedo, which ran true and hit. *Messudiyeh* settled by the stern and shortly afterwards turned over until her mast touched the bottom. She sank in about ten minutes. The Turks had seen and opened fire on B.11's periscope as Holbrook turned for home. B.11 grounded on a shoal which forced her entire conning tower above water. The Turks redoubled their fire. Fortunately, B.11 slid off into deeper water and retreated to the safety of the Mediterranean. B.11 had been submerged for nine hours and when she eventually surfaced the air in her was so bad that her engine (more particular about the quality of air it breathed than human beings) would not start for some considerable time.

B.11 was cheered into Tenedos and his fellow flotilla officers presented Holbrook with a large cardboard Iron Cross. On 22nd December, only nine days after his exploit, Holbrook was gazetted for a real Victoria Cross. His First Lieutenant, Sidney Winn, was awarded a DSO, and his entire crew got DSMs. They also shared a prize bounty award of £3,500 (£5 for every man of the estimated 700 on board *Messudiyeh*).

Holbrook came of a very distinguished naval and military family whom the newspapers sometimes called (to the family's embarrassment) the 'fighting Holbrooks'. His father was Colonel Sir Arthur Richard Holbrook KBE, and he had four sisters and five brothers, four of whom served in the Army or the Navy. Norman was the fourth son, born in Southsea on 9th July 1888. He was educated privately and at Portsmouth Grammar School before going to HMS *Britannia* in 1903. He became a Midshipman on 9th January 1905, Sub-Lieutenant in 1908 and Lieutenant on 30th September 1909. He joined *Bonaventure*, the sea-going depot ship for submarines in the Home Fleet on 4th April 1911, and was appointed to *Egmont* in Malta for B.11 in command on 30th December 1913. Holbrook was at home for the presentation of his Cross by King George V at Buckingham Palace on 5th October 1915, but he served in the submarines F.3, V.4 and E.41, being slightly wounded on another patrol, and finally in J.2, a class of submarine designed to operate with the Grand Fleet, before leaving the submarine service in August 1918. He also went to Russia as Lieutenant-Commander in the Russian cruiser *Askold*. He retired in 1920 and was promoted Commander on the retired list on 9th July 1928, but was recalled for service in the Admiralty during the Second World War.

On 21st June 1919, Holbrook married Viva, daughter of Frederick Woodin and widow of Mr F.E. Dixon, at Holy Trinity, Brompton, London SW. They had one son, who was killed in action in 1945. After his wife died in 1952, he married Gundula, daughter of Dr A. Feldner of Innsbruck the following year. He died at his home, Stedham Mill, Midhurst, Sussex, on 3rd July 1976, in his eighty-eighth year.

Eric Gascoigne Robinson: *Dardanelles, February 1915*

Early in 1915 the Mediterranean Fleet began a series of operations (ultimately unsuccessful) to force the Dardanelles. The plan was to bombard and knock out the most westerly forts, send minesweepers to sweep a way clear for the bombarding ships to approach and bombard the next forts, and so on, progressively working further into the strait. The first bombardments took place on 19th February. On the 26th, parties were landed to complete the demolition work at Kum Kale on the Asiatic side.

Covered by the guns of the pre-Dreadnoughts *Irresistible* and *Vengeance*, the cruisers *Dublin* and *Cornwallis*, and the destroyers *Basilisk* and *Racoon*, fifty marines from *Vengeance* under Major G.M. Heriot and a demolition party under the ship's Torpedo Officer, Lieutenant-Commander E. G. Robinson, landed at 2.30 in the afternoon at a pier just east of a ruined fort near Kum Kale. They were to deal with the guns in Kum Kale and also to blow up a battery further inland at Orkanie and two anti-aircraft guns close to Achilles' Tomb. They were also to blow up a bridge across the Mendere River.

The marines were soon held up by a very heavy fire from near-by Yeni Shehr which killed a sergeant and wounded two marines. It did not seem possible for Robinson's party to reach Orkanie either. But Robinson believed he could at least get to Achilles' Tomb. Half way there he told his sailors to stay where they were, because their white uniforms made them conspicuous, and went on himself with a charge of gun-cotton. He found the AA battery deserted and, having blown up one gun, he came back for another charge and blew up the second.

Dublin's guns had subdued the fire from Yeni Shehr which had troubled the marines, and Robinson and his party were also able to destroy the remaining gun mountings at Orkanie. The bridge over the Mendere they regretfully had to leave for lack of time, but made their way back in good order to the pier. For this, and for his part in four sorties into the minefields of the Dardanelles, Robinson was gazetted for the Victoria Cross on 16th August 1915, and received his medal from King George V at the Palace on 5th October.

On the night of 26th April 1915, on her way to reconnoitre a new minefield, the submarine E.15 was forced off course by the strong current and ran aground, some eleven miles from the entrance to the Dardanelles. She stuck fast, with her conning tower well above water. The forts ashore opened fire, killing the captain and some of the crew. The rest had no choice but to surrender.

When a patrolling seaplane spotted E.15 and it was realised she might fall almost intact into enemy hands, the most strenuous efforts were made to destroy her. Aircraft dropped bombs, submarines fired torpedoes, battleships and destroyers all shelled, without success. Two small steam picket-boats, one each from the battleships *Triumph* and *Majestic*, were manned by volunteers (of whom there were so many they had to be chosen by lot) and fitted with torpedoes carried in slings on outriggers. Robinson commanded *Triumph's* boat, Lieutenant Godwin *Majestic's*. In spite of heavy fire and disconcerting searchlights from shore, Godwin hit E.15 with his second torpedo and blew her up, but was hit himself. His crew were taken off by *Triumph's* boat and both crews escaped, for the loss of one man. Robinson was specially promoted to Commander. Godwin got the DSO, two other officers the DSC, and every man in both boats the DSM.

Robinson's *Britannia* term, who joined in January 1897 and went to sea in May 1898, was possibly the most successful in the Navy's history. Of the original 65, 31 still survived in May 1948, fifty years later, and they included 2 VCs (Guy and Robinson) and 9 flag officers, including two Admirals of the Fleet (Cunningham and Somerville). Robinson was born on 16th May 1882, the son of John Lovell Robinson MA, Chaplain of the Royal Naval College, Greenwich, and Louisa Aveline (née Gascoigne), at 1 Diamond Terrace, Greenwich. He went to St. John's, Leatherhead, and The Limes, Greenwich, before *Britannia*. As a Midshipman in *Endymion*, he served ashore during the Boxer Rising and was one of Admiral Seymour's expedition to relieve Peking in June 1900. He was wounded in action at Peitsang and was mentioned in despatches. He was promoted Lieutenant on 15th August 1903, specialising in torpedoes, and as a torpedo expert he served in the submarine depot ship *Thames* with the Home Fleet in 1910. Robinson served in M.21 on the Palestine coast and in Egypt, and was awarded the Order of the Nile in 1917. He won the Russian

Order of St Anne in 1919 for his service in coastal motorboats in the Caspian Sea. In November he was made an OBE, and was promoted to Captain on 31st December 1920.

After the war, Robinson was Captain (D) of destroyer flotillas, commanded the cruiser *Berwick* on the China Station, was Captain of *Defiance* the Torpedo School at Devonport, and of the Artificer's Training Establishment at *Fisgard*, Torpoint. Before the formation of the Electrical Branch, the torpedo-men were responsible for the Navy's electrics and Captain Robinson was an Associate Member of the Institution of Electrical Engineers (AMIEE). His last appointment was as Captain of Devonport Dockyard. He retired and was promoted Rear-Admiral on the Retired List in January 1933. In the Second World War, Admiral Robinson was recalled and joined that band of senior officers, retired admirals and captains, RN and RNR, for the arduous and dangerous duties of Commodores of Convoy. He retired from this due to ill-health in 1941.

In 1913, he married Edith Gladys (née Cordeux) and they had two sons and a daughter. The Admiral lived at The White House at Langrish, near Petersfield, Hampshire. He died at the RN Hospital in Haslar, Hampshire, on 20th August 1965.

Edward Unwin, George Leslie Drewry, Wilfred St Aubyn Malleson, William Charles Williams and George McKenzie Samson:
V Beach, Gallipoli, April 1915

In theory, the plan of attack for V Beach, on the southern tip of Cape Helles on the Gallipoli peninsula, seemed sound enough. The battleship *Albion* would bombard the village and fort of Seddul Bahir, to plaster the Turkish defences, subdue the garrison, destroy the trenches and blow holes in the barbed wire on the beach. While the Turk's heads were kept down, the converted collier SS *River Clyde* would run in, accompanied by a small hopper normally used for dredging mud, and three lighters. The hopper would ground on the beach, the lighters would be positioned as a floating pontoon bridge. Some 2,000 men of the 29th Division, men of the Royal Munster Fusiliers, Royal Dublin Fusiliers and the Hampshires, would disembark through special ports cut in *River Clyde's* sides, run down specially-constructed gangways, cross the bridge and storm the beach. There, they would advance inland and join forces with troops who had made similarly successful landings at W, X and Y beaches further up the coast, all four pressing on to take the town of Krithia and the heights of Achi Baba to the north-west.

The reality, which began at 6 am on Sunday 25th April 1915, was somewhat different. *Albion* duly bombarded for an hour, *River Clyde*, the hopper and the lighters ran in and, despite some hitches and premature groundings, the floating bridge was established. The first troops ran ashore in dead silence. The plan seemed to be working. However, as soon as the bombardment lifted, three platoons of Turkish soldiers, with four machine guns, returned to their hardly damaged trenches and their almost intact wire. Just as the disembarkation was gathering speed, they opened fire.

In a moment *River Clyde's* gangways were strewn and choked with dead and dying. The Dublin Fusiliers in the lighters were cut down where they stood. The catastrophe was past comprehension. Unable to believe what was happening, fresh men pressed out of *River Clyde's* hold, tossing the dead bodies into the sea to make way for themselves to go forward to the slaughter. A few men got ashore and sheltered under a bank, but there was no question of anybody joining them. After three hours, 1,500 men had tried to land and only 200 had done so. The guns on *River Clyde's* fo'c'sle could make little impression on the Turkish defences, and the main body of troops could not get ashore until after dark that evening.

That anybody got ashore at all was almost entirely due to the great gallantry and physical stamina of *River Clyde's* officers and men. At one point, because of the current setting round the Cape and the difficulties of securing the bridge, the lighters began to drift away from the beach. Commander Edward Unwin, in command of *River Clyde*, himself swam ashore with a line, secured the first lighter and towed it to shore. There was nothing suitable to secure the lighter to, so he stood in the water himself, like a human bollard, with the line wrapped around his waist, while the first parties of Munster Fusiliers rushed over his head. The men who assisted Unwin had to swim from lighter to lighter, under very heavy fire. Midshipman Drewry, of *River Clyde*, was wounded in the head but still took lines from one lighter to another until he was exhausted. A sailor from *River Clyde*, Able Seaman Williams, stood neck-deep in the water for over an hour, under murderous fire, but he held on to his line until he was killed where he stood. Another seaman, George Samson, worked in the lighters all day, under constant fire, eventually he was very badly wounded by Maxim machine-gun fire. He carried thirteen pieces of bullet shrapnel in his body to the day of his death. Another Midshipman, Wilfred Malleson, took over from Drewry, and swam with lines from the hopper to the lighters and succeeded in securing the nearest lighter. When the line broke he made two more attempts to secure it.

Unwin was in his fifties and the cold and immersion were too much for him. Numbed and helpless he was obliged to return to his ship, where the doctor wrapped him up in blankets. But as soon as his circulation had returned he ignored the doctor's advice and went

Above: William Maillard (Photo by West, Southsea)
right: Israel Harding (Author's Collection)
t: Lewis Halliday (Photo by Maull & Fox, London)

w: A tribute by the *Illustrated War News* of 25 August 1915 to the
al heroes of the Dardanelles

MIDSHIPMAN G. L. DREWRY,
(AFTER THE ACTION)

COMMANDER EDWARD UNWIN,
R. N.

MIDSHIPMAN GEORGE L. DREWRY, R.N.R.

MIDSHIPMAN GEORGE L. DREWRY, R.N.R.

MAN GEORGE Mc. KENZIE SAMSON,
R. N. R.

ANDER ERIC G. ROBINSON,
R. N.

George Samson, who on his
way to a public reception in his
home town was presented by a
stranger with a white feather
(Author's Collection).

A. W. St C. Tisdall (Photo by F.
Russell, Deal)

back to the lighters, where he was wounded three times. Later in the morning he decided that something must be done for the wounded, lying in the shallow water by the beach. He commandeered a launch, secured her stern to *River Clyde* and punted her to the shore. He rescued seven or eight wounded men, manhandled them into his boat and hauled them back to *River Clyde*. He was in the end forced to stop through sheer physical exhaustion.

Unwin, Drewry, Malleson, Williams and Samson were all gazetted for the Victoria Cross on 16th August 1915, Williams's award being posthumous. Williams and Samson were the first men from the lower deck to win the VC since Seeley and Pride in Japan over half a century earlier. Only Peel's *Shannon*, and *Vindictive* at Zeebrugge, can equal *River Clyde*'s individual record of five Victoria Crosses. *River Clyde*'s were all won within a few hours, four of them within minutes of each other.

When the great invasion fleet for Gallipoli gathered at Mudros in February and March 1915, Unwin was in command of the old torpedo gunboat *Hussar*, which had been converted for use as a yacht and communications centre for the C-in-C Mediterranean. Unwin had been the Fleet Coaling Officer on Jellicoe's staff in *Iron Duke*, the Grand Fleet flagship, and he had special knowledge of the construction and design of colliers and considerable expertise in the handling of lighters alongside. The idea of filling *River Clyde* with assault troops and running her ashore was largely Unwin's, as were the special ports and gangways and the use of the hopper and the lighters to make a floating bridge. He was himself appointed to command *River Clyde* with the rank of Acting Captain.

Unwin started his career in the Merchant Navy. He was born on 17th March 1864, the son of Edward Wilberforce Unwin JP and Henrietta Jane (née Carmac) at Forest Lodge, Fawley, Hampshire. He went to the *Conway* training ship in the Mersey and first went to sea in Donald Currie's clippers and in the P & O. In October 1895, when the Navy were short of deck watchkeepers and navigating officers, Unwin was one of a hundred officers from the Mercantile Service who transferred to commissions in the Royal Navy. He served in the punitive expedition to the Benin river in 1897, in the Port Guard ship *Thunderer* for the Fleet Manoeuvres of 1899, and in South Africa in 1900. He retired from the Navy with the rank of Commander in 1909 but was recalled at mobilisation on 29th July 1914.

After his injuries in *River Clyde*, Unwin went home for an operation in Haslar Hospital, Alverstoke, in Hampshire, but he was back in Mudros on 1st July and commanded the cruiser *Endymion*. He was beach-master for the Allied landings at Suvla Bay on 7th August and for the evacuations in December; he was awarded a CMG for his services, in March 1916. He was the last to leave the beaches and as he was leaving a man fell overboard; Unwin jumped in and rescued him. He was invested with his Cross by King George V at the Palace on 15th January 1916. From March to October 1916, he commanded the light cruiser *Amethyst* on the South-East America Station. In January 1917 he was appointed Principal Naval Transport Officer in Egypt (and received the Order of the Nile). A year later he was PNTO for the Eastern Mediterranean and was promoted to Commodore in 1919. He retired with the rank of Captain in 1920, his seniority back-dated to 11th November 1918 for his war service.

Edward Unwin was a large, bluff, cheery man, with broad shoulders and a blunt manner. His plan of using *River Clyde* was discounted by more orthodox officers and it was only put into effect at all through the personal decision of Admiral Wemyss. In 1897 Unwin married Evelyn Agnes Carew, daughter of Major General Dobrée Carew of Guernsey. They had two sons and two daughters. In retirement Unwin lived at Ashbourne in Derbyshire and later at Hindhead in Surrey. He died on 19th April 1950.

Midshipman George Leslie Drewry RNR commanded the hopper when it drove ashore on *River Clyde*'s port bow. When he saw Unwin hauling in on the line to bring the nearest lighter to shore, Drewry jumped in the water to help him. He came across a wounded soldier, picked him up and tried to drag him ashore, but the man was hit again and died in his arms. While standing on one of the lighters, Drewry was hit by shrapnel in the head which knocked him to the ground. His face covered with blood, he bound up the wound with a soldier's scarf and went on with his work. He was presented with his Cross by King George V at the Palace on 22nd November 1916.

Drewry also joined the Navy from the Merchant Service and was the first Royal Naval Reserve officer to win the VC. He was born on 3rd November 1894, at Forest Gate, Essex, the son of Thomas Drewry, works manager of P & O Steam Navigation Co. and Mary (née Kendall). He went to Merchant Taylor's School, Blackheath, and seems to have been somewhat accident-prone. As a young boy he was knocked down in the street by a car. As an apprentice on board the sailing ship *Indian Empire*, he fell from a mast into the sea and was nearly drowned. Rounding Cape Horn, the ship was wrecked on remote Hermit Island. The crew managed to get ashore but their lifeboat was smashed by heavy seas. Stranded, they lived for a fortnight on roots and shellfish until rescued by a Chilean gunboat.

In 1912 Drewry joined the P&O and travelled the world. He joined the RNR on 1st July 1913 and when at Port Said he was called up for active service on 3rd August 1914 and appointed as a Midshipman RNR to *Hussar* and then to *River Clyde*. He was promoted Acting Lieutenant on 2nd September 1916 and appointed to the battleship *Conqueror*. The Imperial Merchant Service Guild presented him with a Sword of Honour, as the first RNR officer and Merchant Service to win the VC.

His last accident was at Scapa Flow on 2nd August 1918, when he was in command of HMT *William Jackson*. A block fell from the end of a derrick and struck him on the head, injuring his skull, and breaking his left arm. He died a short time later, aged twenty-four. His brother officers of the Northern Patrol erected a window to his memory in All Saints Church, Forest Gate. In April 1940, his brother Mr H.P. Drewry donated £10,000 to found scholarships for the sons of Merchant Navy officers killed in action.

After winning his VC, Wilfred St Aubyn Malleson expressed the wish to be allowed to live as quietly and obscurely as possible, which he did until his death at St Clements, Truro, on 21st July 1975. He did not join the VC or GC Associations, and attended no dinners, garden parties or other functions in honour of VC winners. In his opinion, far too many books had been written about the VC, especially in his generation. He was born at Kirkee in India on 17th September 1896, the son of Wilfrid Malleson. He joined the Navy as a Cadet in 1912 (two younger brothers, Rupert and Hugh, also joined in due course) and was promoted Midshipman on 7th August 1914, serving in *Cornwallis* in the Mediterranean. Malleson may well have been appointed to join *River Clyde* from her. He was promoted Acting Sub-Lieutenant on 15th May 1916 and joined the battleship *Lord Nelson* in October (his brother Rupert was also serving in her). He was confirmed Sub-Lieutenant on 30th December 1916 and appointed to *Dolphin* for submarine training on 15th October 1917. He was promoted Lieutenant on 30th March 1918 and joined the depot ship *Lucia* (commanded by Nasmith) on 5th November. He served in L.7 in 1921 and later as First Lieutenant of L.19. After passing the 'periscope course' for prospective submarine COs, he was appointed in command of H.50 on 23rd August 1923. Malleson went back to general service for a commission as a seaman divisional officer in the battleship *Iron Duke* on 1st January 1925, was promoted Lieutenant-Commander on 30th March 1926, and appointed to another battleship, *Royal Oak*, on 10th November.

Malleson returned to submarines to command L.69 on 1st August 1927, but his career lost momentum, and thereafter he was relegated to back-waters: on the staff of the Drafting Commander at *Vivid* in Devonport in 1928; as watchkeeping officer in the cruiser *Berwick* on the China Station in 1930; and finally some years in the Dockyard, Devonport, including an appointment to the cruiser *Caledon* in the Reserve Fleet in 1936. By 1941 he was on the Retired List, with the rank of Commander, but later had the war service rank of Captain.

On 28th February 1927, at St Mark's, Hamilton Terrace, St Marylebone, London, Malleson married Cecil Mary Collinson, daughter of Colonel Frank Graham Collinson. He was presented with his Cross by the King at Buckingham Palace on 2nd January 1918.

Able Seaman William Charles Williams died in the arms of Unwin, who called him the bravest sailor he ever knew. Williams was born on 15th September 1880, at Stanton Lucy, Shropshire. He joined the Navy as a Boy at Portsmouth on 17th December 1895 when his father, his next-of-kin, was given as William Williams of 11 Upper Nelson Street, Chepstow (known in the town as 'Williams the Gardener'). After three years' service as a Boy, Williams (Official No.186774) signed a twelve-year engagement in the Navy on his eighteenth birthday, 15th September 1898. He was recommended for bravery by his commanding officer, Captain Percy Scott, for his part in the landings of *Terrible's* Naval Brigade at Natal 1899-1900, and in the Boxer Rising. He had the China Medal 1900, and the South Africa Medal with Relief of Ladysmith and Tugela Heights clasps. After his regular engagement expired he was recommended for enrolment in the Royal Fleet Service Reserve (Official No. B3766) and joined *Vernon* on 19th September 1910. He was recalled to active service at the outbreak of war and joined *Hussar* on 24th September 1914, serving in her until listed as 'Discharged Dead' on 25th April 1915. His medal was given to his father at Buckingham Palace on 16th November 1916. The town of Chepstow presented a bronze war medallion in Williams's honour to his sister and next-of-kin, Mrs F.M. Smith. In Chepstow Parish Church there is a memorial of a painting of *River Clyde*, and red and white ensigns from the Dover Patrol.

'As long as I live', wrote George Samson, the fifth *River Clyde* VC winner, 'I shall treasure memories of the bravery of these men [Unwin, Malleson, Drewry and Williams]. They hurried hither and thither, giving a hand when needed, just as if they were aboard the *Hussar* in peacetime. Every moment they were risking their lives and really it was nothing short of a miracle that they were not hit.' They *were* hit: Williams was killed, Unwin and Drewry were both wounded and Samson himself, after staying and working on the beaches for over thirty hours, was very badly wounded (contemporary reports variously said in thirteen, seventeen and nineteen different places). The *River Clyde's* surgeon, Dr P. Burrowes Kelly, who tended Samson, said: 'He was in great agony when I saw him, and whether he lived or died I knew he had won the VC.'

George McKenzie Samson (Official No. 2408A) was the first RNR rating to win a Victoria Cross. He was born on 7th January 1889, at Carnoustie, Fife, in Scotland, the son of David Samson, a shoemaker, of 63 Dundee Street, Carnoustie. He went to Carnoustie School (with another VC winner from the burgh, Corporal Charles Alfred Jarvis, Royal Engineers, who won his VC in Flanders on 23rd August 1914). Samson also joined the Army, after leaving school, but was bought out and went to sea in the Merchant Navy. He had a varied and adventurous life, sailing to Greenland and to the Argentine, where he tried his hand at cattle ranching. When war

100

broke out he was in Smyrna, working on a railroad, and could speak Turkish. At some time he had joined the RNR and he went to Malta to join up. He was drafted to *Hussar* as a seaman.

After some time in hospital in Port Said and Haslar, Samson went home on sick leave, arriving on 17th August 1915, the day after his VC was gazetted. His train was met by the Provost, Burgh and Town Councillors, a military band and guard of honour. Samson himself was in plain clothes, his uniform apparently not yet having been replaced. A clergyman sitting in the same railway compartment had said loudly: 'Look at that fine-looking young fellow. He ought to be serving his country instead of being a slacker.' Samson was dogged by such misunderstandings. He received his VC from King George V at the Palace on 5th October. On the 29th, he and Jarvis arrived at Carnoustie to be fêted by their home town. Samson's exploits were eulogised, he was cheered through the streets, and presented with a handsome smoker's cabinet and a solid silver rose-bowl. Yet a few hours earlier a complete stranger had come up to him and handed him a white feather.

On 31st December 1915, George Samson married Miss Catherine Glass, a farmer's daughter, at the Huntly Arms Hotel, Aboyne, near Carnoustie, and they had one son.

After discharge from the Navy as a Petty Officer, Samson went to sea again. He sailed from Dundee in the new merchant ship SS *Docina* in February 1922. In the course of the voyage, when the ship was in the Gulf of Mexico, Samson complained of feeling unwell. He was transferred to a sister ship, SS *Stromlus*, which took him to Bermuda. He died of pneumonia at St George's, Bermuda, on 23rd February 1923 and was buried with full military honours in the Military Cemetery. On a kerbstone at the end of his grave the lines from Tennyson are inscribed, 'Oh! for the touch of a vanished hand, and the sound of a Voice that is still.'

Arthur Walderne St Clair Tisdall:
V Beach, Gallipoli, April 1915

Sub-Lieutenant A.W. St Clair Tisdall RNVR won the sixth VC from *River Clyde*, although he was not a member of her ship's company. He took passage in her, commanding 1 Platoon, Anson Battalion, Royal Naval Division, to V Beach where his platoon was to land and serve ashore with the Army.

Tisdall was the first RNVR officer to win the VC, and in his way he was a typical member of that great class of British families who lost so many of their sons between 1914 and 1918. He was a classical scholar and a poet, like Rupert Brooke whom he knew. A young giant, six foot tall and broad-shouldered, Tisdall was one of those lucky men who could do anything; he was a brilliant scholar, a very fine athlete, and a supremely brave fighting man. *Burke's Irish Landed Gentry* lists the Tisdalls as coming from Charlesfort, Kells, Co.Meath. Arthur's paternal grandfather was Major William Tisdall, of the 42nd Foot. His mother Marian's father was a clergyman, the Reverend W. Gray MA, and his father was the Reverend Dr William St Clair Tisdall, an authority on comparative Eastern religions who published books on the religions of Persia and India, and translated the four Gospels into Kurdish; a scholar in Hebrew, Greek and Latin, he also wrote grammars in Gujarati, Punjabi, Urdu and Persian.

Arthur Tisdall was born in Bombay, second son of a large family of brothers and sisters, on 21st July 1890. His father was then in charge of the Church Missionary Service's Muhammadan Missions. In 1892, the family moved to Isfahan, Persia, where Dr Tisdall was head of the CMS Persia-Baghdad Mission. In 1900, the family came home by sea, passing through the Dardanelles and in sight of the very beach where Tisdall won his VC fifteen years later. Tisdall went to Bedford School, where he was possibly the best scholar of his year, rowed for the school and joined the Officers' Training Corps. He had a knack of acquiring nicknames: to the family he was 'Pog', at school he was 'Pussy', because he came from Persia; in the RNVR he was 'Tizzy'. He won a scholarship to Trinity College, Cambridge, where he also joined the OTC and rowed in the First Trinity boat. He graduated in 1913 with a Double First BA Honours degree and the Chancellor's Gold Medal for Classics. He passed the combined examination for the Indian and Home Civil Service and accepted an appointment in the Home Civil Service late in 1913. But for the war, Tisdall would undoubtedly have become a Permanent Secretary, a Whitehall mandarin, with a knighthood in due course.

He joined the RNVR in May 1914 and was called up when the RNVR mobilised in August. His training began at Walmer Camp on the 14th. On 4th October he went to Antwerp with the Naval Division. His commission to Anson Battalion was gazetted on 11th when he returned, back-dated to 1st October. He went to Blandford Camp, where on 27th February his battalion entrained for Bristol, sailing for the Dardanelles from Avonmouth in the trooper *Grantully Castle* the next day.

On 25th April, while waiting his turn to land from *River Clyde*, Tisdall witnessed the Munster and Dublin Fusiliers disembarking and the carnage that followed when the Turkish machine gunners ashore opened fire. He could hear the groans and cries from the beach, and see the men lying wounded and dying in the open. At last, he turned to the Major in charge of *River Clyde's* Maxim guns and said, 'I can't stand it, I'm going over'. The Turkish fire was still heavy and accurate, but Tisdall jumped into the water and waded ashore to where he could see Unwin standing on a spit of rock, pushing a small white boat in front of him.

The wounded Fusiliers on the beach were hardly capable of helping themselves and Tisdall called back to *River Clyde* for a volunteer to assist him. Leading Seaman Malia responded and helped Tisdall rescue two boat-loads of wounded. They were joined by Chief Petty Officer Perring and Leading Seamen Curtiss and Parkinson, for four or five more trips, all under the same heavy and accurate fire. Tisdall's platoon landed the next day and on 27th he sent a postcard to his family '. . .Have been under fire and am now ashore; all day spent in burying soldiers. Some of my men are killed. We are all happy and fit. Plenty of hard work and enemy shells, and a smell of dead men. Will tell you more when possible. . . Best love to all, Pog.'

On 6th May, Tisdall's platoon took part in the first battle of Achi Baba. They set off at 8.30 that morning and by the afternoon had advanced about a mile. As one Able Seaman later wrote to Tisdall's father. 'When we got nicely settled in the enemy trench your son stood up on the parapet of the trench looking for the enemy, but was not there long before he was shot through the chest, and he never said one word. We put him away as well as possible, and on June 4th I was wounded myself.' The Chaplain also wrote to Dr Tisdall, quoting another letter from one of the men: 'He was one of England's bravest men. All his men about cried when he went because all the boys thought the world of him.'

News of Tisdall's death reached Deal, where his father was Vicar of St George's, on 10th May. A memorial service was held on 13th and a memorial tablet later erected in the church. Tisdall's posthumous citation was delayed until 31st March 1916, because of the time needed to establish the facts. Malia, Perring and Parkinson were all awarded the CGM. Curtiss would also have won one, but he was reported missing on 4th June 1915. The Reverend Tisdall and his wife received their son's Cross from King George V at Buckingham Palace.

Verses, Letters and Remembrances of Arthur Walderne St Clair Tisdall VC, Sub-Lieutenant RNVR with a foreword by Dr Butler, the Master of Trinity, was published by Sidgwick & Jackson (who also published Rupert Brooke) in April 1916. The book was actually planned and written before his VC was gazetted and it contained a biography, reminiscences of his life, letters from brother officers, and photographs. Tisdall's own diary, poems, and letters written in Gallipoli were destroyed on the peninsula. The published poems are mostly *juvenilia*, but do show the first stirrings of what might have been a poetic talent.

Walter Richard Parker:
Gaba Tepe, Gallipoli, April/May 1915

On 28th April 1915, the Portsmouth Battalion of the Royal Naval Division landed at Anzac Cove, on the western coast of the Gallipoli peninsula, to relieve an Australian brigade who had been fighting ashore since the first landings on the 25th, and who were occupying a line of trenches about a mile inland near Gaba Tepe. These trenches were less than two feet deep, and the nearest Turks were only about fifty yards away, over a ridge. On the night of 30th April / 1st May the Portsmouth Battalion received a message asking for ammunition, water and medical stores to be sent to an isolated trench position at a place called MacLaurin's Hill. Several men had already been killed or wounded while attempting to reach this isolated trench, which could only be approached across an open space about 400 yards wide, constantly swept by Turkish rifle and machine-gun fire. A party of NCOs and men were detailed to carry the water and ammunition. Volunteers were called for from the Battalion stretcher bearers, and amongst those who volunteered was Lance-Corporal Parker of the RMLI, who had already distinguished himself in charge of a party of stretcher bearers in the previous three days' action.

By Parker's own account, their mission seemed so hopeless that an Australian officer threatened to shoot him if he tried to pass. But, as it seemed to Parker he was likely to be shot by the Turks anyway, he ignored the Australian and went on. It was already broad daylight when Parker's party emerged from the shelter of their trenches and ventured out on to the open space. One man was hit and wounded at once. Parker organised the stretcher party for him and went on, eventually reaching the beleaguered position alone, the other water and ammunition carriers having been killed or wounded. He gave first-aid treatment to the wounded lying in the trench and remained cool and collected, according to a masterly piece of understatement in his VC citation, 'in very trying circumstances'. When the position was finally evacuated, Parker helped to move the wounded, although he had been seriously wounded himself while crossing to the trench and later in the trench itself.

Parker's exploit was not gazetted for the VC until 22nd June 1917, over two years later, because of the difficulty there had been in finding officers who could confirm his brave conduct according to the regulations which governed the award of the Victoria Cross. He was eventually invested by King George V at Buckingham Palace on 21st July 1917, by which time he had been a civilian for over a year. His eyesight which had never been good and which had resulted in him being posted as stretcher bearer, had deteriorated since his injuries, and after treatment at Netley, Southampton, he was discharged as unfit on 17th June 1916.

Walter Richard Parker was a Lincolnshire man, born on 20th September 1881 at 5 Agnes Street, Grantham, the eldest son of the eight children of Richard and Kate Parker. He went to Grantham elementary school, and was then employed as a coremaker at Stanton Ironworks Foundry. He enlisted in the Royal Marine Light Infantry, becoming Marine Parker (Official No. PO/S 229) on 7th September 1914.

After leaving the Marines, Parker lived at 14 Brookhill Terrace, Stapleford, Nottingham. In 1902 he had married Olive, daughter of the late Joseph Orchard, the station-master of Stapleford. They had two daughters, Eva and Vera Constance. In 1917, the RMLI subscribed for a marble and gilt clock, a gold regimental brooch for Mrs Parker and a cheque, which were presented to Parker at Forton Barracks by Brigadier-General C.N. Trotman CB, Lance-Corporal Parker was a special correspondent for *The Observer* at the dinner for VCs given by the British Legion on 9th November 1929 at the House of Lords. For the last ten years of his life he worked for what later became the Ministry of Pensions. He died at his home on 28th November 1936 and was buried in Stapleford Cemetery. His widow died in 1963.

Edward Courtney Boyle:
Sea of Marmara, April/May 1915

Gallipoli was seven days by land from Constantinople, but only about twenty-four hours by ship, down the Sea of Marmara. Both sides realised the importance of the coastal shipping routes in the Marmara. The Turks reinforced the Dardanelles defences with gun and mine until it was impossible for a major surface ship to pass. But Allied submarines might penetrate where surface ships could not. With Holbrook's success in B.11 as an example of what could be done, Allied submarines made several attempts to reach the Sea of Marmara. After initial misfortunes (the French *Joule*, the Australian AE.2 and the British E.15 were all lost) the first prolonged and highly successful patrol in the Marmara was made by E.14, commanded by Lieutenant-Commander E.C. Boyle.

The E-boats were among the most successful fighting submarines ever produced for the Royal Navy. Fifty-seven of them were built between 1913 and 1917. They were 660-ton boats, 181 feet long, with 2 periscopes, 2 diesels to give a maximum surface speed of 16 knots (batteries gave a maximum submerged speed of 10), armed with 5 torpedo tubes and 10 torpedoes (5 loaded and 5 reloads), and a crew of 30.

Edward Courtney Boyle was a very experienced submariner. He

joined the depot ship *Thames* for submarine training as a Sub-Lieutenant (on the same day as Nasmith) in July 1904 when the Navy still operated the early Holland boats. Boyle had first commanded a Holland boat and then C.4, C.29, D.2, and D.3, in which he was mentioned in despatches for patrols in the Heligoland Bight in August 1914. W. Guy Carr, who served with Boyle later in the war, described him as 'Tall and dark, with slightly greying hair, very reserved and immensely self-contained. Off duty, you would find him immersed in some technical book or other most of the time. He had a sense of humour, but it never ran away with him.' Boyle was appointed to E.14 in October 1914. Three E-boats - E.11, E.14 and E.15 - left Portsmouth together in March and reached Mudros at various dates in April (E.11 being detained at Malta with defects).

E.14 left the main fleet on 27th April 1915, to run the gauntlet of the minefields, sunken blockships, surface patrols, shore batteries and searchlights of the Dardanelles. While on passage through the straits, Boyle saw through his periscope the 700-ton ex-German torpedo gunboat *Paykisevkei* and sank her with his second shot. This alerted all the Turkish defences along the coast. E.14 arrived in the Sea of Marmara having spent sixteen of the previous seventeen hours submerged, including one continuous period of over twelve hours.

Turkish patrol activity was so intense that Boyle had the greatest difficulty in finding clear space and time to recharge the batteries. On the 28th he received a signal ordering him to reserve his torpedoes for transports, and the very next day he sighted two transports, escorted by three destroyers. Boyle evaded the escort and though he missed the first transport with his first torpedo, hit and sank the second ship with the second torpedo. That evening Boyle met Lieutenant-Commander H.G.D. Stoker in AE.2 but could not spare him any torpedoes (it was as well, for AE.2 was lost the following day and Stoker taken prisoner).

By 1st May, the knowledge that a British submarine was at large in the Sea of Marmara was already causing the Turks to reroute their troops by land. Boyle reinforced the point the same day by sinking the 200-ton gunboat *Nour el Bahr*. On the 8th Boyle took E.14 into Rodosto harbour to look for targets but found nothing and after exchanging rifle fire with troops on shore (E.14 had no gun; later boats were fitted with 6-pounders) Boyle withdrew. Two days later, Boyle scored his greatest success when he torpedoed and sank the 5,000-ton ex-White Star liner *Guj Djemal*, carrying over 6,000 troops and a complete battery of artillery to Gallipoli. By 13th May, Boyle had only one defective torpedo left but forced a small steamer ashore near Panedos after a running rifle battle. The C-in-C ordered him to stay on patrol because 'the moral effect of your presence is invaluable'. E.14's success had paralysed all coastal traffic in the Sea of Marmara. Boyle spent much time on the surface, a few miles off the coast, watching the signal fires and columns of smoke carrying the news of his presence along the coast. The submarine ran through the Dardanelles and rejoined the fleet on 18th May. It made two more patrols and spent a total of seventy days in the Sea of Marmara between June and August.

Boyle was promoted Commander at once for his bravery and gazetted for the Victoria Cross on 21st May 1915. His two officers, Lieutenant Edward Stanley and Acting Lieutenant Lawrence RNR, were both awarded the DSC, and every member of the crew the DSM. Boyle received his Cross from the King at Buckingham Palace on 1st March 1916.

Later, Admiral Boyle lived at the Sunningdale Hotel, Sunningdale, Prize Court awarded £375 for the two gunboats and the small steamer, but a much larger claim for £31,000 for *Guj Djemal* was disallowed because the Court decided that she was not an 'armed ship' within the meaning of the Naval Prize Act of 1864.

Edward Boyle was born on 23rd March 1883, at 3 Chatsworth Square, Carlisle, the son of Major (later Lieutenant-Colonel) Edward Boyle of the Army Pay Department and Edith Julia (née Cowley). He went to HMS *Britannia* in 1897 and became a Midshipman in 1898. He was promoted Captain on 30th June 1920, while in command of the depot ship *Platypus*, of the Australian submarine flotilla. He commanded the light cruisers *Birmingham* from 1922 to 1924 and *Carysfort* from 1924 to 1926. He was King's Harbourmaster at Devonport 1926-28 and his last active appointment was in command of *Iron Duke* from 1929 to 1931. He was promoted Rear-Admiral on 18th October 1932 and retired the next day. He was a Chevalier of the Légion d'honneur and was also awarded the Italian Order of St Maurice and St Lazarus. During the Second World War, Admiral Boyle was recalled to service and was Flag Officer in Charge, London, from 1939 to 1942.

Later, Admiral Boyle lived at the Sunningdale Hotel, Sunningdale, Berkshire. He attended various VC functions, including the Centenary Review in Hyde Park in June 1956. On 15th December 1967 he was knocked down by a lorry on a pedestrian crossing in Sunningdale and received serious injuries, from which he died in Heatherwood Hospital, Ascot, the following day. He was cremated at Woking on 22nd December. He had married, but there were no children and his wife predeceased him.

William Guy Carr, *By Guess and By God* (London: Hutchinson, 1930).

Martin Eric Nasmith:
Sea of Marmara, May/June 1915

'Go and run amuck in the Marmara' was the order Commodore Roger Keyes, the C-in-C, gave to Lieutenant-Commander Nasmith, CO of E.11. Nasmith was the most dominant personality of the submarine COs in the Mediterranean, and he needed no second urging. He waited to confer with Boyle (*qv*), who returned on 18th May, and set off the next day on a submarine patrol which was the stuff of legend.

In cold figures, E.11 sank eleven ships - a large gunboat, two transports, three store ships, an ammunition ship and four other vessels. But the patrol's effect on the enemy was as much psychological as physical. E.11 twice penetrated Constantinople harbour (like a Turkish submarine appearing in the Pool of London) to sink a troop-carrying barge and throw the population into a panic. Many people were convinced that the Allied fleet was off the Bosphorus and fled into the country. Nasmith improved the moment by taking the first-ever photographs shot through a periscope.

A curious blend of caution and aggression, Nasmith flew over the Dardanelles and the Marmara beforehand in a Farman biplane 'to look at the jumps'. He pursued a paddle steamer which was running itself ashore so close to land that his bridge party were taken under rifle fire by mounted men: one of the few occasions when submarines have been in action against cavalry. He torpedoed a gunboat which, while sinking, shot a hole in his periscope. Nasmith carried out rough repairs at sea and signalled suggesting that a replacement periscope should be flown out from England - not a normal proceeding in 1915. He lashed a sailing ship alongside E.11 to act as camouflage, and had a much-publicised conversation with an American newspaper reporter before sending his First Lieutenant across to blow up the ship in which the American was taking passage. He told her captain that there were at least eleven Allied submarines operating in the Marmara. Most torpedoes, after they had missed, sank to the bottom. Nasmith arranged it so that his torpedoes could be picked up when they surfaced. He then swam out, unwound the small vane in its nose which cocked the firing pistol, and had the torpedo handled through a flooded tube back into E.11.

Martin Nasmith was an extraordinarily self-reliant, self-disciplined man. He was a very fine games player and always kept himself superbly fit with hard physical exercise. He said that he would not touch alcohol or smoke until he had sunk an enemy warship - and kept the vow. Bringing E.11 back through the Dardanelles, he had reserved two torpedoes for a battleship he hoped he would find in the Straits. The battleship was not there. A lesser man would not have pressed his luck, but Nasmith remembered a large transport he had passed further up the passage. He turned E.11 through 180° (itself a fine feat of seamanship in the Dardanelles currents), went back, and sank the transport.

The Dardanelles held one last trial. Nasmith heard a grating sound forward and, looking through the periscope, saw a mine entangled by its cable in E.11's port forward hydroplane. Nasmith could not slow down, for fear the mine would swing against the ship's side. He could not surface, because he was in the narrowest part of the channel, covered by enemy shore batteries. So, for eleven miles E.11 towed the mine. Nasmith did not mention it to another person on board. Clear of the Straits, he ordered E.11 full astern and brought the submarine to the surface stern first. The mine floated free.

On his first night back, Nasmith attended a dinner party and gave the C-in-C, the Chief of Staff and staff officers a full description of his patrol. It was, according to a man who was there, one of the most enthralling stories any man ever told his fellows. Not surprisingly, Nasmith was gazetted for the Victoria Cross, on 25th June 1915. His First Lieutenant, G. Doyly-Hughes, and Lieutenant Robert Brown RNR won DSCs, and the crew DSMs.

Nasmith returned twice more to the Sea of Marmara. In July and August he sank the Turkish Battleship *Heireddin Barbarossa*, a gunboat, six transports, one steam and twenty-three sailing vessels. In a 47-day patrol in November and December, Nasmith sank or disabled five large and three small sailing vessels and sank the Turkish destroyer *Yar Hissar*. By January 1916, thirty passages of the Dardanelles had been made or attempted by one Australian and nine British submarines. They sank 2 battleships, 1 destroyer, 2 gunboats, 7 transports and 197 other vessels of various sorts and sizes, steam and sail, for the loss of 1 Australian and 3 British submarines.

Nasmith went home after his third patrol and was presented with his Cross by King George V at Buckingham Palace on 15th January 1916. He was a close contemporary of Boyle, joining HMS *Britannia* in the same term of May 1898. Together they served as Midshipmen in the Battleship *Renown* and volunteered for submarines on the same day in 1904. Nasmith had command of various submarines from the early days of the first A-boats. In 1914, as a Lieutenant-Commander, he commanded the Portsmouth submarine depot ship *Arrogant*. For a time he was responsible for the training of future submariners.

Nasmith was born on 1st April 1883 at 13 Castelnau Gardens, East Barnes, London, the eldest son of Martin Arthur Nasmith, a London stockbroker, and Caroline (née Beard). His two brothers served in the First World War, both as Army officers, both winning the DSO and one being killed in action. Nasmith was promoted Commander for his bravery on 30th June 1915 and from there on he was rapidly promoted into a distinguished naval career. He became a Captain after only a year, on 30th June 1916, and was promoted Rear-Admiral on 16th January 1928, at the age of forty-seven, one of the youngest men ever to hold active flag rank. He was Captain of the Royal Naval College, Dartmouth, from 1926 to 1928 and Admiral (Submarines), the head of his submarining profession, from 1929 to 1931. He was promoted Vice-Admiral on 12th October 1932, was C-in-C East Indies 1932-4 and Second Sea Lord 1935-8, being promoted Admiral on 2nd January 1936. He was C-in-C Plymouth and Western Approaches from 1938 until 1941 and then relieved Boyle as Flag Officer in Charge, London, from 1942 until 1946.

In 1920, Nasmith married Beatrix Justina, elder daughter of Commander Harry Dunbar Dunbar-Rivers, of Glen Rothes, Morayshire, and took the name Dunbar-Nasmith. They had two sons - one of whom, David, joined the Navy and became a Commodore - and one daughter.

After the Second World War, Admiral Dunbar-Nasmith was Vice-Chairman of the Imperial War Graves Commission, and Vice-Admiral of the United Kingdom and Lieutenant of the Admiralty. For the last twenty years of his life he lived in Morayshire, where he was Vice-Lieutenant of the County, and interested himself in sailing, skiing and forestry. Lady Dunbar-Nasmith died in 1962. The Admiral died in Dr Gray's Hospital, Elgin, on 29th June 1965 and was buried in Elgin on 2nd July.

Rudyard Kipling, 'Tales of the Trade', in *Sea Warfare* (London: Macmillan, 1916).

Reginald Alexander John Warneford:
Belgium, June 1915

Of some men it could obviously be said that they would either be killed, or win the VC, or both. For 'Rex' Warneford it was both, and in the most spectacular manner. On the night of 6/7th June 1915, he singlehandedly destroyed a Zeppelin over Ghent. He became a national hero overnight and was awarded the Victoria Cross. Ten days later he was dead.

In his own family, Warneford was known as 'always a daredevil and knew no fear, mad on adventure, disliked school and went to sea quite young'. Of his flying days many stories later circulated: that on his very first flight he tapped his instructor on the shoulder and said, 'Can I have a go now?', that an Observer in No.2 Squadron, after landing white-faced and shaken, swore that he would never fly with Warneford again. They had chased a German Taube from Dunkirk to Zeebrugge and driven it virtually into the ground; when the gun jammed, Warneford left the flying controls and repaired it himself, while the aircraft flew itself. His squadron commander sent him across to No.1 Squadron in France with a covering note for his new commander, Wing Commander (later Air Marshal) Arthur Longmore, that 'he hoped Warneford would become a Hun killer, but he was a darned nuisance at Eastchurch'.

Warneford's first encounter with a Zeppelin was early in the morning of 17th May 1915 when he and Squadron Commander Spenser Gray sighted LZ.37, 38 and 39 off Dunkirk, heading east, shortly before 3.30 am. They attacked LZ.39 from below with machine-gun fire. The Zeppelins' best defence was their remarkable rate of climb. By jettisoning water ballast they could rise 1,000 feet a minute. LZ.39 simply soared upwards out of reach and, though later sighted and attacked again, landed safely at her shed.

On the night of 6/7th June the same three Zeppelins made a bombing raid on Calais and then turned for home. Longmore sent Warneford and another pilot, Rose, up to intercept. Rose had engine trouble and had to land hurriedly. Warneford went on alone. He was flying a French machine, a Morane-Saulnier Type L 'Parasol' scout armed with a Vickers machine gun firing forwards through the propeller, and six 20-lb bombs, which the squadron armourer had fitted with a toggle and release wire.

Warneford first caught sight of his opponent as she slipped across the coast in the mist north of Ostend. LZ.37 was 520 feet long, with a framework of aluminium struts and some 8,000 cubic feet of hydrogen contained in eighteen drum-shaped balloons. She was painted green on top and yellow below, with the Iron Cross on her nose. She had a top speed of about 75 mph, the same as Warneford's Morane. Her crew of three officers and ten men were carried in a gondola slung below the hull and she was armed with five high-incendiary 110-lb bombs, twenty incendiaries, and four Maxim machine guns.

As soon as he was sure LZ.37 had seen him, Warneford's preoccupation was to close her without alarming her into jettisoning all blast and shooting up and away from him. How he succeeded was best expressed in his own report:

I left Furnes at 1 am on June the 7th on Morane No.3253 under orders to proceed to look for zeppelins and attack the Berchem St Agathe Airship Shed with six 20-lb bombs.

On arriving at Dixmude at 1.05 am I observed a zeppelin apparently over Ostend and proceeded in chase of the same.

I arrived at close quarters a few miles past Bruges at 1.50 am and the Airship opened heavy maxim fire, so I retreated again to gain height and the Airship turned and followed me.

111

At 2.15 am he seemed to stop firing, and at 2.25 am I came behind, but well above the zeppelin; height then 11,000 feet, and switched off my engine to descend on top of him.

When close above him(at 7,000feet) I dropped my bombs, and, whilst releasing the last, there was an explosion which lifted my machine and turned it over. The aeroplane was out of control for a short period, but went into a nose dive, and the control was regained.

I then saw that the zeppelin was on the ground in flames and also that there were pieces of something burning in the air all the way down.

LZ.37 crashed on top of a convent on the ouskirts of the Mont St Amand suburb of Ghent, killing two nuns and two orphaned children and injuring many more people. Her crew were all killed except the coxswain who, by a miracle, survived.

Warneford's engine would not restart, so he landed close to a farmhouse at about 2.40 am. He repaired a joint on a petrol pipe from the pump on the rear tank and, after some difficulty starting the engine by himself, took off again at about 3.15 am. He lost his way, landed for petrol at Cap Gris Nez, and returned to his squadron at about 10.30 am that morning.

The great national roar of acclamation which went up as soon as the news of Warneford's *coup* reached England contained as much relief as hero-worship. Zeppelins had been attacking towns on the east coast since the beginning of the year and only a week earlier had dropped bombs on London, causing serious alarm amongst ordinary people and arousing a furious storm of propaganda directed against these 'bombers of women and children'. Count Zeppelin himself had said, and many experts agreed with him, that Zeppelins were immune to attack by aircraft. But here was young Warneford to slay the dragon. On 8th June the King himself expressed his people's feelings in a personal telegram to Warneford: 'Most heartily congratulate you on your splendid achievement of yesterday, in which you, single-handed, destroyed an enemy Zeppelin. I have much pleasure in confering upon you the Victoria Cross for this gallant act. George R I.' This was by far the shortest interval in the VC's history between the deed and the award. The citation appeared officially on 11th June.

Warneford became a world-wide hero overnight. President Millerand of France presented him with the Légion d'honneur. An American freelance journalist, Henry Needham, came to interview him and on the afternoon of 17th June Warneford took Needham for a flight in a Farman biplane at Bouc, near Versailles. The aircraft turned over and both men were thrown out and killed. Warneford's body was taken home and 50,000 people lined the streets of London when he was buried in Brompton Cemetery. The *Daily Express* opened a shilling fund for a handsome memorial dedicated to him in July 1916. The Warneford family, reputedly some sixty-eight of them, subscribed to their own memorial at Warneford Chapel, Highworth, Wiltshire.

Warneford won the first VC for the Royal Naval Air Service, which had only been in existence a few months. He was born on 15th October 1891, the son of Reginald William Henry Warneford and Alexandra (née Campbell) at Darjeeling in Upper Bengal when his father was consulting engineer to the Cooch Behar Railway. He was sent home for his education to King Edward VI Grammar School, Stratford-on-Avon, and joined the Merchant Navy in 1907. At the outbreak of war he was navigating officer in the *SS Mina Brea* when she ran aground on the coast of Chile on 19th September. He played his part with great coolness and gallantry in getting her back to Liverpool, with only about a foot of freeboard. He joined the Sportsman's Battalion, Royal Fusiliers, on 7th January 1915 and on 10th February transferred to the RNAS, with probationary rank. He was sent to the Central Flying School, Upavon, for flying training, qualified on 25th February (Royal Aero Club Certificate No.1098) and was promoted Flight Sub-Lieutenant on the 12th.

In No.2 and then in No.1 Squadron, Warneford had a reputation for boldness, not to say foolhardiness. M.S. Marsden, a squadron colleague, later wrote to Warneford's mother, 'Your son's exploits were wonderful. He was always doing good work somewhere. He was never happy unless under heavy shell or rifle fire; and I know of one case where he came down to 300 feet to drop his bombs and came home with about 40 rifle bullet holes in his machine.'

On 5th October 1915 the King wrote to Warneford's mother, Mrs Corkery (his father had died some years previously and she had married again):'It is a matter of sincere regret to me that the death of Flight Sub-Lieutenant Reginald Alexander John Warneford deprived me of the pride of personally conferring upon him the Victoria Cross, the greatest of all Naval Distinctions. George RI.'

Captain W.E. Johns, *The Air VCs* (London: John Hamilton, 1930).

Frederick Daniel Parslow:
Atlantic, July 1915

Lieutenant Frederick Parslow RNR was in his sixtieth year when he performed the act of gallantry for which he was posthumously awarded the Victoria Cross, and he was one of the oldest of all VC winners. He was in command of HM Horse Transport *Anglo Californian* on passage home from Montreal to Avonmouth, with 927 horses on board, when at about eight o'clock on the morning of 4th July 1915, some ninety miles south-west of Queenstown, Ireland, a large U-boat surfaced about a mile on *Anglo Californian's* port beam.

Anglo Californian was a 7,533-ton nitrate carrier with a crew of 150, on Admiralty charter from the Nitrate Producers Steamship Co., the ship's owners and Parslow's employers, and had been converted with stalls, fodder stores, and veterinary staff to carry horses bound for the Western Front. She was unarmed, but had a fair turn of speed.

When he saw the U-boat, Parslow turned *Anglo Californian* to starboard to show his stern, and told his engine-room to put on all the speed they could. They eventually achieved about fourteen knots. As the U-boat turned, so Parslow turned to keep stern-on. Eventually, at about nine o'clock the U-boat commander, obviously exasperated by Parslow's refusal to stop, ordered his deck gun to open fire. The Germans kept up a steady fire, occasionally scoring a hit on *Anglo Californian's* hull and superstructure. Parslow continued to outmanoeuvre the U-boat, turning stern-on whenever she tried to approach up either beam. *Anglo Californian* had begun to transmit SOS signals from the moment the U-boat opened fire. She continued to transmit, giving her position and saying that she was being attacked by a U-boat.

At about 10.30 am the U-boat commander lost patience and hoisted the flag signal 'Abandon ship'. Parslow decided to obey, to save as many lives as possible, and ordered the engines to stop and the crew to take to the lifeboats. Meanwhile *Anglo Californian's* distress signals had been picked up by the destroyers *Mentor* and *Miranda*, which both happened to be within interception range. They signalled Parslow, asking him to delay abandoning ship, and urging him to hold on for as long as he could. Obediently, Parslow got under way again while *Anglo Californian* continued to transmit, acting as a kind of live radio homing beacon for the destroyers.

However, when it was obvious that *Anglo Californian* was not stopping after all, the U-boat opened a very heavy fire on her bridge and superstructure. The bridge was wrecked, the port-side lifeboats reduced to matchwood, and one boat's occupants were tipped into the sea. At last, having used enough heavy ammunition, or having none left, the U-boat came within fifty yards of *Anglo Californian's* side. A dozen of her crew, armed with rifles, fired at anything that moved.

Parslow by this time was dead. The bridge was totally unprotected and Parslow and his eldest son Fred, who was also with him, had had to lie flat on the deck. Young Parslow steered, and when the rim of the wheel was shot away he used the spokes. But Parslow himself had had to pop up his head from time to time to con his ship. A shell hit him, blowing off his head and one arm. When the destroyers arrived at about 11 am, the U-boat dived and escaped. But *Anglo Californian* was saved with her valuable cargo. On 5th July young Parslow brought her into Queenstown, where his father was buried with full military honours.

Parslow had set what his citation called 'a splendid example to the officers and men of the Merchant Marine'. But the VC was not gazetted until long afterwards, when the war was over, and the conditions governing VC awards were widened to admit the Merchant Marine. Parslow was gazetted on 24th May 1919, with another Merchant Navy hero, Bisset Smith (*qv*). Young Fred was given the DSC and promoted to Sub-Lieutenant.

Frederick Daniel Parslow was born on 14th April 1856 at 16 Salisbury Terrace, Islington, London, the son of Eliza (née Pizey) and Charles Parslow, whose profession was given as 'Oil-man (Master)'. He married Frances Parslow at St Mary's, Islington, on 18th November 1885. Frances, as a widow, received the Cross from the King at the Palace on 19th July 1919. They had six children, three boys and three girls. The second son, Frank, was killed in action while with the Machine Gun Corps in France in 1915.

Young Frederick, the eldest son, who had followed his father to sea, continued to serve the same Company after the war. In 1938 he was Master of the 5,456-ton *Anglo Australian*, bound for Vancouver via the Panama Canal. On 14th March, she radioed that she was passing the Azores, and then disappeared. Though she was a well-found ship, with two radio sets, no distress signals were picked up, and nothing more was ever heard of her or her crew.

'The Fighting Parslows', *Sydney Mail*, 18th May 1938.
'Mystery of the Anglo Australian', *The Syren and Shipping*, 18th May 1938.

Edgar Christopher Cookson:
Kut-el-Amara, September 1915

After Turkey entered the war, British strategic objectives in Persia were to secure Arab neutrality, to safeguard British possessions including the oil-fields in Persia, and generally to uphold the credibility of the British flag in the East. By July 1915, Shatt-el-Arab, where the two great rivers Tigris and Euphrates flowed together into the sea, had been captured, the oil-fields were safe, and the province of Basra had been occupied. This should have been enough, but in the minds of the British commanders lurked the dream of going on to capture Baghdad. This turned out to be too much for British and Indian arms to accomplish.

Throughout their operations in Persia the Army were supported by a naval flotilla consisting of an amazing gallimaufry of vessels: river gunboats, paddle-steamers, stern-wheelers, armed launches, tugs and barges. This flotilla made possible a daring sortie to capture El Amara, on the Tigris, in June. The next objective was Kut, 120 miles further up river, where the battle began on 26th September. Two days later, the main battle for Kut was virtually over and General Townsend, commanding the British and Indian troops in the field, asked the naval flotilla to try and force a passage upstream and reach a bridge built by the Turks just short of Kut.

As part of their defence line, the Turks had thrown a formidable boom across the river at a place called Es Sinn, some eight or nine miles as the river flows from Kut. Two iron barges had been run aground, one on each bank, and linked by a heavy iron cable to a native *mahela* or dhow, sunk in midstream. That whole reach of the river was commanded by Turkish artillery, and the barrier itself was under point-blank rifle and machine-gun fire from Turkish troops in trenches on the banks.

Just before dusk on 28th September the armed paddle-steamer *Comet*, commanded by Lieutenant-Commander E.C. Cookson, and two armed launches, *Sumana* and *Shaitan*, approached the barrier and attempted to destroy the central *mahela* by gunfire. When this had no effect, *Comet* worked up to full speed and charged the barrier. The ship hit the chain cables full tilt, but they held, so Cookson ran *Comet* alongside the barrier. Turkish fire had disabled *Comet's* guns and wounded many of the crew. Cookson jumped down himself with an axe to try and cut the cables from the *mahela* in midstream. He was hit at once and then again several times. He was dragged back on board, and died a few minutes later. His last words were reputed to be, 'I'm done, it's a failure, get back at full speed.' *Comet* and the two launches retreated downstream under heavy fire. Kut was occupied the next day. The Turks had vanished, and ironically the barrier for which Cookson had given his life was then dismantled in perfect safety. Cookson's posthumous VC was gazetted on 21st January 1916.

Only ten days before his death in action, Cookson had been gazetted for the DSO, won for his bravery in command of the armed launch *Shushan* in a daring river reconnaissance under heavy fire on 9th May 1915. His DSO was sent to his mother, and his VC was also presented to her by the King on 29th November 1916. She was Cookson's only near relative. He had no wife, and his father, Captain William Edgar Cookson RN, had died some years before. Edgar Cookson was born on 13th December 1883 at Cavendish Park, Tranmere, Cheshire. He went to school at Hazlehurst and entered HMS *Britannia* in September 1887. He was promoted Midshipman on 15th February 1899 and served in *Dido's* Naval Brigade in the Boxer Rising in China in 1900. He was promoted Lieutenant on 30th September 1906 and Lieutenant-Commander on 30th September

1913. At that time he was second-in-command of the sloop *Clio* on the China Station, and came in her to Basra in 1915 to take part in the war in Persia.

Richard Bell Davies:
Ferrijik Junction, Thrace, November 1915

'Rescuing His Friend From The Jaws Of Danger' is a favourite theme of boys' adventure stories. The hero returns, galloping up on his horse or swooping down in his aeroplane, to snatch his fallen comrade out of the clutches of the advancing enemy. On 19th November 1915, on a stretch of marshland in Thrace, it actually happened.

Squadron Commander Richard Bell Davies and Flight Sub-Lieutenant Gilbert Formby Smylie, both of No.3 Squadron RNAS, were on a mission to bomb Ferrijik Junction, a railhead on the mainland of Thrace, where the Maritsa River flows into the Gulf of Enos. Davies was flying a Nieuport, Smylie a Henri Farman, and both had six 20-lb bombs. Their target lay north and west of Gallipoli, across the Gulf of Saros, and their attack was to be co-ordinated with a similar sortie against Burges Bridge nearby.

Smylie's aircraft was hit approaching the target and he planed over the station, releasing all his bombs except one, which hung up. He glided on and force-landed safely on a broad stretch of marshland at the river estuary which was baked into hard dry mud after the long hot summer. Smylie was in enemy territory, and to prevent his machine falling into their hands he set fire to it. He then set out to walk back towards Turkish territory, but he soon saw Davies circling above him, and realised that Davies was preparing to land knowing nothing of the bomb still on board his Farman. Smylie went back, fired his pistol at the bomb and detonated it. This took Davies by surprise but he 'saw Smylie come out of a hollow and wave. There was no difficulty in landing. I put my plane down on a dry water course and waited for Smylie to reach me. He had to crouch under the cowling, in the space where the passenger seat had been. It took me about 150 yards to get the plane in the air again.' Both men were gazetted on 1st January 1916, Smylie for the DSC and Davies for the VC, which he recieved from the King at the Palace on 15th April 1916, 'for a feat of airmanship that can seldom have been equalled for skill and gallantry'.

Richard Bell Davies was a very modest, unassuming man. In his own memoirs and in the rare interviews he gave to newspapers he always skated as quickly as he could over his VC exploit. The above *verbatim* account from the *Portsmouth Evening News* to mark the fiftieth anniversary, in November 1965, is typical. He was a professional naval officer, who chose to fly as his specialisation, and his naval career virtually traces out the history of the Fleet Air Arm's early days. He was born on 19th May 1886 at 3 Topstone Road, Kensington, the son of William Bell Davies, civil engineer, and Mary Emma (née Beale), of Croxley Grove, Rickmansworth, Hertfordshire. He joined the Navy in 1901, and first learnt to fly in 1909, gaining Royal Aero Club certificate No.90. In 1913 he was appointed to the Naval Flying School at Eastchurch and promoted Flight Commander. At the outbreak of war he served in Somaliland and then in Belgium, where he won a DSO for his part in an air attack, on 23rd January 1915, on German submarine bases at Ostend and Zeebrugge. The aircraft had to endure heavy and accurate fire and Davies was hit by a bullet in the thigh, but he handled his machine for an hour in spite of loss of blood and pain, and dropped eight bombs on the target.

Davies had joined the RNAS when it first formed in July 1914, and he was promoted Squadron Commander by the time he arrived in the Dardanelles in May 1915, to win the VC. He was one of the pilots who took Nasmith (*qv*) and other submarine captains on flights over the Dardanelles to show them the obstacles they faced. He was awarded the Croix de Guerre avec Palme, and the Légion d'honneur. In 1916 he commanded Killingholme Air Station and the following year he was Senior Flying Officer, Grand Fleet, in command of the air units operating from the seaplane carrier *Campania*. He became a Lieutenant-Colonel when the RAF was formed but he returned to the Royal Navy in May 1919, winning the AFC the same year. He was promoted Commander in January 1920, and for the next four years was in charge of the Air Section of the Naval Staff.

Post-war, Davies nicely balanced his appointments between the air world and general service. He was executive officer of the battleship *Royal Sovereign* in the Atlantic Fleet from 1924 to 1926, was promoted Captain in 1926 and served in the Admiralty for two years in the Naval Air Section. From 1928 to 1930 he commanded the cruisers *Frobisher* and *London* as Flag Captain and Chief Staff Officer to the Rear-Admiral Commanding First Cruiser Squadron in the Mediterranean. From 1931 to 1933 he was Fleet Air Arm liaison officer to the Air Ministry and then commanded the cruiser *Cornwall* in the Far East. He was Commodore RN Barracks, Devonport, 1936-8, and promoted Rear-Admiral. When the Fleet Air Arm was finally wrenched from the Air Ministry's control and returned officially to the Navy in 1937, Davies was the first Rear-Admiral Naval Air Stations, with responsibility for the air stations at Lee-on-Solent (*Daedalus*), Ford (*Peregrine*), Worthy Down (*Kestrel*), Donibristle (*Merlin*) and in Bermuda (*Malabar*). He retired in 1941, but in 1944 he was in command again, of the ex-Union Castle liner

Pretoria Castle, converted as a test aircraft carrier which carried out deck landing trials for the Spitfire, modified for fleet service and renamed Seafire.

On 29th September 1920 he married Mary Montgomery, only daughter of Major-General Sir Kerr Montgomery KCMG, CB, DSO. They had one daughter and one son, who also joined the Navy, becoming a submariner. He died in Haslar Naval Hospital on 26th February 1966, and was cremated at Swaything Crematorium.

Sailor in the Air: the Memoirs of Vice-Admiral Richard Bell Davies VC, CB, DSO, AFC (London: Peter Davies, 1967).

Humphrey Osbaldeston Brooke Firman and Charles Henry Cowley:
River Tigris, April 1916

After General Townsend captured the town of Kut-el-Amara on the River Tigris in September 1915, he went on to defeat the Turks again at Ctesiphon, only twenty miles from Baghdad. But it was a pyrrhic victory. Townsend could only retreat to Kut where, by the end of December, he and his troops were besieged by the Turks. As the months passed, the situation of the garrison in Kut deteriorated from unpromising to desperate. Several attempts were made to relieve the besieged troops. The last, in the SS *Julnar*, can really only be described as suicidal.

The river steamer *Julnar* was specially fitted with iron plating and sandbag protection at Amara. Her cabins, saloons and upper-deck stanchions were removed and her masts cut down. Her destination was supposed to be secret but everybody knew where she was going, including the enemy. *Julnar* was obviously the most forlorn of all forlorn hopes but there were plenty of volunteers to go in her. Only bachelors were chosen: Lieutenant H. O. B. Firman RN in command, Lieutenant-Commander C. H. Cowley RNVR of the Lynch Bros. steamer *Mejidieh* as second-in-command, Sub-Lieutenant W. L. Reed RNR, also of Lynch Bros., as chief engineer, and twelve ratings chosen from the gunboats of the river flotilla. *Julnar* was loaded with 270 tons of desperately needed supplies for Kut where optimistic preparations were made to berth her near No.12 Picquet, beside the fort.

Julnar sailed from Fallahiya at about 8 pm on the evening of 24th April 1916 under cover of the most intense artillery and machine-gun bombardment, to distract the Turks' attention. It was a dark night, slightly overcast, with no moon, but *Julnar* was discovered within half and hour by the light of star-shells. The River Tigris was high, because of spring floods, and fast-flowing, so that *Julnar* could not make more than about six knots against the current, and all Cowley's experience of those waters was needed to keep her in the channel.

Considering the odds against them Firman and Cowley got *Julnar* surprisingly far. They had twenty-five miles to go. They were riddled with machine-gun fire in the first few miles and came under heavy artillery bombardment at Es Sinn (where Cookson, *qv*, had won his VC the previous year). But still *Julnar* survived and kept on steaming until she reached Magasis, where there was a fort, a sharp right-hand bend in the river, steel hawsers stretched across and the Turks waiting in force. *Julnar* arrived at about midnight and the Turkish guns opened fire at point-blank range. Her bridge was smashed, and Firman was killed with several of his crew. *Julnar's* rudder was entangled in the steel hawsers and she ran aground. That was the end. The Turks swarmed on board, capturing the survivors and the supplies for Kut.

The Kut garrison had expected *Julnar* at about 4 am but the gunfire at midnight told them the worst. When the sun came up, they could actually see *Julnar* lying aground. Magasis was only four miles across the marshes from Kut. Townsend surrendered to the Turks four days later, at 1.30 pm on 29th April. Firman and Cowley were both gazetted for a posthumous Victoria Cross on 2nd February 1917.

Cowley was only slightly wounded when the Turks took him from *Julnar*. He was soon separated from the other survivors. Later, the Turks said he had been killed while trying to escape. But there seems no doubt that the Turks executed him. Cowley himself had said that the Turks would kill him if they ever caught him. The reason lay in Cowley's unusual background. He had lived in Mesopotamia for most of his life and the Turks regarded him as an Ottoman subject, and hence a traitor. Knowledge of this made Cowley's volunteering for *Julnar* doubly brave. He was born in Baghdad on 21st February 1872, the son of Commander Henry V. Cowley, and went as a cadet to HMS *Worcester*, the training ship, from January 1885 to July 1888. When he left *Worcester* he joined McDiarmid & Co as an apprentice and went to sea in the sailing ship *Pendragon*.

At some time he went back to Baghdad where his family lived. His father was (possibly) employed by the Eastern Telegraph Service. Charles Cowley joined the firm of Lynch Bros., who operated a steamship service up and down the Euphrates and Tigris rivers. By the time war broke out in Mesopotamia he had an unsurpassed knowledge of local conditions on the rivers, fluent Arabic, and many friends amongst the local Arab population. He became, in effect, a first-class river pilot, interpreter and Intelligence agent for the British, and so earned the hatred of the Turks. He was promoted to the temporary rank of Lieutenant-Commander RNVR on 2nd August 1915, distinguishing himself in the river flotilla in command of *Mejidieh*. His body was never recovered but his name, with Firman's, is on the Basra Memorial. His Cross was presented to his mother at Basra by Rear-Admiral Wake, Senior Naval Officer, Persian Gulf, on 25th August 1917.

Firman's Cross was presented to his father, Mr Humphrey Brooke Firman, by the King at Buckingham Palace on 28th February 1917. In contrast to Cowley, Firman's background was that of the regular naval officer. He was born on 24th November 1886, at 26 Queensberry Place, Kensington, and joined the Navy as a Cadet on 15th May 1901. As a Midshipman and Sub-Lieutenant he served in the battleship *Glory* on the China Station, the battleships *Albion* and *Illustrious* in the Channel Fleet, and in the Royal Yacht *Victoria and Albert*. He was promoted Lieutenant on 31st August 1908, and had service medals for the Persian Gulf and Somaliland.

Edward Barry Stewart Bingham, John Travers Cornwell, Loftus William Jones and Francis John William Harvey:
Jutland, May 1916

On 31st May 1916, in the North Sea off Jutland, there came at last the fleet engagement for which two navies had been hoping and dreaming. The British called it the 'Great Day', the Germans '*Der Tag*'. At Jutland, the Grand Fleet lost 14 ships, with 6,097 men killed and 510 wounded. The High Seas Fleet lost 11 ships, with 2,551 men killed and 507 wounded. Thus in terms of enemy ships sunk and men killed, the Germans just shaded the victory. But strategically the Royal Navy still held the command of the sea. As someone said, the High Seas Fleet had beaten its gaoler but remained in gaol.

Jutland was a complicated, conclusive, yet controversial battle in which the actual fog of war was far exceeded by the metaphorical steam generated by the reminiscences and post-war analyses of many of the participants. But, as so often in British naval history, the smoke of war was lightened by many acts of sublime personal gallantry.

The two fleets met late in the afternoon. The first major engagement was between the 1st and 2nd Battle Cruiser Squadrons under Beatty and Pakenham and the German battle cruisers under Hipper. Both sides opened fire at 3.47 pm at a range of 15,500 yards. The German gunnery was magnificent. At 4.05 pm *Von der Tann* landed three shells out of a four-gun salvo on *Indefatigable's* upper deck. The next salvo also hit, and *Indefatigable* literally blew apart.

There were two survivors of a ship's company of 1,017. At 4.26 pm the same fate overcame *Queen Mary*. Twenty survived of her company of 1,266, and Beatty made his famous remark, 'There seems to be something wrong with our bloody ships today...'

There was indeed something wrong - a defect in ship design. At action stations, the men in the magazines and handling rooms were naturally anxious to supply the gun-turrets with shells and cordite charges as quickly as possible. Magazine doors were open, cordite charges were removed from their canisters and lay, ready for use, on the deck or in the cages inside the turret. There was what amounted to a trail of bare cordite from the turret to the trunking, down which any flash from a hit on the turret could travel and detonate the contents of the magazine. This is what almost certainly happened in *Indefatigable* and in *Queen Mary* (and later in *Invincible*: 6 survivors out of 1,206) and it very nearly happened in Beatty's own flagship *Lion*. Unnoticed by him at the time, *Lion* was hit amidships on 'Q' turret, at the joint between the front armour plate and the roof plate. The shell penetrated into the turret and exploded, blowing the roof out like 'an opened sardine can', killing the gun's crew and starting a fire in the gun-house. Major F.J.W. Harvey RMLI, in charge of 'Q' turret, though shocked by the blast, very badly burned and dying, collected himself enough to give the order to shut the magazine doors and flood the magazines. The fire ignited cordite in the turret and the flash passed down through the ship to the magazine, killing every man in the handling room. The handlers, the switchboard men, the doctor and his stretcher party all died where they stood. But the magazine was safe. Major Harvey's order undoubtedly saved the ship. He died shortly afterwards and was awarded a posthumous Victoria Cross.

At 4.15 pm, the destroyers went ahead to engage the enemy destroyers and to try to torpedo the German battlecruisers. In a sharp action two German destroyers were sunk, and the 13th Destroyer Flotilla, of *Nestor*, *Nomad* and *Nicator*, led by Commander The Hon. E.B.S. Bingham in *Nestor*, pressed in to within 3,000 yards range to fire their torpedoes. They were taken under heavy fire by the battlecruisers' secondary armament. *Nomad* was hit and crippled, and forced to stop. *Nestor* was also hit and badly damaged, swerving out of line and narrowly missing a collision with *Nicator*, which managed to escape.

Lying helpless and broken down, *Nestor* and *Nomad* watched the battlecruiser retracing their course to the north-east. But they were not left alone for long. Soon, to the south-east appeared the great shapes of Scheer's main battle fleet. The two destroyers lay directly in their path. *Nomad* was first. In Bingham's own account, the Germans

...literally smothered her with salvoes. Of my divisional mate nothing could be seen - great columns of smoke and spray alone gave an indication of her whereabouts. Of what was in store for us there was not now the vestige of a doubt and the problem was how to keep all hands occupied for the few minutes that remained before the crash must come.

Bingham kept his men busy ditching confidential books and equipment and preparing the lifeboats for launching. Still nothing had happened. The First Lieutenant, Maurice Bethell, 'by a brilliant inspiration then suggested to me that the anchor cables might be ranged on deck - ostensibly for use in case of a friendly tow but in reality to keep the men busy to the last; just about this time we fired our last torpedo at the High Seas Fleet and it was seen to run well...'

The end was not far off:

It was a matter of two or three minutes only before the *Nestor*, enwrapped in a cloud of smoke and spray, the centre of a whirlwind of shrieking shells, received not a few heavy and vital hits, and the ship began slowly to settle by the stern... I gave my last order as her commander, 'Abandon ship'... Bethell was standing beside me and I turned to him with the question, 'Now where shall we go?' His answer was only characteristic of that gallant spirit, 'To Heaven, I trust, Sir!' At that moment he turned aside to attend to a mortally wounded signalman and was seen no more amid a cloud of fumes from a bursting shell.

A boat-load of survivors got away from *Nestor* and watched her go down.'Reverential pause, broken almost immediately by the voice of a typical AB, "Are we down 'earted? NO!" Then, "Wot abart Tipperary?" His words and spirit were infectious and all joined lustily in the chorus of that hackneyed but inspiring modern war song'. Bingham and some others were picked up by a German ship and became POWs. Bingham himself was gazetted for the VC, 'for the extremely gallant way in which he led his division in their attack'.

At 5.30 pm the 3rd Battle Cruiser Squadron under Rear-Admiral Hood sighted gun flashes to the south-west and the light cruiser *Chester*, scouting on the squadron's starboard bow, was sent to investigate. At 5.40 pm *Chester* found herself in action against the four German light cruisers of the 2nd Scouting Group. *Chester's* six 5.5-inch were no match for the thirty 5.9-inch guns in the German cruisers. *Chester* was hit seventeen times in a few minutes. Her fire control and half her guns' crews were knocked out. 30 men were killed and 46 wounded - 1 in 5 of her ship's company. Amongst the casualties was the entire crew of the forward 5.5-inch turret. After the shock of the battle, only one figure was still standing by the turret. He was Boy First Class Jack Cornwell, the sight-setter, who took his orders from fire control and applied the necessary range corrections to the gun. He was, literally, a boy, not yet sixteen and a half years old, and he had been in the Navy less than a year. But the short months of naval discipline told. Though he was mortally wounded, Cornwell remained, in the words of Beatty's despatches, 'standing alone at a most exposed post, quietly awaiting orders, until the end of the action, with the gun's crew dead and wounded all round him'. Cornwell lived long enough to be taken ashore, but he died of his wounds in Grimsby Hospital on 2nd June. His posthumous VC was gazetted, with Bingham and Harvey, on 15th September 1916.

Jinking like a lively snipe, *Chester* reached the safety of Hood's battlecruisers, which burst through the mist and damaged three of the German light cruisers. Hood's squadron was considerably to the eastward of where they had been expected by the disconcerted Germans, who despatched destroyers from their disengaged side to attack the battlecruisers. On their way, they met a counter-attack by British destroyers including a division of the 4th Flotilla led by Commander Loftus Jones in *Shark*. The German destroyer B.98 was damaged in the action, but much worse damage was done to *Shark*. Her fo'c'sle was wrecked and her forward 4-inch gun blown away, with the loss of all but one of its crew. Another shell hit *Shark's* bridge, putting the steering wheel and control position out of action. Seeing *Shark* in such a state, the destroyer *Acasta* closed her and signalled: 'Can I give any help?' Loftus Jones hailed back, 'No, don't get yourself sunk for us.'

With the bridge steering wheel out of action Loftus Jones and his Coxswain, Petty Officer W.C.R. Griffin, began to make their way aft to the emergency steering position. On the way he was told that another shell had damaged the main engines and severed a main steam pipe in the boiler-room. *Shark* was now under very heavy fire from three German cruisers. Loftus Jones ordered everybody to come on deck and start turning out the boats. But *Shark* was now lying helplessly between the two fleets, just as *Nestor* had done, under fire from both sides. The boats were blown away as soon as they were got out.

Shark's situation now looked hopeless. Loftus Jones ordered confidential documents to be destroyed and rafts and collision mats to be got ready. He had been badly wounded in the leg as he left the bridge. The doctor had been killed, and the wound was bound up by Chief Stoker Hammel. The after gun had been put out of action and most of its crew killed, so Loftus Jones went to the midships gun. With three surviving Able Seamen - Hope, Smith and Howell - he kept up such an effective fire that he assisted in damaging the German destroyer V.48. German destroyers now closed to within 600 yards of *Shark* and poured a storm of fire on her upper deck. Loftus Jones's leg was shot away, just above the knee. He was sitting on deck while Petty Officer Griffin and A.B. Hope were trying to apply a tourniquet to stop the bleeding, when he noticed *Shark* had no ensign. When he was told it had been shot away he ordered a new one to be hoisted at once. *Shark* was now settling in the water and Loftus Jones gave the order, 'Everybody, save yourselves'. At about 7 pm a German destroyer administered the *coup de grâce* to *Shark* with one torpedo. Loftus Jones was later seen on a liferaft, wearing a life-jacket and encouraging other survivors to sing. But, like many of *Shark's* ship's company, Loftus Jones succumbed to loss of blood and exhaustion. He was not among the seven survivors picked up by the Danish steamer *Vidar* later that night. One died on the way, and only six were landed at Hull the next day. The full facts of Loftus Jones's bravery and devotion to duty were not established for some time and his posthumous VC was gazetted later than the other Jutland awards, on 6th March 1917. Griffin, Hope, Smith and Howell were among those who received the DSM.

It was some time after the battle was over, when darkness had fallen, before rescuers working by the poor light of torches found Major Harvey in the shattered, flame-gutted wreckage of 'Q' turret. He did not (as frequently reported in accounts since) have both legs shot away. He was very badly burned and died of his wounds soon afterwards, but he was not dismembered in any way. He was buried at sea.

Major Harvey's bravery at Jutland was in the tradition of his family, who had served the Crown at sea and on land for at least 150 years. He was a direct descendant of Captain John Harvey, who was mortally wounded in command of HMS *Brunswick* at the Glorious First of June, 1794. John's grandson, also John Harvey, served in *Leviathan* when she forced the self-destruction of the French ships *Robuste* and *Lion* in the Mediterranean in October 1809. Francis John William Harvey was born on 29th April 1873 at Kirkdale Villa, Sydenham, Kent, the son of Lieutenant John William Francis Harvey RN and Elizabeth Edwards Lavington (née Penny). He went to Portsmouth Grammar School and joined the RMLI as a Second Lieutenant on 1st September 1892. He was promoted to Lieutenant on 1st July 1895, and served on the Pacific Station; Captain on 16th January 1900; appointed Instructor of Gunnery at Chatham in November 1910; and promoted to Major on 22nd January 1911. He joined *Lion* as Officer Commanding the marine detachment on board on 12th February 1913 and served in the ship until he died. He was on board for the previous actions in the Heligoland Bight in August 1914 and off the Dogger Bank in January 1915. His Cross was presented to his widow Ethel Marguerite (née Edye) by the King on 20th November 1916. They had a son, Lieutenant-Colonel John Malcolm Harvey of the King's Regiment, born in 1905.

For some time it was thought that Commander Bingham, too, had been killed in the battle. But he had become a prisoner of war, and was repatriated some time after the Armistice, receiving his Cross from King George V in the ballroom at Buckingham Palace on 13th December 1918. He used his time in captivity to prepare his memoirs. He had had a busy war before Jutland, as the title of his book *Falklands, Jutland and the Bight* shows.

The Hon. Edward Barry Stewart Bingham was born on 26th July 1881 at Bangor Castle, Bangor, Ireland, the third son of the 5th Baron Clanmorris and Maude, Lady Clanmorris. He went to Arnold House School and then to HMS *Britannia*. He became a Midshipman in 1897, and was promoted Lieutenant on 30th June 1903. At the outbreak of war he was serving in the battlecruiser *Invincible* and was on board her for the action in the Heligoland Bight in August 1914. He was promoted Commander for his services during the battle off the Falkland Islands in December 1914, when Admiral Sturdee's squadron took revenge for Spee's defeat of Admiral Cradock off Coronel by sinking *Scharnhorst* and *Gneisenau*. Bingham was promoted Captain on 31st December 1919. He was also awarded the OBE and the Russian Order of St Stanislaus. After the war, he commanded the Admiralty yacht *Enchantress*, which was a miniature liner of some 4,000 tons, fitted with a board room, a good cellar and accommodation for wives and guests. But he was a destroyer man at heart and in 1922 commanded *Montrose*, leader of the 8th Flotilla in the Mediteranean. From 1925 to 1929 he commanded the Nore Destroyer Flotilla. From the Nore he went to command the battleship *Resolution*. His last active appointment was to *Comus*, as Senior Officer of the Devonport Division of the Reserve Fleet. He was made ADC to the King in 1931 and was promoted Rear-Admiral on his retirement on 4th July 1932.

In May 1915 at St Martin's in the Fields he married Vera, daughter of Edward Temple Patterson. They had a son and a daughter. The marriage was dissolved in 1937. Rear-Admiral Bingham died in a London nursing home on 24th September 1939.

Because of his youth, Boy Cornwell rapidly became one of the most celebrated of all Victoria Cross winners. John Travers Cornwell was born on 8th January 1900, at Clyde Cottage, Clyde Place, Leyton, Essex, the son of Eli Cornwell, a tram driver, and Lily (née King). It was to his mother that Captain Lawson of *Chester* wrote of her son's conduct:

His devotion to duty was an example to all of us. The wounds which resulted in his death within a short time were received in the first few minutes of the action. He remained steadily at his most exposed post on the gun, waiting for orders. His gun would not bear on the enemy; all but two of the ten crew were killed or wounded, and he was the only one who was in such an exposed position. But he felt he might be needed and indeed he might have been; so he stayed there, standing and waiting, under heavy fire, with just his own brave heart, and God's help to support him.

Cornwell had always been keen to join the Navy, but his parents refused to allow him to at first. When he left school he became a delivery van boy for Brooke Bond & Co. The war persuaded his parents, and Cornwell joined at Devonport on 27th July 1915, becoming Boy Second Class John Travers Cornwell (Official No. J/42563). He found seamanship comparatively easy, but when he went to HMS *Vivid* for gunnery training the going was more difficult. He joined *Chester*, a new light cruiser, on commissioning day, 1st May 1915, at Cammell Lairds & Co, Birkenhead. Despite the many fulsome compliments paid him after his death, he seems to have been an ordinary, steady, reliable boy; a mess-mate who joined the Navy, and *Chester*, on the same day as Cornwell said he 'was a most likeable lad, a credit to the Royal Navy'.

At first, Cornwell was buried in a common grave in Grimsby, but when the news of his bravery spread, his body was reinterred in Manor Park Cemetery, East Ham, London. His funeral on 29th July 1915 was an occasion of almost Victorian splendour. The gun carriage, with a White Ensign draped over the coffin, was drawn by boys from the Crystal Palace Naval Depot. The route was lined by Boy Scouts. Following carriages contained Mr. T. J. Macnamara, Financial Secretary to the Admiralty, the Bishop of Barking, the Mayor of East Ham, Sir John Bethell, MP for the Romford division, and members of East Ham Borough Council. Six boy seamen from *Chester* followed the coffin carrying wreaths from the ship's company and there were wreaths from the Lord Mayor of London and one inscribed 'With deep respect' from Vice-Admiral Sir David Beatty.

At the spectacle of Jack Cornwell's extreme youth and bravery, the nation enjoyed a convulsive spasm of collective commemoration. Cornwell's portrait was painted by the Chief Scout, Sir Robert Baden-Powell, by Frank Salisbury for the Admiralty, by F. Matania for the *Sphere*, and by many others. (Cornwell's brother Ernest was Salisbury's model.) Grimsby and District Hospital named a special cot with a tablet in his memory. A full-page picture of Cornwell on board *Chester* was presented with every copy of *Answers* on 28th October 1916. A poem 'John Travers Cornwell', with the couplet 'Fate set his name in honour grim/And even death is proud of him', was published (amongst many others) by 'X', in a book of war poems. His story was included in *The Scouts Book of Heroes* by F. Hayn Dimmock. Lord Beresford got up in the House of Lords in July 1916 to ask whether it was proposed to award the VC posthumously to Jack Cornwell and the Duke of Devonshire replied that at present no recommendation had been received. A brass plate was put up to commemorate Cornwell in Walton Road School, Manor Park, which he had attended. Thursday, 30th September 1916 was nominated 'Jack Cornwell Day' in the elementary schools of Great Britain. Stamps bearing Cornwell's portrait were printed and cost a penny each. They were bought by no less than seven million school-children. A portrait of Cornwell was presented to any school where the children's contribution was more than £1. A public Jack Cornwell Fund was launched and reached £18,000 in a few months for the Star and Garter Home for Disabled Servicemen at Richmond. A separate fund was opened in East Ham to provide naval scholarships and homes for disabled sailors. Six cottages were erected in Cornwell's memory at Hornchurch, and were occupied by retired sailors. Chester's Union Jack, and White Ensign, with an oak roll of honour carved with the names of those who fell in the ship at Jutland, and a photograph of the ship, were set up as a memorial in Chester Cathedral. The picture of Jack Cornwell standing by his gun became a nationally known image, as famous as any advertising symbol. The gun itself, a Mark 1 5.5 inch breech-loader, was erected in the Imperial War Museum.

One of Cornwell's friends in *Chester*, who was himself wounded, later wrote: 'He was my chum, and no fellow could wish for a better; in fact, he was a *real* Scout. We often used to sit under one of the guns in the evening, chatting about Scouting.' Cornwell was a keen member of the St Mary's Mission (Manor Park) Troop until the outbreak of war, when the scoutmasters enlisted and the troop dissolved. After his death, the Boy Scouts awarded Cornwell the Bronze Cross, their highest award, and instituted a Cornwell Badge, awarded for high character and devotion to duty. *The Scout* had a special 'Cornwell Memorial' number, to launch a Cornwell Memorial Fund for scholarships for Cornwell Badge winners.

Cornwell's mother received the Cross from the King at Buckingham Palace on 16th November 1916. His father, who had been a Private in 57th Company, Royal Defence Corps, had died on 25th October and was buried in the same grave as his son. £500 of the Fund was set aside for Cornwell's mother, until she died in 1918. Another brother, Arthur Frederick, was killed in action in France in August 1918. A sister, Lily, emigrated to Canada with her husband after the war and a certain amount of the Memorial money was used to assist her. In retrospect, it seems that much more of the money raised for Jack Cornwell might have been used to help his own immediate family.

Loftus William Jones came of an old naval family. There had been Loftus Joneses in the Navy List for generations. He was born on 13th November 1879, the second son of Admiral and Mrs Loftus Jones, of Hylton House, Petersfield, Hampshire. Like other members of his family, he went to Eastman's Royal Navy Academy, Fareham, which was loathed by all the Jones who went there, and then to

A reconstruction by the *Illustrated London News* of 6 May 1916 of 'Rex' Warneford's VC-winning exploit

Below left: Charles Cowley, who was killed attempting to reach Kut and was subsequently awarded the VC posthumously (Author's Collection).

Below right: The Hon. Edward Bingham, awarded the VC for his bravery at Jutland (Central Press)

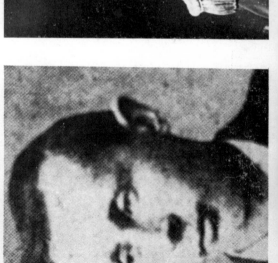

Boy Cornwell, the youngest and perhaps most famous of naval VCs (*Sphere*, 18 November 1916; illustration by F. Matania)

HMS *Britannia* in 1894. He appears to have been a somewhat restless officer: from the time he went to the cruiser *Flora* as a Midshipman in 1897 until he was appointed in command of *Shark* in 1914, he had twenty-eight appointments. He was obviously uneasy in anything bigger than a torpedo-boat destroyer. His time of service in cruisers and battleships was never long and he was a temporary watch-keeper in the cruiser *Argonaut* for ten days. He joined destroyers as a Sub-Lieutenant in *Spiteful* in 1901. He was promoted Lieutenant on 1st April 1902 and his first command was the torpedo-boat destroyer *Sparrowhawk* in 1903. His next was the river gunboat *Sandpiper* in China and he then had a succession of destroyer commands: *Success* from 1905 to 1908, *Chelmer* from 1908 to 1910, *Gurkha* from 1910 to 1912 when he was promoted Lieutenant-Commander. He was in command of the new destroyer *Linnet* at the outbreak of war and his was one of four ships which sank the German minelayer *Koningen Louise* in August 1914. He was promoted Commander on 30th June 1914.

In *Shark* he took part in the preliminary moves of the action which was later known as the Scarborough Raid by elements of the German High Seas Fleet in December 1914. Loftus Jones led *Shark*, *Lynx*, *Ambuscade* and *Hardy*, in foul weather and against a superior force of German light cruisers and destroyers, in a gallant manner which Beatty later commended.

In 1910, Loftus Jones married Margaret Annie, daughter of Richard Francis Dampney, of Netherbury, Dorset. They had one daughter, Linnette, named after her father's ship. Mrs Loftus Jones survived her husband by over half a century. On 23rd October 1916 the Admiralty wrote to tell her that her husband's body had been recovered off the coast of Sweden and he had been buried at Fiskebakskil Churchyard on 24th June. The funeral was well attended by the local townspeople and the fishermen of the place had subscribed to a monument, 'the whole proceedings being marked by every sign of sympathy and reverence'.

Bingham: Commander the Hon. E.B.S. Bingham VC, *Falklands Jutland and the Bight*, (London: John Murray, 1916).

Harvey: Lieutenant-Colonel F.R. Jones's letter to the *Globe and Laurel*, October 1956.

Cornwell: *The Scout Association Headquarters Gazette*, August 1916.

Loftus Jones: Petty Officer W.C.R. Griffin DSM, 'Loftus Jones: VC Hero of Jutland', *Sunday Graphic and Sunday News*, 16th June 1935.

Gordon Campbell, Ronald Niel Stuart, William Williams, Charles George Bonner and Ernest Herbert Pitcher: Atlantic and Bay of Biscay, 1917

In 1917 the *London Gazette* began to publish curiously laconic and uninformative citations for certain naval VCs. On 21st April, for example, it was announced that Commander Gordon Campbell DSO, RN, had been awarded the VC 'in recognition of his conspicuous gallantry, consummate coolness and skill in command of one of HM Ships', and nothing more. On 22nd June a similar citation, with exactly the same guarded wording, announced a VC for Acting Lieutenant W.E. Sanders RNR (*qv*). On 20th July, Lieutenant R.N. Stuart RNR and Seaman W. Williams DSM were 'selected by the officers and ship's company respectively of one of HM Ships to receive the Victoria Cross under Rule 13 of the Royal Warrant dated 29th January 1856'. On 2nd November, a VC was recorded for Lieutenant C.G. Bonner RNR and Rule 13 was mentioned again in respect of a VC for Petty Officer Ernest Pitcher. An alert reader could also have noticed in the Court Circulars that year that Campbell and Bonner both had an audience with the King before any public announcement was made of their Victoria Crosses.

Obviously, there was some mystery about these men - appropriately, for they were all serving in Q-ships, or 'mystery ships' as they were known, and it was essential that the names of the ships and the kind of service they were engaged on should be kept from the enemy (details did not actually appear until 20th November 1918, after the Armistice).

The best defence against U-boats was the convoy system but the Admiralty did not introduce it until the end of April 1917, by which time the U-boats had brought the United Kingdom to within a few months of starvation and the Allies to the brink of losing the war. On 1st February the Germans declared unrestricted submarine warfare against all merchant ships in certain areas, and by the end of that year U-boats had sunk 354 ships of 834,549 tons. Amongst many anti-submarine expedients tried (with initial success, until the enemy inevitably tumbled to them) were the Q-ships - converted tramps, colliers and sailing ships, apparently harmless but once a U-boat had been lured within range revealing that they were in fact heavily armed with concealed guns, torpedoes and depth-charges, with highly trained crews. The Q-ships used many ruses - crews in plain clothes, a Captain's 'wife' to be seen on the bridge, altering the ship's appearance, painting and repainting the funnel, a 'Panic party' taking hastily and clumsily to the boats, ostensibly abandoning ship at the first alarm, whilst leaving the Captain and the guns' crews still concealed on board.

It took a particularly cold-blooded kind of courage to serve in

Q-ships. The crews had to stay quiet, motionless and out of sight while the enemy closed them. The guns' crews had to lie flat on the deck beside their guns. The Captain had to manoeuvre his ship as though trying to avoid the submarine, whilst actually allowing it to close, and steer so as to invite a torpedo hit which might sink his ship before it ever had a chance to fire back. After a hit, the crews still had to stay concealed. In the engine-rooms, the staff crouched above their engines while the water level rose to the hatches. The 'Panic party' would pull away, followed in the later stages when the U-boat commanders became more suspicious by a second and sometimes even a third 'Panic party'. Then, when the moment came, up went the White Ensign, down came the camouflage screens, out jumped the guns' crews, and the guns opened fire at the closest possible ranges. The first Q-ship success was in July 1915, when the *Prince Charles* (Lieutenant Mark-Wardlow) sank U.36. *Baralong* (Lieutenant-Commander Herbert) sank U.27 a month later, and Q-ships sank another four submarines by the end of 1916 for the loss of five of their number.

As so often happens in war, a particular weapon found its own *virtuoso*. Until the war came, Gordon Campbell's naval career had been adequate, but no more distinguished than that of hundreds of other lieutenants. He was born on 6th January 1886 in Upper Norwood, Croydon, the second surviving son of Colonel Frederick Campbell and Emilie Guillaume (née MacLaine); there were actually eleven sons and five daughters, of which eight sons and two daughters survived infancy. He went to Dulwich College and then in 1900 to HMS *Britannia*, becoming a Midshipman in 1902. He served in *Prince George* in the Channel Fleet, *Flora* in the Pacific, *Irresistible* in the Mediterranean and *King Alfred* on the China Station, and was promoted Lieutenant on 1st October 1907, with the unremarkable record of four 'seconds' and two 'thirds' in his examination results. In 1910 he went to the boy's training ship *Impregnable* in Devonport and his first command was the destroyer *Ranger*, also at Devonport. When war broke out he was in command of the destroyer *Bittern* at the same port.

In September 1915, Campbell's career took a decisive turn when he was appointed for special service under Admiral Sir Lewis Bayly at Queenstown, Ireland. On 21st October he commissioned the ex-collier *Loderer*, converted at Devonport with all the devices of a Q-ship and armed with a 12-pounder gun in a 'steering house' aft, two more concealed behind hinged flaps on the main deck, and a further two in dummy 'cabins' on the upper deck. A 6-pounder was hidden at each end of the bridge and a Maxim placed in a 'hencoop' amidships. She had a complement of eleven officers and fifty-six men, and Campbell himself was the only 'regular' RN officer on board.

On passage from Devonport to Queenstown, *Loderer's* name was changed quietly to *Farnborough* and it was under this name that she fought and sank her first U-boat. At 6.40 am on 22nd March 1916 in the Atlantic, a submarine was sighted, hull awash, and soon afterwards a torpedo missed astern. *Farnborough* steamed on, as if she had noticed nothing, until the submarine surfaced, whereupon the 'Panic party' took to the boats (the 'Captain' carrying a stuffed parrot in a cage). The submarine U.68, incautiously closed *Farnborough* to finish her off but *Farnborough's* guns opened fire at 800-yards range. Several shells hit U.68 before she could submerge. Campbell finished her off with two depth-charges. There were no survivors. Campbell was awarded the first of his three DSOs and promoted Commander over the head of 700 others in the Navy List.

After a 'near-miss' on another U-boat on 15th April, Campbell had to wait almost a year for his second kill, by which time *Farnborough* had been officially renamed Q.5. At 9.45 am on 17th February 1917 west of Ireland, a torpedo track was sighted, and Campbell altered speed and steered so as to allow it to hit Q.5 aft by the engine-room bulkhead. While the 'Panic party' got away convincingly, the ship rapidly settled by the stern. The machinery spaces were eventually flooded so deep that the Chief Engineer and his men, to keep out of sight, had to lie on their faces on the gratings at the top of the compartments. Meanwhile, Campbell and the guns' crews were lying prone on the upper deck while the U-boat came within fifteen or twenty yards of Q.5, so close that Campbell, peering out from behind his screen could see the whole shape of her submerged body in the water.

At 10.5 am the submarine broke surface about 300 yards away on the port bow, but where none of Q.5's guns could bear on her. She began to pass down the port side, heading for the 'Panic party's' boats on the port quarter. As she passed abeam, Campbell saw that she was fully surfaced, with her conning tower open and her Captain on the bridge. He would never get a better chance and so, at 10.10 am he gave the order to open fire. The range was 100 yards – point blank. Forty-five shells were fired, almost all of which hit. One officer and one seaman, 'a sample of each' as someone said, were picked up. The submarine, U.83, sank.

Q.5 herself was now so low in the water that it looked as if she too would sink and Campbell made the mournful signal: 'Q.5 slowly sinking respectfully wishes you goodbye'. However, the destroyer *Narwhal* and the sloop *Buttercup* arrived in time to take Q.5 in tow and eventually she was safely beached. Campbell was awarded the VC, and his First Lieutenant, Stuart, the DSO. Amongst the guns' crews awards Seaman William Williams was awarded the DSM and Petty Officer Pitcher was mentioned in despatches. Q.5 herself was refloated, renamed *Holypark* and ended life under new owners in May 1928. Campbell was decorated by the King on 17th March 1917, before his VC was publicly announced.

Q-ships' crews had the option of leaving after any voyage but almost the whole of Q.5's ship's company followed Campbell to his next command, another converted collier, the 3,000 ton *Vittoria* which was renamed (for some reason Campbell could never discover) *Pargust*. She had one 4-inch, and four 12-pounder guns, two 14-inch torpedo tubes, and an outfit of depth-charges. Commissioned on 28th March 1917, she was converted with all the dodges and devices that experience had taught Campbell and his men. There was improved wireless equipment, better accommodation for the men, and better and quicker-acting concealment for the guns. Late in May *Pargust* went to sea, with the intention of being torpedoed.

On 6th June, well out into the Atlantic, a bird flew into Campbell's cabin. This was a sure omen, for it had happened on the day before the other U-boats were sunk. At 8 am on the 7th, a torpedo was fired at *Pargust's* starboard side from such close range that Campbell could not have avoided it even had he wished. The 'Panic party' went away with their stuffed parrot, and at about 8.15 am, as the last boat was leaving, the U-boat's periscope was sighted broad on the port bow. The U-boat cruised round the stern and out to port again. The U-boat captain was misled by the antics of Lieutenant Hereford DSC in the 'Panic party', who began to row towards *Pargust's* starboard side hoping the submarine would follow him, as it did. The submarine surfaced and her Captain came out on to the bridge. She was about fifty yards away on the starboard beam when, at 8.36 am, Campbell gave the order to open fire. Thirty-eight rounds were fired and most of them hit. The submarine tried to get under way but blew up and sank, at about 8.40. Two survivors were picked up and it was learned that the U-boat was UC.29, a minelayer. *Pargust* was lying helpless in the water but she was towed back to Queenstown, arriving at 3 pm the next day.

The King awarded the Victoria Cross to the whole ship. Under Rule 13, the men involved could ballot for one officer and one seaman to receive the Victoria Cross on behalf of them all. They chose Lieutenant R.N. Stuart DSO, RNR and Seaman William Williams DSM, RNR. Hereford got a DSO to add to his DSC, Campbell got a Bar to his DSO and was promoted Captain over 500 others in the list. Pitcher got the DSM.

Pargust was towed to Plymouth and paid off. Apart from a few changes due to sickness, the same crew accompanied Campbell to his next ship - except Stuart, who had left to command his own Q-sloop. Bonner, the Second Lieutenant, took his place as First. The next ship, Campbell's third and last, was also a collier from Cardiff, slightly bigger than the others. Her name was *Dunraven* and Campbell thought her 'a beautiful ship, and all her arrangements in every detail were as perfect as we could wish for'.

Submarines had been active in the Bay of Biscay and so, when

Dunraven sailed on 4th August 1917, Campbell made a large detour into the Bay on his way to Queenstown. As Admiral Bayly said, Campbell 'had a genius for foretelling whereabouts a submarine was likely to be found', and on 8th August, some 130 miles south-west of Ushant, he did it again. At 10.58 am a submarine was sighted on the horizon. *Dunraven* played the part of the unobservant merchantman and the submarine did not dive for some minutes. She eventually surfaced dead astern of *Dunraven* (the most awkward bearing for a Q-ship, showing that the U-boats were growing wary) and opened fire at 11.50 am, at a range of about 5,000 yards.

Campbell made smoke, and sent off frantic panicky distress signals (without giving any position), whilst on the poop Williams and the others on the 2½-pounder token gun gave a brilliant demonstration of poor shooting.

The U-boat (UC.71) shelled for about half an hour, without hitting. Campbell hoped to lure him much nearer before opening fire himself. Slowly, the submarine closed to within 1,000 yards and Campbell took advantage of a very near miss a few feet off the port side to stop his ship, cover the whole midships section with steam from a donkey boiler, send away the 'Panic party' and turn hard to port, bringing the submarine abeam of him. All might have been well, except that the submarine, now closing very rapidly, scored three quick hits on *Dunraven's* poop.

The first detonated a depth-charge which actually blew Bonner out of his hiding place. The others started a fire on the poop so that Bonner, Pitcher, Williams and the others had to stay in hiding whilst a major fire raged in the ammunition store immediately below them.

Meanwhile, UC.71 was crossing *Dunraven's* stern, close to, and was enveloped in the thick black smoke billowing from her poop. Although his after guns' crew might be blown up at any time, Campbell decided to wait until the submarine emerged from the smoke. At 12.58 pm, just as the submarine appeared, there was a tremendous explosion aft. The 4-inch gun and its crew were blown into the air. One man landed in the sea, and the others on mock railway trucks made of wood and canvas which cushioned their fall and saved their lives.

Dunraven's cover had, literally, been blown and UC.71 crash-dived. Two shots were fired at her, one of which might have hit. Campbell sent away a second 'Panic party' to try and reassure his opponent, but at 1.20 pm UC.71 torpedoed *Dunraven* just abaft the engine-room. Campbell sent away a third 'Panic party' on a raft and the original party came back and picked up a few more men, leaving only two guns in *Dunraven* still manned. The fire on the poop-deck was merrily exploding shells and cordite when the submarine surfaced again and shelled *Dunraven* steadily for about twenty minutes, before diving at 2.50 pm. Using the periscope as an aiming point, Campbell fired two torpedoes at UC.71 but missed.

He then waited, expecting another torpedo, but nothing happened. UC.71 had no torpedoes left and could not surface again because help for *Dunraven* was on the way. UC.71 was not seen again. The destroyer *Christopher* took *Dunraven* in tow for Plymouth, but the weather worsened, her crew had to be taken off and shortly after 3 am the next morning she sank, her ensign still flying.

It was Campbell's last Q-ship action. Admiral Bayly insisted he retire. As for his crew, Campbell himself said of them, 'Not a man failed, not a man could have done more.' Bonner was awarded the VC. So too was Pitcher, the 4-inch gunlayer, by ballot under Rule 13. Campbell himself received a second Bar to his DSO and Seaman Williams a bar to his DSM.

Campbell went on as Admiral Bayly's flag captain and Senior Naval Officer at Holyhead, in charge of Q-boat operations in the Irish Sea. In 1918 the French government awarded him the Croix de Guerre avec Palmes and the Légion d'honneur. He then commanded the light cruiser *Active*, and ended the war as Captain (D) of a destroyer flotilla.

After Q-ships, the peacetime Navy was bound to seem somewhat humdrum. Campbell commanded the cadet training cruiser *Cumberland*, from 1919 to 1921, was Captain in charge of the naval base at Simonstown in South Africa, and commanded the battlecruiser *Tiger* from 1925 to 1927. He was a naval ADC to the King in 1928 and was promoted to Rear-Admiral on 5th October, at the age of forty-two, and retired - as he said, 'the penalty of quick promotion'. He was informed that he would be placed on the retired list in what he called a regular stereotyped letter 'rather less gracious than one would send to a cook who had served you for two years'.

After his retirement, Campbell wrote his story of Q-ships *My Mystery Ships*, in 1928, his memoirs, *Number Thirteen*, so called because he was thirteenth of a family of sixteen, in 1932, and over the years published several other books about the sea. His exploits in Q.5 were dramatised for radio in August 1938. In 1931 he made an unexpected foray into politics when he stood at Burnley, a hot Labour stronghold, against the notable Socialist Arthur Henderson, then Secretary of the Parliamentary Labour Party and Foreign Secretary in the Labour Government. Campbell stood as a National-ist, took the White Ensign as his colours, hung a torn Q-ship flag over the wall of his election office, and polled an astonishing 35,126 votes against Henderson's 26,917. In Parliament he spoke very occasionally, almost always on defence matters. He vehemently supported National Service and the abolition of the use of submarines. He was promoted Vice-Admiral on the retired list on 31st December 1932. After a severe heart illness in 1934 he was beaten by Labour in the 1935 Election.

Admiral Campbell was a vigorous lecturer and public speaker, and took a very active interest in Service and charitable organisations, including the Old Boys of his old school. In the Second World War he lent his presence to Warship Weeks and other fund-raising functions in Plymouth and around. On 14th January 1911 he married Mary Jeanne, daughter of H.V.S. Davids, of Hillier House, Guildford, formerly HM Consul in Batavia. They had one son and one daughter. Admiral Campbell died in the West Middlesex Hospital, Isleworth, on 3rd October 1953.

Ronald Niel Stuart was a professional seaman and the son, grandson and great-grandson of seamen. He himself said his family had been seafarers for at least five generations. His grandfather settled in Prince Edward Island, Canada, and his father sailed in clipper ships from England to Australia. He was born on 26th August 1886 at 31 Kelvin Grove, Toxteth Park, Liverpool, the son of Niel Stuart, master mariner, and Mary (née Banks). He went to Shaw Street College, Liverpool, and then in 1902, aged fifteen, to sea as an apprentice in the barque *Kirkhill*, owned by Messrs Steele & Co. After completing his time he joined the Allan Line and served in various ships all over the world. Control of the Allan Line was acquired by the Canadian Pacific Railway Co. in 1915 and Stuart was employed by the Company for the rest of his working life.

In October 1914, Stuart became a probationary Sub-Lieutenant RNR; he was confirmed in May 1915 and promoted Lieutenant RNR in September 1916, and commanded the destroyer *Opossum* and the Q-sloop *Tamarisk*. In *Tamarisk* he won the United States Navy Cross when he stood by the US destroyer *Cassin* after she had been torpedoed by a U-boat on 15th October 1917 and successfully towed her back to harbour. In 1918 he was promoted Lieutenant-Commander RNR, and awarded the Croix de Guerre avec Palmes.

After the war, Stuart kept up his two parallel careers, in the RNR and with Canadian Pacific. He regularly returned for requalifying training with the RN, was promoted Commander RNR on 30th June 1928, awarded the Reserve Officers' Decoration in November 1929, and became a Captain RNR on 1st July 1935. He was Honorary President of the RNR Officers Club, the Sea Urchins, and by a special Ensign Warrant of 14th May 1927 he was authorised to fly the Blue Ensign on any ship under his command.

In the CPR, Stuart rose to the top of his profession. He was Staff Captain in the RMS *Empress of France* from 1924 to 1926, Master of the *Minnesota*, 1926-29, and as Captain of RMS *Duchess of York* he brought a party of Canadian VCs to the VC Dinner in the Guildhall in November 1929. In July 1934, aged forty-eight, he became Captain of the 42,500-ton liner *Empress of Britain* and Commodore of the CPR Fleet. In July 1938 he came ashore and was general manager of CPR in London until he retired in 1951.

Ronald Stuart was a typical bluff sailor. One reporter described him as 'blond, ruddy, powerful', a hard man and a hard taskmaster. He knew at first hand the dangers of the sea and the violence of the enemy, and was philosophical about both. The *Kirkhill* barque spent forty-two days trying to round the Horn and eventually foundered off the Falklands; Stuart and the rest of the crew were in the lifeboats for some days before reaching shore. He bore to his death the scars on his fingertips of an early accident handling sugar in the days of sail. Of Q-ships he said that the men in them 'were lucky and far better off than the poor fellows in the lines'. He described the press as 'always trying to find out things they should leave alone'.

In the spring of 1919, Ronald Stuart married Evelyn Wright of West Derby, Liverpool, at St Clement's Church, Toxteth, Liverpool. They had three sons and two daughters. Two of the sons served in the RN and RCN, carrying on the Stuart family tradition. In retirement, Stuart lived with his three sisters, (his wife having died in 1930) at Beryl Lodge, Charing, in Kent, where he died on 8th February 1954.

Lieutenant Stuart and Seaman William Williams RNR received their Crosses from the King on the forecourt of Buckingham Palace on Saturday 21st July 1917, the day after the awards had been publicly announced. The ceremony was watched by Williams' father and mother, who, summoned by Admiralty telegram, had come up by train from their home in Anglesey.

William Williams came from a humble background, one of a family of six or seven children, in Amlwch Port, on the island of Anglesey. He was born on 30th October 1890. He joined the RNR as a Seaman, (Official No. 6224A) in 1914. In Q-ships he seemed to have the perfect employment for himself. He handled his gun with great skill and coolness and once, for which he was elected to receive the VC, he saved the ship from betraying herself. When *Pargust* was first torpedoed by UC.29 on 7th June 1917, the force of the explosion freed the securing pins and balance weights which held the starboard side gun-covers in place. Had the covers fallen down, the presence of the guns would have been prematurely revealed to the U-boat. But Williams, with great presence of mind, took the whole weight on himself and physically prevented the covers from falling. But for Williams, as Campbell said. 'The action might never have taken place.' Worse, the U-boat might have simply stood off and shelled *Pargust* to destruction.

Williams finished the war with the VC, the DSM and bar, and the French Medaille Militaire. He went back to Anglesey and worked as a seaman on the Holyhead-Greenore steamers. In 1925 he married Elizabeth Jane (née Wright). They had one daughter. Williams died in Holyhead on 22nd October 1965 and was buried in Amlwch.

After his exploits in *Dunraven*, Lieutenant C.G. Bonner VC, DSC, RNR was appointed to command his own Q-ship, what Campbell called the 'dangerous-looking' *Eileen*. Campbell knew that Bonner was about to go to sea in *Eileen* and had a young wife in Plymouth

137

and, fearing that Bonner like Sanders (qv) might never live to collect his VC and give it to his wife, asked the Admiralty if it would be possible for Bonner to be decorated before sailing.

At 10 pm on Friday 6th October 1917 Bonner had an Admiralty telegram at his digs in Saltash ordering him to report to the Fourth Sea Lord in London at 10 am the next day. Thinking there was to be an Investiture at the Palace and he would be back the next night, Bonner took just a small bag and his sword, only to be told he was to spend the weekend with the King at Sandringham. However, all went well and George V presented Bonner with his VC in the study at York Cottage that Saturday evening. (It was not gazetted until 2nd November.)

Charles George Bonner was a professional seaman, who came from a Midlands farming background. He was born on 29th December 1884, at Shuttington, Warwickshire, the youngest son of Samuel Bonner JP, of Aldridge, near Walsall, Staffordshire, where the family moved when Bonner was an infant, and Jane, daughter of Charles Hellaby, of Bramcote Hall. He went to Bishop Vesey's Grammar School, Sutton Coldfield, and Coleshill Grammar School, and then in 1899 to the training ship *Conway*. He joined the firm of George Milne & Co in 1901 and went to sea as an Apprentice in the sailing ship *Invermark*, then as Second Mate and Chief Mate in the barque *Ashmore*. He took his master's certificate at the age of twenty-two. Changing from sail to steam, he joined the Johnston Line, serving in their ships in the Black Sea trade. He was in the *Incemore* when she collided with the German liner *Kaiser Wilhelm* off the Isle of Wight.

After the war, Bonner was a First Officer with the Furness Withy Line for a few months and then, for the next twenty-one years, worked for the Leith Salvage and Towage Co. and became an expert in ship salvage. In 1925, as Captain of the tug *Bullger*, he successfully refloated the Copenhagen steamer *Elizabeth* from a reef at Johnstone's Point, Campbeltown, Argyll. In the Second World War he salvaged the *Caledonia* in the Firth of Forth and in 1948 he flew to Norway to advise on the salvage of the German battleship *Tirpitz*.

He married Alice Mabel, daughter of Thomas Partridge of Walsall, at St Matthew's Church, Walsall, on 17th June 1917. They had one son, Gordon Dunraven Bonner, who later became a Surgeon Lieutenant in the RNVR. Bonner died at his home, 12 Netherly Road, Edinburgh, on 7th February 1951.

Although he won the VC by ballot, to add to his DSM and his Mention, Petty Officer Ernest Pitcher, the 4-inch gunlayer, was probably the most disappointed man on board *Dunraven*. He waited with the rest of the gun's crew, concealed on the poop, while the battle went on overhead and around them. When the magazine below them caught fire, they still waited, taking up cartridges and holding them on their knees to prevent the heat of the deck igniting them. But they never fired a shot against UC.71 after all. The magazine blew up before they were ordered to fire and the whole crew were blown into the air, Pitcher himself landing near the engine-room. Like Bonner and several others of the guns' crew, he was injured by the blast.

Unusually for the Q-ships' crews, Ernest Herbert Pitcher was a regular RN sailor. He was born on 31st December 1888, son of George Pitcher, a coast guard, and Sarah (née Beverstock), at Mullion, in Cornwall, although the family soon moved to Swanage in Dorset, where Ernest went to the Primary School. He joined the Navy at Portsmouth, (Official No. PO/227029) on 22nd July 1903, at the age of fifteen. At the outbreak of war he was serving in the super-Dreadnought *King George V* and volunteered for Q-ships in 1915. He received his Cross from King George V himself at an Investiture at Buckingham Palace on 5th December 1917. He also received the French Medaille Militaire and the Croix de Guerre.

Pitcher was rated up to Chief Petty Officer on 1st August 1920 and retired from the Navy on pension, after twenty-five years' service, on 30th December 1927. He went back to Swanage, where he was groundsman and taught woodwork at a boys' preparatory school. He is also said to have been licensee of the Royal Oak, Herston, Swanage, at some period between the wars.

He rejoined the Colours on 5th August 1940 and served in various naval establishments in Poole and Portland and in HMS *Attack* at Yeovilton, until the end of the Second World War. He died in the RN Auxiliary Hospital, Sherborne, of tuberculosis, on 10th February 1946. His last years were spent in a house called Dunraven, at 4 Richmond Road, Swanage. In 1918 he married Lily (née Evers) at Wareham and they had one daughter, named Ruth Mary Dunraven. In 1963 some friends and townspeople of Swanage subscribed to a memorial tablet to Pitcher, which was unveiled in the Parish Church on Armistice Day that year.

Vice-Admiral Gordon Campbell VC, DSO, *My Mystery Ships* (London: Hodder & Stoughton, 1928).
Vice-Admiral Gordon Campbell VC, DSO, *Number Thirteen* (London: Hodder & Stoughton, 1932).
E. Keble Chatterton, *Q Ships and their Story* (London: Hurst & Blackett, 1923).

Archibald Bisset Smith:
Atlantic, March 1917

On 10th March 1917, the New Zealand Shipping Company's cargo steamer *Otaki*, 7,520 tons, was about 350 miles east of St Miguel in the Azores, outward bound from London to New York. She was in ballast and making about fourteen knots. There was a long swell running and the visibility was poor in heavy rain squalls when, at about 2.30 pm, a strange ship was sighted at about three miles on the port quarter. *Otaki's* Master, Archibald Bisset Smith, suspected an enemy and did not stop or challenge, but held his course and increased to full speed, about fifteen knots.

The stranger was the German raider *Möwe*, a fruit carrier converted while building into an auxiliary commerce raider, with guns, torpedoes, armour plating and mines. Commanded by Count Nikolaus zu Dohna-Schlodien, she had been at sea (on her second raiding trip of the war) since November 1916 and had already sunk or captured twenty-one ships, mostly British. She was smaller than *Otaki*, but faster, and carried four 5.9-inch, one 4.1-inch and two 22-pounder guns to *Otaki's* single stern-mounted 4.7-inch. At first, Dohna-Schlodien held off, hoping the weather would clear, but when it was obvious that *Otaki* was not stopping, *Möwe* set off in chase. *Möwe* was rolling heavily, and Dohna-Schlodien wanted to get close to give his gunners a better chance.

At a range of just under 2,000 yards, *Möwe* fired a warning shot across *Otaki's* bows, which Bisset Smith ignored. *Möwe's* gunners could see *Otaki's* stern gun being manned and trained, and so opened fire in earnest. Both ships exchanged shells for some twenty minutes. *Möwe* hit *Otaki* several times, set her on fire and killed four of her crew, including a Boy Apprentice, Basil Kilner, serving the gun.

But *Otaki* had what the Germans themselves called 'an excellent gunner'. He hit *Möwe* seven times, on the signal bridge, and beside the funnel, and along the superstructure and put one shell in a portside coal bunker, starting a fire which burned for three days. *Möwe's* officers were amazed by such opposition. Their ship was quite badly damaged, and with a little more luck on *Otaki's* side, might even have sunk.

Otaki had now been hit some thirty times and was heavily on fire. Although a big sea was running and darkness was coming on, Bisset Smith was forced to order the lifeboats away. There was no point in losing more lives in a hopeless action.

When the survivors of the crew of seventy-one had taken to the boats, only the Chief Officer, Roland H.L. McNish, the ship's carpenter and Bisset Smith himself were left on board. The Chief Officer and the carpenter both jumped into the water, thinking that the Master was following them. But Bisset Smith stayed on board, evidently deciding that he preferred to go down with his ship, which sank with the Red Ensign still flying. *Möwe* picked up the survivors and took them back to Germany, arriving at Kiel on 20th March, where they were interned for the rest of the war. *Otaki* had six killed and nine wounded. *Möwe* had fifteen killed or wounded. McNish was awarded the DSO, Leading Seaman A.F. Worth RFR and A.B. Ellis Jackson RNVR, of the guns' crew, both got the DSM; two Apprentices, Basil Kilner and W.E. Martin, were mentioned in despatches. Bisset Smith's VC was gazetted posthumously with Parslow's (*qv*) on 24th May 1919. He was given the honorary rank of Temporary Lieutenant RNR, back-dated to 26th February 1917, to make him eligible for the VC, but he remained a Merchant Navy officer and was proud to be so. His name appears as 'Master A.B. Smith RNR' on the Merchant Navy Memorial on Tower Hill. His Cross was presented to his widow by the King at a private ceremony at the Palace on 7th June 1917.

Archibald Bisset Smith was a Scot, born at Cults, Aberdeen, on 19th December 1878. He went to school at Robert Gordon's College, Aberdeen. In 1937 the family presented the school with a shield to be given annually to the boy with the highest qualities of character, leadership and athletic ability. The winner had a three-month visit to New Zealand, with his return passage provided free by the New Zealand Shipping Co.

On 9th March 1951, at Glendinning's auction rooms, the New Zealand Shipping Co. paid £125 for Bisset Smith's VC, which was then mounted in a special display case in a new MV *Otaki*, launched at John Brown's on the Clyde on 24th October 1952. The Cross is now at P & O headquarters in London.

Crossed Flags (house magazine of the New Zealand Shipping Co.) Vol.1, No.1, May 1965.
Sydney D. Waters, *Clipper Ship to Motor Liner: The Story of the New Zealand Shipping Company 1873-1939* (London: NZSC, 1939).

Frederick William Lumsden:
Francilly, France, April 1917

Major F.W. Lumsden RMA was awarded the DSO for gallantry in France in the New Year's Honours List of 1917. Between that date and his death from a sniper's bullet on 3rd June 1918, Lumsden won a VC, a CB, three more DSOs and a Croix de Guerre. The soldiers who served under him said it should have been at least two VCs.

Lumsden was a thinking soldier. He passed the Staff College Course and spent as much time as a staff officer as a soldier in the line. He was a first-class shot, but he was also a first-class interpreter in German. He might have been reckless with his own life, but never with those of his men, and he always tempered valour with discretion. His numerous citations pay due credit to the discreet and skilful way in which he carried out withdrawals. Once the objective had been achieved, he was careful not to squander any more lives.

141

He was born in India, at Fyzabad, on 14th December 1872, the son of John James Foote Lumsden, of the Indian Civil Service, and Marguerite (née White). He came home for his education, as was customary, and went to Bristol Grammar School. He joined the Royal Marine Artillery as a Subaltern on 1st September 1890, specialising in signals and gunnery, but his career in the Corps was unremarkable: Lieutenant on 1st September 1891, Captain on 16th June 1897, Brevet Major on 1st September 1911. He had an appointment on the staff in the Straits Settlements from 1911 to the outbreak of war. As Acting Major RMA he went to France in February 1915 in command of the RMA No.1 Howitzer Battery and took command of the RMA Howitzer Brigade in April. He also served on the staff and was GSO2 when promoted to the substantive rank of Major in January 1916.

He was still on the staff of 32 Division when he was temporarily appointed to take command of the 17th Battalion (3rd Glasgow Battalion) of the Highland Light Infantry and won two more DSOs in daring personal reconnaissances, each time making a careful withdrawal. These two bars to his DSO were gazetted in the same issue of the *London Gazette*, of 11th May 1917.

By then Lumsden had already won the VC, when his battalion took part in the British and French advance on the Hindenberg Line, prior to the great battle at Arras which opened on 9th April. When the village of Francilly, just west of St Quentin, was captured by the British on 3rd April, it was discovered that the Germans had left behind a battery of six field guns, dug in about 300 yards forward of the front line. Lumsden determined to bring the guns back although the Germans were shelling the place, being equally determined that the guns should be destroyed before they could be captured.

That night Lumsden led four gun-teams of horses and a covering force of infantry through the barrage towards the guns. In no-man's-land, one team sustained such casualties that they were unable to go on. Lumsden left the other three under cover and then led the infantry through heavy artillery and machine-gun fire to capture the gun positions. He sent two teams back with their guns and himself took the third to his own lines. He returned and took another two guns away. The Germans now counter-attacked and disabled the one remaining gun. Lumsden returned again and drove off the enemy so that even the sixth gun was also captured.

A few days later Lumsden was promoted Temporary Brigadier-General in command of 14th Brigade. He was gazetted for his VC on 8th June 1917 and received it from the King at Buckingham Palace on 21st July. He returned to France again, and was promoted Lieutenant-Colonel RMA for distinguished service in October. The following spring he won a third bar to his DSO, leading an assault on a group of seven pill-boxes, showing, as his citation said, 'such coolness, determination to succeed and absolute disregard of danger

142

...as afforded a magnificent example to all ranks, the value of which can hardly be exaggerated.'

Lumsden was awarded the CB on 1st June 1918 but it is unlikely that he ever knew of it. On 3rd June, there was an alarm in his sector of the line at Blairville, some six miles from Arras, and,as usual, he went forward to see for himself. He was hit in the head by a sniper's bullet and killed instantly. He was buried in Berles New Military Cemetery, and a memorial to him was later erected at the RM Barracks, Eastney, Portsmouth.

In 1894 he married Mary Ellen Harward, daughter of Lieutenant-General Harward RA, and they had one daughter.

An Epic of Glasgow: History of the 15th Battalion the HLI, ed. Thomas Chalmers (Glasgow: John McCallum & Co., 1930).

William Edward Sanders:
Atlantic, April 1917

Sanders was another Q-ship 'Mystery VC' and his citation in the *London Gazette* of 22nd June 1917 was as laconic as Campbell's (*qv*): 'In recognition of his conspicuous gallantry, consummate coolness and skill in command of one of HM Ships in action.'

Like many VC citations, that was something of an understatement. On 30th April 1917 the Q-ship *Prize*, under Acting Lieutenant W.E. Sanders RNR, was about 180 miles south of Ireland, looking for U-boats.She was a 200-ton three-masted topsail schooner, originally called *Else*; she had been the first prize captured from the Germans in the war (and her first name had actually been *First Prize*). She had been converted into a Q-ship early in 1917, being fitted with two 12-pounder and two Lewis guns, because the U-boat captains had become suspicious of tramp steamers but were still attacking sailing ships with confidence.

Shortly after eight o'clock that evening a submarine broke surface some distance off *Prize*'s port quarter. She was the new, large U.93, on her first war patrol, commanded by Freiherr Speigel von und zu Peckelsheim, who had already sunk eleven ships and thought this would be his twelfth. U.93 opened fire at 8.40 pm at a range of some 3,000 yards (although Speigel later admitted he had absolutely no suspicions about *Prize*). *Prize* was holed in three places along the waterline, twice in her mainmast and her engine-room was set on fire. Sanders and his crew kept out of sight, while the 'Panic party' took to the boats.

At 9.05 pm, when *Prize* appeared to be sinking, U.93 approached within eighty yards of her port quarter. The last forty minutes had been a very trying time for Sanders, but his moment had now come. The White Ensign was run up, the gun ports fell open, and the first shot from the forward 12-pounder hit the U-boat's forward 4.1-inch gun, knocking gun and crew into the sea. The 12-pounders scored several more hits whilst the Lewis guns sprayed the U-boat crew on deck. U.93 turned to port to try and ram *Prize* but then sheered off hard to starboard. Another shell hit and wrecked her conning tower. Fires could be seen raging inside her hull, and her bows rose in the air. *Prize's* 'Panic party' meanwhile picked up Speigel, who had been blown into the water, his Navigating Officer and a Stoker Petty Officer. In spite of her own damage, *Prize* reached Kinsale on 2nd May (prisoners assisting in the pumping out and plugging of holes) and was eventually towed to Milford Haven.

Sanders was promoted to Lieutenant-Commander (a remarkably rapid rise from Sub-Lieutenant in eighteen months) and presented with a Sword of Honour by the officers of the naval base at Milford Haven.

William Edward Sanders was yet another of the adventurous professional seamen who found their way into Q-ships. He was a New Zealander, born in Auckland on 7th February 1883, the eldest son of Edward Helman Cook Sanders, a bootmaker, and Emma Jane (née Wilson). Both his parents had emigrated from London. He first went to sea in the coasting steamer *Hinemoa* in 1900 and joined the Craig Line, being First Mate in the barque *Joseph Craig* when she was wrecked inside Hokianga Bar. He joined the Union Steamship Co. and gained his master's and extra master's certificates. He volunteered at the outbreak of war but when he was not called up he gave up his job and worked his passage to the UK as Second Officer of a troopship in 1915. He joined the RNR, becoming a Sub-Lieutenant on 19th April 1916. He served in Q-ships, gaining the DSO for action against an enemy submarine in undisclosed circumstances and which was not gazetted until 14th September 1917. He commissioned *Prize* at Falmouth early in 1917, supervising her conversion and fitting-out; he and his second-in-command, Lieutenant W.D. Beaton DSO, RNR, had done a course of special instruction in gunnery at Whale Island.

In the mist and confusion of the action everybody (including Speigel) believed that U.93 had been sunk. But she was still afloat (as was revealed much later when the Germans made enquiries about the three survivors through the Red Cross). Meanwhile, brilliant seamanship and leadership by her First Lieutenant brought her back to Germany, though her conning tower was wrecked and she could not dive. This meant that *Prize's* true nature became known to the enemy. When U.48 sighted her in the Atlantic on 14th August 1917, she torpedoed her without surfacing. *Prize* was lost with all hands.

Sanders's VC was presented to his father at Auckland Town Hall by the Governor-General, the Earl of Liverpool, on 19th June 1918.

He was commemorated in his native land by the Sanders Cup, New Zealand's premier sailing trophy, and by a Sanders Memorial Fund, which provided a scholarship for children of members of the Mercantile Marine Service or the Royal Navy resident in New Zealand, valued at £75, and tenable for three years at Auckland University College.

Lieutenant-Commander Harold Auten VC, *Q Boat Adventures* (London: Herbert Jenkins, 1919).
Account by Lieutenant W.D. Beaton DSO, RNR in *Imperial Merchant Service Guild Gazette*.
E. Keble Chatterton, *Q-Ships and their Story* (London: Hurst & Blackett, 1923).
Vice-Admiral Friedrich O. Ruge, 'The Submarine War: a U-Boat Commander's View', *Purnell's History of the First World War, Vol. 5*, p.2092.

Joseph Watt:
Straits of Otranto, May 1917

There was an 'Alice in Wonderland' element about the concept of the submarine net barrage. Because salmon could be caught in nets stretched across river estuaries, so (it was reasoned) bigger fish such as U-boats could be caught in bigger nets stretched across bigger passages such as the Straits of Dover or Otranto. This belief persisted for years, in the face of conspicuous failure.

The Otranto Barrage, set up at the beginning of 1916, stretched across the opening of the Adriatic, between Otranto on the 'toe' of Italy and the island of Corfu. It had the admirable object of sealing off the Mediterranean from the U-boats at their base at Cattaro, but intercepted only two of the hundreds of U-boat passages made through the Straits.

The Barrage consisted of 120 net drifters and 30 motor launches, all equipped with depth-charges to drop on the submarines, supported by Italian destroyers, sloops, and kite-balloons. The drifters had a crew of ten and were armed with a small defensive gun.

The Austrian Navy, though normally a passive force, were sufficiently irritated by the Barrage to attack it four times in March and April 1917 and made a much more determined attempt on the night of 14/15th May 1917. Three light cruisers, *Novara*, *Saida* and *Helgoland* each took a third of the drifter line and set out systematically to destroy it. The drifters were, of course, ludicrously small targets. To their credit the Austrians gave their opponents every opportunity to surrender and to take to their boats whilst their drifters were sunk by gunfire. Some did surrender.

But most of the drifter crews would have none of it. *Admirable's* crew only abandoned ship after the boiler blew up and the wheel-house had been shot away; even then the Second Hand, A. Gordon, scrambled back on board and fought the gun singlehanded until he was killed. *Novara* approached within 100 yards of *Gowan Lea* and ordered her crew to abandon ship. Her Captain, Skipper Joseph Watt, ordered full speed ahead, called upon his crew to give three cheers and fight to the finish. *Novara* was engaged by *Gowan Lea's* single 57-mm gun which got off one shot before it was disabled by answering 4.1-inch fire from *Novara*. Under heavy fire from the cruiser, *Gowan Lea's* crew struggled to get their gun working again, although a box of ammunition exploded on deck, wounding the gun-layer, Fred Lamb, in the thigh and laming him for life. *Novara* steamed on down the line, convinced that *Gowan Lea* must be sinking after the damage she had sustained. But *Gowan Lea* was still under way and soon went alongside another drifter, *Floandi*, most of whose crew were dead or dying; the Signalman, A.B. Douglas Harris RNVR, stayed at his post to the end and was found dead in his chair. *Gowan Lea's* crew rendered what assistance they could to *Floandi* and eventually limped into Otranto.

There were forty-seven drifters in the line that night, in eight divisions of about six drifters each. Together, they put up what the Austrians themselves called 'this united mad resistance'. *Girl Rose*, *Coral Haven* and *Selby* were only abandoned by their crews when they actually foundered. The crew of the sinking *Taits*, counting heads in the boat, found one man missing, so all went back to look for him. The crews of *Garrigill*, *Bon Espoir*, *Christmas Daisy* and *British Crown* refused to abandon ship even when outranged and under heavy broadside fire, and brought their ships safely out of the action. Fourteen drifters were sunk and three badly damaged. Seventy-two men were taken prisoner (although Joseph Hendry, Second Hand of *Serene*, did not fancy being captured and stayed on board until she sank under him and was picked up an hour later by *British Crown*). The driftermen won a VC, five DSCs, a bar to a DSC, five CGMs, eighteen DSMs, and a bar to a DSM.

Skipper Watt was awarded the VC in the *Gazette* of 29th August 1917 and received his medal from the King at the Palace on 6th April 1918. He also received the Croix de Guerre, a Serbian Gold Medal, and an Italian silver Military Medal for Valour. He was promoted to Chief Skipper, back-dated to 15th May 1917, the day of the action. *Gowan Lea* was repaired and saw service again as a fishing vessel after the war.

Joseph Watt was a fisherman, of a fishing family, and after a working life spent combating the whims of God, the sea and the fish, the attentions of the Austrian Navy must have seemed of very

146

small importance. He was born on 25th June 1887 in the tiny fishing village of Gardenstown, in the parish of Gamrie, in Banffshire, the third child of a family of two boys and three girls. He went to school at Bracoden. His father was drowned at sea when Joseph was about nine years old, and his mother moved with her family to Fraserburgh, where Joseph went to sea in the fishing boats when he grew up. At the outbreak of war he was skipper of the motor drifter *Girl Alice*, which he took to Scapa Flow to act as a tender for the ships of the Grand Fleet.

After the war Joseph Watt returned to his trade as a fisherman, fishing for herring along the East Coast, from Fraserburgh and then from Lowestoft, in his own steam drifter *Benachie* (named after the highest hill in Aberdeenshire). He was a very modest man in spite of his fame, with a most equable temper and a very generous nature, and was known along the east coast of England and both coasts of Scotland as 'Gamrie Joe' or 'VC Joe'.

On 5th August 1915, he married Jessie-Anne Noble, the eldest daughter of a Fraserburgh fisherman, at Fraserburgh, and they lived at 7 Finlayson Street there for many years. They had one daughter, and a son who joined the Gordon Highlanders in 1939, was wounded in France in 1940 and invalided home. He joined his father, who was once again commanding a drifter serving ships of the Home Fleet and who was quoted in a newspaper in 1942 as saying, 'Ah'm not allowed to go to sea and fecht, they think ah'm tae auld.' In his later years Joseph Watt's main recreation was walking on the hills with his gun and dog. He died of cancer of the gullet in Fraserburgh on 13th February 1955 and was buried in the local cemetery at Kirkton, where his wife had been buried four years earlier.

Thomas Crisp:
North Sea, August 1917

In 1915, when German submarines began attacking the fishing fleet in the North Sea, the Lowestoft skipper F.W. Moxey offered his smack *G & E* (named after his two children Gladys and Edward) to the Admiralty, suggesting that she be armed with a gun for self-defence. That offer was refused, but it was not long before the Admiralty took up numbers of trawlers, changed their names, enrolled their crews in the RNR, and fitted them with small guns. On 11th August, off the Sussex coast, HM Special Service Smack *G & E*, commanded by Lieutenant-Commander Hamond, sank UB.4 and brought the U-boat's ensign and flagstaff back to Lowestoft.

On 1st February 1917, the day the Germans declared virtually unrestricted U-boat warfare, the same smack, now called *I'll Try* and commanded by Skipper Thomas Crisp RNR, was fishing in company with *Boy Alfred* (Skipper Wharton DSC, RNR) when a U-boat hailed them and ordered them to abandon ship. Wharton and Crisp took their time, during which another U-boat surfaced near them. When one of the U-boats was near enough, Wharton opened fire and his second shell hit its conning tower, which then disappeared, while the other U-boat submerged. For some two hours Crisp stalked the U-boat, and then pretended to give up and turn for home. The U-boat surfaced and followed, as he had hoped it would. *I'll Try* opened fire and scored a probable hit. Skipper Crisp was awarded the DSC, and Wharton a Bar.

On 14th August 1917 the same fishing smack, now called HM Special Service Smack *Nelson*, was fishing in company with the *Ethel and Millie* off the Jim Howe Bank in the North Sea. She was on the port tack, with the trawl shot, when Crisp came on deck at about 2.45 pm and sighted a submarine between three and four miles away, coming down through the mist from the north-west. Crisp just had time to shout 'Sub Oh! Clear for action!' when the U-boat's first shell fell about 100 yards off *Nelson's* port bow.

Nelson's gunlayer, Leading Seaman P. Ross, manned the gun, but the range was too great. Crisp held his fire, hoping the U-boat would come closer. The U-boat's fourth shell holed *Nelson* below the water-line, and the seventh hit Crisp himself, shattering both his legs at the hips and partially disembowelling him, before penetrating the deck and passing out through the ship's side. In spite of his frightful wound, Crisp still retained command of himself and his ship. He told Ross not to wait any longer and to open fire, and gave orders for the ship's carrier pigeon to be released, with the message, '*Nelson* being attacked by submarine, Jim Howe Bank. Send assistance at once.' *Nelson's* Second Hand, who was Crisp's son Tom, took the tiller and steered south-east, while the U-boat turned her attention to *Ethel and Millie*.

When *Nelson* had only five rounds of ammunition left, Crisp gave orders to abandon ship. *Nelson* was settling by the bows. Tom asked his father if they should take him in the boat. Skipper Crisp replied, 'No, Tom, I'm done. Throw me overboard.' This Tom naturally could not bring himself to do, and as his father was clearly beyond all help they left him on board. Tom and seven others got into the boat, and *Nelson* sank fifteen minutes later, her White Ensign still flying. *Ethel and Millie* had disappeared and her crew were last seen lined up on the U-boat's casing. *Nelson's* party did not wish to be picked up by a U-boat and rowed off into the mist and escaped. On the second day, they secured their boat to the Jim Howe Bank buoy, Tom jumped on to the buoy, where the destroyer *Dryad* saw him waving and picked them all up, after forty-one hours in the boat. Skipper Crisp's posthumous VC was gazetted on 2nd November

1917, with those of Bonner and Pitcher (*qv*) of the Q-ships. Ross got a Bar to his DSM (which he had won in *I'll Try's* action). Son Tom got a DSM which he received from the King at the same time as his father's VC, at the Palace on 19th December 1917.

Thomas Crisp was born in Alma Street, Lowestoft, on 28th April 1876, the son of William Crisp, shipwright and boat-maker, and Mary Ann (née Patterson). He went to the Baptist and St John's Schools in Lowestoft. In 1895 he married Harriet Elizabeth Alp, and they had two sons and a daughter. *Nelson's* taffrail was dredged up after the war and made into a seat in Lowestoft Library, but it was destroyed when the Library was bombed by the Luftwaffe in the Second World War. The seventh (tenor) bell in the ring of eight in St Margaret's, Lowestoft, was named the 'VC Bell' and dedicated to Skipper Crisp.

Nelson's pigeon came safe to land and survived the war. It had a place of honour at the East London Federation of Homing Pigeons Show in December 1921.

John Henry Carless:
Heligoland Bight, November 1917

The battle in the Heligoland Bight of November 1917 was the last 'big-ship' engagement of the First World War. It might have led to a major action, but in fact it was not much more than a skirmish, between British light battlecruisers and cruisers, under Admiral Napier, covered by battleships, and German cruisers under Admiral von Reuter, covered by the battleships *Kaiser* and *Kaiserin*. By November 1917 the most important task of the German Navy was to keep submarine bases free of mines. German minesweepers, with heavy ship support, were operating over 100 miles from their bases. Knowing this, Beatty despatched Napier's force into the Bight in the hope of action.

The German minesweepers were first sighted at 7.30 am on 17th November. Von Reuter immediately turned away under smoke. Due to misunderstandings about the positions of German minefields, von Reuter was not followed as closely as he might have been. In the action that followed, the light cruisers *Calypso* and *Caledon* were straddled and hit by salvoes from *Kaiser* and *Kaiserin*, while the battlecruiser *Repulse* hit von Reuter's flagship *Königsberg*. The Germans also lost the torpedo boat *Kedingen*.

It was a disappointing action for the British (and it contributed to Jellicoe's resignation) but it was redeemed by an act of outstanding gallantry in *Caledon*. One of her guns was hit and almost the whole crew became casualties. The rammer, Ordinary Seaman Carless, was mortally wounded in the stomach. In spite of his wound, Carless carried on serving his gun and helping to clear away the casualties. He collapsed once, but got up again. He cheered on the new guns' crew who arrived to take the place of the casualties, but then fell again and died. In the words of his VC citation, 'He not only set a very inspiring and memorable example but he also, while mortally wounded, continued to do effective work against the King's enemies.'

The citation appeared in the *London Gazette* of 17th May 1918, and the Cross was presented to Carless's parents by King George V at Buckingham Palace on 22nd June 1918.

John Henry Carless was born on 11th November 1896, at Renwick Terrace, Frederick Street, Walsall, Staffordshire, the son of John Thomas Carless, a journeyman brass caster, and Elizabeth (née Smith). He went to St Mary's the Mount Roman Catholic School, Walsall, and joined the Navy on 1st September 1915 (Official No. J43703). He did not marry.

In 1920 a bronze bust of Carless, executed by R.J. Emerson of Wolverhampton and mounted upon a base of Portland stone, was unveiled outside Walsall Free Library. Every year on Armistice Day, which was also Carless's birthday, a service of remembrance was held at the memorial.

Geoffrey Saxton White:
Dardanelles, January 1918

The escape of the German battlecruiser *Goeben* and the light cruiser *Breslau* through the Dardanelles and up to Constantinople in August 1914 was an embarrassing tactical failure for the Royal Navy and a major strategic success for the Central Powers, helping to bring Turkey into the war on their side. Both ships made occasional forays into the Black Sea, but lack of coal virtually immobilised them from 1916 onwards. At 4 am on 19th January 1918, they left Constantinople to play what was to be their final part in the war.

There was little opposition for them in the Dardanelles. On the 20th they shelled and sank the monitors *Lord Raglan* and *M.28* in Kusu Bay. There seemed nothing to prevent them going on to attack Mudros, when *Breslau* hit a mine. *Goeben* stopped to assist her and also struck a mine. *Breslau* hit several more mines and sank in about ten minutes. *Goeben* re-entered the Dardanelles and ran aground off Nagara Point. No Allied ships could reach her where she lay, but aircraft flew some 270 sorties over her and reported sixteen direct bomb-hits.

A passenger in one of the aircraft was Lieutenant-Commander

G.S. White, commanding Boyle's old submarine E.14, to see *Goeben's* position for himself and plan his method of attack. E.14 had been recalled from patrol in the Otranto Straits, to attempt to torpedo *Goeben* and sink her where she was.

No Allied submarine had penetrated the Dardanelles for over two years, in which time the defences had been greatly strengthened. The guns, searchlights, nets and minefields were still there, and the straits were constantly patrolled by motor launches fitted with depth-charges and hydrophone listening gear.

Air reconnaissance showed that *Goeben* was still there on 27th January, and E.14 left Mudros the same day. However, *Goeben* was refloated that evening and when E.14 had struggled up through the nets at Chanak and evaded all the patrols, White found that his bird had flown. On his way down, at about 8.45 am on the 28th, he attacked a Turkish ship, but only eleven seconds after the torpedo left the tube there was a tremendous explosion just forward of E.14, either the torpedo detonating prematurely or a depth-charge attack. The defences now knew that an Allied submarine was once more in the straits and from that moment things began to go wrong for E.14. The force of the explosion sprung open the forward torpedo hatch, admitting hundreds of gallons of water, the lights went out and the submarine lost trim, swimming up towards the surface. She was in plain sight and easy range of the shore batteries, which at once opened fire. Fortunately the hull was not hit, and E.14 was able to dive again. But soon the boat became out of control, and as the air was extremely bad in the submarine after a long period submerged, White decided to try running on the surface. E.14 was hit again and again, and after about half an hour she was so badly damaged that White decided to ground her, to give his crew a chance of survival. He himself was killed by a shell which blew his body out of the conning tower. E.14 sank and, in the event, only seven survivors were picked up by the Turks.

White's posthumous VC was gazetted on 24th May 1919 and the Cross was presented to his widow by the King at the Palace on 12th June. E.14 was the only ship in the Navy's history in which two different Captains won the VC.

Geoffrey Saxton White was born at Bromley in Kent on 2nd July 1886, went to Bradfield School and then to *Britannia*, passing out in 1901. He became a Midshipman in November 1902 and served in the cruiser *Amphitrite* in China in 1904 and in *Glory* in the Channel Fleet in 1905.He was promoted Sub-Lieutenant on 15th February 1906 and appointed to the battleship *Venerable* in the Channel Fleet in 1907. He became a Lieutenant on 1st October 1908 and joined the old cruiser *Mercury*, at that time depot ship at Portsmouth for submarine training, on 11th January 1909. His first command, for a few months in 1911, was the aged A.4, and then on 30th November he was appointed in command of C.27 until April 1914, when he joined the battleship *Monarch* on commissioning. In 1915 he went back to submarines and commanded D.6 in the Harwich Flotilla. He was promoted Lieutenant-Commander on 1st October 1916 and went to the Mediterranean to take command of E.14.

In 1911 he married Sybil (née Thomas) and they had two sons and a daughter (the girl was born after White left for the Mediterranean and he never saw her).

Arthur Francis Blakeney Carpenter, Norman Augustus Finch, Arthur Leyland Harrison, Edward Bamford and Albert Edward McKenzie:

Zeebrugge, April 1918

'St George', said Mrs Keyes, 'can be trusted to bring good fortune to England.' She was right. At one minute past midnight on 23rd April, St George's Day, 1918, the cruiser *Vindictive's* port side ground against the Mole at Zeebrugge. The great attempt to seal off the U-boat base at Bruges from the sea was under way. That night the Royal Navy and the Royal Marines between them won eight Victoria Crosses, more than in any other single operation in their history. *Vindictive's* people won five VCs inside one hour, putting her in the same league as Peel's *Shannon* and the *River Clyde* at Gallipoli.

At Bruges, in Flanders, there was a base for over thirty destroyers and torpedo boats, and about thirty U-boats. They could reach the North Sea either through the canal exit at Zeebrugge or, if they were of shallower draught, at Ostend. Plans to seal off Zeebrugge and Ostend had been discussed since 1914. The Flanders ports had been major objectives of Haig's great offensive in 1917. After that failure, Vice-Admirable Roger Keyes, who had taken over command of the Dover Patrol on 1st January 1918, was authorised to try a direct attack from the sea.

The Zeebrugge canal exit was protected by the curve of a 1½-mile-long Mole, on which the Germans had mounted batteries of heavy guns, with more guns along the near-by coast and in the town. Zeebrugge was nearly seventy miles from England, and a very difficult passage, through probable minefields, narrow channels and sandbanks, from which the Germans had removed all navigational aids. The plan was to sink blockships in the entrance, under cover of a smoke-screen and a diversionary infantry attack on the Mole batteries. A section of the Mole near the shore would be blown up, to prevent the Germans bringing up reinforcements. Clearly, the plan called for superb navigation, well-trained forces, exact timing, favourable weather and very great courage.

The assault force consisted of the 4th Battalion, Royal Marines, and some 200 bluejackets who had been given intensive training in close combat with rifle, bayonet and bombs. Fifty more bluejackets, volunteers from the Grand Fleet, received special training in demolition. The assault ship was the old (1899) *Arrogant* class cruiser *Vindictive* (Commander Alfred Carpenter RN), which was specially prepared for the job, with special ramps built on her port side to allow a large number of men to disembark together, and special fenders and derricks to keep her alongside. Her bridge was given extra protection, with a fighting top with Lewis and pompom guns above the conning position. She also had an 11-inch howitzer on her quarterdeck and two extra 7.5-inch guns to deal with the guns on the Mole, and flame throwers to discourage enemy personnel. She was supported by two ex-Mersey ferry-boats, *Iris II* and *Daffodil*, each carrying troops.

The night chosen was 22nd/23rd April, when there was high tide at Zeebrugge near midnight, and no moon. In spite of the darkness and smoke, *Vindictive* was sighted a few hundred yards off the Mole and the Germans opened a tremendous fire on her at ever-closing ranges. Her funnels, ventilators, bridge and wheel-house were riddled with dozens of shell and splinter holes. Her superstructure was hit repeatedly by shells of various calibres. Captain Halahan, in command of the naval assault force, and Colonel Elliot, commanding the Marines, were both killed outright, and many other officers were killed or wounded. A shell in the forecastle killed or wounded most of the cable party.

That *Vindictive* got alongside at all was largely due to the coolness of Carpenter himself. By an amazing piece of navigation, he brought his ship in only sixty seconds late, and he kept calm although men were falling on either side of him and his bridge was under fire from rifles, machine guns and heavy batteries from the town. Although the flame-throwers were out of action, and the scend of the sea much greater than expected, making it extremely difficult for the assaulting parties to get ashore, Carpenter walked round the upper deck, directing operations and encouraging the men in the most dangerous and exposed positions.

As *Vindictive* neared the Mole the marines in the fighting top under Lieutenant Rigby kept up a continuous fire with their pompoms and Lewis guns. Although *Vindictive* herself was being hit by shrapnel and splinters every few seconds and it was difficult in the darkness to locate the enemy guns which were causing the most trouble, Rigby and his guns' crews changed rapidly from target to target, spraying the Mole with bullets, and keeping down the enemy's heads and fire to a considerable extent. When *Vindictive* got alongside, the fighting top was hit by two heavy shells, possibly from guns in the town. Rigby was killed, and everybody else killed or disabled except Sergeant Finch, the second-in-command, who remounted a Lewis gun, got it into action again and kept up rapid fire on the Mole once more. He was badly wounded himself but he kept his gun firing, undoubtedly saving many lives amongst the storming parties on the Mole, until another direct hit destroyed the fighting top, and he had to evacuate his position.

Vindictive had actually come alongside some 300 yards further from the seaward batteries than planned. Carpenter did what he could by going astern to close this distance, but the water disturbance caused by *Vindictive*'s arrival, the rise and fall of the swell against the Mole, and the fact that the starboard anchor was jammed and could not be dropped, all made it difficult for Carpenter to get his ship close in. Fortunately, *Daffodil* came up on his starboard side and nudged *Vindictive* in (although *Daffodil* had just received a direct shell hit which half-blinded her Captain).

Now it was all up to the storming parties, led by Lieutenant-Commander A.L. Harrison, who took over after Halahan's death. Harrison had been hit during *Vindictive*'s approach by a shell splinter which broke his jaw and knocked him out, but he recovered in time to take charge of A and B Companies of bluejackets on the Mole. Although he was badly wounded and in great pain, he placed himself at the head of his men and led them towards the seaward batteries. Harrison was killed, and every man with him was killed or wounded, including Able Seaman Albert McKenzie of B Company, who was in charge of a Lewis gun. Although he was badly wounded, McKenzie advanced down the Mole with Lieutenant-Commander Harrison and used his machine gun to great effect, killing several Germans running for shelter to a ship alongside the Mole.

When Captain Edward Bamford RMLI landed on the Mole at the head of No.5 Platoon there was, as one of the marines said, 'all hell let loose'. It was pitch-black, with rolling thick smoke clouds, and the men could only see one another by the flashes of the guns. As one said, 'We would just as soon have bolted home again'; but then they heard Bamford's voice calling. 'Come on chaps, follow me.' Led by Bamford, the marines doubled to the right down the upper promenade of the Mole and attacked some snipers who had been giving the men on *Vindictive*'s upper deck some trouble. They arrived abreast of *Iris II* and hailed her. She replied with cheers, but they could see she was being shelled and was not likely to be able to get her men ashore. Having retired from the right Bamford climbed down some scaling ladders abreast of *Vindictive* and, crossing the Mole, collected men from Nos. 7 and 8 Platoons. With these and a few survivors left from his original No.5 Platoon, Bamford led an attack on the batteries at the end of the Mole. They heard the recall signall from *Iris II* and *Daffodil*'s sirens (*Vindictive*'s having been carried away by shell-fire) and retreated across the Mole. They were still under heavy fire but they kept their discipline, only crossing the Mole in small parties so as not to clog the ladders.

154

Carpenter had given the recall signal at 12.50 am. Helped by *Daffodil* again, *Vindictive* swung away from the Mole. By the light of exploding shells, Carpenter had seen the shapes of the blockships gliding by on the other side of the Mole. Two of them had successfully penetrated to the canal entrance, and Zeebrugge was blocked.

Carpenter was selected by the officers of *Vindictive*, *Iris II*, *Daffodil* and the naval assaulting force to receive the Victoria Cross under Rule 13 of the Royal Warrant of 29th January 1856. Able Seaman McKenzie was similarly selected by the men, and both were gazetted on 23rd July 1918. Captain Bamford and Sergeant Finch were elected by the officers of the RMA and RMLI, and the marines of 4th Battalion respectively, and received the Victoria Cross under Rule 13. They too were gazetted on 23rd July 1918. Harrison's posthumous VC, was not gazetted until 17th March 1919.

Captain Carpenter (his rank back-dated to 23rd April 1918) received his Cross from the King at Buckingham Palace on 31st July 1918. Besides his VC and his promotion he also received the Croix de Guerre and was made a Knight of the Légion d'honneur. Carpenter was an old ship-mate of Admiral Keyes, having served with him as Navigating Officer in the cruiser *Venus* and he was a navigating specialist who (to his very great joy) had been taken away from his desk with the Director of Planning in the Admiralty to command *Vindictive*.

Alfred Francis Blakeney Carpenter came of a naval family. He was born on 17th September 1881, the son of Lieutenant (later Captain) Alfred Carpenter RN and Henrietta Maude (née Shadwell) at Byfield Cottage, Barnes, in London. His father won the DSO for service in Burma in 1887 and also won a medal for lifesaving. His grandfather, Commander Charles Carpenter, joined the Navy in 1810 and took part in the capture of the American privateer *Rattlesnake* in 1814.

Alfred Carpenter was educated privately and then went to HMS *Britannia* in 1896. His active service started very early. As Midshipman and then as Sub-Lieutenant he served in the operations in Crete in 1898 (when Maillard, *qv*, won a VC) and also in the Boxer Rising in China, for which he received the China Medal. He was promoted Lieutenant on 1st October 1903 and took a specialist course in navigation. In 1913 he won the Royal Humane Society's medal for lifesaving, thus again following a family tradition. He passed out from the War Staff Course in that year and served under Jellicoe from July 1914 until November 1915, when he joined *Emperor of India* for two years as Navigating Commander.

After his exploits Captain Carpenter went on a lecture tour in USA and Canada in 1918 and 1919, and on his return was in charge of the Junior Officers' War Course at Cambridge. In 1921 he published his own authentic account of Zeebrugge, *The Blocking of Zeebrugge*.

155

Between the wars, Captain Carpenter commanded the light cruiser *Carysfort* in the Atlantic Fleet from 1921 to 1923, directed the Senior Officers' Technical Course at Portsmouth and was Captain of the Dockyard and King's Harbourmaster at Portsmouth from 1924 to 1927. He commanded *Benbow* in 1926 and *Marlborough* in 1928, before being promoted Rear-Admiral on 3rd August 1929 and retiring. He was promoted Vice-Admiral on the retired list on 31st July 1934.

In retirement, Admiral Carpenter lived in Gloucestershire, where he became a JP in 1936. As a director of the South American Saint Line he took a great interest in Merchant Navy affairs and especially in the selection and training of cadets; the seagoing training vessel *St Briavel*, in which young men gained practical ship-handling experience, was largely his conception. From 1940 to 1944 the Admiral commanded his local Home Guard, the 17th Gloucestershire (Wye Valley) Battalion, and in 1945 became Director of Shipping at the Admiralty.

In 1903, Alfred Carpenter married Maud, daughter of the Reverend Stafford Tordiffe, and they had a daughter, Iris. His wife died in 1923, and in 1927 he married Hilda Margaret, daughter of W. Chearnley Smith. After an operation in November 1955, the Admiral died at his home Chanterslure, St Briavels, Lydney, Gloucestershire, on 27th December 1955 (Lydney appropriately meaning 'Sailor's Island').

Sergeant Finch was in hospital recovering from his wounds for some time after returning from Zeebrugge, but he was fit enough to go to the Palace to receive his Cross from the King with Captain Carpenter on 31st July 1918.

Norman Augustus Finch was born at 42 Nineveh Road, Handsworth, Birmingham, on 26th December 1890, the son of Richard William John Finch and Emma Amelia, and went to Benson Road Board School and Grove Lane Council School. He joined the Royal Marine Artillery at Portsmouth on 15th January 1908 and the dates of his various promotions reveal much about the career structure of the Corps in his day: Acting Bombardier, 22nd November 1912; Bombardier, 1st May 1913; Corporal, 2nd January 1915; temporary Lance Sergeant, 3rd February 1916; Corporal, 20th April 1916, Sergeant, 15th March 1917. He was promoted Colour Sergeant on 12th August 1920 and re-engaged for further service on 8th January 1921. He was promoted to Barrack Quartermaster Sergeant on 23rd December 1925 and finally retired from the Corps on 26th December 1929. In retirement he went to live in Southsea, where he became a postman and was later a messenger for a bank in Portsmouth North End. On 1st January 1931 he was made a Yeoman of the Guard. When the Second World War broke out, Sergeant Finch rejoined and was promoted Quartermaster Sergeant on 24th October 1939. His final promotion in the Corps was to Temporary Lieutenant (QM) on 24th February 1943. His last promotion of all was to Sergeant-Major in the Queen's Bodyguard of Yeomen of the Guard on 1st February 1961.

On 3rd April 1919, he married Elizabeth Jane Ross in Portsmouth and they had one son, who became a warrant officer in the RAF. Lieutenant Finch died on 15th March 1966 in St Mary's Hospital, Milton, Portsmouth, and was cremated at Porchester on the 21st. He left his medals to the Royal Marine Museum, Eastney, where they now comprise an impressive row: VC, 1914-15 Star, War Medal, Victory Medal, Defence Medal 1939-45, War Medal 1939-45, Jubilee Medal 1935, Coronation Medal 1937, Coronation Medal 1953, Long Service and Good Conduct Medal, Meritorious Service Medal.

In *The Blocking of Zeebrugge* Captain Carpenter wrote that 'Harrison's charge down that narrow gangway of death was a worthy finale to the large number of charges which as a forward of the first rank he had led down many a Rugby football ground.' The comparison was apt, for as his jutting jaw and pugnacious features imply, Harrison was a brilliant forward, playing for the Navy, United Services and for England (gaining two caps), against France and Ireland, in 1913-14). He played for the Navy against the Army in a celebrated match at the Queen's Club in March 1914, said to have been one of the finest ever played, when the players were afterwards presented to the King. 'With Harrison's death', says Carpenter, 'the Navy lost an officer who was as popular and keen as he had been invaluable to the success of this particular operation, especially in the preparatory work.'

Arthur Leyland Harrison was born at Torquay on 3rd February 1886, the son of Lieutenant-Colonel Arthur J. Harrison of the 7th Royal Fusiliers, and Mrs Harrison of Wimbledon, London SW. He went to Dover College and then joined the Navy as a Cadet in September 1902. He was promoted Lieutenant on 1st October 1908, his first command being Torpedo Boat No.16 that same year. He served in Beatty's flagship *Lion* at the battles of the Heligoland Bight and the Dogger Bank and was mentioned in despatches for his services at Jutland. He volunteered for special 'hazardous services' at the end of 1917 and so joined Carpenter in *Vindictive*. His address when he was killed was Waddon Cottage, Durham Road, Wimbledon. Mrs Harrison received her husband's Cross from the King at the Palace on 17th May 1919.

Years later, in 1934, Harrison was somewhat unexpectedly honoured by a Belgian ex-soldiers' organisation, the Union des Fraternelles de l'Armée de Campagne, who named a room after him in a new club in Ghent. Every room was named after some Allied hero who lost his life in the war; Harrison was chosen as the English hero.

Able Seaman McKenzie was one of the very few men to survive Harrison's last desperate charge along the Mole. The heavy swell had smashed all but two of the gangways, one forward and one aft. 'I tucked my Lewis gun under my arm,' McKenzie said,

...and nipped over the gangway aft. Two of my guns' crew were killed inboard, so that left me with only two - turned to my left, advanced about fifty yards and then lay down. There was a spiral staircase which led down into the Mole and Commander Brock fired his revolver down and dropped Mills bombs. You should have seen them nip out and try to get across to the destroyer tied up against the Mole, but I met them halfway with the box of tricks and ticked off about twelve before I checked. My Lewis gun was shot spinning out of my hands - leaving me with stock and pistol grip which I kindly took a bloke's photo with - he looked too business-like for me with a rifle and a bayonet. It half-stunned him and gave me time to get out my pistol and finish him off. Then I found a rifle and bayonet and joined up our crowd who had just come off the destroyer. All I remember was pushing, kicking and kneeing every German who got in the way. When I was finished I couldn't climb the ladder so a mate lifted me up and carried me up the ladder and then I crawled on my hands and knees inboard (*Vindictive*).

Like Harrison, Able Seaman McKenzie was a superb athlete and won medals for boxing in the training ship *Arethusa*; later, when he joined the fleet, he became the 4th Battle Cruiser Squadron lightweight champion. He was a Londoner, in spite of his name, born at 10 Alice Street, Bermondsey, London SE, the son of Alexander McKenzie, a photographer, and Eliza (née Marks), on 23rd October 1898. He went to Webb St School, Bermondsey, and then to Mina Street L C C School there. He joined the Navy as a Boy Second Class on 20th June 1914, and was rated Boy First Class on 18th December 1914. He was rated Able Seaman on 23 April 1916 and served in minesweepers, patrol work and convoy escort duties at various times. In the battleship *Neptune* he won another boxing medal and volunteered for the service which led to Zeebrugge.

McKenzie was still on crutches when he received his Cross from the King with the other Zeebrugge VCs on 31st July 1918 and when he returned home to Shorncliffe Road, Southwark (where his mother had moved when her husband died while McKenzie was still an infant) for a civic reception. He seemed to be recovering well from his wounds when he caught influenza during the great epidemic of 1918 and died on 3rd November. He was buried in Camberwell Cemetery on the 9th of that month. Captain Carpenter and Mr T. J. Macnamara, Financial Secretary to the Admiralty, attended his funeral. 'Mrs McKenzie has lost a son,' said Mr McNamara in his oration, 'but the nation has found a hero.'

As a note of local historical interest, McKenzie was one of 'St

Mark's Little Army', the 4,286 from that London parish who joined the Colours in 1914-18, of whom 518 died or were killed on active service and 81 won war decorations.

Edward Bamford took over No.5 Platoon at the end of February from another officer who had not been a success as platoon commander. Bamford's first words to the men were, 'Well, fellows, if you will be right with me I'll be right with you.' And, as one of his platoon said 'We got on very well indeed. Very strict, but what was very uncommon then in the forces - the Human Touch.' Bamford was a tall man, over six foot in height and with ginger hair. He was another good athlete: he played golf, hockey and tennis and he was an enthusiastic fisherman and yachtsman. He was a shy man, who could never be brought to talk about his experiences, but the marines liked him: 'He knew how to get the best out of his men without bullying.'

Bamford had already won the DSO for his bravery at Jutland, when he was OCRM in *Chester*. In the same action in which Boy Cornwell (*qv*) won his VC, a shell hit the after control tower where Bamford was in charge, and the tower was wrecked and set on fire. Bamford was wounded in one leg and his face was burned, but he helped to serve one gun, controlled another and assisted in putting out the fire, behaving, as his citation said, 'with great coolness and courage when exposed to a very heavy fire'.

Edward Bamford was born at Highgate, London N., on 28th May 1887, the son of the Reverend Robert and Blanche Edith Bamford. He went to Sherborne School and then to Malvern House at Kearnsey, near Dover. He joined the RMLI as a Subaltern in July 1905 and was promoted Lieutenant in 1906. He served in *Bulwark*, *Magnificent* and in *Britannia* and was on board her when she ran aground near Inch Keith after going out to support the Battle Cruiser Squadron in the fight off the Dogger Bank. He was attached to the Guards Brigade during the battles on the Ypres salient of April 1916 and joined *Chester* on commissioning in May, being promoted temporary Captain RMLI. He was in *Chatham* when he volunteered for the Zeebrugge raid, and was given the Brevet of Major, dated 23rd April 1918, for his services there. Besides his VC, he was awarded the Légion d'honneur, the Russian Order of St Anne (3rd Class) and the Japanese Order of the Rising Sun (4th Class). He joined *Royal Sovereign* in August 1918 and was present in her for the surrender of the German High Seas Fleet in the Firth of Forth. He received his Cross with Carpenter, Finch, and McKenzie from the King at th. Palace on 31st July 1918 and he seems to have been the only one of the quartet unwounded.

After the war, Bamford served in *Highflyer* in the East Indies, did the naval war staff course at the Naval College, Greenwich, and served for a year with the 11th RM Battalion in the Mediterranean. In 1926 he was appointed Small Arms Instructor at *Tamar*, the naval base in Hong Kong, and was promoted full Major on 1st March 1928. Whilst at Wei Hai Wei in September he mysteriously fell ill and was taken on board the cruiser *Cumberland* for passage to Hong Kong. On 29th, his condition worsened. The ship connected all boilers and made all possible speed through a heavy swell to the nearest port, which was Shanghai, but Major Bamford died on the 30th when the ship was still at Woosung, about ten miles from Shanghai. He was buried in Bubbling Well Road Cemetery, Shanghai. He never married, and his sister presented his medals to the Royal Marines.

Captain Alfred F.B. Carpenter VC, RN, *The Blocking of Zeebrugge* (London: Herbert Jenkins, 1921).

Percival Hislam, *How we Twisted the Dragon's Tail* (London: Hutchinson, 1918).

Barrie Pitt, *Zeebrugge, St George's Day, 1918* (London: Cassell, 1958).

Admiral Sir Roger Keyes, *Naval Memoirs* (London: Thornton Butterworth).

C. Sanford Terry (ed), *Ostend and Zeebrugge, 23 April to 10 May 1918, The Despatches of Vice-Admiral Sir Roger Keyes KCB, KCVO, and Other Narratives of the Operation* (London: Oxford University Press, 1919).

George Nicholson Bradford:
Zeebrugge, April 1918

'He had been a splendid fighter in the ''ring'', ' Captain Carpenter wrote of Bradford after Zeebrugge, 'and it was against his nature to give in as long as there was the remotest chance of winning through; his death brought us a great loss of a great gentleman'. The action which won Bradford his VC was, as his citation said, 'one of absolute self-sacrifice; without a moment's hesitation he went to certain death, recognising that in such action lay the only possible chance of securing *Iris II* and enabling her storming parties to land'.

Bradford was in command of the naval storming party in *Iris II*, the ex-Mersey ferry-boat used for special service at Zeebrugge. In planning the raid, it had been realised that the main assault ship, the converted cruiser *Vindictive*, drew enough water to strike a minefield or even to run aground on her way to the Mole. Other ships were needed to support her and take enough men in them to storm the Mole if anything should happen to *Vindictive* en route. An unobtrusive survey of UK ports revealed the ferry-boats *Daffodil* and *Iris II*, plying to and fro across the Mersey between the Wirral and Liverpool. Both were handy vessels, fitted for running alongside jetties, capable of transporting large numbers of people, and drawing only eleven feet. For the raid, they had protective armour

Above: Gordon Campbell (Imperial War Museum)

Below left: William Sanders (Imperial War Museum) Below right: William Williams (Central Press)

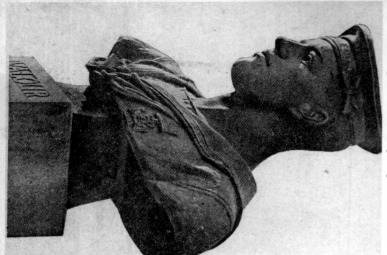

Above: Ernest Pitcher at a Naval Exhibition in London in 1918, with King George V, Queen Mary and the Dowager Queen Alexandra (Imperial War Museum)

Below left: The memorial erected to John Carless outside the public library in his native Walsall (Author's Collection).

Below right: Thomas Crisp (Imperial War Museum)

fitted on the upper deck, partitions stripped out below, and certain engineering alterations (to make the change from cross-river to cross-Channel trips). Special anchors were fitted to catch the parapet of the Mole and claw the ships alongside. Both ships could take 1,500 men.

While *Daffodil* played her part in nudging *Vindictive* in, *Iris II* came alongside the Mole 100 yards ahead of *Vindictive* at about 12.15 am. The swell made *Iris II* toss and pitch so much that it was clearly going to be very difficult to use the parapet anchors. One of the storming party's officers, Lieutenant Claude Hawkings, got up on to the Mole by a scaling ladder. He could be seen sitting astride the wall, fixing an anchor, but then he was apparently attacked by somebody on the Mole. He was defending himself with his revolver when he was killed.

It did not look as if anybody would get ashore. Although it was not part of his duties to secure the ship alongside, Lieutenant-Commander Bradford climbed a large derrick which was projecting out over the Mole. The ship, the derrick and he were all under heavy fire, and the derrick was crashing and grinding against the Mole because of the violent tossing of the ship. Picking his moment, Bradford jumped, taking the anchor with him. He had placed the anchor in position when he was killed. Riddled by machine-gun bullets, his body fell into the water between *Iris II* and the Mole. Strenuous efforts were made to recover the body, but without success. It was his thirty-first birthday.

Iris II was still under heavy and constant fire, and Carpenter, seeing this from *Vindictive*, had signalled her to leave, when the anchor slipped, or the cable broke or was shot away, and *Iris II* came off the Mole. So, ironically, Bradford had given his life in vain. Nobody was able to follow him. Commander Valentine Gibbs, commanding *Iris II*, decided to put his ships alongside *Vindictive* so that his men could disembark across her. A few men had scrambled across when the recall signal was given and *Iris II* was ordered to leave. Backing off from *Vindictive*, *Iris II* was hit twice by heavy shells. Gibbs was killed, and there was a terrible carnage among the sailors still waiting below. *Iris II* retired under cover of smoke from her damage and from a screen thoughtfully put up from a motor launch. Although they thought in *Vindictive* that *Iris II* must have been sunk, she reached Dover that afternoon to tumultuous cheers from the survivors in all the other ships there.

Bradford's posthumous Victoria Cross was gazetted on 17th March, 1919, and his mother, Mrs Amy Bradford, received the medal from the King at Buckingham Palace on 3rd April 1919. It was the second time she had done this - surely a unique record for one family. Another son, Lieutenant Roland Boys Bradford MC, had won a posthumous VC with the 9th Battalion Durham Light Infantry at Eaucourt l'Abbaye in France on 1st October 1916. A third son,

161

James Barker Bradford won an MC, also with the DLI and died of his wounds after the Battle of Arras in May 1917. The eldest son, Thomas Andrews, who won a DSO, survived the war. Mrs Bradford never failed to put In Memoriam notices in *The Times* on the anniversaries of her three sons' deaths until her own death, at the age of ninety-one, at Folkestone in 1951.

As Carpenter's reference to 'the ring' shows, Bradford was a boxer and an athlete, Navy officers' welterweight champion, and twice in the finals of the Army and Navy Officers' championships. The naval writer 'Bartimeus', two terms above Bradford in *Britannia*, described a boxing bout between Lieutenant Adams (Bradford) and Seaman Hands (Hayes) in the chapter 'Arma Virumque' of his book *The Long Trick*, which actually took place when Bradford was serving in the flagship *Orion*.

George Nicholson Bradford was born on 23rd April 1887 at Wilton Park, Durham, second son of Mr and Mrs George Bradford, of Milbanke, Darlington. He went to Darlington Grammar School, the Royal Naval School, Eltham, and Eastmans, before joining *Britannia* in 1902. As Cadet and Midshipman he served in the battleships *Revenge* and *Exmouth* in the Channel Fleet, as Sub-Lieutenant in the destroyer *Chelmer*, where he distinguished himself in rescuing the crew of a trawler after a collision, and was promoted Lieutenant in her in December 1909. He also served in the battleship *Vanguard* in 1910 and the destroyer *Amazon* in 1912, before joining *Orion*.

His body was recovered a few days after the raid at Blankenburghe in Belgium and buried by the Germans.

Richard Douglas Sandford:
Zeebrugge, April 1918

'We only got there at all because every bally thing went wrong,' said Lieutenant Sandford of his own part in the Zeebrugge raid, which was to blow up the road and rail viaduct connecting the Mole to the shore.

Destruction of the viaduct, a 300-yard-long structure of steel girders under which the North Sea tides raced to scour out the canal entrance, would prevent the Germans bringing up reinforcements from the town, and would add to the main diversion. It would also reduce Zeebrugge's effectiveness as a base by preventing the Germans using the railway out to the Mole for military purposes.

Keyes first thought of floating rafts against the viaduct but then decided to use two old obsolete submarines, C.1 and C.3, packed with five tons of Amatol explosive with delay fuses and manned by volunteer bachelor crews of two officers and four men, and fitted with special gyroscopic steering gear so that the crews could set the submarines on final course and then abandon them, taking to the motor skiff provided, before they hit the target. But special scaling ladders were provided, in case the crews had to get up on the Mole and join *Vindictive*.

The two submarines were towed to the area, but on passage the towing hawser of C.1 (Lieutenant Aubrey C. Newbold) broke and C.1 was unable to take part. C.3 (Lieutenant Richard D. Sandford) slipped on time and in position. When she emerged from the smoke-screen at midnight she was sighted by the enemy and illuminated by star-shell and searchlights, but strangely the enemy did not fire. The glare behind showed up the girders of the viaduct clearly in silhouette. Sandford disdained to use the gyro steering gear and conned the submarine right into its target. He made his last alteration of course only 100 yards short. He ordered the crew to come up on deck, so that nobody could be trapped below.

At about 12.15 am C.3 ran in under the viaduct at nine and a half knots and hit it with such an impact that her bows projected out from the other side and her conning tower was wedged in the steel web of the girders. Sandford ordered the crew to lower the motor skiff and get into it, whilst he fired the fuses, which had a twelve-minute delay.

Now at last the enemy woke up and began to fire from the top of the viaduct. Sandford, his coxswain and the stoker were all hit. The skiff's engine would not start, so they got out two paddles and began to row, literally, for dear life. Sandford was hit again, as were the two paddlers. Two others carried on. They were only 300 yards away from C.3 when the Amatol blew up with a roar that everybody on the raid heard and afterwards remembered. A hundred feet of the viaduct were blown out and no reinforcements were brought up that night. Meanwhile, Sandford and his crew were picked up by a picket boat (incidentally commanded by his elder brother, Lieutenant Francis Sandford) and taken out to the destroyer *Phoebe*.

Sandford was gazetted for the VC on 23rd July 1918 and, after three months in hospital with hand and thigh wounds, was fit enough to receive his Cross from the King with the other Zeebrugge VCs on 31st July. His second-in-command, Lieutenant John Howell-Price, got the DSO, and Petty Officer Coxswain Walter Harner, Leading Seaman William Cleave, Engine-Room Artificer Allan Roseburgh and Stoker Henry Bindall all got the CGM.

Ironically, having survived Zeebrugge, Sandford died of typhoid fever in Cleveland Hospital, Grangetown, Yorkshire, on 23rd November 1918 and was buried in Exton Cemetery near by. It was a great blow to the Service and his friends, for Sandford - known for some reason as 'Baldy' - was 'the perfect companion: interested, simple-hearted, faithful and wonderfully understanding'. When his VC was gazetted, it 'snowed telegrams' on his family. He was

163

Percy Thompson Dean:
Zeebrugge, April 1918

born at 15 The Beacon, Exmouth, on 11th May 1891, the seventh son of the Venerable Ernest Grey Sandford, Archdeacon of Exeter, and Gabriel (née Poole). He went to Clifton College and then to HMS *Britannia* in 1904. He was promoted Lieutenant on 30th August 1913, joined the Submarine Service in February 1914, and served in submarines until his death.

Dean was the archetypal volunteer naval officer. Before the war, he worked in his family business in the town where he was born and where he and his family were prominent citizens. He was a town councillor, and chairman of the local Conservative party. He enjoyed sailing and was a member of several yacht clubs. When war came it was only natural that Dean should join the RNVR, where he endured the dangers of the sea and the violence of the enemy. And when the war was over he went back to his business and political life in his home town, to enjoy the blessings of the land and the fruits of his labours. He had, however, in the meantime done something that no other RNVR officer had done - won a Victoria Cross when he was over forty years of age.

While Carpenter, Harrison, Finch, McKenzie and Sandford and all the men of *Vindictive, Iris II, Daffodil* and *C.3* were causing a diversion on the seaward side of Zeebrugge Mole, the real objective of the expedition was being carried out on the other side. At about 12.20 am that night the three blockships, the light cruisers *Thetis, Intrepid* and *Iphigenia*, rounded the lighthouse at the end of the Mole and headed for the canal entrance. They were sighted, and the Mole guns opened fire at 100 yards' range. *Thetis*, leading, caught the brunt of the fire, missing the gap in the net defences, which entangled round her screws and caused her to run aground short of the entrance. But *Thetis* had shielded *Intrepid*, which arrived in the canal mouth virtually unharmed. Her Captain, Lieutenant S.S. Bonham-Carter, had his ship perfectly placed across the channel when *Iphigenia* unfortunately collided with her. Bonham-Carter hurriedly blew the charges and *Intrepid* settled, almost blocking the canal. *Iphigenia*, commanded by Lieutenant E.W. Billyard-Leake, was scuttled almost alongside her. The canal was, for all effective purposes, blocked.

After the blockships had been scuttled, their crews were taken off by Motor Launch No 282, commanded by Lieutenant P.T. Dean RNVR who had followed them right into the channel. Under constant and deadly fire from heavy and machine guns firing at point-blank range from the sides of the Canal and from the Mole, Dean handled his motor launch 'as calmly as if engaged in a practice manoeuvre' and took off more than 100 officers and men. Three men were shot down at his side and at one point he looked upwards and saw German guns and their crews just above him. He had six revolvers on the bridge, and as his launch gathered speed he emptied them all at the German gunners. Keeping close over to that side, so that the Germans could not depress their guns enough to fire at him, Dean was about to clear the canal when the steering gear broke down. Unabashed, he manoeuvred on his engines and was actually clear of the entrance when he was told there was an officer in the water. He turned back, going ahead on one engine and full astern on the other, and picked the man up. Incredibly, ML.282 was hit many times but not sunk and eventually transferred her passengers to the destroyer *Warwick*. As Dean's citation said, it was solely due to his courage and daring that ML.282 succeeded in saving so many lives. The citation appeared on 23rd July 1918 and Dean received his Cross from the King with the other surviving Zeebrugge VCs at Buckingham Palace on the 31st.

Percy Thompson Dean was born on 20th July 1877 at Witton Bank, Witton, Blackburn in Lancashire, son of John Dean, a slate merchant and Ellen (née Thompson). He went to King Edward's School, Bromsgrove, and then into the family businesses as slate merchants and cotton spinners, becoming a town councillor in Blackburn in 1913. He joined the RNVR and became a Temporary Sub-Lieutenant in June 1916, being promoted to Lieutenant in June 1917. For his exploit at Zeebrugge he was promoted Temporary Lieutenant-Commander RNVR with seniority as of 23rd April 1918.

He was elected one of two Coalition Unionist MPs for Blackburn in December 1918 and sat for the constituency until 1922. He married three times: in 1905, Mabel Ratcliffe of Didsbury, by whom he had one son, John Ratcliffe Dean, who himself served as Lieutenant RNVR in the Second World War. When his wife died in 1907, Dean married Jeanne Marie Klein, daughter of Jacques Klein, wine merchant, on 1st October 1908, and they had a daughter. This marriage was annulled in 1921 and in 1927 Dean married Mrs M.R. Hardicker, widow of Lieutenant-General J.O. Hardicker.

Dean died at his London home, 36 Avenue Close, Avenue Road, London NW, on 20th March 1939.

Victor Alexander Charles Crutchley, Geoffrey Heneage Drummond and Roland Richard Louis Bourke:

Ostend, May 1918

On the same night as Zeebrugge was raided, and as part of the same operation, a similar attempt was made to block the harbour entrance at Ostend, using the light cruisers *Brilliant* (Commander A.E. Godsal) and *Sirius* (Lieutenant-Commander H.N.M. Hardy) as blockships. The Germans, possibly forewarned, had shifted one vital navigation mark and removed another. An unfortunate offshore wind blew away the covering smoke-screen, so that Godsal had to con his ship, by dead reckoning, in towards the shore through a heavy barrage and the intense glare of searchlights. *Brilliant* grounded about a mile out of position and before Godsal could take any action *Sirius* collided from astern, driving *Brilliant* even further on to the sand. The charges were exploded, to blow the bottoms out of both ships, and their crews were taken off by motor launches.

The Ostend party at once pressed Admiral Keyes to be allowed another try. Keyes himself was not a man to leave a job half done and so, on the night of 9th/10th May, another attempt was made to block Ostend harbour, using as blockships the old *Vindictive*, the survivor of Zeebrugge, with Godsal in command, and another old cruiser, *Sappho*, with Hardy in command. Many of the officers and men had taken part in the earlier attempt.

Sappho had to return with engine trouble, but this time Godsal made no mistake in spite of thick fog at a critical moment and took *Vindictive* right into the harbour mouth. He was manoeuvring his ship to place her across the channel when an unlucky shell exploded on the bridge, killing him and badly wounding his navigating officer, Lieutenant Sir John Alleyn. The First Lieutenant, Lieutenant V.A.C. Crutchley (who had already won a DSC for his gallantry in *Brilliant* at the first attempt) took charge of the ship and tried to swing her stern across the channel. Unknown to him, *Vindictive* was actually aground amidships and could not be moved. Crutchley ordered his crew to abandon ship and get into the motor launches waiting to take them off. He himself toured the ship with an electric torch, to satisfy himself there was no one alive left on board, before getting into ML.254.

As ML.254 drew away, the charges set in *Vindictive* blew up and the ship settled on the bottom, partially blocking the entrance. ML.254 (Lieutenant G.H. Drummond RNVR) had been hit by a shell as she followed *Vindictive* in. Her second-in-command and one sailor were killed, Drummond and his coxswain were badly wounded. In spite of his wounds Drummond had taken ML.254 alongside *Vindictive* and embarked the survivors of her crew. 2 officers and 38 men were taken off although some were killed or wounded whilst on board ML. 254. Drummond retained consciousness long enough to back the motor launch away from the piers and towards the open sea. He then sank exhausted from his wounds, and Crutchley assumed command of ML.254 as he had done in *Vindictive*. The motor launch was badly damaged and flooding by the bows. Crutchley organised a bucket brigade to bale as hard as they could, and told every man not employed and all the wounded who could move to stand aft so as to counteract the flooding. Enemy fire pursued ML.254 until she was some way out to sea, where Crutchley brought her alongside Keyes's flagship, the destroyer *Warwick*, and the survivors were taken on board.

As ML.254 came out of the harbour she was passed by ML.276 (Lieutenant R. Bourke RNVR) on the way in. The two launches actually collided, but without doing any damage to each other. Bourke (who had already won a DSO for his bravery in taking off *Brilliant*'s crew at Ostend in the earlier attempt) took ML.276 near *Vindictive* to check that everybody had got away. He stayed for about ten minutes, under very heavy fire, and was just leaving when he heard cries from the water. He returned and found Lieutenant Sir John Alleyn and two sailors, all very badly wounded, clinging to an upturned boat. In spite of the fire being poured on the motor launch, Bourke picked up all three men and made for the open sea. ML.276 was hit by one 6-inch shell, which killed two of her seamen and did considerable damage, and she was hit fifty-five times in all. Bourke eventually came alongside a monitor and was successfully taken in tow.

Crutchley, Drummond and Bourke were all gazetted for the Victoria Cross on 28th August 1918 and received their medals from the King at Buckingham Palace on 11th September.

Crutchley's citation was one of the very few which specifically mentioned seamanship as well as gallantry - 'this very gallant officer and fine seaman throughout these operations off the Belgian coast...' It was a perceptive comment, for Crutchley had a long, eventful and successful naval career in which he saw action in both world wars and seldom had a shore appointment.

Victor Alexander Charles Crutchley was born on 2nd November 1893 at 28 Lennox Gardens, London SW, the son of Percy Edward Crutchley JP and the Hon. Frederica Louisa (née Fitzroy), second daughter of the 3rd Baron Southampton. He went to the RN Colleges at Osborne and Dartmouth. His first ship as Midshipman was *Indomitable* in the 1st Cruiser Squadron of the Home Fleet in 1911, and from there on he served almost continuously at sea until he became Flag Officer Gibraltar in 1945. He was promoted Sub-Lieutenant on 30th April 1914, Lieutenant on 30th September 1915 and Lieutenant-Commander on 30th September 1923. He was at Jutland in *Centurion*, in both Ostend raids, and took part in operations in the Black Sea in 1918-19.

In the 1920s, Crutchley served in *Petersfield* on the South American Station 1919-21; in HM Yacht *Alexandra* 1922-3 for the season; and was Cadets' Divisional Officer in *Thunderer* 1922-24; he served in HM Yacht *Victoria and Albert*, 1924; in *Queen Elizabeth*, flagship of the Mediterranean Fleet, 1924-6; and in *Ceres* in 1926-8.

In 1929 he became Training Commander at the RN Barracks, Devonport.

Crutchley had been promoted Commander on 30th June 1928, and Captain on 31st December 1932 and it was in the 1930s that he began a long association with the navies of New Zealand and Australia. From 1930 to 1933 he was lent to the New Zealand Division and commanded *Diomede*, assisting in rescue work during the Napier earthquake in February 1931 and having a remarkable escape when *Diomede* was swept by very heavy seas returning to New Zealand from Sydney in March 1932.

After taking the Senior Officers' War Course in 1934, Captain Crutchley was Senior Officer, 1st Minesweeping Flotilla, from 1935 to 1936 and Captain (Fishery Protection and Minesweeping Flotilla) until taking command of the battleship *Warspite* in 1937.

As Captain of *Warspite*, one of the most famous ships in the Navy, Crutchley saw close action again in the Second Battle of Narvik, on 13th April 1940, when *Warspite's* 15-inch guns avenged Warburton-Lee (*qv*) and cleaned out a nest of German heavy destroyers, sinking eight of them, whilst her aircraft sank U.64. Crutchley was promoted Rear-Admiral on 6th February 1942 and appointed to command the Royal Australian Squadron. In the South-West Pacific, under General MacArthur, he commanded the screening force for the invasion of the Solomons at Guadalcanal in August 1942. On the night of 8/9th August, he was urgently summoned to a conference with Admiral Turner, the American commander of the Amphibious Force, so that he and his flagship, the cruiser *Australia*, were absent that night when a force of Japanese cruisers made one circuit of Savo Island and sank tye American cruisers *Vincennes*, *Astoria* and *Quincy* and the Australian *Canberra*. Crutchley was later exonerated by Admiral Nimitz, and went on to command a cruiser squadron in the US Seventh Fleet during operations in New Guinea.

Besides the VC and DSC, Crutchley also had the Croix de Guerre, the Polish order of Polonia Restituta (1942), was Commander of the US Legion of Merit in 1944, CB in 1945 and KCB in 1946. He retired in 1947 and went home to live in Dorset, where he was later Deputy Lieutenant and High Sheriff. He led the naval contingent at the VC Centenary Parade in Hyde Park in June 1956. In April 1930 he had married Joan Elizabeth Loveday Coryton, and they have one son and one daughter.

When King George V presented Lieutenant Drummond with his VC he asked him what he had done before the war. Drummond replied, 'I was a professional invalid, sir.' It was almost true. He had broken his neck in a fall when he was twelve years old and was never out of pain, although a number of treatments were tried (including one which involved fastening his head to the ceiling). At Ostend, Drummond, by his own account, suffered 2½ inches of copper driving-band in the back of my left thigh', 'a piece of shrapnel, which lodged behind my collar-bone within a fraction of my lungs', and said he 'must have bled the best part of a gallon and a half'.

Geoffrey Heneage Drummond was born on 25th January 1886 at 13 St James's Place, London SW, the third of seven sons of Captain Algernon Heneage Drummond, of the Rifle Brigade, and Margaret Elizabeth (née Benson). He went to Evelyn's School, Eton, and Christchurch, Oxford, and the South-East Agricultural College, but he failed to complete a number of courses because of his physical disabilities. However, he joined the RNVR in 1915 on his own doctor's recommendation.

Drummond himself described the action in vivid terms:

The firing seemed to grow in intensity, machine guns' rattle piercing the deeper roar of the batteries. Star shells, searchlights, the glare of the bombardment gave us plenty of light. One could clearly see figures on the piers, and even the hotel buildings along the shore. But a sea mist had fallen, and actually visibility was so bad that I had to rip open the canvas roof of the bridge and stand on the shelf with my head and shoulders out, and work the telegraphs with my feet. By this time I was getting rather numb from loss of blood. A machine gun about twenty yards away on the other pier was doing its level best. It gave me two bullets in the right forearm, but they dropped out on the way home, having penetrated only about half an inch; my theory is that, fired point-blank, they had not picked up their spin, and so were held up by my duffel coat.

When ML.254 was hit, 'The wardroom was burning merrily, a pom-pom having landed in one of the bunks, and our 150 gallons of petrol was right aft, only separated from the fire by a sheet of galvanised iron. Crutchley was a tower of strength. He reduced the fire, bound up the wounded and put a tourniquet round my leg.'

After the war Drummond was director of a firm of builders' merchants, and then joined ICI. In 1918 he married Maude Aylmer Tindal Bosanquet and they had a son and two daughters.

In 1939 Drummond again volunteered for the RNVR but was not accepted because of his age and disabilities, and so joined the Thames River Patrol Service as a Seaman. He still hoped for a commission, and his old friend Admiral Keyes was doing all he could to help it along, when in April 1941 he slipped whilst loading coal, or perhaps his wounded leg collapsed under him, and he fell, hitting his head. He suffered serious concussion and died in St Olave's Hospital, Rotherhithe, on 21st April. His name on the Commonwealth War Grave Commission's list is given not as Lieutenant RNVR but 'LT/JX211029, Second Hand G.H. Drummond

VC, RNPS, Chalfont St Peter Cemetery, Bucks., England.' His son joined the Royal Navy and served in the Second World War.

The bespectacled, studious features of Roland Richard Louis Bourke were markedly unheroic, but Keyes called him 'the bravest of all holders of the Victoria Cross'. He was born on 28th November 1885 at 40 Redcliffe Square, London SW, son of Isidore McWilliam Bourke MD retired Surgeon Major of the 72nd Highlanders, of Curraleegh, Co. Mayo, Ireland, and Marianna (née Carozzi). Aged seventeen, he went to Canada to try his hand at gold mining in the Klondyke and as a fruit farmer near Nelson, British Columbia. He was rejected by all the armed forces of Canada on the outbreak of war because of his poor eyesight, but came to England and joined the RNVR as a Sub-Lieutenant in command of ML. 276 at Ostend in the first blocking attempt. It was Bourke who took off the majority of the crew of *Brilliant*. He was promoted Lieutenant RNVR in 1917 and Lieutenant-Commander with seniority back-dated to 23rd April, in 1918.

In 1920 he was demobilised and went back to his farm in British Columbia, but by 1931 his eyesight had deteriorated so much that he believed he was going blind and he had to give up farming. He moved to Victoria, British Columbia, and was employed at the Royal Canadian Naval Barracks at Esquimault. Later he was appointed to organise the British Columbia Fishermen's Naval Reserve in Vancouver. He himself joined the RCNVR and served throughout the Second World War. He retired from the Canadian Civil Service in 1950. In 1919 Bourke married Rosalind Barnet of Sydney, New South Wales. He was a very quiet, reserved gentleman who disliked having a fuss made of him. He went to few of the functions organised for VCs, and he would only allow his photograph to be taken under the strongest protest. He died on 29th August 1958 at his home, 1253 Lyall Street, Esquimault, and was buried in Royal Oak Burial Park.

Lt.-Cdr. Geoffrey Drummond VC, 'When HMS Vindictive "Stormed" Ostend Piers', *The Daily Telegraph*, 9th May 1936.

Harold Auten:
English Channel, July 1918

When King George V was presenting the Victoria Cross to Lieutenant-Commander Auten DSC, RNR in the quadrangle at Buckingham Palace on 18th September 1918, the band played 'Hush, Hush, Hush, Here Comes the Bogey Man', to the great amusement of the King, Auten and the spectators.

Auten was the last of the Q-ship VCs, and his citation in the

London Gazette of 14th September 1918 was the most laconic of them all, consisting only of his name and rank.

Harold Auten very probably served in Q-ships longer than any other man. He joined the ex-collier Q-ship *Zylpha* as a Sub-Lieutenant RNR in the early days of September 1915. He took over his first Q-ship command, Q.16, or *Heather*, in April 1917 when his predecessor as Captain had been killed in action against a U-boat. He had just commissioned the Q-ship *Suffolk Coast* and was taking her to sea for gunnery trials when the Armistice was signed in November 1918. His most famous Q-ship, in which he won the Victoria Cross, was HMS *Stock Force*, a 360-ton collier which he himself picked out after she had taken his fancy in a Cardiff dock. 'This was the ship for me', he later wrote.

At about 5 pm on 30th July 1918, in the English Channel about twenty-five miles south-west of Start Point, *Stock Force* was torpedoed by a U-boat. The torpedo hit forward on a main bulkhead and did tremendous damage. Had it not been for her specially stowed cargo of wood, the ship would have gone down at once. The forward end of the bridge disappeared, Auten himself was blown under the chart table, and derricks were blown overboard. Pieces of shattered planking, unexploded 12-pounder shells and other debris rained down on the bridge for some time, followed by a deluge of water which drenched everybody on deck to the skin. One officer's steward called Starling was pinned under the wreckage of a gun and there he stayed until the action was over. A coloured seaman, specially chosen by Auten to give his crew verisimilitude, was covered in white paint.

Stock Force settled by the bows, water flooding the forward magazine and between decks to a depth of three feet, while the 'Panic party' took to the boats. Auten, the crews of two 4-inch guns and the engine-room staff, stayed on board.

The U-boat surfaced half a mile ahead and stayed there for about fifteen minutes whilst her Captain studied his target. The 'Panic party' began to row back, hoping the U-boat would follow them. It did, until it lay about 300 yards away on *Stock Force's* port beam, where both guns would bear. They opened fire at about 5.40 pm, the first shot carrying away one periscope, the second hitting the conning tower and blowing it and its occupant into the sea, and the third ripping a hole in the U-boat's hull. Her bows rose into the air for a time, as repeated shots hit her, and then she slid backwards out of sight.

Stock Force was kept afloat until 9.25 pm that night but finally sank with her White Ensign still flying. Auten and his crew were taken off by a torpedo boat. Starling and the other wounded survived.

Harold Auten was born at The Shrubberies, Leatherhead, Surrey on 22nd August 1891, the son of William Blee Auten, Paymaster RN (Retd) and Edith Fanny (née Ross). He went to Wilson's Grammar

School, Camberwell, and then to sea as an apprentice with the P&O Line when he was seventeen. He joined the RNR in 1910, became Sub-Lieutenant in June 1914 and was promoted Lieutenant RNR in 1917. He won the DSC commanding *Heather*. After the war he was promoted Lieutenant-Commander RNR on 2nd August 1925 and Commander on 29th August 1939. He served in the RNR again in the Second World War, routing convoy shipping leaving New York for Europe.

In 1919, Harold Auten published his memoirs *Q Boat Adventures*, and from 1922 he worked in the film business. In 1929 he replied on behalf of the naval VCs at the Prince of Wales' dinner for VCs at the Guildhall. He and his wife Margaret had one son and one daughter. After the war he was executive vice-president of the Rank Organisation in New York and for thirty years he lived in Bushkill, Pennsylvania, where he owned and operated the Bushkill Manor Hotel and Playhouse. He died in Monroe County Hospital, Pennsylvania, on 3rd October 1964.

Lt.-Cdr. Harold Auten VC, *Q Boat Adventures* (London: Herbert Jenkins, 1919).

Daniel Marcus William Beak:
Logeast Wood, France, August/September 1918

In August 1918 the Allied armies in France - British, French, Australian, Canadian and American - began a great offensive against the Hindenberg Line. The Royal Naval Division was still in the field, its Drake Battalion led by Commander Beak RNVR, an almost legendary figure, who had already won a DSO and two MCs and was about to win a VC.

Beak's VC was not awarded for a single exploit, but for a sustained show of bravery carried on over four days and repeated again ten days later. His citation only hints at what was involved: the confusion of a long battle, the constant gun-fire, the capture and consolidation of objectives and the scouting for new, the rallying of exhausted and wounded men, the physical and mental effort needed to ignore personal pain and to go on, and still go on, long after it would have been reasonable to stop, long after indeed the VC had already been won.

On 21st August, Beak led the Drake Battalion's attack on a place called Logeast Wood, near Bapaume, where his 'skilful and fearless leadership' resulted in the capture of four enemy positions, gained under very heavy machine-gun fire. The tide of the war was now with the Allies and four days later the Drakes were advancing again. Beak himself had been wounded and was still dazed, with a shell fragment actually lodged in his skull. However, in the absence of the Brigade Commander, he reorganised the whole 63rd Brigade under 'extremely heavy gunfire' and led them with splendid courage to their next objectives. At one point, an attack was held up and Beak himself rushed forward to lead it, accompanied by only one runner, and 'succeeded in breaking up a nest of machine guns, personally bringing back nine or ten prisoners'. With this example in front of them, Beak's bluejackets and adjoining units were encouraged to go on. On 4th September, Beak again 'displayed great courage and powers of leadership, coupled with the confidence with which he inspired all ranks'. His VC was gazetted on 15th November 1918 and was presented to him by King George V at Vincent Barracks, Valenciennes, on 6th December.

Daniel Marcus William Beak was born in a modest little house at 42 Kent Road, St Denys, Southampton on 27th July 1891. He went to St Denys School and then to Taunton's School. When he left he became a schoolmaster at St Mary's, Southampton, but feeling that he 'was not too good at it' he became a private secretary to a parson in Bristol. Then came the war, and Beak went with a friend to enlist in the RNVR at the Crystal Palace, joining as an ordinary seaman on 26th January 1915. He was rated Petty Officer before being commissioned as a Sub-Lieutenant RNVR on 8th May 1915. He seems never to have had a sea-going appointment, but served at various times with the Drake, Anson and Howe Battalions. He was at the evacuation from Gallipoli, won his first MC as Adjutant of Drake Battalion in January 1917, and his second in March when he was commanding the Battalion. After command of Howe and Anson, he returned to Drake, with the rank of Temporary Commander on 12th March 1918 and commanded the battalion until its disbandment in June 1919, winning his DSO in July 1918.

With such a fighting record, it was not surprising that Beak found civilian life post-war 'rather tame' and after one year rejoined as a regular army officer, being commissioned as a Captain in the Royal Scots Fusiliers. In 1932 he went to India as a Major and served with the 1st Battalion, King's Liverpool Regiment there for seven years. In 1938, as a Colonel he commanded the 1st Battalion, South Lancashire Regiment and as a Major-General was mentioned in despatches again for service in France in 1940. In 1942 he went to Malta as GOC Troops and was once more under fire, this time from the Luftwaffe, who knocked down his house and very nearly killed him. He retired from the Army in 1945 and went to live at Lambourn in Berkshire. In 1923 he married Matilda-Catherine Frances Ritchie, only daughter of Lieutenant-Colonel Hugh Robert Wallace DSO, JP, DL of Busbie, in Ayrshire. They had two sons. General Beak died at the Princess Margaret Hospital, Swindon,

Wiltshire on 3rd May 1967. The Drake Battalion Society, of which he was President, held a reunion every year until his death.

George Prowse:
Pronville, France, September 1918

'The extreme of heroism', wrote Frederic Manning in *Her Privates We*, 'is indistinguishable from despair.' His words aptly applied to Chief Petty Officer G. Prowse VC, DCM, RNVR, of the Royal Naval Division, whose behaviour in the last month of his life was like that of a man determined to die.

Prowse was serving in the Drake Battalion which was part of 63rd Division in the great advance upon the Hindenburg Line in August 1918. By 1st September the Canadians of General Horne's 1st Army, and the 17th Corps of General Byng's 3rd Army (which included the 63rd Division) had established a six-mile front from Etaing to Queant. The 63rd Division attacked Pronville, east of Queant, on 2nd September. Prowse's conduct on the 2nd and subsequently is tersely but well described in his citation:

For most conspicuous bravery and devotion to duty when, during an advance, a portion of his company became disorganised by heavy machine-gun fire from an enemy strong-point. Collecting what men were available he led them with great coolness and bravery against this strong point, capturing it together with twenty-three prisoners and five machine guns.

Later, he took a patrol forward in face of much enemy opposition, and established it on important high ground. On another occasion he displayed great heroism by attacking single-handed an ammunition limber which was trying to recover ammunition, killing three men who accompanied it and capturing the limber.

Two days later he rendered valuable services when covering the advance of his company with a Lewis-gun section, and located later on two machine-gun positions in a concrete emplacement, which were holding up the advance of the battalion on the right.

With complete disregard of personal danger he rushed forward with a small party and attacked and captured these posts, killing six of the enemy and taking thirteen prisoners and two machine guns. He was the only survivor of this gallant party, but by this daring and heroic action he enabled the battalion on the right to push forward without further machine-gun fire from the village. Throughout the whole operation his magnificent example and leadership were an inspiration to all, and his courage was superb.

174

The citation appeared in the *London Gazette* of 30th October 1918, by which time Prowse was dead. He was killed in action on 27th September during the battle of Cambrai, when the 63rd Division attacked and cut the Bapaume-Cambrai road. He knew he had been recommended for the VC. In one of his last letters to his wife he wrote: 'To know I have been recommended for such an award is the greatest of honours and you can quite imagine I must have done something very great. You say I shall not be half "swanking" now, but you know there is not very much "swank" attached to me.'

George Prowse was a coalminer, born in 1886 in the West Country, possibly in Bath, or in Paulton, between Bath and Bristol. His father John was also a coalminer. In areas of local unemployment, large rural families normally dispersed, the girls into service in the houses of gentry, the boys to find work where they could. In 1907 a new coal-mine opened at Grovesend, Swansea and George Prowse was one of those men who came from all parts of the country looking for work. For a time he lodged with a family called Nock in Station Road, Grovesend. Later he worked in the Mountain Colliery, Gorseinon (and played for their football team). On 8th November 1913 at Swansea Registry Office he married Sarah Lewis, reputedly a barmaid, of 65 Pentreharne Road, Landore, Swansea. Prowse gave his own address as 22 New Road, Grovesend, Pontardulais.

His marriage was supposed locally not to be a happy one, leaving him with the sense of 'having nothing to come home to', which might account for his recklessness. He joined the Navy at Swansea Naval Recruiting Office on 26th February 1915 and served in the Naval Division from 1916 onwards, being rated Petty Officer and then Chief Petty Officer on 28th April 1918. He was one of the very few naval ratings to win a DCM, a military award, the Naval Division being under Army command.

Prowse's body was never found. His name is commemorated on the Vis-en-Artois Memorial. His widow received the Victoria Cross from King George V at Buckingham Palace on 17th July 1919.

Augustine Willington Shelton Agar:
Kronstadt, June 1919

In 1919, months after the Armistice, Great Britain was still at war with the revolutionary Bolshevik regime in Russia. A large expeditionary force guarded British interests in Murmansk and Archangel, and a naval squadron operated in the Baltic, blockading the naval base at Kronstadt, at the entrance to the channel leading to Petrograd (St Petersburg) in the Gulf of Finland. In June 1919 the British naval commander Rear-Admiral Sir Walter Cowan established a base at Bjorko Sound, thirty miles east of Kronstadt on the Finnish shore, where he eventually had some eighty ships of various kinds under his command.

Not for the first time in naval history, the Admiralty had no clear political guidance from the Cabinet, and for some time Cowan was not sure whether his forces were at war with the Bolsheviks or not. Meanwhile, Lieutenant A.W.S. Agar, who was on special service under the Foreign Office, set up a secret base at Terrioki, on the Finnish shore north of Kronstadt, and began to operate a 'courier' service, ferrying secret agents and information in and out of Kronstadt Harbour in his shallow draught, 35-knot Coastal Motor Boat, CMB.4.

When an anti-Bolshevik insurrection broke out in Kronstadt in June, Agar dropped his clandestine role, and hoisted the White Ensign. On the night of 16th/17th June (although Kronstadt had actually surrendered to the Bolsheviks earlier that day) Agar made a daring solo sortie into Kronstadt Bay. He penetrated a destroyer screen and was closing a larger warship further inshore when CMB.4 broke down. Her hull had been pierced by gunfire and Agar had to take her alongside a breakwater to make repairs. These took twenty minutes, during which CMB.4 was in full view of the enemy. Agar then resumed his attack and with his single 18-inch torpedo hit and sank the 6,550-ton Russian cruiser *Oleg* in Kronstadt Bay. Agar retired under a very heavy fire and reached the safety of the open bay, skirting the fringes of a Russian minefield and returned to Terrioki. Because of his secret role, Agar's VC citation of 22nd August 1919 was non-committal: "In recognition of his conspicuous gallantry, coolness and skill under extremely difficult conditions in action."

The Bolsheviks put a price of £5,000 on Agar's head but this did not deter him from taking part in the raid on Kronstadt Harbour on 18th August in which Dobson and Steele (*qv*) won their VCs. With his great navigational experience of those waters, Agar led one column of CMBs in CMB.7 to their destination and remained on patrol at the mouth of the harbour. For this he was awarded a DSO. He was invested with it and his VC by the King at Buckingham Palace on 9th October 1919 (although the DSO was not actually gazetted until 11th November).

Augustine Willington Shelton Agar was born on 4th January 1890 at Kandy, Ceylon, son of John Shelton Agar, a planter, of Woodmount, Co. Kerry, Ireland. He went to Framlingham College, Eastman's Naval Academy and HMS *Britannia*, joining the Navy in October 1905; his term were the last of the old *Britannia* scheme before the new college at Dartmouth was opened. He was promoted Lieutenant on 30th June

1912. He served in the battleship *Hibernia* in the Grand Fleet from 1914 to 1915, and was at Gallipoli for the evacuation. He then served in *Iphigenia* (later blockship at Zeebrugge) before leaving for special service in CMBs in 1918.

Agar was promoted Lieutenant-Commander on 30th June 1920, Commander on 31st December 1925 and Captain on 31st December 1933. In 1932 when he was commanding the sloop *Scarborough* on the American and West Indies Station, he was badly injured in a seaplane accident on the Acushnet River in Massachusetts. He commanded the cruiser *Emerald* (with Fogarty Fegen, *qv*, as his commander). In August 1941 he took command of the cruiser *Dorsetshire*. On 1st December, south-west of St Helena, *Dorsetshire* sighted a suspicious ship and closed her at high speed. She was the U-boat supply ship *Python*, whose crew abandoned and scuttled her.

Early in the afternoon of Easter Sunday, 5th April, 1942, *Dorsetshire* and her sister ship *Cornwall* were south-west of Ceylon, steaming hard to rejoin the Eastern Fleet, when they were attacked by fifty Japanese bombers launched from Admiral Nagumo's carriers, then operating in the Indian Ocean. Both ships were overwhelmed with many bomb-hits and sank in a few minutes. Agar went down with his ship, literally, so deep that one of his lungs was permanently damaged, but he surfaced again to encourage and cheer his men through a 24-hour ordeal by heat and shark attack. 1,122 officers and men from the two ships were picked up next day; 424 lives were lost.

Agar's last appointment was as Commodore and President of the Royal Naval College, Greenwich, from 1943 until 1945, when he stood unsuccessfully as a Conservative (Nationalist) in the July election. In his retirement he went home to Alton in Hampshire and grew strawberries.

In 1920, at St George's, Hanover Square, he had married Mary Petre, Baroness Furnivall (a title which had been in abeyance since 1777 but was determined in her favour in 1913). They divorced in 1931, and the following year Agar married Mrs Ina Margaret Hurst in Bermuda. He published his autobiography *Footprints in the Sea* in 1960. He died at his home, Anstey Park House, Alton, Hampshire, on 30th December 1968. Coastal Motor Boat No. 4 lay neglected at Hampton Wick for nearly thirty years. In 1967 it was placed on display at the Shipbuilding Industry Training Board's centre at Southampton, later being removed to the Imperial War Museum.

Commodore A.W.S. Agar VC, DSO, RN, *Footprints in the Sea* (London: Evans Bros., 1960).
Geoffrey Bennett, *Cowan's War: The Story of British Naval Operations in the Baltic, 1918-1920* (London: Collins, 1964).

Claude Congreve Dobson and Gordon Charles Steele: Kronstadt, August 1919

'The Scooter Raid', as it was called, when fast Coastal Motor Boats entered Kronstadt Harbour on 18th August 1919, was in the Royal Navy's great tradition of raiding and cutting-out parties - a small, fast-moving, highly-trained force penetrated an enemy stronghold, inflicted a numbing blow on a much larger opponent and got clear away again, for slight casualties.

In 1919, although Great Britain was officially at war with the Bolshevik revolutionary regime in Russia, the political situation was by no means cut and dried and British forces were often uncertain about what they were permitted to do. For instance, Rear-Admiral Sir Walter Cowan, commanding the British Baltic Force, pointed out to the Admiralty that he was required to blockade the Russian naval base on Kotlin Island at Kronstadt, where there were two Bolshevik battleships, without being allowed to take offensive action with aircraft monitors or motor boats. The ban on offensive action was lifted in July. Agar ($q\nu$) had shown what could be done with CMBs. Eight more were towed across the North Sea to join Cowan. They were 55-feet-long, 35-knot craft, armed with Lewis guns and one or two 18-inch torpedoes.

At 1 am on 18th August, the eight CMBs led by Commander C.C. Dobson in CMB.31, left Cowan's base at Bjorko Sound, thirty miles east of Kotlin Island. The CMBs were manned by two officers and an engine-room artificer, and each had a Finnish smuggler on board with local knowledge of the Bay. They reached the north side of the island at about 4 am just as a diversionary bombing attack by twelve RAF Sopwith Camels was taking place, and slipped past a row of forts which were supposed to be armed with heavy 11-inch, 9-inch and 6-inch guns (in fact, at least two forts had only rifles and machine guns). However, the guns' crews were caught completely napping and even when the CMBs roared into the inner harbour at about 4.25 am, many of the guns could not fire because they feared to hit each other or because they could not depress far enough.

Three CMBs had been detailed to sink the destroyer *Gavriil* at the entrance but their torpedoes ran too shallow and missed. Assisted by searchlights from the forts *Gavriil* retaliated and eventually sank three CMBs. Meanwhile, the others swept into the harbour in two columns. CMB.31, conned by Lieutenant McBean, reached the inner jetty and torpedoed the battleship *Andrei Pervozvanni*. The CMB stayed for a time in the harbour, under heavy machine gun fire, whilst Dobson directed the other CMBs, before retreating under the shelter of the harbour walls to the open bay.

On the run into the harbour the C O of CMB.88, Lieutenant Dayrell-Reed, was shot through the head and killed. His body

178

slumped over the steering wheel so that the motor boat began to career out of control. The second-in-command, Lieutenant G.C. Steele, manhandled his dead Captain's body away from the controls and took charge himself, steadying the boat on course once more for her target, the battleship *Andrei Pervozvanni*. Steele fired one torpedo at 100-yards range, and then had to manoeuvre the CMB in a very confined space to get a clear shot at the other battleship, the *Petropavlosk*, which was obscured by the hull of *Andrei Pervozvanni* and shrouded in the smoke from her. Steele only just had enough room to turn but headed for the entrance, firing at the machine guns along the wall as he went, and he too gained the safety of the bay outside, where Agar in CMB.7, who had been acting as a kind of traffic marshal, was waiting. There, Lieutenant Bremner in CMB.24 also arrived, having torpedoed and sunk the submarine depot ship *Pamyat Azova*. Both battleships sank in the inner harbour, as the remaining CMBs roared across the water back to their base.

This brilliant *coup de main* severely embarrassed the Cabinet, who were at that very moment conducting delicate negotiations with the Bolsheviks for the withdrawal of the large British land forces then in Archangel. The raid also had another unexpected and unfortunate political effect. The Russian Baltic Fleet, and especially the Kronstadt garrison, had been scornfully critical of the Bolsheviks. The audacity of the raid caused them to turn temporarily over to the Bolshevik side. However, Victoria Crosses are happily not awarded by politicians, and Dobson and Steele were duly gazetted on 11th November 1919, the first anniversary of Armistice Day.

Dobson, a submariner of distinction, had already had an eventful war and won the DSO. He served in the submarine campaign in the Dardanelles in 1915, when such captains as Nasmith, Boyle, Herbert, Cochrane, Brodie and Dobson terrorised the seaways, bringing traffic to a halt, torpedoing ships, and shelling trains on coastal railways. On 20th July 1915, off Fair Island in the Atlantic, Dobson took part in one of the first successful anti-U-boat 'ruses'. Commanding C.27, he was being towed by the trawler *Princess Marie Jose* when U.23 surfaced and began to shell the trawler. The tow was cast off while the trawler's men abandoned ship and took to their boat. As the U.23 closed the trawler, so Dobson stalked U.23 and sank her with his second torpedo.

Claude Congreve Dobson was born on 1st January 1885 at Barton Regis, near Bristol, youngest of the four sons of Nelson Congreve Dobson FRCS of Halifax, Nova Scotia, who was House Surgeon at Bristol General Hospital from 1867 to 1871 (where he performed the first appendectomy operation outside London) and was later in practice at Clifton from 1871 to 1898. Dobson went to Clifton College and then to HMS *Britannia* in 1899, joining the Fleet in 1901. He was promoted Lieutenant on 30th March 1906, having gained all 'first classes' in his examinations. He joined submarines in 1910, later commanding B.5, B.11 and, in 1913, C.27. He had a spell in general service in the battleship *Monarch* in 1912. He was promoted Commander on 30th June 1918 and for a time served in the Anti-Submarine Division at the Admiralty. He received his Cross from the King at Buckingham Palace on 18th December 1919. Like the other VCs from Bristol, he received a gold watch and an illuminated address from the city in 1920.

After the war Dobson served for three years, from 1922 to 1925 with the Royal Australian Navy at Flinders Base, and was promoted Captain on 31st December 1925. He commanded *Colombo*, *Canterbury* and *Malcolm* before retiring at his own request on 1st January 1935. His eyesight had been failing for some time. In retirement, Dobson went to live in Walmer, Kent, when he was manager of a lending library. He married Edith, daughter of Professor Archibald Mac-Mechan, also of Halifax, Nova Scotia, at Bristol on 17th October 1920 and they had twin daughters, Anne and Joan, born in Melbourne, Australia on 8th October 1923. Dobson was promoted Rear-Admiral on the retired list in 1936. He died in Chatham Hospital on 26th June 1940.

Steele was also an ex-submariner and had just as adventurous a war as Dobson. He served in submarines, in Q-ships and at Jutland. Like the majority of the Q-ship crews, Steele was a professional sailor in civilian life, from a sea-going family background. He was born on 1st November 1894 at Exeter, the son of Captain H.W. Steele RN and Selina May, daughter of Major-General J.C. Symonds RMLI. He went to Vale College, Ramsgate, and then to HMS *Worcester*, the training ship on the Thames, where he was an excellent student, winning thirteen prizes and a P & O Scholarship, and became a Cadet Captain. He left in 1909 to become an Apprentice Cadet in the P & O ship SS *Palma*, becoming a Midshipman RNR on 12th August 1909. He joined up at the outbreak of war and served in the battleship *Conqueror* in 1914. In October 1914 he joined submarines and served in D.8 and E.22. He was promoted Acting Sub-Lieutenant on 10th July 1915, when he was serving as Gunnery Officer of the old Great Eastern Railway ship *Vienna*, renamed as the Q-ship *Baralong*. Steele was mentioned in despatches as Gunnery Officer when *Baralong* sank U.27, and transferred to a permanent RN commission as a Sub-Lieutenant for distinguished service in action, with seniority as of 17th August 1915. He was promoted Lieutenant on 19th November and served in the battleship *Royal Oak* at Jutland, before transferring to *Iron Duke* in 1916-17. He was then given two commands of his own, the ocean escort P.63 and the sloop *Cornflower*.

Steele was promoted Lieutenant-Commander on 19th November 1923 and might have had a long career in the Royal Navy in front of him, but he chose instead to go on half pay in 1929 (being too young at that time to retire) to become Captain-Superintendent of his 'old school' HMS *Worcester*, a post he held until retirement in 1957. He was placed officially on the retired list in 1931 and promoted Commander (Retd) on 1st November. Steele was a man of many parts, with an astonishing range of interests; in 1935 he introduced into the *Worcester* syllabus courses on civil aviation and air navigation, and was made a Member of the Central Board for the training of Officers for the Merchant Navy; he was also an interpreter in Russian; a Younger Brother of Trinity House; a Member of the Worshipful Company of Shipwrights; a Fellow of the Institution of Navigation, of the Royal Geographical Society, and the Royal Meteorogical Society; an author of books about HMS *Worcester* and ships' electrical systems; a Naval Member of the Royal Yacht Squadron; a lay reader in the diocese of Canterbury; borough councillor in Folkestone from 1958 until 1961; and a Freeman of the City of London. He has never married and now lives in retirement at Winckleigh Court, near Okehampton, Devon.

Gerard Broadmead Roope:
Norwegian Sea, April 1940

The first naval Victoria Cross of the Second World War (though not the first gazetted) was awarded for a hopelessly gallant attack against overwhelming opposition in the tradition of Sir Richard Grenville and the *Revenge*. The action took place in April 1940 during the opening stages of the Norwegian campaign, but the details only became known at home when the survivors were repatriated after the war. Until then, there was only Winston Churchill's epitaph, spoken in the House of Commons: '*Glowworm*'s light has been quenched. We can only conclude she has been sunk by greatly superior enemy forces.'

On 7th April 1940 the battlecruiser *Renown* was steaming northwards in the Norwegian Sea in a rising gale when one of her four escorting destroyers, *Glowworm* (Lieutenant-Commander G.B. Roope), reported a man overboard and asked permission to turn aside and search. Roope spent nearly two hours vainly looking for the man and in so doing lost touch with *Renown*. During the night the weather deteriorated and *Glowworm* had to reduce speed, dropping further behind *Renown*, and when, shortly after daybreak on 8th April she sighted an unidentified destroyer to the north, *Glowworm* was quite alone.

The stranger at first identified herself as Swedish, and then opened fire. She was in fact the German destroyer *Paul Jakobi*, and after *Glowworm* had got off two salvoes against her she was joined by another German destroyer, *Bernd von Arnim*, whose mess decks

181

were crammed with German troops for Trondheim, her Captain's main preoccupation being to get them safely ashore. He attempted to evade *Glowworm*, but being less seaworthy made heavier weather of it and had to reduce speed. Roope believed that the enemy were trying to lure him on to a more powerful force, but decided to follow to see what big ships the Germans had at sea. By this time *Glowworm's* gun-director control tower had been flooded by heavy seas, two more men had been lost overboard and several more injured by the ship's violent rolling.

Shortly afterwards, a much larger enemy ship appeared to the north-west, bearing 320 degrees, range five miles. It was the heavy cruiser *Admiral Hipper*, also bound with troops for Trondheim, returning to assist her destroyer escort.

As usual, the German initial gunnery ranging was excellent and *Hipper* hit *Glowworm* with her first salvo. The weather made escape or evasive shadowing almost impossible, so Roope sent off an enemy sighting report (his second, both of which were received by the C-in-C) and closed his enemy. The destroyer *Glowworm*, 1,345 tons and armed with four 4.7-inch guns, therefore advanced upon the 10,000-ton *Admiral Hipper*, armed with eight 8-inch and twelve 4.1-inch guns. *Glowworm* was hit again, in the Captain's day cabin, where the doctor and his action sick-bay party were all killed or wounded. Another shell brought down part of the foremast and the wireless aerials, which fouled the siren on the funnel, and *Glowworm* went into action with the strange mournful banshee wailing of her steam siren. She fired a spread of five torpedoes, all of which ran wide, and was hit again, forward and in the engine-room, where a large fire broke out. *Glowworm* made smoke and prepared for another torpedo attack. At some time now, Roope decided to ram his enemy. *Glowworm* emerged from the smoke-screen, crossing *Hipper's* bows from port to starboard, and fired another spread of five torpedoes, four of which got away and one of which only just missed *Hipper* by yards. *Glowworm* was still making about twenty knots when Roope ordered a sharp turn to starboard and headed for *Hipper's* starboard side. Helmuth Heye, *Hipper's* Captain, alarmed by the possibility of another torpedo attack, also tried to turn to starboard and ram *Glowworm*, but *Hipper* was much slower under helm and *Glowworm* struck her amidships, tearing away about 100 feet of her armoured plating, damaging the starboard side torpedo tubes, killing one man at his gun and puncturing two fresh-water tanks.

Glowworm drew clear after the collision and although her decks were swept by a storm of fire from *Hipper's* 4.1-inch and 37-mm close-range weapons, *Glowworm* got off another salvo and hit *Hipper* from a range of about 400 yards. She was by then losing way, settling by the bows, with a major fire raging amidships and all steam pressure lost. Roope ordered his ship's company to abandon ship. He stayed on the bridge, smoking a cigarette.

Heye chivalrously stayed for over an hour to pick up *Glowworm's* survivors. Roope was seen in the water, helping men to put on their lifejackets and he actually reached *Hipper's* ship's side, where a rope was thrown to him. He caught it, but was not able to hang on. He sank back exhausted and was drowned. One officer and 30 men of *Glowworm's* total ship's company of 149 were picked up. Two men died in captivity.

Roope's posthumous VC was gazetted on 10th July 1945. The sole surviving officer, the Torpedo Officer Lieutenant R.A. Ramsay, was awarded a DSO and three of the ship's company the CGM. Roope's VC was presented by King George VI to his widow, accompanied by his son, Cadet Michael Roope RN, at Buckingham Palace on 12th February 1946.

Gerard Broadmead Roope was at Dartmouth during the First World War and was just too young to take part, having been born on 13th March 1905 at Hillbrook Trull, near Taunton in Somerset, son of Gerard and Florence (née Broadmead) Roope. He was a Midshipman in 1923 and served in the gunroom of the battlecruiser *Revenge*. He was promoted Lieutenant on 30th September 1927 and, apart from a commission in the cruiser *Caradoc* in 1930, he was essentially a 'small ship' man, and a 'salt-horse', i.e. having no specialist gunnery, torpedo or navigation qualification. He was First-Lieutenant of the minesweeper *Tiverton* in 1932, and of the destroyer *Boreas* in the Mediterranean in 1933. His first command was the destroyer *Vidette* in the 1st Anti-Submarine Flotilla at Portland. He was promoted Lieutenant-Commander on 30th September 1935 and appointed in command of *Glowworm* on 22nd July 1938, commissioning her for the 1st Flotilla in the Mediterranean, and he served in her until the day of his death.

In 1928 he married Faith Clarke at Long Ashton in Somerset. In addition to their son Michael, they also had a daughter, Felicity.

Gerard Roope was a large, burly man, with a broad face, firm jaw and a forthright manner. He was a career naval officer, devoted to the Service. His ship's company called him 'Old Ardover', for his habit of altering course violently towards his objective whether or not it was the men's mealtime or any other consideration. It was typical of him to go straight for *Hipper*. It was Gerard Roope and his generation of professional naval officers who held the ring in the early years of the war at sea, while the thousands of later RNVR officers were learning their new trade.

The Times, 9th July 1945.
Tim Carew, 'Stand By to Ram', *Sunday Express*, 7th January 1962.

Bernard Armitage Warburton Warburton-Lee:
Narvik, April 1940

The first VC of the Second World War, in the sense that it was the first to be recognised and gazetted at the time, was won for a brief but furious naval action during the Norwegian campaign by a man who saw and acted upon what is sometimes known in the Navy as 'the Golden Moment'. He chose to go on and inflict the maximum damage upon the enemy, in circumstances where he could equally well have been cautious and nobody on earth would have criticised him. But he saw his chance and took it.

On 9th April 1940 the C-in-C Home Fleet, Admiral Forbes, ordered Captain Bernard Warburton-Lee, commanding the 2nd Destroyer Flotilla, to 'send some destroyers up to Narvik to make certain that no enemy troops land'. At noon that day the Admiralty signalled direct to Warburton-Lee telling him that the enemy had already landed at Narvik and he should sink or capture their transports. Warburton-Lee took all four destroyers of his Flotilla, himself in *Hardy*, with *Hotspur*, *Havock* and *Hunter*. He was later joined by *Hostile*.

At 4 pm that afternoon, *Hardy* stopped off the pilot station at Tränoy, at the entrance to Ofotfjord leading to Narvik, and there Warburton-Lee learned that the enemy were in much greater strength than reported. Six large destroyers (there were ten) had been going up, and a U-boat. The Norwegians said that Warburton-Lee would need twice as many ships to deal with them. But Warburton-Lee decided to go on, and take advantage of surprise. He signalled, 'Intend attacking at dawn high water.' The Admiralty approved the plan, but evidently had second thoughts, for the First Sea Lord later signalled more details of German strength and added: 'You alone can judge whether, in these circumstances, attack should be made. We shall support whatever decision you take.'

By the time that signal was received Warburton-Lee's ships were already feeling their way up Ofotfjord, in pitch darkness, thick mist and frequent snow squalls. They arrived off Narvik Harbour entrance, just after 4 am, as the snow showers were clearing and dawn breaking. There was no sound or movement from the enemy. The surprise was complete.

Hardy went in first alone, at about 4.30 am, and her torpedoes sank one German destroyer, the *Schmidt*, blew the stern off a second, the *Heidkamp*, and sank or damaged several merchant ships, while her guns severely damaged a third destroyer, the *Roeder*. *Hardy* withdrew, while *Hunter* and *Havock* took her place, firing more torpedoes into the harbour and hammering *Roeder* again. *Hotspur* and *Hostile* had stayed outside, to patrol the entrance and

184

provide counter-battery fire if needed. They laid a smoke-screen to protect the others as they retired and then joined in a second attack, shelling the harbour and firing torpedoes through the entrance. Leaving Narvik Harbour behind them in a chaotic confusion of smoke, fires, sporadic shelling, criss-crossing torpedo wakes streaking at random through the water, and several destroyers and German-held merchant ships sunk or sinking, Warburton-Lee's ships retired two or three miles down the fjord to regroup and consider the situation.

Some ships still had torpedoes on board, and as most of the German destroyers known to be present seemed to have been accounted for, Warburton-Lee decided on a third attack, and once more led his ships past the entrance, to shell targets of opportunity and fire the remaining torpedoes into the harbour. They then retired down the fjord towards the open sea.

But Warburton-Lee had stretched his luck too far. Three German destroyers, *Zenker*, *Gliese* and *Koellner*, appeared out of the mist in Herjangsfjord to the north-east, and while Warburton-Lee cracked on to thirty knots, a running battle developed. Warburton-Lee might still have got away, but two more German destroyers, *Thiele* and *Bernd von Arnim*, appeared ahead from Ballangen fjord.

Warburton-Lee had just hoisted the signal 'Keep on engaging the enemy' when a shell burst on *Hardy*'s bridge, killing or wounding every man on it. The first officer to recover was her Captain's Secretary, Lieutenant G.H. Stanning, who came to his senses to find *Hardy* steaming down the fjord with nobody steering her or in command. He took over the wheel himself until relieved by an Able Seaman. Successive salvoes hit *Hardy* in the engine-room and severed main steam pipes. As *Hardy* lost speed, Stanning directed her towards the shore, to beach her before she sank.

Warburton-Lee, terribly wounded, was floated ashore on a stretcher by the Gunner, Mr McCracken, but died on the way. The survivors of *Hardy* gathered in a hut ashore, where they were looked after by the Norwegians. They were taken off by *Ivanhoe* three days later.

Hunter was also sunk in the battle and *Hotspur* severely disabled, so that *Hostile* and *Havock* came back to help her. The German destroyers did not press their advantage and the three escaped, *Havock* sinking the German ammunition ship *Rauenfels* on the way out. Warburton-Lee's posthumous VC, for 'gallantry, enterprise and daring in command' was gazetted on 7th June 1940 and presented to his widow, who was accompanied by her fourteen-year-old son Phillip and her brother Colonel Swinton, at a private investiture at Buckingham Palace on 2nd July 1940. Warburton-Lee's body was buried ashore in Ballangen New Cemetery, in Norway.

Bernard Armitage Warburton Warburton-Lee was born on 13th September 1895 at Broad Oak, Isycoed, Flintshire, the son of Joseph

Henry Warburton-Lee, barrister-at-law, and Emmeline Vernon Armitage. He went to Dartmouth and Osborne and on to the training cruiser *Cornwall*, where he passed out top of his term in 1912. Except for eighteen months between 1933 and 1934 in command of the C-in-C Mediterranean's despatch vessel *Bryony*, his service career was spent almost entirely in destroyers: 1st Lieutenant of *Mischief* and *Wrestler* in 1917, command of *Tuscan* in 1924, *Stirling* in 1926, *Walpole* in 1928, *Vanessa* in 1930 and of *Witch* in 1934. He was promoted Commander on 30th June 1930 and Captain on 30th June 1936, and was in command of the cruiser *Hawkins* and Flag Captain to Vice-Admiral Max Horton, commanding the Reserve Fleet until July 1939, when he took command of *Hardy* and was Captain (D) of the 2nd Flotilla. He played polo, tennis and squash racquets for the Navy. In 1924 he married Elizabeth, daughter of Captain G.S. Campbell-Swinton.

Donald Macintyre, *Narvik*, (London: Evans Bros, 1959). 'The First and Second Battles of Narvik, and the Norway Campaign of 1940', Supplement to the *London Gazette* of 3rd July 1947.

Richard Been Stannard:
Namsos, April/May 1940

In the Norwegian campaign of 1940 the Royal Navy experienced determined air opposition for the first time in its history and learned a hard lesson: that it was impossible to maintain the Army on an overseas expedition, or even to operate its own ships off an enemy coast for any length of time, without proper air cover.

One of the fiercest and most prolonged ordeals by air attack was endured by the ships and men at Namsos, about 100 miles north of Trondheim, where troops had been landed on 14th April 1940. Amongst the ships there were the 15th and 16th Anti-Submarine Striking Forces. These splendidly named forces were actually composed of four trawlers each, with RNR officers and crews from the Royal Naval Patrol Service. Their duty was to patrol the fjords for submarines but, slow and lightly armed as they were, they made easy targets for the Stuka dive-bombers, who soon made it impossible for them to operate in daylight.

The 15th A/S Striking Force, under Commander Sir Geoffrey Congreve, arrived at Namsos at 2 am on 28th April, and the trawler *Arab* (Lieutenant R. B. Stannard RNR) was ordered alongside the cruiser *Carlisle* to ferry stores and equipment from the ship to the shore. The first air-raid began at daybreak, when *Arab* was cast off from *Carlisle* and later secured alongside a jetty astern of a French ammunition ship, *Saumur*. She was still there when another air-raid began. A bomb landed on the jetty and set fire to some ammunition which had been disembarked. Stannard ran *Arab*'s bows against the jetty and held her there by running the engines slow ahead. He sent all but two of his crew to comparative safety aft, and then tried for two hours to put out the fire with *Arab*'s hoses. He succeeded in saving a part of the jetty, which was invaluable in the later evacuation.

Arab spent the night of 28th/29th ferrying a battalion of 850 French troops from shore to ship, before facing a long day of air attacks in which sixteen near-misses damaged *Arab*'s rudder and propeller and cracked her main engine castings. Stannard had to find shelter by running *Arab* under the cover of some cliffs. The air attacks continued next day. Stannard took his own crew and the crew of the damaged trawler *Gaul* ashore and set up an anti-aircraft gun position on the cliffs, where he beat off a succession of dive-bombing attacks. The next morning, many of the men, including Stannard, were suffering from frost-bitten feet and Stannard himself was wounded by a bullet. However, when a bomb hit the trawler *Aston Villa* and set her on fire, Stannard went back on board *Arab* and had moved her about 100 yards, just far enough off, before *Aston Villa* blew up.

At last, on 2nd May, when the Namsos evacuation was almost complete, they were ordered to leave and Stannard set *Arab* with her damaged engines gingerly going down the fjord. They had barely cleared the entrance by daybreak when a Heinkel 111 bomber appeared and flew over them. Its pilot, as Stannard said later, 'appeared to be a novice' and signalled *Arab* to 'steer east (i.e. back to Namsos) or be sunk'. Stannard flashed back what he called 'a suitable answer in reply'. The Heinkel then began a series of ineffective strafing runs on *Arab*. Stannard held his fire until the unwary pilot made a pass, banking over them at a range of 800 yards. *Arab* opened fire with every gun and, after the long and grim ordeal they had endured, her people had the satisfaction of seeing the bomber crash into the sea. Stannard then brought *Arab* safely home in spite of her damaged engines. As his citation of 16th August 1940 said, 'his continuous gallantry in the presence of the enemy was magnificent and his enterprise and resource not only caused losses to the Germans but saved his ship and many lives'. *Arab* had survived thirty-one air attacks in five days at Namsos, and in a way it was appropriate that when Stannard went to Buckingham Palace to receive his Cross from King George VI on 3rd September 1940, the first anniversary of the war, the ceremony was switched from the quadrangle to the great hall - because of an air-raid.

He was mentioned in despatches in December 1940 for gallantry in command of *Arab* during an air-raid on a convoy he was escorting. King Haakon awarded him the Norwegian War Cross in 1942 and he was made a Member of the Hon. Company of Master Mariners in 1943.

After *Arab*, Stannard was promoted Lieutenant-Commander RNR on 29th June 1940 and commanded *Ramsay*, one of the fifty 'gift-horse' ex-American destroyers in 1941. In May 1943 he was back at Buckingham Palace, to receive from the Queen a DSO for his part as Captain of the destroyer *Vimy*, which with *Beverly* sank U.18 on 4th February 1943 in the Atlantic.

Richard Been Stannard was the first RNR VC winner of the Second World War and he was a man in the great tradition of all the professional Merchant Service seamen who have served with such distinction under the Crown. He was born on 21st August 1902 at Blyth, Northumberland, one of three sons of Captain George Davis Stannard, master mariner, and Elizabeth Jane (née Knowles). Captain Stannard's ship *Mount Oswald* was lost with all hands on a voyage from Baltimore in February 1912, and Richard and his brothers went to the Royal Naval Merchant School (in Essex, and later in Wokingham, Berkshire) which was founded in 1827 for the orphans of merchant seamen. Stannard was captain of the school and in 1943, as a VC and one of its most famous 'old boys', he sponsored a £1 million appeal for the school.

Stannard went to sea as an apprentice in the Port Line ship *Port Victor* in 1918 and advanced from Fourth to Second Officer from 1922 to 1928. In March 1929 he joined the Orient Line and also became a Probationary Sub-Lieutenant in the RNR. He was promoted Lieutenant RNR in 1932 and Second Officer in the Orient Line in 1937. After *Arab* and *Vimy*, he commanded *Peacock*, *Prince Henry* and *Stanley*. He was promoted Commander RNR on 30th June 1947 and left the Reserve in September, rejoining the Orient Line as Chief Officer, and serving as Staff Commander in 1949, Captain RNR in May 1952, and Marine Superintendent of the Orient Line in Sydney, New South Wales, in 1955. In 1960 he became Marine Superintendent of the P&O Orient Lines of Australia.

In 1928 at West Ham he married Phyllis May (née Tomkin), daughter of G.P. Tomkin, printer, of Leytonstone, Essex, and they had two daughters. Captain Stannard lived in Balmoral Heights, Sydney, New South Wales, where he died on 22nd July 1977.

Donald Macintyre, *Narvik* (London: Evans Bros, 1959).

188

Jack Foreman Mantle:
Portland, July 1940

Of all the VCs won by the Navy, only one was awarded for an act of gallantry in the United Kingdom itself. By July 1940, the Battle of France was over and, as Churchill said, the Battle of Britain was just beginning. Soon, Messerschmitt Me109s, Dornier bombers and Junkers Ju 87 Stuka dive-bombers, operating from airfields in France, less than an hour's flying time away, were raiding and strafing towns, harbours and installations all along the south coast. On 4th July the C-in-C Portsmouth, Admiral Sir William James, wrote that 'Bombing has started in earnest and Portland has had a bad time from the dive-bombers, and we have lost six ships out of one convoy.' On the same day as Admiral James was writing, a force of some twenty Stukas raided Portland and attacked the 5,500-ton armed merchant cruiser *Foylebank* in the harbour.

Foylebank's starboard 20-mm pompom was manned by Leading Seaman Jack Mantle, a notable gunner, who was already about to be mentioned in despatches (on 11th July) for his gallantry while serving in the Naval Control Service in the Thames; he was one of the first naval gunners to bring down an enemy aircraft on convoy protection service, whilst handling a Lewis gun on board a French ship. Early in the action on 4th July, Mantle had his left leg shattered by the blast from a bomb exploding near by, but he remained at his gun, and when electric power in *Foylebank* failed he went on training and firing the gun by hand. He was wounded again many times but continued to fire the gun. As his citation said, 'Between his bursts of fire he had time to reflect on the grievous injuries of which he was soon to die; but his great courage bore him up till the end of the fight when he fell by the gun he had so valiantly served.'

Mantle's gallantry had been noted, and although *Foylebank* was sunk, her commanding officer Captain Wilson sent in a report on the conduct of her crew which, as Admiral James wrote, 'would gladden your heart. I am recommending a Leading Seaman, Mantle, who behaved too magnificently for words and died at his gun, for the Victoria Cross.' The posthumus award was gazetted on 3rd September 1940, to Admiral James's delight. The Cross was presented to Mantle's parents by King George VI at the Palace in June 1941.

When those who knew Mantle were interviewed later, they seemed surprised that he had won the VC. 'Jack didn't seem to be the heroic type,' his mother said:

He was so gentle that we all used to say he ought to have changed places with his eldest sister, who is the toughest of the family. He was such a quiet, earnest boy. He never was brilliant at school. He had an intense dislike of pain. He was always afraid of the dentist.

What he liked most as a youngster were days in the country with the Boy Scouts.

Jack Foreman Mantle was born on 12th April 1917 at 11 Harvard Mansions, St John's Hill, Wandsworth, London, the second child of six children (and second of three sons) of Lisle John Foreman Mantle, an insurance company claims assessor, and Jennie May (née Jackson). He went to school at Taunton's, Southampton, where the family moved and his father worked in the Borough Engineer's office. After leaving school, he worked on a farm for a year, thinking of following his elder brother Peter who was farming in New Zealand, but then joined the Navy as a Boy Second Class when he was sixteen, on 2nd May 1933. He was rated Able Seaman on 12th October 1936 and Acting Leading Seaman on 1st February 1940. As his mother said, 'he took to the sea at once, and became a regular swot and studied to get on'. He served in the cruiser *Decoy* before the war, on the China Station, and during the Italian-Abyssinian confrontation of 1938.

He was buried in the RN Cemetery at Portland. In 1954 an appeal was launched to raise £2,500 to build two cottages in his memory on Portland Hill, to be occupied by ex-naval men, but only £500 was collected and it was spent instead on a sun lodge for the patients in the grounds of Portland Hospital. Jack Mantle never married.

Admiral Sir William James, *The Portsmouth Letters* (London: Macmillan, 1946).

Edward Stephen Fogarty Fegen:
Atlantic, November 1940

On the afternoon of 5th November 1940, convoy HX84 was in mid-Atlantic, homeward bound from Halifax to the United Kingdom. The thirty-seven ships were disposed in nine columns, with the Commodore's ship *Cornish City* leading the fifth column, and the convoy's sole escort, HMS *Jervis Bay* (Captain E.S.F. Fegen), a 14,000-ton ex-Aberdeen and Commonwealth Line ship converted into an armed merchant cruiser, in the centre of the convoy, between the fourth and fifth columns.

It was a fine autumn afternoon, with late sunshine, a smooth sea and good visibility. At about 3.40 pm the *Rangitiki*, leading the sixth column, reported smoke bearing north-east. At 5 pm the *Empire Penguin*, leading the fourth column, signalled that she had sighted a ship bearing almost due north, heading towards the convoy. The ship had also been sighted from *Jervis Bay*, which signalled to the

Admiralty six minutes later giving the strange ship's bearing, range, course and position, and also warned the convoy to prepare to scatter.

The ship was the 10,000-ton commerce-raiding pocket battleship *Admiral Scheer* (Kapitan Theodor Krancke), armed with six 11-inch and eight 5.9-inch guns. *Scheer* closed the convoy and at 5.10 pm opened fire at a range of 17,000 yards, her first two salvoes pitching in the middle of the convoy lanes. Although *Jervis Bay's* seven 6-inch guns had been made when Victoria was on the throne, had a maximum problematical range of about 10,000 yards and it was unlikely *Jervis Bay* would ever get within range of her enemy, Fegen hauled out of line and headed straight for *Scheer*, opening fire as he cleared the last column. Behind *Jervis Bay*, the convoy began to scatter under orders from the Commodore, laying a covering smoke-screen from floats dropped as the ships retired.

Scheer hit *Jervis Bay* with her third salvo and from then on it was not a battle but a massacre. *Jervis Bay* was hit on the bridge, setting it on fire, and shattering Fegen's right arm. Her fire control, range-finder, steering gear and wireless were put out of action. Fegen moved for a time to the after bridge, and then went back to the remains of the fore bridge. After that, as one of his officers said later, 'we did not see him again'. *Jervis Bay* was hit repeatedly on her superstructure, her hull was holed in several places, and major fires started down below. However, her guns continued to fire. Her ensign was shot away but, in an episode of pure Elizabethan drama, a sailor climbed the shattered flagstaff and nailed another to it, which was still flying as *Jervis Bay* went down.

Jervis Bay was last seen by the convoy at about 7 pm burning but still afloat. She did not in fact sink until almost 8 pm, nearly three hours after *Scheer* had first attacked. This precious delay saved the convoy, who were separately steaming south-east, south, and west. *Scheer* headed east and then south to skirt the smoke-screen, but most of her prey had escaped. The Commodore's ship, heading west, heard several heavy explosions and saw gunfire flashes to the south in the moonlight, until about 10.30 pm. In the end *Scheer* sank five ships totalling 33,331 tons. The tanker *San Demetrio* was shelled and abandoned, but was reboarded two days later by a boat-load of her own survivors, who, amazingly, brought her back to the United Kingdom. Thirty-one ships of the convoy escaped, three of them back to Canada, and the rest to the UK. Of *Jervis Bay's* complement of 254 officers and men (some Regulars of the Royal and Royal Canadian Navies, some 'hostilities-only', and some Merchant Navy) the Swedish *Stureholm* picked up 68–3 of whom were found to be dead. Fegen himself was not among them.

When the survivors reached safety and told their experiences, the story of *Jervis Bay* thrilled the free world. It became one of the most famous naval sagas of all time, told and retold, commemorated in song, in verse and on film. 'If ever a ship deserved a VC,' said *The Times*, 'that ship is surely the *Jervis Bay*.' 'There she rode like a hero,' said Captain Olander of *Stureholm*. Fegen's posthumous Cross was announced on 17th November and gazetted on the 22nd.

Edward Stephen Fogarty Fegen was the son and grandson of naval officers. He was born on 8th October 1891, at 42 Nightingale Road, Southsea, the son of Commander (later Vice-Admiral) Frederick Fogarty Fegen and Catherine Mary (née Crewse), of Ballinlonty, Co. Tipperary. He went to Osborne and Dartmouth and served at sea throughout the Great War, his active service in fact beginning very early in the war when his ship, the destroyer *Amphion*, was mined and sunk on 5th August 1914. His service was divided between sea-time in destroyers and shore-time in training establishments for young officers and men. He was a Divisional Officer at the boys' training ship *Colossus* at Devonport and at Dartmouth. He was promoted Commander on 30th June 1926 and went out to Australia as commander of the Royal Australian Navy's College at, by a coincidence, Jervis Bay. He won Lloyd's Medal for lifesaving at sea by putting his ship alongside a burning oiler and, as Commander of the cruiser *Suffolk* on the China Station in 1930-32, won a Dutch lifesaving medal and an Admiralty commendation for his handling of the rescue of the crew of the steamer *Hedwig*, aground on the Patras Reef in the South China Sea. He also commanded the cruisers *Dauntless*, *Dragon* and *Curlew* in the Reserve Fleet, had an appointment in the Anti-Submarine Division of the Admiralty and one on the staff at Chatham before becoming Agar's executive officer in the cruiser *Emerald* in 1939. In March 1940 he left to take command of *Jervis Bay*.

Fegen's Victoria Cross was presented to his sister Miss M.C. Fegen by King George VI at Buckingham Palace on 12th June 1941. Memorials to Fegen were set up all over the world: a sundial in Hamilton, Bermuda, a 12-foot column in the grounds of a hospital at St John, New Brunswick, and a wreath of copper and gold laurel leaves with an inscription at the Seamen's Institute in Wellington, New Zealand.

George Pollock, *The Jervis Bay* (London: Kimber 1958).
Lieut. Anthony Thwaite RNVR *The Jervis Bay and Other Poems* (London: Putnam, 1943).
'Personal Tribute', by A.S.W.A., *The Times*, 19th November 1940.
'Suicide – But Magnificent', *Sunday Graphic*, 17th November 1940 (AB. Lane's account).
'HMS *Jervis Bay* Engages Raider': Imperial War Museum tapes, Chief Wireless Officer and Captain of SS *Rangitiki*, No. 3425; Dr Firth, passenger in *Rangitiki*, Nos. 3588-90, recorded 20th November 1940; Second Officer Hawkins of *San Demetrio*, No. 3425, recorded 17th November 1940.

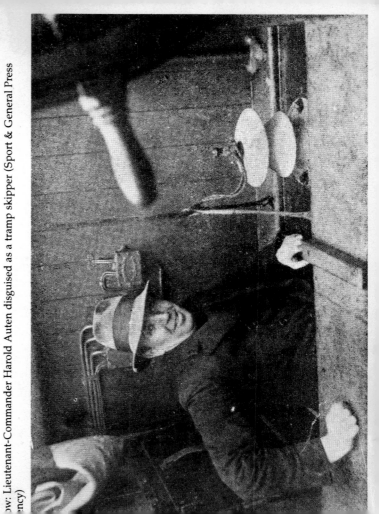

Above left: Edward Bamford (RM Historical Photo Library)

Above right: Admiral V.A.C. Crutchley at the opening of the VC and GC Exhibition at the Imperial War Museum in 1970, fifty-two years after he himself had won his VC (Central Press)

Below: Lieutenant-Commander Harold Auten disguised as a tramp skipper (Sport & General Press Agency)

A.W.S. Agar (Imperial War Museum)

A Buckingham Palace garden party for VC winners, 26 June 1920. From left to right are Lieutenant P. T. Dean, Lieutenant G.C. Steele, Lieutenant A.W.S. Agar, Admiral of the Fleet Sir Arthur Wilson and Commander Unwin (Imperial War Museum).

Kenneth Campbell:
Brest, April 1941

At first light on 6th April 1941, a single Beaufort torpedo bomber flew in low over the quays and docks of the harbour at Brest, the great naval base on the north coast of France. Armed with one 18-inch torpedo, the Beaufort's target was the 32,000-ton German battlecruiser *Gneisenau*, which had come out of dry dock the previous day and was lying alongside the fitting-out jetty in the Rade Abri.

The Germans had been well aware of their vulnerability to air attack and the great ship was formidably defended. She lay alongside the wall on the north side of the harbour, protected by a stone mole which curved round from the west. A total of 270 anti-aircraft guns were placed in batteries on the rising ground behind the ship, on two arms of land which encircled the outer harbour and on board three anti-aircraft 'flak' ships moored near the mole. Even if an aircraft managed to penetrate the flak barrage to make the necessary low-level attack, it would be unlikely to be able to pull up in time to avoid the rising ground.

The Beaufort, piloted by Flying Officer Kenneth Campbell RAFVR, of 22 Squadron Coastal Command, was the only one of six to reach the target. Three had been bogged down by heavy ground on the airfield and never took off. A fourth lost its way in the early-morning haze over the Channel, and a fifth went into the attack a few minutes too late, when the gunners had been thoroughly aroused. The pilot's account gives some idea of what Campbell and his crew endured. He came under fire from shore batteries as he crossed the spit of land at the south-west corner of the harbour. Going low, a few feet above the water, towards the mole protecting the Rade Abri, behind which the *Gneisenau* lay, he passed the three flak ships and as he neared the Mole he came under fire from batteries all round the harbour: 'Continuous streams of fire seemed to be coming from every direction. It was by far the worst flak I have ever encountered. When I was nearly up to the Mole I saw that the battlecruiser herself was completely hidden from me by a bank of haze. I therefore turned away to the east and climbed into cloud.'

Campbell had known of the dangers but, as his citation said, despising the heavy odds, he went cheerfully and resolutely to the task. His Beaufort crashed or was shot down, and he and his crew of three were all killed. Reconnaissance next day showed that *Gneisenau* had been moved back into dry-dock, but it was some months before it was confirmed that Campbell's torpedo had hit *Gneisenau* aft, causing extensive damage and flooding. Because of the delay in finding out the facts, the VC was not gazetted until 13th

193

March 1942, being presented by the King to Campbell's parents on 23rd June.

The intention of the German Kriegsmarine had been for *Gneisenau* and her sister ship *Scharnhorst*, also at Brest, to join *Bismarck* and *Prinz Eugen* at sea in May - with incalculable effects on the Battle of the Atlantic and the war as a whole. Campbell's attack and later successful bombings by the RAF prevented them. Campbell's torpedo therefore had as much effect on the progress of the war at sea as a heavy ship engagement.

Kenneth Campbell was a 'weekend' flyer in peacetime, who joined the RAFVR just as other men who were 'weekend' sailors joined the RNVR. His crew had also joined 'for the duration'. His Navigator, Sergeant James Scott, was a nineteen-year-old Canadian from Toronto who joined up from school; his Wireless Operator, Sergeant W. Mullis, was a farmer from Larkhall near Bath, Somerset; and his Air Gunner, Sergeant R.W. Hillman, from Edmonton, in London, had driven a car for a doctor in Barnsley, in Yorkshire. All four bodies were recovered by the Germans and buried with full military honours in the Kerfautras Cemetery, Lambezellec, Brest.

Campbell was born on 21st April 1917 at Bank of Scotland House, Saltcoats, Ayr, the son of James Campbell, a solicitor and joint town clerk, and Jane Mather Morton (née Highet). He went to Sedbergh School and then to Clare College, Cambridge, where he read chemistry. He joined the Cambridge University Air Squadron in 1937 and was commissioned as a Pilot Officer in the RAFVR on 23rd August 1938 (Official No. 72446).

Campbell was promoted to Flying Officer on 23rd February 1940 and had an energetic war. Serving in 2 Squadron, he and his crew made a moonlight torpedo attack on a 3,000-ton German supply ship and sank her. On another operation off the Dutch coast he attacked a small ship with bombs in spite of an intense fire from escorting E-boats and went on to strafe some gun positions on the shore from low level. He was intercepted by two Messerschmitt Me 110 fighters and his aircraft was badly damaged. The Wireless Operator and Campbell himself were wounded, the hydraulics shot away and the gun-turret put out of action. Campbell successfully crash-landed the aircraft on their return. His was the first VC for the RAFVR and for Coastal Command.

Coastal Command (London: HMSO, 1943).

Alfred Edward Sephton:
Mediterranean, South of Crete, May 1941

'We must not let the army down,' Admiral Cunningham signalled his Mediterranean Fleet before the evacuation from Crete in May 1941. When his staff demurred at the likely cost in ships, he said: 'It takes the Navy three years to build a ship. It would take three hundred to rebuild a tradition.' To uphold that tradition, Cunningham's fleet had already suffered a long and terrible casualty list of ships sunk or damaged by air attack. He was speaking at a time when the Luftwaffe had just knocked out the fleet's one aircraft carrier, *Formidable*, and the ships would have to do the best they could with their own anti-aircraft fire.

There were many acts of heroism on board Cunningham's ships off Crete, and one which won the Victoria Cross. On 18th May, south of Crete, the hospital ship *Aba* signalled that she was under attack from Stuka dive-bombers (although red crosses were painted quite visibly on her sides) and the cruiser *Coventry* (Lieutenant-Commander Dalrymple-Hay) was sent to help her.

Coventry was an old First World War light cruiser which had been converted as an anti-aircraft ship; with ten 4-inch high-angled guns and multitudes of pompoms and Oerlikons, she was a floating flak battery. Her guns were directed on to their targets by two director-towers, whose crews observed the flight of enemy aircraft and predicted their height, speed, course, range and rate of change of bearing, passing the information to the guns' crews.

The forward director was on top of the foremast tripod and the after one in a tower just aft of the mainmast. Both were extremely exposed positions and needed highly trained and disciplined crews to keep on operating their instruments and passing information to the guns during an action. The officer in charge of one director was Lieutenant J.M.Robb, with Chief Petty Officer Davenport, Petty Officer Alfred Edward Sephton, Able Seaman Stanley Fisher and Marine Corporal Bill Symmons.

As *Coventry* closed *Aba*, they could see the hospital ship under attack and more Stukas were reported approaching on the radar screens. Some of the dive-bombers broke off their attack on *Aba* and went for *Coventry* herself. Attacking in pairs, the Stukas swooped down like great black hawks, with that characteristic moaning sound which chilled the blood. Dalrymple-Hay threw his ship violently from side to side, weaving in and out of the bomb bursts, whilst every gun that would bear put up a tremendous barrage of steel. One Stuka penetrated the barrage and, flattening out over *Coventry*, raked her upper decks, bridge and director-towers with machine-gun fire. One burst smashed into Lieutenant Robb's director and mortally wounded Petty Officer Sephton. A bullet actually passed through his body and injured A.B. Fisher sitting immediately behind him. Though in great pain, losing blood rapidly, and partially blinded, Sephton was director layer and, as one of the team, stuck to his instruments and carried out his duties until the attack was over. *Coventry* was not hit during that attack and Cunningham himself later wrote that 'Sephton's action may well have saved the *Coventry* and the *Aba*.'

After the action Sephton insisted that Fisher be carried down out of the director tower first. He himself was taken to the sick-bay, where he died of his injuries next day and was buried at sea. As his citation said, 'Until his death his valiant and cheerful spirit gave heart to the wounded. His high example inspired his ship-mates and will live in their memory.' His posthumous VC was gazetted on 2nd December 1941 and the Cross was presented to his parents by King George VI at an Investiture at Buckingham Palace on 23rd June 1942.

Alfred Edward Sephton was born on 19th April 1911 at 30 Collier Street, Warrington, Lancashire, one of six children of Alfred Joseph Sephton, a journeyman blacksmith, and Annie (née Ryder). The family moved to Wolverhampton and he went to the Dudley Road Council School there. He joined the Navy in 1927 as a Boy. A regular rating, as his mother said, 'he was wrapped up in the Navy'. He was rated Petty Officer on 1st May 1939. He was a diver, a good footballer, a well-liked and respected shipmate, and a very competent and conscientious rating.

C.E. Lucas-Phillips, *Victoria Cross Battles of the Second World War*, Chapter 2, 'Ordeal in Crete' (London: Heinemann, 1973)

Malcolm David Wanklyn:
Mediterranean, South of Sicily, May 1941

'The ship and her company are gone, but the example and the inspiration remain.' Thus, while admitting that 'it was seldom proper to draw distinction between different services rendered in the course of naval duty', the Admiralty ended their statement of 22nd August 1942, announcing the loss of the submarine *Upholder* with her Captain, Lieutenant-Commander M.D. Wanklyn VC, DSO, and his crew.

So passed a submariner who had become a naval celebrity. His name was known to thousands who had only the haziest notion of what a submarine was, and his death came as a personal loss. The war correspondent Anthony Kimmins called him 'one of the greatest men I ever met'. The Admiral Submarines, Sir Max Horton, wrote to his widow, 'his name, qualities and record will remain always in the front of our memories as an example of a splendid man, of whom the Royal Navy and the Submarine Service are most justly proud.'

Yet, there was a time when Wanklyn - 'Wanks' as he was known - was not hitting targets and the Captain (S) at Malta, 'Shrimp' Simpson, had serious doubts about his competence and his marksmanship. *Upholder*, a 700-ton U-Class submarine, armed with eight torpedoes and a 12-pounder gun, with a crew of four officers and twenty-eight men, was built at Barrow-in-Furness, commissioned in December 1940 and joined the Malta Submarine Force, going on her first patrol in January 1941.

Wanklyn's first five patrols had negligible success. It was not until his sixth patrol in April, in the Lampedusa Channel, that Wanklyn got his eye in and sank three transports, one of them the 8,000-ton *Leverkusen*. On 24th May, during his next patrol, Wanklyn performed the exploit which was later picked out for his VC.

At dawn that day four large ocean liners - *Conte Rosso*, *Marco Polo*, *Victoria* and *Esperia* - all packed with troop reinforcements for Rommel in Libya, had sailed from Naples escorted by four destroyers. By that evening they had cleared the Straits of Messina and were heading at high speed for Tripoli. The sun had set, the light was fading, and Wanklyn was preparing to surface for the nightly battery charge when he noticed an aircraft to the north-west. This could well be an escort. Wanklyn stayed submerged and steered for the bearing. *Upholder's* listening gear was defective, so that Wanklyn was blind whenever the periscope was down, and the submarine was very nearly run down by a destroyer as she penetrated the screen. When Wanklyn next put the periscope up he saw the silhouette of a very large ship with two funnels against the afterglow of the sunset. He fired two torpedoes, which were sighted by the close escort leader in the destroyer *Freccia*, who fired a Very alarm light. But it was too late for the 17,879-ton *Conte Rosso*, which sank with 2,800 men on board, 1,300 of them being drowned. *Upholder* then endured a sharp counter-attack, in which thirty-seven depth-charges were dropped in twenty minutes, before getting clear.

As the year of 1941 went on, Wanklyn developed into one of the deadliest killers the submarine service had ever seen. His VC was gazetted on 16th December 1941 and he also won a DSO and two Bars. By the end, he had made 36 attacks, of which 23 were successful, and had sunk nearly 140,000 tons of enemy shipping, including a destroyer, the Italian U-boats *Ammiraglio St Bon* and *Tricheco*, and over a dozen assorted troopships, tankers, supply and store ships. He sank two 20,000-ton troopships, the *Oceania* and the *Neptunia*, in one evening attack on 16th September 1941, hitting them both with one salvo.

Upholder sailed from Malta for her twenty-fifth patrol, and her last before she was due to go home for refit, on 6th April 1942. She successfully landed a clandestine agent on the North African coast, and kept a rendezvous with *Unbeaten* on the 11th. On the 14th, *Urge* heard heavy prolonged depth-charging from the area off Tripoli where *Upholder* should have been. On the 18th the Italians claimed that one of their torpedo boats had sunk a British submarine. *Upholder* was overdue, presumed lost. It had been her first and only commission. Wanklyn had been her first and only commander.

Although 'Wanks' had a somewhat piratical appearance, with his lean figure, beaked nose and biblical black beard, he was a quiet, unassuming man, who wore his fame very lightly. He had a good mathematical brain, was a cool calculator of chances and he had the strength of character to withstand the pressures of both early failure and later success. He was a reassuring leader, imperturbable under depth-charging, and had developed to an unusual degree the submarine CO's essential gift of the 'periscope eye', the ability to see and remember the contents of a whole room by looking through the keyhole. He was a successful killer and yet, as Kimmins noticed, 'He hated killing, and when he had sunk a supply ship he would toss and turn in his bunk for nights afterwards, trying to shut out the picture of the death and suffering he had caused.'

Wanklyn was an expert at dry-fly fishing, a sport he adored, and first met his wife during a fishing holiday in Scotland. She was Elspeth, known as Betty, daughter of James Kinloch of Ellangowan, Meigle, Perthshire, and they were married at Holy Trinity, Sliema, Malta, on 5th May 1938. They had a son, Ian, who was present, aged three and a half, with his mother and grandmother for the presentation of his father's Victoria Cross by the King at Buckingham Palace on 4th March 1943 (and in due course, joined the Navy himself).

Malcolm David Wanklyn was born on 28th June 1911 in Calcutta, the third son of Mr and Mrs W. L. Wanklyn. He went to Parkfield Preparatory School, (where he is supposed to have been nicknamed 'Mouse'), near Haywards Heath, Sussex and went to Dartmouth in January 1925. He passed out fifth in his term in the summer of 1928, gaining second prize for science, and then went to the *Marlborough*, was promoted Midshipman on 1st May 1929 and became senior Midshipman in the battlecruiser *Renown*. He took five first class passes in his examinations for Lieutenant, was confirmed Sub-Lieutenant on 1st January 1932 and Lieutenant on 1st February 1933. He joined the Submarine Service in May and was fourth hand in *Oberon* in the Mediterranean. From October 1934 until August 1939, he was in L.56 as Third Hand, and in H.50, *Porpoise* and *Otway* as First Lieutenant. His first command was H.31, in January 1940. He was appointed in command of *Upholder* in August 1940.

Kenneth Hare-Scott, *For Valour*, 'Malcolm David Wanklyn' (London: Peter Garnett, 1949).

Anthony Kimmins, *Half Time*, 'A Patrol with Wanklyn' (London: Heinemann, 1947).

Eugene Esmonde:
Straits of Dover, February 1942

'In my opinion,' Admiral Sir Bertram Ramsay, Flag Officer Dover, signalled to the Admiralty, 'the gallant sortie of these six Swordfish constitutes one of the finest exhibitions of self-sacrifice and devotion to duty that the war has yet witnessed.' But a day later *The Times* was thundering, 'Vice-Admiral Ciliax has succeeded where the Duke of Medina Sidonia failed. Nothing more mortifying to the pride of sea-power has happened in home waters since the seventeenth century.'

The gallantry and the mortification were both results of the escape of the German battlecruisers *Scharnhorst* and *Gneisenau* and the heavy cruiser *Prinz Eugen* from Brest and their dash through the Straits of Dover back to Germany in February 1942. The battlecruisers had been at Brest, and under frequent air attacks, since March 1941. They had been joined by *Prinz Eugen* in June, after her voyage with *Bismarck*. It was Hitler himself, obsessed with the notion of an Allied attack on Norway, who had ordered the Kriegsmarine to bring the ships back to Germany, or have them reduced to hulks where they lay, and their crews dispersed into the Luftwaffe. Allied Intelligence had been reporting German plans to break out for months past. Their route was anticipated. Some even guessed the date, but few the *time of day*; it was not thought that Ciliax, the German fleet commander, would risk passing Dover in broad daylight.

Operational plans were laid to intercept the ships, but when they did make their break on the night of 11th/12th February, a combination of bad luck, bad briefing, bad practice and bad weather sent almost everything awry. Attempts were made, by destroyer, motor torpedo boat, bomber and torpedo-bomber, to sink or hinder the German ships, but they were all hurriedly mounted and not properly co-ordinated. The bravest and most hopeless of all was the gallant sortie by six Swordfish torpedo-bombers of 825 Squadron, Fleet Air Arm.

Lieutenant-Commander Eugene Esmonde, the CO of 825, who led the Swordfish, had an unusual background for a Fleet Air Arm pilot. He came from an Irish Roman Catholic family of Dromenagh, Borrisokane, Co. Tipperary. A great-uncle, Captain Thomas Esmonde, of the 18th Royal Irish Regiment, won a VC for gallantry at the attack on the Redan, Sebastopol, in June 1855. Eugene and his twin brother James were born on 1st March 1909, at Huthwaite House, Thurgoland, Wortley, Yorkshire, sons of Dr John Esmonde MP, and his second wife, Eiliy Josephine (née O'Sullivan). (Dr Esmonde, MP for North Tipperary, who practised medicine in England for some twenty-four years, had a total of eight sons and three daughters.) Eugene went to Wimbledon College, the school run by Jesuits in South London, and then studied at St Peter's College, Freshfield, Liverpool, and Burn Hall, Durham, with the intention of joining St Joseph's Foreign Missionary Society of Mill Hill, London, a religious society founded by His Eminence Herbert Vaughan in 1866.

Something made Esmonde change his vocation, for he was commissioned as a Pilot Officer in the RAF on 28th December 1928 and served a short service engagement of five years. On leaving the RAF he joined Imperial Airways as a First Officer on 9th August 1934. Those were the pioneering days of commercial aviation and Esmonde flew on early mail services from London to Glasgow and other cities, later on routes to the Continent, and, as Imperial Airways expanded its service, to the Middle East and across India. In 1935 he flew on a regular service between Rangoon and Mandalay in Burma, and survived a serious accident when his aircraft crashed into the Irrawaddy. He was promoted to Captain on 3rd July 1937 and was one of the first to fly the giant flying boats which introduced the first airmail service between the United Kingdom and Australia. He might have made a career with the air-line, but on 3rd May 1939, he resigned to take up a commission as a Lieutenant-Commander in the Fleet Air Arm.

Esmonde was in action several times before his death, being a survivor of the carrier *Courageous* when she was torpedoed and sunk in the Western Approaches on 17th September 1939, and in *Victorious* for the action against *Bismarck* in May 1941. At 10 pm on the evening of 24th May, he led a strike of nine Swordfish aircraft, armed with torpedoes, to make a 120-mile flight in foul weather and into head-winds to attack *Bismarck*. As Esmonde's aircraft took off and flew away into the darkening sky there were not a few in *Victorious* who thought that that would be the last of them.

Guided by his own radar and directions from the cruiser *Norfolk*, Esmonde found *Bismarck* (in spite of having come down out of cloud prematurely, to sight the US Coast Guard cutter *Modoc*). However, *Bismarck* herself was also in sight only eight miles away, with all her gunners alert. Esmonde's aircraft attacked through intense AA fire and scored one hit, amidships on the starboard side. The crews' return was as hazardous as the attack. The radio beacon failed and in the pitch dark they overran *Victorious*, which ignored the dangers from U-boats and shone every possible light. Esmonde's men eventually landed again at 2 am in driving rain and spray. For his part in the *Bismarck* action, Esmonde was awarded the

DSO and received it from King George VI at Buckingham Palace on 11th February 1942. That evening he went down to Manston, in Kent, where his squadron had been moved, specifically in case the German ships broke out. It was well after eleven the next morning, 12th February, before it was definitely confirmed that the German ships were out. It was decided to attack with Esmonde's six Swordfish - a suicidal course in broad daylight, without adequate fighter cover, which Esmonde had been promised. He took off at 12.25 pm, spurred by reports that the enemy were approaching the straits of Dover. By 12.29 pm only ten Spitfires of 72 Squadron, under Squadron Leader B. Kingcombe, had arrived. Esmonde's Swordfish had a maximum loaded speed of 90 knots. The ships were making 27. Unless he hurried, Esmonde would never catch them. He decided not to wait and took departure at 12.30 pm. In the event, the other four fighter squadrons never did join him, although they all did their best in poor visibility (and with very incomplete briefing).

Esmonde was well aware of his likely fate. The station commander at Manston saw his face when he wished him luck: 'Although his mouth twitched automatically into the semblance of a grin and his arm lifted in a vague salute, he barely recognised me. He knew what he was going into. But it was his duty. His face was tense and white. It was the face of a man already dead. It shocked me as nothing has ever done since.'

Esmonde's six Swordfish, flying in two 'vics' of three aircraft each, sighted the German ships about ten miles north of Calais. They were already themselves under fierce attack from Me 109s and Focke-wulfe Fw 190 fighters. In a rare bout of co-operation with the Kriegsmarine, the Luftwaffe had provided massive fighter cover for the ships. Kingcombe's Spitfires fought a succession of dog-fights to protect Esmonde, but the Swordfish had to attack through a barrage of fire from the 3 heavy ships, 6 destroyers, 34 E-boats and a cluster of flak ships, and were constantly harassed by fighters above them. The Swordfish's slow speed baffled the German fighter pilots, who overshot frequently and had to try attacking from astern. The Swordfish observers then stood up in their cockpits and turned round, to spot the closing fighters and shout warnings to the pilots.

Esmonde's own Swordfish was hit crossing the destroyer screen and hit again approaching *Prinz Eugen*. Just after launching its torpedo, the Swordfish was shot down, followed by the two other Swordfish of his flight. Kingcombe saw them from above: 'The Germans were firing heavy guns which threw up mountains of spray like water spouts. The Swordfish flew straight into them. Mostly they were caught by *Prinz Eugen's* flak and I saw the leader and two others go into the drink.' *Prinz Eugen* evaded the torpedo. Of the other 'vic' of three, led by Lieutenant Thompson, all the Swordfish were shot down and their crews killed. Five men of

Esmonde's flight survived, four of them wounded. The four officers received the DSO, the sole rating received the CGM.

Esmonde's posthumous VC was gazetted on 3rd March 1942. His mother, a widow, was wheeled into the Investiture at Buckingham Palace on 17th March by two of her four serving sons, Captain Patrick Esmonde and Pilot Officer Owen Esmonde. Her son's body was recovered from the Medway the following month and buried on 30th April in the Roman Catholic section of Woodlands Cemetery, Gillingham, Kent.

The Escape of the Scharnhorst and Gneisenau, Report of the Board of Enquiry presided over by Mr Justice Bucknill, Cmd. 6775 (London: HMSO, 1946).

John Deane Potter, *Fiasco* (London: Heinemann, 1970).
Terence Robertson, *Channel Dash* (London: Evans Bros., 1958).
'Attack on German Battleships', Imperial War Museum Tape No. 26153, Bk 4; personal narrative by Korvetten Kapitan Friehse, gunnery officer of *Prinz Eugen*, recorded 15th February 1960; talk by Lt.-Cdr Pumphrey, Tape No. 4123, recorded 13th February 1942.

Thomas Wilkinson:
Java Sea, February 1942

For the Navy, as for the other Services present, the fall of Singapore was a dark and terrible episode. But even that tragedy, as so often in British military history, was illuminated by astonishing acts of individual bravery. One of them was the story of HMS *Li Wo*.

Li Wo was a 1,000-ton flat-bottomed passenger steamship built in Hong Kong in 1938 for service on the upper Yangtse River. In December 1941, after the outbreak of war against the Japanese, she was requisitioned by the Admiralty and commissioned as an auxiliary patrol vessel. She was armed with one old 4-inch gun, two machine guns and a depth-charge thrower.

On Friday, 13th February 1942, two days before the fall of Singapore, HMS *Li Wo*, commanded by Temporary Lieutenant T. Wilkinson RNR, was ordered to Batavia in Java, and sailed from Singapore that day. She had on board eighty-four officers and men, including survivors of other HM ships which had been sunk such as *Prince of Wales* and *Repulse*, men from Army and RAF units, and one civilian. They had thirteen rounds of practice ammunition for the 4-inch gun and some rounds for the machine guns.

By the afternoon of the 14th, when *Li Wo* was in the Java Sea, she had survived four air attacks, one of which was by fifty-two Japanese aircraft, but was considerably damaged. Later in the afternoon two Japanese convoys were sighted, the larger being escorted by Japanese warships, including a heavy cruiser and some destroyers. These were the advance guard of the Japanese invasion fleet heading for Sumatra. After the Japanese ships had been sighted, in the presence of the enemy, Wilkinson gathered his scratch ship's company together and told them that, rather than try and escape, he had decided to engage the convoy and fight to the last, hoping at least to inflict some damage. His decision 'drew resolute support from the whole ship's company'.

Li Wo was small but handy, with twin rudders, and Wilkinson was a superb ship-handler. The 4-inch gun, manned by volunteers, was used with such purpose that a Japanese transport was badly hit, set on fire and abandoned by her crew. *Li Wo* stayed in action against a heavy cruiser for over an hour, the convoy masking her from the fire of the warships for some time. Wilkinson tried to ram the nearest transport but eventually *Li Wo* was hit at point-blank range and sunk. Wilkinson ordered his crew to abandon ship, but himself went down with *Li Wo*. He and his crew had behaved magnificently, to set on fire a Japanese ship using only practice ammunition and machine-gun bullets. There were ten survivors, not all of whom survived captivity and came safely home in 1945.

Wilkinson was mentioned in despatches posthumously on 14th December 1945, but on 17th December 1946, a year later almost to the day, this award was cancelled and Wilkinson received a posthumous VC instead, the last of the Second World War to be gazetted. His brother, William Wilkinson, received the Cross at an Investiture at Buckingham Palace on 28th January 1947. Temporary Sub-Lieutenant R.G.G. Stanton RNR, *Li Wo's* only surviving officer, received a DSO. Temporary Lieutenant E.N. Derbridge RNZNVR, and Temporary Sub-Lieutenant J.G. Petherbridge, Malayan RNVR, were both posthumously mentioned in despatches. The gunlayer, Acting Petty Officer A.W. Thompson, got the CGM, and the port machine-gun's crew, Leading Seaman V. Spenser and Able Seaman Albert Spendlove, both got the DSM.

Thomas ('Tam') Wilkinson was a professional seaman in the great tradition of the RNR. He was born on 1st August 1898 at West Bank, Widnes, in Lancashire, the youngest of five brothers. He went to West Bank School, working as a grocer's errand boy after school hours. He left school at fourteen and joined his brothers as cabin boy and deckhand in the sailing sloop *Irene*, captained and partly owned by his father, carrying salt along the canals and the River Mersey from Northwich in Cheshire to the chemical factories in Widnes of the United Alkali Co. Ltd (later merged into ICI).

Wilkinson served in the Merchant Navy during the First World War, as quartermaster in the Blue Funnel ship *Alcinous*, employed as a troopship. He stayed at sea after the war, and went to the Far East, where he joined the Indo-China Steam Navigation Co., better known as 'Jardines', possibly in 1922. He sat for and obtained a

Master's Certificate in Liverpool in about 1936 and commanded SS *Hang Sang* on the China Coast a year later and saw the Japanese army in action during the occupation of Tsingtao in January 1938.

Years later, Tam's Chief Officer in *Hang Sang*, John Littler, remembered him

...as a ruddy-faced man of Lancashire. He did not drink, which was remarkable in China. He was tremendously keen on physical fitness and he was universally liked. He never spoke of his marriage [Wilkinson is supposed to have got married in the 1930s, and divorced]. I was aware that he had contracted TB when he first arrived in China, and that for some time he had manfully struggled to regain his health, and had succeeded. This, perhaps, would explain his abstemious and non-smoking nature. He enjoyed life immensely, read widely, was very fond of music, and liked to play the 'market' when it appeared sensible to do so. He loved to bake in the sun at a time when few dreamed of doing such a thing in the tropics.

Wilkinson was at home on leave in September 1939 but soon returned to the East. With his knowledge of Far Eastern waters, and his experience of the Japanese at war, he was commissioned in the RNR (possibly in 1940). Wilkinson did not, by upbringing, training or outlook, resemble the Regular naval officer. He had probably never had any instruction in naval tactics in his life or undergone any form of Regular naval training. Yet he fought a splendid naval action in the highest traditions of the Service. He was a Lancastrian from a working-class family, who had knocked about the China Coast for nearly twenty years, and he undoubtedly possessed powers of leadership of a very high order. He had assembled his ship's company, in the presence of the enemy, and obtained their wholehearted assent for what must have looked like, and indeed for most of them was, a suicidal course of action.

John Littler, *Naval Review*, Vol. LX (1972), 'Benbow's Column' and 'Thomas Wilkinson VC'.
A.V. Sellwood, *Stand By to Die*, (London: New English Library, 1961; White Lion, 1971).

Peter Scawen Watkinson Roberts and Thomas William Gould:

Mediterranean, North of Crete, February 1942

About midday on 16th February 1942, HM Submarine *Thrasher* (Lieutenant H.S. Mackenzie) on patrol off Suva Bay, on the north coast of Crete, torpedoed and sank an Axis supply ship of some 3,000 tons, strongly escorted by five anti-submarine vessels. The escorts counter-attacked, with support from aircraft, and dropped 33 depth-charges, some of them very close indeed. *Thrasher* survived the attacks and, that evening after dark, surfaced to recharge batteries. Later, in the early hours of the morning, when *Thrasher* altered course across the swell and began to roll more heavily, some unusual banging noises were heard from the deck above, as though some heavy object was loose and rolling about. It was found that there was a bomb, between 3 and 4 feet long, 5-6 inches in diameter, probably weighing about 100lb, lying on the submarine's casing in front of the 4-inch gun mounting.

Lieutenant P.S.W. Roberts, the First Lieutenant, and Petty Officer Gould, the Second Coxswain, volunteered to go on deck and remove the bomb. As Second Coxswain, Gould was in charge of handling wires when entering or leaving harbour and of the care and stowage of gear inside the casing (which was a light metal free-flooding structure, erected as an upper deck, on top of the submarine's pressure hull; normally there was about two or three feet of clearance between the casing and the hull, enclosing a tangle of pipes, wires and other gear).

At any moment the bomb might roll off the casing on to the saddle tank below and detonate. While Gould held the bomb still, Roberts fetched an old potato sack, which they put round the bomb and tied with a length of rope. The bomb was too heavy to be thrown clear of the saddle tanks, so they manhandled it 100 feet forward to the bows and dropped it overboard, whilst *Thrasher* went full astern to get clear.

Looking more closely at the casing they found a jagged hole in the metal and inside, another bomb, resting on top of the pressure hull. There was no possibility of handling the bomb up through the hole it had made. The only approach was through a hinged metal grating trap-door about twenty feet away. The two men lowered themselves through the trap-door and wriggled on their stomachs to where the bomb lay. If the bomb exploded they and the submarine would be lost. Furthermore, *Thrasher* was off an enemy coast, and the enemy knew there was an Allied submarine in the area. If a surface vessel or aircraft were sighted now, Mackenzie would have to dive, and the two men would be drowned.

Gould lay flat on his back with the bomb in his arms. Roberts lay in front of him, dragging him by the shoulders as he crawled along. By the faint light of a shaded torch, the two of them worked the bomb through the narrow casing, easing its weight around obstacles and up through the trap-door. Now and then, the bomb made a disconcerting twanging noise as it was moved. It was forty minutes before they had the bomb clear, and could wrap it in the sack, carry it forward and drop it over the bows like its predecessor.

Understandably, both men were recommended for and awarded the Victoria Cross, gazetted on 9th June 1942, and Roberts was invested by the King the same month.

Peter Scawen Watkinson Roberts was born on 28th July 1917 at Bessaloan, Chiltern Road, Chesham Bois, Buckinghamshire, the younger son of George Watkinson Roberts, an incorporated accountant, and Georgina Dorothy (née Tinney). He went to Falconbury School, Bexhill, and to King's School, Canterbury, before joining the Navy in September 1935 as a 'special entry' cadet (i.e. joining at seventeen years old, after public school, instead of at thirteen and going to RNC Dartmouth). He went to the training ship *Frobisher* and as a Midshipman to the cruiser *Shropshire*. He served as Sub-Lieutenant in *Saltburn* and joined the submarine service in September 1939, being promoted Lieutenant in November. He was Navigating Officer of H.32, Torpedo Officer of *Tribune* and then joined *Thrasher* as First Lieutenant in January 1941. He had already been recommended for the DSC for his distinguished conduct in *Thrasher*. The award was announced after his Victoria Cross.

Later in 1942 Roberts left *Thrasher* to do the 'periscope course' for submarine captains and, to his great disappointment, he failed. This meant the end of service in submarines, and he then went over to the other side of the fence, with appointments at *Vernon*, the torpedo and anti-submarine school at Portsmouth, and *Defiance*, the torpedo and diving school in Devonport. He was with the cruiser *Black Prince* in the Pacific in 1945–6, and saw active service again in the frigate *Cardigan Bay* in Korea in 1952–3. He retired from the Navy in 1962. His elder brother, Lieutenant James G.F.W. Roberts RN, was lost in the destroyer *Exmouth*, torpedoed and sunk in the North Sea in January 1940.

Roberts married Brigid Victoria Lethbridge at Plymouth in February 1940, and they had a son and a daughter. He lives at Membland, Newton Ferrers, in Devon.

Thomas William Gould was the only Jewish VC of the Second World War. He was born in Dover on 28th December 1914, son of Reuben Gould, who was killed in action in 1916. His mother's maiden name was Irons. She married a second time, to Petty Officer Cheeseman. Gould went to St James's School, Dover, and joined the Navy on 29th September 1933. He was an experienced submariner, having joined submarines in 1937 and served in *Regent*, *Pandora* and *Regulus*. He was rated Acting Petty Officer on 17th August 1940. On 13th January 1943 Gould was made an Honorary Freeman of his birthplace of Dover; and in March, after his Investiture at Buckingham Palace, he went home to St Albans, where he then lived, to a civic reception by the Mayor and Corporation. In 1941, in St Albans, he married Phyllis Eileen Eldridge, and they had one son, born soon after Gould's VC was awarded.

After his discharge on 21st December 1945, Gould kept up his interests in the Navy and with the Jewish community. He took part in Jewish ex-Servicemen's marches and in July 1946 was in the front row of a march of Jews through London to protest against the government's policy towards Palestine. He was Lieutenant of the Sea Cadet Corps with a local unit at Bromley in Kent, where he was then living. Gould lived in several addresses in London and in the Home Counties before moving back to Dover. He was a business consultant and for some years chief personnel manager with Great Universal Stores Ltd.

In 1943, as a VC hero, Gould was interviewed by the Marquess of Donegal, who asked him what he was thinking while busy with those bombs. Gould said: 'I was hoping the bloody thing would not go off.' In May 1965, Gould's name appeared in the papers again, this time as 'a VC on the dole'. He had lost his job as personnel manager, because of 'a clash of personalities'. He was finding his VC a liability. 'Incredible though it may seem, people in top management seem to shy away from me. I think it might be because they are afraid that a man with such a record could show too much embarrassing initiative. If it is the VC which is frightening people away from me, I wish they would forget it. Those days are over.'

'Exploits of HMS Thrasher: Talks by Members of the Crew', Imperial War Museum Tape No. 5427, recorded 5th January 1943.

Robert Edward Dudley Ryder, Stephen Halden Beattie, William Alfred Savage:
St Nazaire, March 1942

In early 1942, Intelligence reported that the new German battleship *Tirpitz* had been completed and was growing restless. If she broke out into the Atlantic and then, like *Bismarck*, headed for France, there was only one dock on the western European seaboard which could take her - the Normandie graving dock in St Nazaire, at the mouth of the River Loife, in France. On 3rd March 1942, the Chiefs of Staff Committee approved Operation Chariot, a daring scheme to crash the dock gates and blow them up.

The plans were strikingly similar to those for the attack on Zeebrugge almost a quarter of a century earlier. The explosive - twenty-four depth-charges with a time fuse - was carried in an ex-American destroyer, HMS *Campbeltown* (Lieutenant-Commander S.H. Beattie), which had been specially lightened to cross the estuary sandbanks and had a strengthened superstructure to protect personnel during the approach. Besides *Campbeltown*, the force consisted of MGB.314, carrying Commander R.E.D. Ryder, the

Naval Force Commander and his staff; two escorting destroyers, *Atherstone* and *Tynedale*; sixteen motor launches in two columns carrying Commandos under Lieutenant-Colonel A.C. Newman; and MTB. 74 with delayed-action torpedoes for use on the inner dock gates if *Campbeltown* failed. The total number of men involved was 630, not including the two escort destroyers.

The Chariot Force left Falmouth on the afternoon of 26th March 1942 and made a wide circuit out into the Atlantic to allay suspicion, during which they sighted and attacked U.593, which later reported them heading *west*. With this misleading report, great good luck and brilliant navigation, the Force arrived off the estuary at 12.30 am on 28th March unmolested and, led by MGB.314, headed up the river. *Campbeltown's* four funnels had been cut to two, with their tops sloped, to resemble a German destroyer, and she wore a German ensign. With these ruses, and by behaving as if they belonged in the Loire, they were not challenged until 1.20 am. Even then, a bold reply to a challenge, an almost-correct Very light recognition, a long unintelligible signal in German by Leading Seaman Pyke, and, of course, the sheer *unlikelihood* of an attack on St Nazaire, caused the Germans to hold their fire for another eight minutes. Then the searchlights stabbed out from all over the harbour, *Campbeltown* struck the Iron Cross and hoisted the White Ensign, and the batteries opened fire from both sides of the river.

The guns and lights concentrated on *Campbeltown*, the largest ship, which was hit on her foc's'le, blowing away her 12-pounder gun, and many times in the hull, where shells penetrated the decks below and killed or wounded half her company. On the bridge, Beattie had picked out his aiming point, a lighthouse on the end of the Old Mole to port, passed it at twenty knots and gave the order 'Stand by to ram'. Two hundred yards from the Normandie dock entrance, MGB.314 turned aside, leaving the way clear for *Campbeltown*. Half-blinded by searchlights, but with all his own remaining guns firing, Beattie headed *Campbeltown* towards the outer gate. Her bows cut through an anti-torpedo net and crashed into the dock. Over thirty feet of the bows crumpled back, but the foremost part projected over the inner face of the dock gate. *Campbeltown* was well and truly wedged in position. The time was 1.34 am - four minutes late.

While Beattie and his surviving ship's company prepared to scuttle their ship, Newman's Commandos in *Campbeltown* landed and fanned out into the dock area to their assigned objectives in the U-boat pens, the harbour installations and the operating gear for the great dock. Defensive positions were stormed, searchlights extinguished and guns silenced. The main dock pumphouse was blown up and the gate winding house wrecked. The Germans replied with gunfire from rooftops and machine-gun positions by the dockside. The battle was fragmented, individual demolition parties

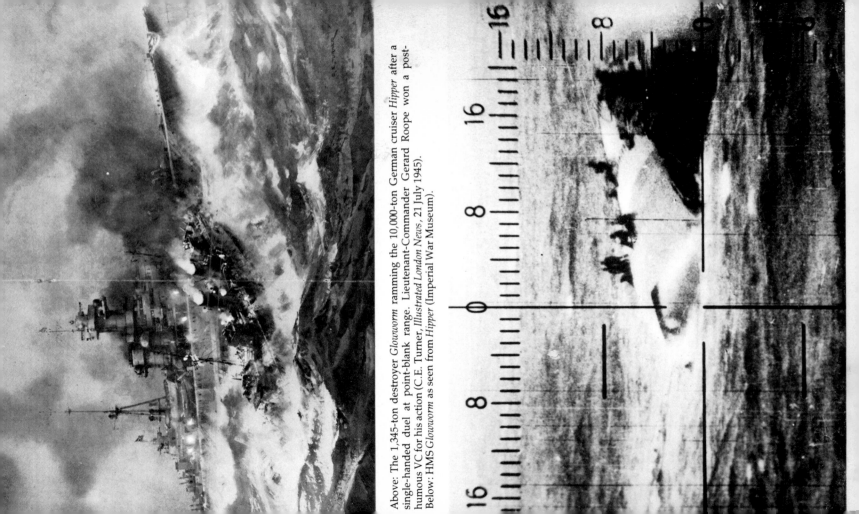

Above: The 1,345-ton destroyer *Glowworm* ramming the 10,000-ton German cruiser *Hipper* after a single-handed duel at point-blank range. Lieutenant-Commander Gerard Roope won a posthumous VC for his action (C.E. Turner, *Illustrated London News*, 21 July 1945). Below: HMS *Glowworm* as seen from *Hipper* (Imperial War Museum).

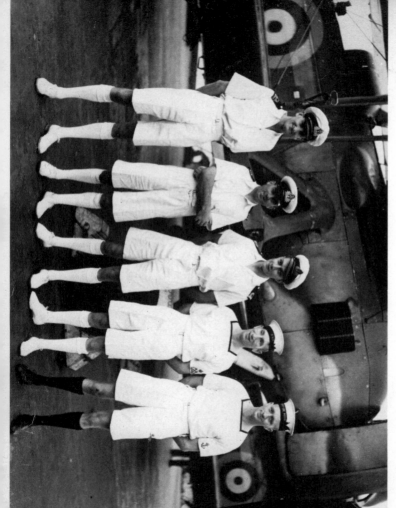

Above left: B.A.W. Warburton-Lee (Imperial War Museum)
Above right: Jack Mantle (Imperial War Museum)
Below: Officers and ratings of 825 Squadron on board *Ark Royal*, decorated for attack on *Bismarck*, May 1941. Eugene Esmonde is second from left (Imperial War Museum).

Above left: M.D. Wanklyn (Keystone Press)
Above right: William Savage (Imperial War Museum)

Below: HMS *Onslow* in action in the Barents Sea, as a result of which Captain Robert Sherbrooke won the VC (C.E. Turner, *Illustrated London News*, 23 January 1943).

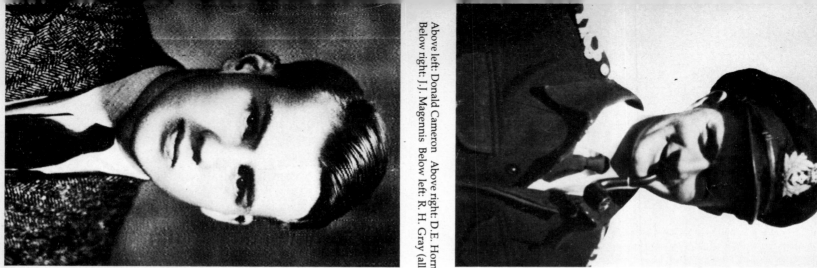

Above left: Donald Cameron Above right: D.E. Hornell
Below right: J.J. Magennis Below left: R. H. Gray (all Imperial War Museum)

searching out their objectives in the smoke and darkness, and lit by flashes from guns and exploding charges. Men came pelting round a corner into their enemies and fought there and then to the death.

Most of the Commandos in the motor launches never got ashore at all. The German resistance at the Old Entrance to the dock was so fierce that only two motor launches of the starboard column got alongside, and one of those was hit and abandoned. A third withdrew, badly damaged, and three more blew up and sank. Of the port column attacking the Old Mole, four had to withdraw without coming alongside, and three were disabled or sunk. Only ML.177 at the Old Entrance got her Commandos ashore, and came off with survivors from *Campbeltown*.

Lieutenant Curtis RNVR, commanding MGB.314, took his gun-boat into the Old Entrance, where Ryder went ashore to look round. Once he had seen that *Campbeltown* was satisfactorily scuttled, Ryder came back to MGB.314 and told Curtis to take her out into midstream so that he could see how the battle was going. Off the Old Mole one motor launch was going to the assistance of another, and both were under fire from the shore. MGB.314 went to support them, closing to within 250 yards of the shore. Able Seaman Savage and Able Seaman Smith on the forward pompom engaged the most troublesome gun, which was hidden in a concrete emplacement. Savage's shooting was so good he put several shells through the slit of the position and silenced the gun. Savage then turned his gun on other targets along the skyline and on top of near-by buildings, directed by Curtis wielding the searchlights. Although Savage had no gunshield to protect him and was in a most exposed position, right forward on the gunboat's deck, when he saw Germans running to man the gun he had just silenced he coolly put another round through the same embrasure and knocked out the gun again. Meanwhile the two motor launches had blown up, and Ryder could see that there was nothing more he could do. Regretfully, he had to leave Newman ashore with his surviving Commandos and head down river. As they did so, Savage was cut down by a burst of shrapnel and killed. Curtis took MGB.314 down river, leaving behind a scene of devastation, wrecked and sinking motor launches, explosions and gunfire, past bodies and wreckage floating in the water, with fires burning ashore and in patches of fuel on the surface down to the safety of the open sea.

It was now 2.40 am. Ryder, as his citation said, had been in close action under heavy fire for an hour and sixteen minutes, supervising operations, arranging for the evacuation of *Campbeltown's* people, and dealing with German strongpoints at almost point-blank range. The main object of Chariot had been carried out. There was nothing more he could do. MGB.314, full of dead and wounded, withdrew; that she was able to, and survive an intense barrage of close-range fire, was 'almost a miracle'.

209

Ryder and MGB.314 reached England but Newman became a prisoner-of-war, and Beattie was also captured when the motor launch carrying him down river was blown up and her survivors rescued by a German trawler. The next morning Beattie was questioned by a German Intelligence Officer, who remarked on the futility of trying to destroy such a massive dock by ramming it with a destroyer. Shortly afterwards, the charges in *Campbeltown* exploded, shattered the dock gates and killed an inspecting party of Germans on board. MTB. 74's delayed action torpedoes, fired into the Old Entrance gates, blew up a day later.

Ryder, Beattie and Savage (posthumously) were gazetted for the VC on 21st May 1942, Beattie 'in recognition not only of his own valour but also that of the unnamed officers and men of a very gallant ship's company, many of whom have not returned', and Savage also not only for his own gallantry and devotion to duty, but also for 'the valour shown by many others unnamed, in motor launches, motor gun boats and motor torpedo boats who gallantly carried out their duty in entirely exposed positions against enemy fire at very close range'. Beattie's and Savage's VCs were therefore a variant of the 'ballot' practice, which was, perhaps not strictly covered in the VC warrants. The VCs of Newman, and of Sergeant T.F. Durrant, of the Commandos (posthumous), were gazetted on 19th June 1945, when Newman and the other survivors were repatriated. 169 men were killed during the raid. Besides the 5 VCs, the participants won 4 DSOs, 17 DSCs, 11 MCs, 4 CGMs, 5 DCMs, 24 DSMs and 15 Military Medals. 51 were mentioned in despatches, 22 posthumously.

The choice of Robert Ryder as Naval Force Commander for St Nazaire proved that the processes of naval selection, moving as they do in mysterious ways, not infrequently produce the right man. Ryder was a restless, adventurous man, a proven leader, an excellent seaman, with great powers of physical endurance and a taste for the unorthodox. He could bear hardship much more easily than he could ceremonial. He thrived in small ships, stifled in large.

Robert Edward Dudley Ryder was born in India on 16th February 1908, the son of Colonel Charles H.D. Ryder CB, DSO, CIE, RE, a noted military engineer and surveyor who later became Surveyor-General of India. Ryder was sent home for his education and went to Cheltenham, where he passed in bottom of his class but was eventually made captain of his house, thus establishing the pattern of his life: little interest in academical or theoretical distinction, but great force of character and powers of leadership. Because he had found that it would allow him to leave school a year early, Ryder made up his mind to sit the examination for the Navy but was discouraged by his parents, who wanted him to join the Army, and by his masters, who believed he had no chance.

Ryder duly passed, top of all public school candidates, and

became Chief Cadet Captain and won the King's Dirk in the training ship *Thunderer*. He was a Midshipman in the battleship *Ramillies* from 1927 to 1929 and then studied for his Lieutenant's examinations, in which he came top in all except seamanship. He volunteered for submarines and went out to China in 1930 to join *Olympus*. On 1st May 1933, he and four other officers left Hong Kong to sail home in the 30-ton ketch *Tai-Mo-Shan*, specially built for the voyage. Ryder, who had considerable experience of sailing and had taken part in the Fastnet race, was sailing master, and *Tai-Mo-Shan* completed the 16,217-mile voyage in one day under a year. The five (who went on half pay for the voyage) later won one VC and four DSOs between them.

In the meantime Ryder had volunteered to join John Rymill's expedition to Grahameland in the Antarctic and to his great joy was accepted. He spent the next three years as skipper of the three-masted schooner *Penola* and was awarded the Polar Medal with clasp. The outbreak of war found Ryder languishing as a general purpose Lieutenant-Commander in the battleship *Warspite* and he accepted with alacrity an invitation to serve in a newly-formed force of decoy, or 'Q', ships. This was a temporary aberration of the Admiralty's, in which they tried to revive a ruse which had been fully exposed in the previous war. Ryder, commanding the 'Q' ship *Willamette Valley*, a converted Cardiff tramp, was torpedoed in June 1940 and spent four days in the water, clinging to a piece of wreckage, before he was picked up.

In July 1940 Ryder was appointed in command of the frigate *Fleetwood* and on 31st December 1940 was promoted Commander. He was selected for special duties in Combined Operations Command, as Captain of the Belgian cross-Channel steamer *Prince Philippe*, which was fitted out at Penarth to carry infantry and their landing craft for raids on the Norwegian coast. Unhappily, she was rammed and sunk in thick fog in the Firth of Clyde by the *Empire Wave* in July 1941, shortly after she was commissioned. Ryder came ashore, and once more languished, as Naval Liaison Officer on the staff of the GOC Southern Command, General the Hon. Sir Harold Alexander, at Wilton House, near Salisbury. It was there in February 1942 that he received another glad summons, to attend a conference at Combined Ops HQ in London, which led to St Nazaire.

Ryder also took part in the planning for the Dieppe Raid in August 1942 and was present in the river gunboat *Locust*. Later in the war he was in command of the destroyer *Opportune* in operations off the Norwegian coast. It was just after the war, in August 1946, that Ryder experienced one of the peculiar hazards of a VC. He was in court at Richmond in Surrey to give evidence if required (on his own behalf in a way,) at the trial of one Edward Andrew Pennington, forty-three of no fixed address, who was sentenced to three months' hard labour for wearing unauthorised medal ribbons and three months for obtaining credit by fraud, the sentences to run consecutively. Pennington had claimed to be Robert Ryder VC and stated that he was entitled to the numerous medals he wore and had been blinded at Dunkirk.

Ryder was promoted Captain on 30th June 1948 and spent the last two years of his naval career as Naval Attaché in Oslo, retiring in 1950. At the General Election that year he won Merton and Morden for the Conservatives, and represented the seat until 1955. In 1941, at Windsor, while *Prince Philipe* was being fitted out, he married Hilare Constance Green-Wilkinson, daughter of the Reverend L.C. Green-Wilkinson of Lovel Hill, Windsor. They had a son and a daughter. Captain and Mrs Ryder live at Wolferton, King's Lynn.

Lieutenant-Commander Beattie's part at St Nazaire was not only, as his citation said, a display of great gallantry and determination, but a superb piece of ship-handling. *Campbeltown*, the ex-USN four-funnel *Buchanan*, was not the easiest ship to handle. In Beattie's own words, she was a 'bitch', with a turning circle almost as large as a battleship. Specially lightened as she was, she made a lot of leeway in any wind, and was skittish and skidded all over the place when the helm was put over. She did run briefly aground, and there were anxious moments when her speed dropped to five knots, but Beattie kept her going, and to hit the target so exactly was a magnificent feat of seamanship on his part.

Beattie was a contemporary of Ryder's and joined the training ship *Thunderer* in the same term of September 1925. He was born on 29th March 1908 at Leighton, Montgomeryshire, eldest son of the Reverend Prebendary E.H. Beattie MC, Rector of Madley, in Herefordshire, and Ethel (née Knowles). He went to Abberley Hall, Worcestershire, and then to Rugby, before joining the Navy as a 'special entry' cadet. He was a destroyer man, and was First Lieutenant of *Zulu* when war broke out. His first destroyer command was *Vivien*, on the East Coast and Atlantic convoy routes; he was mentioned in despatches for good work against E-boats, and his gunners shot down two Junkers aircraft in the North Sea in November 1940. In January 1942, Beattie was appointed to stand by the destroyer *Petard* while building, but was suddenly sent to *Campbeltown* in mid-March, when planning for St Nazaire was well under way, after the C-in-C had decided that the present Captain was too old. Beattie therefore only had a few days to get used to *Campbeltown* and accustom himself to her idiosyncrasies.

He was taken prisoner and went to Marlag und Milag Nord, near Bremen. When his VC was announced the German camp commandant, unconsciously carrying out the spirit of Queen Victoria's original wishes, called a special camp parade which he and his officers attended in full regalia with medals, and announced the award to the assembled prisoners, adding his own congratulations to the 'wild applause' of the POWs. In 1946 Beattie was mentioned in despatches again, for his gallant bearing in prison. He was also awarded the Croix de Guerre avec Palmes and became a Chevalier of the Légion d'honneur in 1947. By then Beattie had resumed his naval career and was commanding the destroyer *Zodiac*. He was promoted Commander on 30th June 1946. After a staff course, he commanded *Hawke*, the training establishment for Upper Yardmen Officer Candidates. He commanded another destroyer, *Whirlwind*, in 1949, was Commander of the RN College Greenwich 1950-51 and promoted Captain in June 1951. He went to Australia as Captain of 1st Frigate Squadron, serving in *Shoalhaven* and *Quadrant*. He was at the Admiralty with Admiral Commanding Reserves from 1954 to 1956 and then Senior Naval Officer, Persian Gulf, until 1958. He commanded the cruiser *Birmingham*, his last appointment and his last command, from 1958 until his retirement in 1960.

In 1933 at Gosport, Beattie married Philippa Blanchflower, daughter of Paymaster Rear-Admiral Blanchflower, and they had four sons. Captain and Mrs Beattie lived at Mullion, Cornwall, where he died on 24th April 1975.

Photographs of 'matelots' like Able Seaman Bill Savage, with his cheerful, round face, his smile, his beard and his sailor's cap with its HMS ribbon flat aback on his head, must have stood on thousands of mantelpieces in homes all over Great Britain. William Alfred Savage was born at 7 Raglan Avenue, Raglan Road, Smethwick, Warwickshire, the youngest of the twenty-two children of James Savage and Catherine (née Dobson), on 30th October 1912. His father had been a boatman with the Shropshire and Worcestershire Canal Company and then a drayman with William Butler's Brewery (later to become Mitchells & Butlers) locally in Birmingham. He worked for M & B's for thirty-seven years and his youngest son, after attending the Cape Hill Schools, followed his father into the bottling department of the same brewery. He was a popular man in his work and was a member of the swimming club, reserve for the water-polo team, secretary of the bottling stores darts club, fond of weight-lifting, cats, and his firm's product. On 27th March 1937 he married a girl he had known at school, Doris Hobbs at St Matthew's, Smethwick (so that he was actually on his way to St Nazaire and his death on his fifth wedding anniversary). But for the war, Savage might have lived and died obscurely in his home in Durban Road. He was called up, and joined the Navy (Official No. C/JX 173910) at Chatham Barracks on 18th December 1939 and was rated Able Seaman a year later. As gunlayer of a 20-mm pompom, Savage served in Motor Gunboats, making clandestine high-speed trips across the Channel to France.

Savage's widow received the Cross from the King at Buckingham Palace on 23rd June 1942. She has since remarried, and still lives in Smethwick.

Kenneth Hare-Scott, *For Valour*, 'Robert Edward Dudley Ryder and William Alfred Savage' (London: Peter Garnett, 1949).

C.E. Lucas-Phillips, *The Greatest Raid of All* (London: Heinemann, 1958).

Commander R.E.D. Ryder VC, RN, *The Attack on St Nazaire* (London: John Murray, 1947).

'The Attack on St Nazaire, 28th March 1942', Supplement to the *London Gazette*, 30th September 1947.

Combined Operations 1940-1942 (London: HMSO, 1943).

'Commander Ryder VC describes the raid in which he won the VC', Imperial War Museum Tape No. 9671, recorded 21st March 1946.

Anthony Cecil Capel Miers:
Corfu Roads, March 1942

Of all the twentieth-century naval VCs, Anthony Miers perhaps most closely resembles those nineteenth-century officers who won the VC and went on to flag rank and knighthoods. His VC, like theirs, was the most dramatic incident of his career, but it was only one incident of many in a naval service which lasted, in his case, for thirty-five years. Miers's naval career had an almost Victorian symmetry: a hectic youth and an active middle age, followed by a later phase in which he became an 'elder statesman' and the 'senior submariner' of the Navy.

Anthony Cecil Capel Miers comes from a Scottish military background. He is very proud of the fact that through his grandmother Mary Ann Macdonald he is a direct descendant of Donald Macdonald, 16th Chief of Clanranald. He was born on 11th November 1906, younger son of Captain D.N.C. Capel Miers and Margaret Annie (née Christie), at Birchwood, Inverness, where his father was adjutant of the 3rd Battalion Queen's Own Cameron Highlanders, the same regiment in which his grandfather, Lieutenant-Colonel Capel Miers, also served. Captain Miers went to France in 1914 with the 1st Battalion and was killed in action at Bourg on the Aisne on 25th September.

Anthony Miers went to Stubbington House, Edinburgh Academy and Wellington College, before joining *Thunderer* as a Special Entry Cadet in 1924. He was promoted Sub-Lieutenant on 1st January 1928 and joined the Submarine Service in April 1929. In 1931-2 he served in M.2, the giant submarine-monitor, fitted first with a 12-inch gun and later with an aircraft hangar (through which, in January 1933, she flooded and sank off Portland). Miers by then was in H.28 as First Lieutenant. He was a good athlete, a tennis and squash racquets player, and a very fine rugby footballer, playing for London Scottish, Combined Services and Hampshire and being chosen for trials for the Navy and for Scotland. He was keen, competitive and, as one of his captains said, 'frighteningly loyal'. Life in the Navy, a life of sport and duty, within a framework of discipline and loyalty, had much to offer him, but in 1933, when he was a Lieutenant serving in the fishery protection vessel *Dart*, he himself voluntarily put his future in jeopardy. In the heat of the moment of an incident on the football field he threatened to strike a rating. The matter was soon common knowledge on board but would have rested there had not Miers himself voluntarily reported it. He was inevitably court-martialled and dismissed his ship. But the affair did him no lasting damage and in a month he was appointed First Lieutenant of the submarine *Rainbow* in the Far East. He passed the 'periscope' or 'perisher' course for submarine captains in 1936 and his first command was L.54, which he commanded at the 1937 Coronation Review at Spithead.

Miers was promoted Lieutenant-Commander on 1st January 1938 and when war broke out he was serving in battleships, on the staff of the C-in-C Home Fleet. In 1940, he returned to submarines, with the command of *Torbay*. In *Torbay*, one of a new class of larger submarine, Miers became one of the most successful submarine 'aces' in the Mediterranean. Operating mainly from Alexandria, he was mentioned in despatches and won two DSOs while sinking or damaging over 70,000 tons of Axis shipping.

On 20th February 1942, *Torbay* sailed from Alexandria for a patrol off the west coast of Greece. Early in the morning of the 26th, while *Torbay* was surfaced recharging batteries, Miers sighted a tanker escorted by a destroyer. He dived, surfaced astern and fired one torpedo, which was spotted. *Torbay* herself was also seen and forced to dive again. Eleven depth-charges were dropped. It had been a narrow escape, because Miers had had great difficulty in shutting the upper hatch when the destroyer was heading straight towards him. Later, he found the hatch had been jammed by his own pillow.

On 1st March and again on the 2nd, in what was turning out to be a strenuous patrol, *Torbay* was depth-charged by destroyers and six near misses lifted her several feet. Miers himself spoke of the effect of depth-charging on him, and like so many submarine captains under stress, of the serenity and reassurance he gained from his crew: 'I am bound to confess that on many occasions I have felt extremely frightened when the depth-charges have been going off around us. Yet even then the crew of the *Torbay* has never failed to amaze me. In fact they almost seem to enjoy themselves keeping a scoreboard of the number of enemy depth-charges dropped.'

Miers moved his patrol area to Corfu Island where, on 3rd March, he sighted a large enemy convoy escorted by three destroyers entering Corfu harbour. The harbour is a stretch of water thirty miles long from north to south and twelve miles across at its widest point, formed between the island of Corfu and the Greek mainland. The southern entrance is five miles long, with an effective width reduced by shoals for submarines to about two and a half miles. Miers followed the convoy at slow speed until dusk, when he surfaced and entered the southern channel. He had to dive again to avoid a small motor-ship but then surfaced and followed it in.

At 10 pm *Torbay* was trimmed down, with only her conning tower showing above water and her hull turned stern on to the brilliant moon which had just risen, while recharging batteries about five miles east of the main anchorage. A signal was received recalling *Torbay* from patrol. Miers remarked in a somewhat Nelsonian manner that he was 'relieved to find that this signal did not conflict with the present operation'. At 1 am, Miers had to dive to avoid a patrolling trawler, and then took *Torbay* slowly across the harbour towards the anchorage. By 2.35 am Miers found himself actually in the roads, having been carried across by a strong westerly set. He could see no sign of ships, and decided to wait until daylight.

Dawn showed that the convoy had apparently sailed again. There were two 5,000-ton transports and a destroyer still in the anchorage. Firing as *Torbay* swung round, Miers shot one torpedo at each, missing the destroyer but hitting the transports. He and *Torbay* then endured another forty depth-charges while making their escape to the open sea, after being in closely patrolled enemy waters for seventeen hours.

Miers's VC was gazetted on 7th July 1942. He himself wished that the medal could be awarded to the whole ship, but in a remarkable and unprecedented Investiture at Buckingham Palace on 28th July, the King presented Miers with the VC, his engineer officer, Lieutenant (E) Hugh Kidd DSC, with a DSO, Lieutenants Paul Chapman and D.S. Verschoyle-Campbell with bars to their DSCs, and twenty-four ratings of Torbay with DSMs or Bars to their DSMs.

On 30th June 1942, Miers was promoted Commander and appointed as submarine Staff Liaison Officer on the Staff of Admiral Nimitz, C-in-C Pacific, and of Commander Submarines Pacific, Admiral Lockwood. He made a 56-day war patrol with the US submarine *Cabrilla*. In 1944 he was Commander S/M in the depot-ship *Maidstone*, of the 8th S/M Flotilla, when she arrived in Australia. On 20th January 1945, at Perth, Western Australia, Anthony Miers married Patricia Mary Millar, who was serving in the WRANS. They had a daughter and a son, who followed his father into the Navy.

Miers was promoted Captain on 31st December 1946. He commanded *Blackcap*, the RN Air Station at Stretton (gaining a pilot's 'A' licence) from 1948 to 1950, *Forth* and 1st Submarine Flotilla 1950-2, RN College Greenwich 1952-4 and the aircraft carrier *Theseus* 1954-5. He was promoted Rear-Admiral on 7th January 1956 and appointed Flag Officer, Middle East, until he retired on 4th August 1959. In 1945 he had been made an Officer of the US Legion of Merit, a CB in

1958 and a KBE in 1959, and in 1955 a Burgess and Freeman of the Royal and Ancient Burgh of Inverness.

In retirement, Admiral Miers was far from retired. He had several business interests and kept his links with the Navy, becoming President of the RN Lawn Tennis Association and the RN Squash Racquets Association, and, in 1967, National President of the Submarine Old Comrades Association. Sir Anthony and Lady Miers live in Roehampton, London.

Frederick Thornton Peters:
Oran Harbour, November 1942

'He was one of the rare "romantic" Adventurers, one of those complete "Pirates" that the Navy occasionally produces. These types are completely without fear, dedicated to duty or their own interpretation of it, and tough as old ropes.' So wrote Commander David Joel, a *Britannia* term-mate of Peters, long after Peters's VC and death in an air accident.

Frederick Thornton Peters made an orthodox start to life and to his naval career but followed it with one of the most unorthodox lives and naval careers any man ever had. He was a Canadian, born on 17th September 1889 in Charlottetown, Prince Edward Island. His father, Frederick Peters, was called to the Bar of Prince Edward Island and Nova Scotia in 1876 and was Prime Minister and Attorney-General of Prince Edward Island from 1891 until 1897. His mother, Bertha, was the youngest daughter of the Hon. John Hamilton Gray, one of the Fathers of the Confederation. Peters went to St Peter's School in Charlottetown and, when he was nine years old and the family moved to British Columbia, to school in Victoria, British Columbia, where his father was a member of the Bering Straits Boundary Commission. He joined HMS *Britannia* in 1904 where he was nicknamed for some reason 'Tramp'. He was promoted Lieutenant on 26th March 1912 and served in destroyers on the China Station from 1910 to December 1913 when he resigned from the Navy, giving his reason the fact that 'his family's coffers needed filling'. He then joined the Canadian Pacific Railways as a Third Officer.

Peters rejoined the Navy in September 1914 and had an energetic and distinguished war, winning the DSO for his gallantry in the destroyer *Meteor* during the Battle of the Dogger Bank in January 1915, in which *Meteor* was hit and badly damaged by an 8.2-inch shell from the German cruiser *Blucher*. He was also gazetted for the DSC in March 1918.

In June 1919 he attended a staff course and did well enough in it to be offered an appointment as Assistant Staff Officer (Operations) in the *Queen Elizabeth*, flagship of the Home Fleet. It was one of the best

217

staff appoinments for a junior officer but Peters never took it up and retired again in June 1920.

Between the wars, Peters did various things. He went back to Canada and was reported to be selling boots to the Russians. He was connected with Commander Cromwell Varley, an old friend, who was the original inventor of the one-man submarine. In the 1930s, Peters went out to the Gold Coast to grow cocoa. His friends used to see him in London every two or three years, spending his money until it ran out and going back to the Coast to make more.

At the outbreak of war, Peters rejoined once again and was again gazetted for a bar to his DSC, for good service in *Thirlmere*, as early as July 1940. An insight into his doings and his character that summer comes from an unexpected source. Peters, then a Commander, was commandant of a school for training special agents at Brickendonbury Hall, a former school near Hertford. Two of his colleagues there were Guy Burgess and Kim Philby, who later wrote of Peters that he

. . . had faraway naval eyes and a gentle smile of great charm. Against all the odds, he took a great and immediate fancy to Guy, who ruthlessly swiped the cigarettes off his desk. He was later awarded a posthumous VC for what was probably unnecessarily gallant behaviour in Oran Harbour. When I heard of the award, I felt a pang that he should never have known about it. He was the type of strong sentimentalist who would have wept at such honour. Our trainees came to adore him.

Peters hated the political intrigues that went with the work. Philby soon noted that his 'aspect changed for the worse. He became more than usually taciturn and withdrawn.' Eventually, Peters

. . . fell into a deep depression. It was no surprise when he summoned Guy and myself one morning and told us that he had spent the previous evening composing his letter of resignation. He spoke sadly, as if conscious of failure and neglect. Then he cheered up and the charming smile came back, for the first time in many days. He was clearly happy to be going back to his little ships after his brief baptism of political fire.

He was indeed happier in his little ships, and his friends soon heard that when he took his ship up to Tobermory for anti-submarine training and work-up under Vice-Admiral Sir Gilbert (Puggie) Stephenson, 'the face that launched a thousand ships', Peters did not like the look of it and 'gently sailed away again'.

In October 1942, Peters arrived in Greenock with a lorry full of explosives and an unaccustomed fatalism. 'I am probably going to be killed,' he told Joel, 'but it's well worth it.' Operation Torch, the Allied landings in North Africa, were in the offing and those of Peters's friends in the know guessed that his mission was connected with Torch. He himself said he had had his instructions from Mr Churchill.

On the night of 8th November 1942, the two 1,000-ton Lease-Lend ex-US Coast Guard cutters *Walney* (Acting Captain F. T. Peters) and *Hartland* (Lieutenant-Commander G.P. Billot) approached the harbour of Oran, in North Africa. They had on board parties of US Rangers, to seize port installations and prevent the Vichy French from sabotaging them and scuttling ships in the harbour, and specially trained technicians to operate the harbour once it had been taken. *Walney* had no sooner crashed through the harbour boom than a searchlight picked her out and the harbour defences opened fire at point-blank range. Peters was blinded in one eye but was the only one of the seventeen men on *Walney's* bridge to survive. He ordered the cutter alongside a French warship, where grapnels were thrown out and the surviving Rangers with tommy guns and revolvers stormed on board. *Walney* was still raked from end to end by constant and heavy fire at close range. Her boilers blew up, and she turned over and sank, with her ensign still flying. *Hartland* also reached the jetty, but there were too few men left alive to handle her lines and she drifted out again into the harbour, where she too blew up and sank.

Peters and a handful of men reached shore on a Carley float and were imprisoned by the Vichy garrison. They were released a few days later when the Allies took Oran. Peters was carried through the streets, where the people of Oran hailed him with flowers. On 13th November, when he was flying home, his aircraft crashed taking off from Gibraltar and he was killed. His posthumous VC was gazetted on 18th May 1943.

A.D.Divine, the author and war correspondent, later wrote to Peters's mother: 'I do know that the men who were with him, the survivors of the exploit, spoke of your son in the very highest possible terms. They would, I know, have gone with him again knowing that the same future was in store for them.' Mr Divine heard the news of his death 'with a great sense of shock for I knew - as I think few others did at that time, the brilliance and dash of this Zeebrugge in miniature'.

Commander David Joel RN Retd, 'Notes for a Memoir of F.T. Peters' (unpublished).
Kim Philby, *My Silent War* (London: MacGibbon & Kee, 1968).

Robert St Vincent Sherbrooke:

Barents Sea, December 1942

When, in A. P. Herbert's words, Hitler 'leaped upon his largest friend' and attacked Russia in June 1941, it soon became necessary for the Allies to send supplies to Russia by sea round the North Cape. Whatever political or moral justifications for the Russian convoys there might have been, as naval undertakings they were always basically unsound. The merchant ships and their escorts had to make their way to and from north Russian ports along a route often restricted by polar ice, and always within reach of enemy air, U-boat and surface ship bases, where Allied heavy covering forces could not protect them. To the dangers of the enemy were added the appalling violence of the Arctic weather and the hostility of a suspicious and ungrateful ally.

Convoy JW51B, of fourteen merchantmen, British and American, left Loch Ewe for Russia on 22nd December 1942. Though by no means a large convoy (it was in fact only half of JW51) it carried 2,046 vehicles, 202 tanks, 87 fighters, 33 bombers, 24,150 tons of fuel and aviation spirit, and 54,321 tons of miscellaneous stores. The escort was 3 *Hunt*-class destroyers, 3 corvettes, 2 trawlers and 1 minesweeper, which were joined at 2.30 pm on Christmas Day, far out in the north Atlantic, by the 17th Destroyer Flotilla under Captain R. St V. Sherbrooke DSO in *Onslow*, with *Obedient*, *Orwell*, *Obdurate* and *Achates*. *Achates* was an old destroyer but the others were new, although only *Onslow* had new 4.7-inch guns (the rest had 4-inch guns with '1915' stamped on their breeches).

The three *Hunts* and the corvette *Circe* turned for home, leaving Sherbrooke's destroyers to take the convoy on to Murmansk. Also at sea was a covering Force R, of the cruisers *Sheffield* and *Jamaica*, under Rear-Admiral Burnett, and in the deep field the battleship *Anson*, flying the flag of Admiral Fraser, C-in-C Home Fleet, with the cruiser *Cumberland* and two destroyers.

The convoy, blown south of its course by a gale, was sighted and reported by U.354 on 30th December. The German Admiral Kummetz, with the heavy cruiser *Hipper*, the pocket battleship *Lützow* and six destroyers, sailed from Altenfjord to intercept. At 9.15 am on the 31st the three destroyers with *Hipper* sighted *Obdurate* on the fringe of the convoy and opened fire.

Sherbrooke had anticipated that surface ship attack was the most likely - the weather would deter the U-boats and the short daylight the Luftwaffe - and prepared a plan: if the convoy were attacked, his destroyers would concentrate on the threatened side. The convoy would turn stern-on to the danger and retire under cover of smoke, while Sherbrooke's destroyers sallied out to threaten torpedo attack. Four times *Hipper* approached the convoy and four times the

220

destroyers drove her off, whilst *Achates* laid a smoke-screen in front of the convoy. At 10.19 am, during the fourth attack, *Hipper* hit *Onslow* abaft the bridge with an 8-inch shell which split open the funnel and sprayed the radar office and bridge with splinters. One hit Sherbrooke in the face, smashing his left cheekbone and cutting open his nose, so that his eyeball hung dangling down his cheek. Sherbrooke's voice gave no sign that he was hurt. Lieutenant-Commander T.J.G. Marchant, the Flotilla Torpedo Officer, had no idea anybody had been touched until he turned round and saw Sherbrooke's face. *Onslow* was hit again forward, putting 'B' gun out of action and holing the hull under 'A' gun-mounting. Sherbrooke carried on for half an hour until his medical officer insisted he go below for treatment. 'He was temporarily blind,' said Marchant, 'and in great pain, but he retained all his other faculties and ordered that the ship be kept as far as possible between the enemy and the convoy and that everything was to be done to get the fires under control.'

Command of the flotilla devolved on Lieutenant-Commander Kinloch in *Obedient*, who led the remaining four destroyers out to beat off yet another attack by *Hipper* in which she hit *Achates*, killing her Captain and doing damage from which she subsequently sank. Once again *Hipper* turned away for fear of torpedoes. At 11.37 am when she herself was under fire and hit by the cruisers *Sheffield* and *Jamaica* who had arrived on the scene, Kummetz, broke off the action and headed back to Altenfjord. One of her destroyers, *Friedrich Eckholdt*, mistook *Sheffield* for *Hipper* and was sunk.

The Germans, too, had a plan. When *Hipper* and her three destroyers attacked from the north, they would force the convoy south - towards *Lutzow* and her destroyers. The plan worked. *Lutzow* encountered the convoy when all the escorts were beating off *Hipper* But Stange, *Lutzow*'s Captain, hesitated and missed his chance. He made no attack. The convoy escaped intact. As Sherbrooke himself said, 'Had the roles been reversed, the convoy would not have arrived at its destination complete and practically undamaged.' Lacking sea-time, hamstrung by Hitler's own cautious orders, and hag-ridden by doubts and fears, Kummetz and Stange had let a great chance go. Their failure was a catastrophe for the German Navy. A furious Hitler ordered the big ships to be scrapped. Raeder, the C-in-C, resigned.

After being patched up in Russia, *Onslow* reached Scapa Flow on 4th February, to be cheered by the Home Fleet. Sherbrooke had already come home in *Obedient* to endure a series of operations on his face. His Victoria Cross was gazetted on 12th January 1943. Mrs Sherbrooke worked in the Operations Division signal room in the Admiralty and was on duty on 31st December. She read the signals and saw the plot while the action in the Barents Sea was being fought, and so was the only naval wife in history to 'watch' her husband winning the Victoria Cross.

Robert St Vincent Sherbrooke, always known to his family as 'Rupert', was born on 8th January 1901 at Oxton Hall, Newark, Nottinghamshire, where his forebears had lived since the fifteenth century, the son of Lieutenant (later Captain and DSO) Henry Graham Sherbrooke and Flora Maud (née Francklin). His grandfather was also a naval officer and his grandmother was a Jervis, directly descended from Lord St Vincent, hence Sherbrooke's middle name.

Sherbrooke went to Osborne in September 1913 and was promoted Midshipman on 1st January 1917. He served in the battleship *Canada*, was promoted Sub-Lieutenant on 15th July 1919 and appointed to the torpedo gunboat *Hussar*. After the war he was one of the officers an understanding Admiralty sent to Cambridge to study for a period and to recover some 'civilising influence' after the exertions of the First World War. He was promoted Lieutenant on 15th April 1921 and joined the battleship *Iron Duke* in 1924. Until shortly before the Second World War, Sherbrooke was not really a destroyer man at all. He was appointed to the cruiser *Capetown* in 1922 and was a divisional officer in the old monitor *Erebus* for duties with Special Entry Cadets in 1926. Promoted Lieutenant-Commander on 15th April 1929 he served in the battleship *Queen Elizabeth* in the Mediterranean. That same year he also got married at St George's, Hanover Square, to Rosemary Neville, née Buckley; they had two daughters. From the *Queen Elizabeth* he went to another battleship, *Rodney* in the Atlantic Fleet in July 1930, and then to the cruiser *Dauntless* on the America and West Indies Station as First Lieutenant and Senior Watchkeeper in July 1932. He was promoted Commander on 31st December 1935 and went to Malta in August for duties with the Base Defences.

His first destroyer appointment after the First World War was his first command, *Vanoc*, in the Gibraltar Local Defence Flotilla, and in her Sherbrooke saw service in the Spanish Civil War. He was appointed in command of *Cossack* on 29th December 1939. When Vian's own ship was damaged, he took over *Cossack* for the first few months of 1940 (including the *Altmark* Incident in February) but Sherbrooke was once more in command and won a DSO at the second battle of Narvik on 13th April 1940, when *Warspite* and nine destroyers entered the fjord and 'cleaned out' a nest of eight German destroyers. *Cossack* herself was hit by four 5-inch shells and ran aground, where she stayed, fifty yards off an enemy coast, for nearly thirteen hours. She eventually got off, having fired over 800 4.7-inch shells and 500 rounds of 20-mm pompom during the action. Sherbrooke later commanded another 'Tribal' Class destroyer *Matabele*, and served in Freetown, Sierra Leone, before becoming Captain (D) of the 17th Flotilla in November 1942.

He received his Cross from the King at Buckingham Palace in June 1943 and, though blinded in his left eye, returned to duty in

February 1944. He commanded a naval air station in Scotland, and was then Senior Naval Officer at Stavanger in Norway in 1945. He went to the Admiralty as Director of Craft and Amphibious Material in 1946, was Commodore RN Barracks at Lee-on-Solent in 1948, and in command of the aircraft carrier *Indefatigable* in 1951, until he was promoted Rear-Admiral on 7th July 1951. His last appointment was as Flag Officer Germany, and British Representative on the Allied Control Commission. He was retired, medically unfit, on 4th March 1954. In 1953, he was made a CB and was Gentleman Usher of the Scarlet Rod. He was also High Sheriff of Nottingham in 1958. He died at his home on 13th June 1972.

Sherbrooke had only commanded *Onslow* and his Flotilla for four weeks before the action and had had little time to get to know his officers and men. To them he was a somewhat austere figure, sparing with words, always courteous, but remote and a difficult personality to assess. With his silver hair, fine features and air of asceticism, he looked more like an artist than a man of battle, a violinist or a sculptor rather than a sea-captain.

Commander Kenneth Edwards RN, *Seven Sailors* (London: Collins, 1945).
Dudley Pope, *73 North* (London: Weidenfeld & Nicolson, 1958).
Alan Ross, *Open Sea* (London: London Magazine Editions, 1975).
'Convoy to Russia', Recording No. 5111, 12th January 1943, by Chief Petty Officer Fuller; No. 5353, 24th January 1943, by Lt. L.E. Peyton-Jones of *Achates*; No. 10248, 9th November 1944, by Lt-Cdr Hudson RANVR, in the Imperial War Museum Library.

John Wallace Linton:
Mediterranean, 1942-43

'Tubby' Linton was a first-class professional submariner, who was devoted to his trade. He looked the part, with his determined face and black beard. Like many successful submarine captains, he was physically a very strong man, a fine athlete, with a good head for mathematics, and an excellent 'periscope eye'. His career had no single high moment. His VC was not won for any brilliant individual action, but was the reward for a man who exerted a relentless pressure on the enemy, conducting his submarine patrols with skill and daring over a period of nearly four years of war.

John Wallace Linton was born on 15th October 1905 at Claresmont, Malpas, near Newport, Monmouthshire, the son of Edward Maples Barron Linton, an architect, and Margaret Gertrude (née Wallace). He went to Osborne in 1919 and then to Dartmouth,

223

passing out in 1922 with the second prize in his term for mathematics. He was a Midshipman in *Dauntless* and *Royal Oak* from 1923 to 1926 and joined the Submarine Service as a Sub-Lieutenant in 1927. Except for a period from 1936 to 1938, when he served in *Iron Duke* and the destroyer *Westcott*, he was in submarines continuously until his death, and spent eight years in command. He was in L.22 and *Oberon*, First Lieutenant in H.43 and *Oswald*, and commanded L.21 and *Snapper*. From 1927 to 1930 he also played rugby football regularly for the Navy, United Services and Hampshire, and had trials for England.

At the outbreak of war Linton was on the China Station, where he had commanded *Pandora* for a year. The large 2,000-ton 'O', 'P' and 'R' boats of the China Station were unsuitable for the North Sea or the Mediterranean, but the pressure of events brought the China submarines to join the 1st Flotilla at Alexandria in 1940. Linton arrived at Suez in May and went on his first patrol, in the Aegean, in June. In July, when British submarines were ordered to torpedo French warships to prevent them falling into German hands, Linton sank the minelaying sloop *Rigault de Genouilly*.

In December 1940, after five patrols, *Pandora* joined the 8th Flotilla at Gibraltar. By the end of May 1941, Linton had done eleven patrols, had spent 196 days on patrol of a total of 251 at sea, and won a DSC for sinking two Italian supply ships in one attack in January. When *Pandora* went to America for refit at Portsmouth, New Hampshire, in June (she was eventually sunk in an air-raid on Malta in April 1942) Linton went home to commission the new 'T' class submarine *Turbulent* on 18th November 1941. He was promoted to Commander in December and could have had a training or staff appointment but chose to remain in submarine command. He was *Turbulent's* first and only captain, and this was her first and only commission. She sailed from the United Kingdom on 3rd January 1942 and arrived at Alexandria to join the 1st Flotilla in February.

In *Turbulent*, as in *Pandora*, Linton showed the same restless, aggressive spirit, always on the look-out for targets and always pressing his attack in close. In one action, mentioned in his citation, he sighted a convoy of two Italian destroyers and two merchantmen in moonlight and mist. He worked *Turbulent* round on the surface until he was ahead of the convoy, and then dived for the attack as the silhouettes of the ships passed through the moon's rays. While he prepared for his attack, Linton was directly in the path of one destroyer steaming towards him. He held on until the destroyer was almost overhead and then, when his sights came 'on', he fired. He sank the large destroyer *Pessagno* and one merchantman. The other caught fire and eventually blew up. On another occasion, *Turbulent* surfaced and sank six sailing ships and a motor vessel, all carrying German troops, by gunfire. In all, Linton sank nearly 100,000 tons of enemy shipping, including *Pessagno* and twenty-eight ships of various kinds. *Turbulent* also destroyed three trains by gunfire. Her eighth patrol, from 28th October to 2nd December 1942, lasted thirty-five days. In September, Linton was awarded the DSO for his courage and skill in successful submarine patrols.

As in Bomber Command, the odds against survivors in submarines mounted the longer they served, and the more operational patrols they did. At thirty-seven, Linton was now the oldest and most experienced Captain and the doyen of the Flotilla, ready to give advice and consolation to the younger captains if they asked. *Turbulent* sailed for her tenth, and Linton's twenty-first patrol, in the Tyrhennian Sea in February 1943. She was sighted off the east coast of Corsica on 14th March. She was supposed to withdraw on the 18th but, ominously, the day before the Italians had announced that an enemy submarine had blown up on one of their mines in a controlled minefield off Maddalena, a harbour which Linton had reconnoitred on a previous patrol. *Turbulent's* homeward route was signalled to her on the 20th, but there was no reply. On the 24th, after six days' silence, it was clear she was lost, almost certainly in that minefield. In his last year, Linton had spent 254 days at sea, and was submerged for nearly half that time. *Turbulent* had been hunted 13 times and 250 depth-charges had been aimed at her. She was reported overdue, and her captain and crew posted missing, presumed killed, on 3rd May. Linton's posthumous VC was gazetted on 25th May 1943.

In 1929 at Lutterworth, Linton had married Nancy Pitts-Tucker, and they had two sons. The eldest, William Linton, then a naval cadet, went with his mother to Buckingham Palace to receive his father's Victoria Cross from the King on 23rd February 1944. William Linton also joined the Submarine Service. Aged twenty-one, a Sub Lieutenant doing his submarine training, he was one of those lost in *Affray* when she failed to surface in the English Channel on 17th April 1951.

Lloyd Allan Trigg:
Atlantic, West of Dakar, August 1943

In 1943 the Battle of the Atlantic took a decisive turn in the Allies' favour, largely through a series of climactic convoy battles fought in April and May, in which the U-boats were comprehensively defeated and were temporarily withdrawn from the North Atlantic. Long-range aircraft played a very important part in the battles - in fact, the Battle of the Atlantic was very nearly lost for want of a few dozen long-range aircraft at a vital time.

The defeated U-boats went south, in search of easier pickings, and it was there that the first VC of the war awarded for the sinking of a U-boat was won, appropriately by a Coastal Command pilot,

Flying Officer Lloyd Trigg, of the Royal New Zealand Air Force. He and his crew were all killed in the action and the VC was awarded on the recommendation of the U-boat survivors, although this aspect was not stressed until after the war.

Trigg's Liberator, of No.200 Squadron, took off from Rufique, near Dakar, in West Africa, just after dawn on 11th August 1943, to carry out a sea-search patrol far out in the Atlantic. The squadron had just re-equipped at Nassau, in the Bahamas, changing from Hudsons to Liberators, and was based at Yuntum in Gambia. This was Trigg's first operational patrol in a Liberator but he was a very experienced Coastal Command pilot who had already flown forty-five operational sorties. In June that year he had won a Distinguished Flying Cross for his successful attacks on two U-boats which had attacked a West African convoy the previous March.

At about 11 am Trigg was diverted from his own search area to look for a U-boat which had been sighted and unsuccessfully attacked by a Catalina. Later, after some eight hours in the air, Triggs sighted the submarine on the surface. The U-boat, U.468, did not dive but, obeying Dönitz's current tactical policy, stayed on the surface to fight it out. She had been specially fitted with three anti-aircraft guns on the bridge and conning tower, and her gunners' fire was fast and accurate. They hit the Liberator several times as it flew in on its bombing run and set it on fire aft. Flames rapidly enveloped the tail-plane. The Liberator became difficult to fly, and Trigg was soon faced with a choice which meant literally life or death to his crew.

Trigg could have broken off his attack and force-landed his aircraft in the sea. If he continued, the Liberator would present an easier and easier 'no deflection' target at ever-decreasing range, while every second in the air allowed the fire to gain a firmer hold and lessen the chances of survival. Trigg chose to go on and flew over the U-boat at a height of less than fifty feet, while the U-boat's gunners were actually firing up through his open bomb doors. Trigg dropped his bombs in a perfect pattern which straddled the U-boat and exploded all round her. The Liberator flew on and crashed into the sea. Of Trigg and his crew, none survived. U.468 sank twenty minutes later.

When Trigg's Liberator failed to return to base, a search was organised, and the following afternoon a patrolling Sunderland sighted a dinghy containing several men floating in the area where Trigg might have gone down. Next morning a corvette reached the spot and found that the dinghy was from the Liberator but the men were the U-boat Captain and six survivors of his ship's company. It was the U-boat commander's account of the action, and his expressed admiration for the way Trigg had pressed home his attack in the face of accurate fire after his aircraft had been badly damaged, that won Trigg the VC, which was gazetted on 2nd November 1943.

Lloyd Allan Trigg was an agricultural machinery salesman from New Zealand, born on 6th June 1914 at Houhora, North Island. He went to Victoria Valley and Kaitaia primary schools, Whangarei High School and Auckland University College. He joined the RNZAF (Official No. NZ 413515) on 16th June 1941, and embarked for Canada for flying training on 22nd September. He was promoted Flying Officer on 1st October 1942 and embarked for the United Kingdom on 5th November. He arrived in West Africa on 13th December 1942, and joined 200 Squadron, and then went on to No. 111 OTU, Nassau, in May.

In 1937, Trigg married Noalla McGarvie and they had two sons. The Victoria Cross was presented to his widow at his brother's farm in Victoria Valley, North Island, on 28th May 1944. The names of Flying Officer Trigg and his crew are commemorated on the Malta War Memorial, Malta GC.

Donald Cameron and Basil Charles Godfrey Place:
Kaafjord, Norway, September 1943

Hitler probably never realised what a trump-card he held in *Tirpitz*, the 44,000-ton battleship which spent most of her life in one heavily defended Norwegian fjord or another. By herself, *Tirpitz* constituted a 'fleet in being'. All she had to do was like Everest, just be there. As Churchill said, her existence influenced naval movements all over the world. She had no need actually to go to sea, indeed it was better if she did not. At sea she was just one battleship, with a Commander bedevilled by political precautions and a ship's company badly in need of sea-time, escorted by an inexperienced destroyer screen and patchy air cover. But in *harbour*, lying up in her northern fastness at Kaafjord in Norway, she became, like Grendel's mother, a creature of legendary menace and almost supernatural powers. Hidden both by Arctic mists and clouds of rumour, *Tirpitz* swelled ever more monstrous and dangerous the more the Allied staffs thought about her.

Obviously such a dragon could not be allowed to stay unmolested. Before the RAF Lancasters and their 'Tallboy' bombs administered the final *coup de grâce* at Tromso in November 1944, there had been a number of attempts by various arms on *Tirpitz*, of which Operation SOURCE, the X-craft attack of September 1943, was the first to inflict serious damage.

The X-craft were midget submarines, ordered in May 1942 and completed early in 1943. They were 51 feet long, weighed 35 tons, could dive to 300 feet, had a speed of 5 knots and a crew of 3 officers and 1 engine-room artificer. They were armed with 2 side-charges of 2 tons of Torpex explosive each, which could be dropped under a target and set to detonate by clockwork time-fuses.

Six X-craft were built, and two crews - a 'passage crew' and an 'operational crew' - trained for each. All crew members were volunteers for 'special and hazardous service'. For SOURCE, the X-craft were allocated targets: X.8, *Lutzow*; X.9 and X.10, *Scharnhorst*; X.5 (Lieutenant H. Henty-Creer, RNVR), X.6 (Lieutenant D. Cameron RNR) and X.7 (Lieutenant B.C.G.Place RN), *Tirpitz*, in Kaafjord.

Tirpitz returned from her last operational sortie, a somewhat pointless bombardment of Spitzbergen, on 10th September. The X-craft left their depot ship *Bonaventure* in Loch Cairnbawn at intervals on 11th and 12th September, each towed submerged, by a parent submarine on the surface. The proposition was that the X-craft should be towed for more than 1,000 miles to the entrance of a land-locked fortified enemy harbour where the tow would be dropped, penetrate the known anti-submarine defences, lay explosive charges exactly underneath their targets, and then, if possible, return to the open sea and rejoin the parent submarines.

X.9 was lost with all hands on passage; and X.8 had to be scuttled because of defects. X.10's target, *Scharnhorst*, was away from her anchorage doing gunnery trials and X.10 eventually abandoned her operation. But the attack on *Tirpitz* went on as planned.

X.6, although her periscope was defective and Cameron had to complete his attack almost 'blind', penetrated the outer and inner anti-torpedo nets, and by 7.05 am on 22nd September was within striking distance of *Tirpitz*. She then ran aground on the north shore of the enclosure and broke surface. She was seen from *Tirpitz*, but there was an astonishing delay during which X.6 got clear but surfaced again, only eighty yards from *Tirpitz*. Her compass was out of action and her periscope was flooded, but Cameron steered towards the great ship, hoping that her shadow would guide him. X.6 was too close for any of *Tirpitz*'s guns to bear, but men on the upper deck opened fire with rifles and revolvers. X.6 surfaced again, under *Tirpitz*'s bows, where men rained hand-grenades down on her. A quick-witted officer took a launch away from the gangway and lassooed X.6's periscope with a line, but the submarine towed his launch through the water. Cameron realised that escape was now impossible, so destroyed the most secret equipment, went astern until X.6 was abreast 'B' turret, released his charges, and opened the hatch. As he and his crew stepped out, X.6 sank to the bottom. Cameron and his crew were taken on board at about 7.30 am and interrogated by *Tirpitz*'s officers, who could hardly believe their eyes.

Place and his operational crew took over X.7 on the 18th and at once found a mine entangled in the towing wire. Place went forward on the casing and kicked it clear. X.7 entered Altenfjord at 12.30 pm on the 21st, and surfaced that evening to charge the battery. X.7 dived at 1 am on the 22nd and found a gap in the outer net at 4 am. Place waited for a minesweeper to come out before

228

taking X.7 in through the opening. X.7 then ran into an anti-torpedo net at a depth of about thirty feet. The water was so clear Place could see the meshes of the net through the periscope. X.7 went full astern and full ahead, flooded and blew tanks, threshed and fought like a struggling salmon, and eventually got through. Place first sighted Tirpitz at 6.40 am at a range of about a mile. There was yet another net in which X.7 stuck at a depth of about 70 feet. Place later said that 'he had no idea how they got there' but X.7 broke surface inside the net about thirty yards from Tirpitz, on her port beam. Place ordered forty feet and, at full speed, X.7 struck Tirpitz's side at a depth of twenty feet, below 'B' turret, slid gently under the keel, swung fore and aft in line with the ship, and jettisoned the starboard side charge. X.7 went slowly astern for about 150 to 200 feet further aft and dropped the port side charge.

The charges had a time delay of about an hour, but the time could not be relied upon precisely and it was essential for X.7 to get away. Place tried frantically to get through the net but X.7 was still stuck in it when the charges went off at 8.12. Tirpitz's log read, 'Two heavy consecutive detonations to port at a tenth of a second interval. Ship vibrates strongly in vertical direction, and sways slightly between the anchors.'

The impact was surprisingly small in X.7 and in fact blew her clear of the nets. But her compasses and diving gauges were out of action, and the boat was difficult to control and broke surface several times, whereupon Tirpitz's guns opened fire and inflicted damage on the hull and the periscope. With almost all her high-pressure air exhausted, X.7 sat on the bottom while Place considered the situation. There was enough air for one more trip to the surface. Place decided he must abandon the craft. X.7 surfaced beside a battle practice target, about 500 yards off Tirpitz's starboard bow. Place got out and began to wave a white sweater. Unfortunately a small amount of water lapped into X.7 and in her low state of buoyancy it was enough to send her to the bottom. Sub-Lieutenant R. Aitken RNVR made a successful Davis Apparatus escape three hours later, but Lieutenant L.B. Whittam RNVR and Engine Room Artificer W.M. Whitley were drowned.

Henty-Creer's X.5 reached a position 500 yards outside the inner net and was sighted on the surface from Tirpitz at 8.43 am, after the charges had detonated. X.5 was sunk by gunfire and depth-charges and none of her crew survived.

Had the charges all exploded directly underneath Tirpitz she would probably have sunk. Her crew managed to move her bows to starboard, away from the charges, so that they blew up more to her port side. Even so, she was badly damaged and unable to go to sea until April 1944. For the loss of four men in X.5, four in X.9, and two in X.7, a major warship had been crippled.

Cameron, Place and the other survivors became prisoners-of-war.

VCs for Cameron and Place were gazetted on 22nd February 1944 and were presented to them by the King when they had been repatriated after the war at an Investiture at Buckingham Palace on 22nd June 1945. Aitken, of X.7 and Sub-Lieutenant J.T. Lorimer and R.H. Kendall RNVR of X.6 were awarded DSOs, ERA E. Goddard also of X.6 won the CGM, and Lieutenant K.R. Hudspeth RANVR of X.10 won the DSC. Other operational and passage crew members were mentioned in despatches or awarded the MBE.

Donald Cameron was a Scot, born in Carluke, Lanarkshire on 18th March 1916. But for the war he might have joined the RAF. He had passed for Cranwell and while waiting to enter he went to sea, aged sixteen, in the Merchant Service. He became a Midshipman RNR in August 1939 and from then on made his life in the Navy. He joined the submarine service in August 1940 and served in *Sturgeon* before becoming one of the first X-craft volunteers in mid-1941. He was First Lieutenant of X.3, the first midget, when she was launched at Varley Marine Ltd on the Hamble River on 15th March 1942, and served in her through the trials and training of the summer of 1942, taking over as Captain in October. The following month he went up to Barrow to take over the operational X-craft X.6, and began training for the attack on *Tirpitz*.

After the war Cameron kept up his connection with submarines. He was First Lieutenant of *Spiteful* when he transferred to a permanent commission in the Royal Navy on 3rd May 1946, and after passing the COs' qualifying course, commanded the 'T' class submarine *Tiptoe* from 1947 to 1948. He then went as a divisional officer to *Ganges*, the boys' training establishment at Shotley, and in April 1950 to America as Senior Officer XE-craft to demonstrate midget submarines to the United States Navy. He commanded the sloop *Gateshead* from November 1950 to June 1951, and the submarine *Trump* from July 1951 until promoted Commander in January 1953. He did a staff course in March and then went to RN Air Station *Goldcrest* as executive officer. In January 1955 he returned to the submarine world, to *Dolphin*, the submarine base at Fort Blockhouse, as Commander (Submarines).

He married his wife Eve(née Kilpatrick), then serving in the WRNS, in 1940, and they had four children - two boys and two girls. His health deteriorated in the last years of his life and he fell ill at his home in Gosport, and was taken to the RN Hospital Haslar, where he died on 10th April 1961. His body was buried at sea from HM Submarine *Thule* on 13th April.

Place was the only Regular naval officer of all the early X-craft volunteers and his were the only RN initials amongst all the RNRs, RNVRs, RNZNVRs, RANVRs and SANF(V)s of the Honours and In Memoriam lists. Basil Charles Godfrey Place was born on 19th July 1921 at Wintercott, Little Malvern, Worcestershire, eldest child and only son of Charles Godfrey Morris Place, barrister-at-law in the Colo-

230

nial Service, and Anna Margaret (née Stuart-Williams). His father was later Solicitor General of Northern Rhodesia, and served in the East Surreys in the First World War, winning the DSO and MC. Place went to The Grange, Folkestone, and then to RNC Dartmouth, aged thirteen. He was a Midshipman in the cruiser *Newcastle* when war broke out, and was promoted Sub-Lieutenant, joining the submarine service in June 1941. He was liaison officer in Malta for the Polish submarine *Sokol* and was awarded the Polish medal Kryzn Walecynicj ('Cross of Valour') in November 1942. Place served in *Urge*, *Una* and *Unbeaten* in the Mediterranean and won a DSC in *Unbeaten* for an action on 17th March 1942. He was promoted Lieutenant in 1942 and as one of the early X-craft volunteers commanded the second experimental X-craft X.4, before taking command of the operational X-craft X.7. After capture and intense interrogation, Place, Cameron and the other X-craft survivors spent the rest of the war in Marlag-Milag Nord.

After the war Place resumed his naval career but unlike Cameron he did not return to submarines and in fact never had another submarine appointment. He was in the frigate *Cardigan Bay* from 1946 to 1948, was promoted Lieutenant-Commander in 1950 and then went over to the Fleet Air Arm, an almost unprecedented action for a submariner. He began a naval flying training course in May 1951 and received his wings at a parade at Syerston, Nottinghamshire, on 1st February 1952. Promoted Commander in 1952, he served as a Pilot and Squadron Commander in the aircraft carrier *Glory* in the Korean War. From then on his appointments were either in the Air Arm or general service surface ships: staff of Flag Officer Flying Training, 1953-5; command of the destroyer *Tumult*, 1955-6; executive officer of the carrier *Theseus*, 1956-7; and command of the destroyer *Corunna* from 1957 to 1958, when he was promoted Captain. His appointments in the new rank showed the same pattern: Chief Staff Officer to Flag Officer Aircraft Carriers, 1958-60; Deputy Director of Air Warfare, 1960-2; command of the frigate *Rothesay* and Captain (F) 6th Frigate Squadron, 1962-4; Captain of *Ganges*, 1964-6; command of the carrier *Albion*, 1966-8; promoted Rear-Admiral, 1968; Admiral commanding Reserves, 1968 until his retirement in 1970. He was also made CB the same year.

In July 1943 in Grimsby, only a few weeks before the attack on *Tirpitz*, he married Althea Tickler, then Second Officer WRNS, daughter of Harry Tickler of Danebury House, Grimsby. Henty-Creer was their best man. They had a son and two daughters. Admiral and Mrs Place live near Sherborne in Dorset. The Admiral is Chairman of the VC and GC Association.

Captain W.R. Fell CMG, CBE, DSC, RN, *The Sea our Shield* (London :Cassell, 1946).
Gervis Frere-Cook, *The Attacks on the Tirpitz* (London: Ian Allan, 1973).

Thomas Gallagher, *Against All Odds* (London:Macdonald, 1971).

C.E. Lucas-Phillips, *Victoria Cross Battles of the Second World War,* 'David and Goliath' (London: Heinemann, 1975).

C.E.T. Warren and James Benson, *Above Us the Waves* (London: Harrap, 1953).

David Woodward, *The Tirpitz* (London:Kimber, 1953).

'Midget Submarine Attack on *Tirpitz*', a talk by Rear-Admiral C.B. Barry, recorded 22nd February (the day the VCs were gazetted) 1944, Tape No. 6934, Imperial War Museum.

'Accounts by Place and Cameron'. Tape No. 8702, recorded 21st June 1945, Imperial War Museum.

'The Attack on the *Tirpitz* by Midget Submarines on 22nd September 1943 (Operation Source)', Supplement to the *London Gazette*, 11th February 1948.

David Ernest Hornell:
Atlantic, North of the Shetlands, June 1944

On the evening of 24th June 1944, the twin-engined Canso 'A' (Catalina) flying boat 'P for Peter' of No.162 Squadron, Coastal Command, was about 250 miles north of the Shetlands, flying at 1,500 feet southwards and homewards to her base at Wick in the north of Scotland. She had been in the air for about ten hours, patrolling what was known as the Northern Transit Area, a wide stretch of the Atlantic between Iceland and Norway where in 1944 several U-boats were intercepted and sunk while on outward passage to their patrol areas. No. 162 Squadron, Royal Canadian Air Force, was a most successful unit, having already sunk three U-boats in the area that June, and a fourth earlier in April. P-Peter's crew of eight were all Canadians, led by an experienced captain and first pilot, Flight Lieutenant 'Bud' Hornell RCAF, and an equally experienced co-pilot, Flying Officer Bernard Denomy, whose own crew were on leave.

The crew's thoughts were drifting towards base and bed, and Hornell was preoccupied by the worsening weather situation when, just after 7 pm, Flight Sergeant Bodnoff, the 2nd wireless-air gunner, sitting in the port 'blister' - a perspex-covered bulge behind the wing - reported a submarine on the surface, five miles away on P-Peter's port beam. It was a U-boat thrashing along at full speed, north-westwards out into the Atlantic.

Although he had over 600 flying hours and 60 operational sorties, this was the first enemy Hornell had ever seen. He pressed the alarm klaxon for action stations and turned his Canso in a wide circle to port, to attack the U-boat in a long shallow dive from astern. P-Peter had four depth-charges - quite sufficient if Hornell could only get close enough to drop them.

232

The U-boat was U.1225, a 750-ton Type VII patrol submarine, armed with one 37 mm and four quick-firing 20 mm AA guns. Following current U-boat practice, she stayed on the surface to fight it out. The Canso's crew could see the U-boat's gunners manning their guns. As usual, the German gunnery was excellent. They opened fire at four miles, and although Hornell flew a weaving course from side to side to throw them off their aim, the U-boat gunners continued to put up an intense and accurate flak barrage as the Canso closed them. The Canso's front gunner, Flying Officer Campbell, opened fire at 1,200 yards and although the starboard gun jammed, caused casualties amongst the guns' crews. But the Canso herself was badly hit several times at half a mile. Flight Sergeant Cole, who was transmitting an enemy sighting report (which, with his later SOS, was never received) was lucky to escape alive: 'The flak was coming in to the fuselage like hail, so thick you could see where it was punching holes in the metal. A large piece exploded beside me and knocked me off my feet. Pieces grazed my leg and my cheek, and the concussion stunned me for a few seconds.' Denomy, sitting beside Hornell, could see that

...we were hard hit. Big holes were torn in the wings and fuselage and the starboard engine caught fire. We feathered this engine and were flying on the one remaining. Bud guided the badly damaged aircraft into the attack. Before long our starboard engine, which was burning, broke loose from the wing and fell into the sea. Bud fought with the controls which were damaged, either from anti-aircraft shells or from fire, we did not know. With one engine gone and the aircraft afire we had a tough time trying to keep the aircraft trimmed and at the same time press home the attack. This, however, he did and we coasted in to within thirty or forty feet above the enemy sub and loosed our depth-charges.

At 200-yards range the U-boat turned violently to port to make a more difficult bombing target, but Hornell managed to follow her. U.1225's bows reared up, and several men were seen to fall into the sea. Intelligence later confirmed that she was lost with all hands.

Hornell tried to keep his aircraft flying on one engine but it was hopeless. He flew up wind and ditched:

We landed on waves twelve feet high [said Cole] and bounced 150 feet. With most of the controls shot away, Bud had to fight with every ounce of strength to bring us down safely at all. We bounced fifty feet the second time we hit the water, but the skipper still had control. By this time the oil and fuel in our starboard tanks caught fire and we could only escape through the port blister. The starboard side was a mass of flames.

Hornell and Denomy went out through the forward emergency hatch, the others through the blister openings. Flight Sergeant St Laurent, Second Flight Engineer, put one dinghy through the starboard opening and jumped into it, but flames prevented anybody following him. When the dinghy inflated, it overturned and St Laurent floated away on his own. Bodnoff and the First Flight Engineer, Sergeant Scott, launched the other dinghy through the port blister and the seven crew members boarded as best they could, some inside, the rest hanging on. When the dinghy inflated, it still took ten minutes' hard work to reach St Laurent's dinghy, and when they reached it, it promptly burst. The eight of them now had to make do with one dinghy designed for four men. By throwing out paddles and the ration box they made extra room for themselves.

Four hours later they were sighted quite by chance by a Catalina of No. 333 (Norwegian) Squadron, which saw their last flare and circled above them, homing rescue craft to the scene for the next twelve hours before being relieved by another Catalina.

Meanwhile below, Hornell and his crew saw evidence from the U-boat - oil, planks and baulks of wood, and the lifejacketed body of a German sailor. 'We didn't know if he was alive or dead and didn't much care,' said Cole. 'We didn't have room in the dinghy for enemy survivors and I grabbed a can of water to bash him over the head if he had tried to come aboard.'

The sea was getting much rougher and waves were climbing to twenty feet. In such conditions, hope meant life, and Hornell did his best to encourage his men with his own cheerfulness and inspiring example. But the next morning, after fourteen hours in the sea, the dinghy overturned. They managed to get it upright but the effort weakened them. St Laurent was the first to die, becoming first delirious and then unconscious. They slipped his body quietly over the side. An aircraft dropped another lifeboat but it was too far for them to reach it. Hornell said he would swim over and get it. His crew could see that he was no longer capable of such an effort and restrained him. Three hours later Scott died and his body, too, was slipped overboard.

Twenty hours after the ditching a Sunderland flying boat appeared, which fired red Very lights and dropped floating flares to guide an Air-Sea rescue launch. Hornell was very weak from exhaustion and was blinded. When Cole saw the launch he 'let out a whoop you could have heard in Ottawa'. The six survivors were picked up. Hornell was in the last stages of exhaustion. The launch crew tried for five hours to resuscitate him but he became unconscious and died. He was buried ashore in Lerwick, in the Shetland Isles. His posthumous VC was gazetted on 28th July 1944 and was presented to his widow at Government House, Ottawa, by

234

the Governor-General, the Earl of Athlone, on 12th December 1944. Hornell was the first member of the RCAF to win the Victoria Cross. Denomy was awarded a DSO, Flying Officers Matheson, the navigator, and Campbell DFCs, Bodnoff and Cole DFMs.

David Ernest Hornell was born in Mimico, Ontario, on 26th January 1910. He was educated in Mimico and at Western Technical School, Toronto, where he was a fine athlete, tennis player and swimmer. He was a founder member of the Lakeside Tennis Club, near Toronto, and superintendent of his local Sunday school in Mimico. He worked in the research laboratory of the Goodyear Tyre and Rubber Co., and joined up on 8th January 1941, volunteering for flying training, although at thirty he was old for a pilot. He learned to fly at elementary school at Goderich, Ontario, and then went to the advanced course at Brantford, getting his wings on 25th September 1941. He was selected for Coastal Command and went to the General Reconnaissance School at Charlottetown, Prince Edward Island. He was posted to a flying boat squadron at Coal Harbour in northern Vancouver Island and flew Stranraers throughout 1942. He went on leave in January 1943 and came back with a wife, a school-teacher from his home town of Mimico. He was promoted to Flight Lieutenant on 15th April, 1943 and posted to 162 Squadron in October. The squadron was later based at Reykjavik, and then at Wick.

Ron Dodds, 'Ordeal by Fire, Ordeal by Water', *The Legionary*, May 1966.
Kenneth Hare-Scott, *For Valour*, 'David Ernest Hornell' (London: Peter Garnett, 1949).
Air Chief Marshal Sir Philip Joubert, 'Fight to the Death–Flying Boat v U-boat', *Sunday Express*, 8th April 1962.

John Alexander Cruickshank:
Arctic Ocean, West of Narvik, July 1944

'Softly, softly, catchee monkey' might have been the Coastal Command motto for attacking surfaced U-boats. The trick was to get over the target fast, before the U-boat could dive and gain depth or her gunners man their guns. For this, centimetric radar was a great advantage to an aircraft, enabling it to dive out of cloud. But once surprise had been lost, it was a brave and skilful pilot who managed to attack successfully. The U-boats were well armed and determined and with their 37-mm and 20-mm guns were quite capable of knocking a Liberator or a Catalina out of the sky.

Shortly before 2 pm on the afternoon of 17th July 1944, a two-engined long-range Catalina flying boat of No.210 Squadron, Coastal Command, piloted by Flying Officer J.A. Cruickshank RAFVR, took off from Sullom Voe in the Shetland Islands for an anti-submarine search patrol of the Northern Transit Area, which was a wide stretch of ocean between Iceland and Norway. Here several U-boats were caught and sunk, whilst on outward passage to their patrol areas, in a most successful air campaign in the summer of 1944. At about 10 pm that evening, the Catalina was some 200 miles west of Narvik. In July, in those high latitudes it was still broad daylight, but the Catalina's first contact was by radar: a single 'blip' showing on the cathode-ray screen. Cruickshank immediately closed the contact and coming down out of cloud, at about 1,000 feet, sighted the vessel on the surface, apparently stopped at a range of some six miles. Cruickshank flew up into cloud again, while still heading for the target, and next sighted it at about two miles. It had got under way and was turning to starboard. It was still possible the vessel was friendly so Cruickshank fired a recognition cartridge followed by the code letter of the day. The strange ship increased speed, turned hard-a-port, began to zig-zag violently, and replied with a burst of AA fire. Cruickshank, now in no doubt, also turned to port in a complete circle and flew along the target's wake, to attack from astern. The target, U.347 outward bound on patrol, now at full speed, kept up a fierce but inaccurate fire as the Catalina approached. Cruickshank's front gunner opened fire at 1,000-yards range and scored hits on the conning tower. Cruickshank pressed home a perfect attack and flew over the U-boat at less than fifty feet. Unfortunately, when the moment came, all the depth-charges 'hung up' and did not drop.

Although all surprise had now been lost and the U-boat crew must have been tremendously encouraged by their escape, Cruickshank climbed, turned and attacked again. This time the Catalina was hit again and again by a fierce and accurate fire. The Navigator/Bomb-Aimer was killed outright, the Second Pilot and two others of the crew were injured. Cruickshank himself was wounded in no less than seventy-two places, with two serious injuries in his lungs, and ten penetrating wounds in his hips and legs. The Catalina itself was becoming hard to fly, and the shattered interior was filled with smoke and fumes. Nevertheless, Cruickshank flew on and, aiming the depth-charges and releasing them himself, straddled U.347 perfectly. Intelligence later reported she was lost with all hands.

After the high climax of the attack, Cruickshank suffered the inevitable reaction and collapsed. The Second Pilot took over the controls. When he recovered Cruickshank was bleeding badly but insisted on taking over command again. Only when he was reassured that the Catalina was flying under proper control, the correct course for base had been set, and all the necessary signals transmitted, did Cruickshank consent to have first aid for his injuries. He refused pain-killing morphia in case it prevented him from carrying on.

The flight back took five and a half hours. Cruickshank passed out

236

several times from loss of blood. When they arrived over Sullom Voe in the Shetlands, Cruickshank could see that the water was too rough for his Catalina, damaged as it was, with badly injured men on board and a less experienced second pilot, who was also wounded. Although for a man in his condition every minute was critical, Cruickshank had himself propped up in the second pilot's seat, and ordered the Catalina to fly round for an hour, until the sea and light conditions improved. He supervised the landing and the taxi-ing, and ordered the aircraft to be beached so that it could be more easily salvaged. When assistance, including a medical officer, finally arrived on board, Cruickshank fainted after his long ordeal and had to be given a blood transfusion on his way to hospital. His VC was gazetted on 1st September 1944, and was presented to him, when he had recovered from his injuries, by the King at Holyrood Palace, Edinburgh, on 21st September 1945.

John Alexander Cruickshank was born at 14 Fonthill Road, Aberdeen on 20th May 1920, the son of James Crane Cruickshank, a civil engineer, and Alice (née Bow). He went to Aberdeen Grammar School and to Daniel Stewart's College, Edinburgh. He worked as clerk in the Commercial Bank of Scotland branch in Edinburgh, and joined the Territorial Army in April 1939, being mobilised with the Royal Artillery in August. Cruickshank transferred to the RAF in 1941, becoming an AC2 on 13th June. He was commissioned as a Pilot Officer on 5th July 1942, promoted Flying Officer on 5th December, and Flight Lieutenant on 5th July 1944. After leaving the RAF on 13th September 1946, he became a bank official on the Eastern staff of the National and Grindlays Bank Ltd, and on 7th May 1955, in Rangoon, married Marian Beverly. They have no children. Mr and Mrs Cruickshank live in Edinburgh.

Thomas Peck Hunter:
Lake Comacchio, Italy, April 1945

By April 1945 the Eighth Army had fought their way up into Northern Italy and, now commanded by General Sir Richard McCreery, stood poised to begin their very last battle of the war - the forcing of the Argenta Gap, east of Bologna. The advance began with an attack by the Commandos and 24th Guards Brigade along the coast road running north across a spit of sandy land which separated Lake Comacchio from the Adriatic.

On 2nd April, the leading 'C' Troop of 43 Commando reached a position some 400 yards south of the Reno River, which flowed into the sea to their right. Their objective was the small town of Porto Garibaldi, five miles to the north. Corporal Tom Hunter, of 'C' Troop, in charge of the bren-gun section, could see that the enemy held a cluster of houses south of the river, which was channelled between banks at this point, like a canal, Hunter also knew that the Troop behind him were lying in the open, because the country was completely devoid of any cover. At any moment enemy machine-gun fire would sweep the area and decimate the Troop. Without any orders or prior consultation of any kind, Hunter took the bren-gun himself, got to his feet and ran alone across 200 yards of open ground towards the houses held by the enemy.

Three Spandau heavy machine guns from the houses and six more from the north bank of the river opened fire, while mortars began to shell the Troop behind. The German gunners seemed fascinated by this single figure, evidently bent on suicide, for Hunter attracted most of the fire on himself. But so determinedly and elusively did he run, firing the bren from the hip as he came on, that the Spandau gunners in the houses were demoralised and six of them surrendered to Hunter, while the rest fled across a footbridge to the other side of the river. Disregarding completely the enemy fire, and their surrenders, Hunter ran through the houses, changing the magazine on his bren as he ran. The Troop meanwhile took the chance to close up behind Hunter, whilst the enemy were distracted.

Hunter flung himself down on a heap of rubble in plain view of the enemy, set the bren-gun up, and fired at the Spandau gun emplacements in concrete pill-boxes on the other side of the river. Most of the Troop had reached the cover of the houses behind him. Hunter shouted encouragement to them and called for more bren magazines to be brought up to him. He kept up his own fire with great accuracy to the end, but could not defy the odds for ever: a burst of Spandau fire hit him in the head and he was killed instantly. His posthumous VC, the first and only VC to be won by the Royal Marines in the Second World War, was gazetted on 12th June 1945 and presented to his parents by King George VI at a special ceremony in the Picture Gallery of Holyrood Palace, Edinburgh, on 26th September 1945.

Thomas Peck Hunter may actually have been born in Hampshire, but that was an accident of his father's posting. He was a Scot from an Army family, born at Louise Margaret Hospital, Aldershot on 6th October 1923, the son of Lance-Sergeant Ramsey Hunter of the 2nd Royal Scots (1st Foot) and Mary (née Wingate). Their home was at Stenhouse, Edinburgh, where Thomas went to school. He worked for a firm of printers and stationers, and joined the local Home Guard, before being called up on 23rd June 1942, aged nineteen, and joined the Royal Marines (Official No. C/HX 111296). He joined the Commandos when they were expanded and reorganised in August 1943, was promoted Lance-Corporal on 6th October 1943 and Corporal on 25th January 1945. He was buried at Argenta Gap War Cemetery.

After the war, £10,000 was raised by public subscription to build five cottages at Stenhouse, Edinburgh, in Tom Hunter's memory. Built under the auspices of the Scottish War Veterans' Association, the cottages were opened by the Commandant General Royal Marines in March 1954. A ship's bell, mounted in a brick monument, is also dedicated to his memory at the Depot RM, Lympstone.

Ian Edward Fraser and James Joseph Magennis:
Johore Straits, July 1945

'You're the little guys with a lotta guts!' the Americans told the men of the 14th Submarine Flotilla, consisting of an improved XE-Class of midget submarine, when they arrived in Australia in their depot ship *Bonaventure* in April 1945. But when Captain W. R. Fell, commanding the flotilla, called on Rear-Admiral James Fife, commanding US submarines in the S W Pacific Area, he was told there were no targets for X-craft. For a time there was a real chance that the flotilla would be paid off and *Bonaventure* used as a supply ship in the Fleet Train.

However, on 31st May, when Captain Fell was attending a staff conference in Sydney, he was asked whether his midget submarines' divers could cut submarine telegraph cables, which at that stage of the war were the only secure means of communication still open to the Japanese. The Flotilla went to Hervey Bay on the east coast of Queensland, to practise on a disused Australia-New Caledonia cable. When Fell reported that cable-cutting was feasible, he was delighted to hear that further targets were suggested: two Japanese heavy cruisers, moored in the Johore Straits, off Singapore dockyard.

Thus by the end of July 1945 the Flotilla had three projected operations: two to cut cables in the Lamma Channel, off Hong Kong, and at Cap St Jacques, off Saigon, and Operation STRUGGLE to sink the 10,000-ton cruisers *Takao* and *Miyoko*, in the Johore Straits. Both had previously been damaged in action but it was believed they might still be repaired, and in any case, could be used as floating gun-batteries to defend the Straits.

STRUGGLE was carried out by XE.1 (Lieutenant J. E. Smart RNVR) and XE.3 (Lieutenant I.E. Fraser RNR) towed by *Stygian* and *Spark* respectively, which sailed from Labuan on 26th July. As in the attack on *Tirpitz*, passage crews, as their name suggested, manned the X-craft for the towed passage and were relieved by the operational crews who were to carry out the attack. Fraser and his operational crew, consisting of Sub-Lieutenant W.J.L. ('Kiwi') Smith RNZNVR, ERA C. Reid and Leading Seaman J.J. Magennis, transferred from *Stygian* to XE.3 by rubber dinghy at 6 am on 30th July. XE.3 slipped her tow at 11 o'clock that night, about two and a half miles from the Horsburgh Light, at the eastern end of the Singapore Channel. Fraser and his crew now faced an intricate and dangerous passage of some forty miles, past shoals and wrecks, across minefields and listening posts, through a buoyed boom and surface patrols, first along the Singapore Channel and then north and west through the Johore Straits which lay between Singapore island and the Johore mainland. If they fell into Japanese hands they were likely to be executed as spies.

Navigated by Fraser, who knew his courses and distances by heart, XE.3 made a steady five knots on the surface and passed the Johore listening posts just after 2 am on 31st July. At 4.30 am Fraser had to dive hurriedly to avoid a tanker and its escort which came looming up out of the dark, and XE.3 hit the bottom at thirty-six feet, damaging the logs which measured speed and distance and on which Fraser relied for his dead-reckoning navigation. In the heat and confinement of the X-craft, conditions were extremely unpleasant. Fraser and his crew kept themselves going by sipping orange juice from the refrigerator and at 6 am they took Benzedrine stimulant tablets. XE.3 was then just off the eastern point of Singapore island, near Changi gaol (whose grim grey towers and roofs, with the Rising Sun flag flying above, Fraser actually saw to port through his periscope).

At 9.30 am Fraser sighted the line of buoys which marked the boom, and, waiting outside, managed to follow a small unwary trawler through at 10.30 am. As XE.3 worked her way steadily up the Straits at forty feet, Magennis began to dress in his rubber frogman's suit, assisted by Fraser. The temperature was 85° F inside the submarine and the air heavy and sticky. At 12.50 pm, Fraser saw the shrubby shore of Singapore island to his left, some buildings ahead, and then quite suddenly the target - *Takao*. As Fraser said, 'Although she seemed to appear with the suddenness of an apparition, I had the feeling that I had been staring at her for a long time. She was heavily camouflaged and she lay in the exact position I had plotted on my chart.'

It was 1.52 pm when Fraser began his attack. He and his crew had been nineteen hours without proper sleep and nine hours submerged in their midget submarine. But now was the time for their supreme effort. *Takao* was anchored with her stern only 50 to 100 yards from the Singapore side of the Straits. The depth of water around her was only 11-17 feet but she lay across a depression in the sea-bed some 500 feet wide. Fraser had somehow to get XE.3 across the shallows and into the hole below *Takao*. (He had already announced to the depot-ship staff that he thought this was impossible.)

The first attack was too fine on *Takao*'s bow. Fraser retired and at 3.03 pm he tried again. This time he slid XE.3 neatly under the target. Magennis went out through the 'wet and dry compartment' (which could be flooded and pumped to let a diver in or out of the submarine) and began to fix limpet mines to *Takao*'s bottom. The plates were covered in weeds and marine growth and Magennis had to chip and clear away for over half an hour before he could place his six mines properly. Their magnets were unaccountably weak and the mines kept floating up and away, with Magennis swimming after them and bringing them back.

When Magennis came back, Fraser's next task was to release the two side-charges, each of two tons of Amatol. The port charge dropped away cleanly but the starboard side stuck. So too did XE.3, underneath *Takao*, and Fraser and his crew had a frantic few minutes' manoeuvring before the submarine came free. The starboard charge was still there. Fraser volunteered to go out and release it but Magennis insisted that he was the diver and he would go. Armed with a spanner, he climbed out again and in five minutes - the longest five minutes of Fraser's life - he released the charge. He came back for the second time and then it was full speed for home. XE.3 rendezvoused with *Stygian* and was taken in tow again, reaching Labuan on 4th August. Smart and XE.1 arrived the next day. Their target *Miyoko* was further up the Straits than *Takao* and they had been delayed by patrol craft. They approached *Takao* shortly before Fraser's charges were timed to detonate, so Smart added his burden to Fraser's under *Takao* and retired. The combined charges duly detonated and blew a great hole in *Takao*'s bottom.

Fraser was dismayed to find there were plans in *Bonaventure* for him to repeat STRUGGLE. He felt he had done enough and more than enough, and was greatly relieved when the end of the war made the operation unnecessary. On his way back to the United Kingdom, Fraser passed through Singapore and was shown over the remains of *Takao*. To his bitter disappointment he found that there had only been a skeleton crew on board her when he attacked. The Japanese Navy had written the vessel off. Nevertheless, he and Magennis were recommended for and awarded the Victoria Cross, gazetted on 13th November 1945, and presented by the King at Buckingham Palace on 11th December. 'Kiwi' Smith got a DSO, and Reid the CGM.

It had been Fraser's ambition to transfer to the regular Royal Navy after the war, but it soon became obvious to him that he was not going to be offered a permanent commission and in August 1946 he withdrew his application. He was discharged on 4th March 1947, to face the uncertainties of civilian life. His VC had changed his life, and so Fraser used his VC intelligently and resourcefully to give himself as good a start as possible in that new life. He was a professional frogman, so with other ex-frogmen and Service colleagues he formed his own company, Universal Divers Ltd, to exploit their skills. Fraser was managing director and later chairman. To help finance their company, Fraser organised what can only be called a performing troupe of frogmen, who appeared in a kind of circus turn in which they went through their underwater paces, re-enacting their wartime experience in a glass-sided tank in such various venues as Belle Vue, Manchester, and the Shakespeare Theatre, Liverpool. Their act, which unashamedly traded on Fraser's VC, was fiercely criticised as 'commercialising the VC'.

Fraser was upset by the disapproval; but unabashed, and rightly so, went on with his performances and with Universal Divers. By coincidence, one of their very first contracts was to refloat the Greek-owned *Matrona*, which had dangerously capsized in Bidston Dock, Birkenhead. She was being converted back again to a passenger ship, from her previous service as hospital ship - she was in fact the Elder Dempster Line *Aba*, in defence of which Petty Officer Sephton (*qv*) had won his posthumous VC off Crete in May 1941. As the years passed, Fraser converted himself from a young 'green' naval officer into a businessman. Universal Divers and his later companies expanded into the field of exploration and maintenance of North Sea oil and gas rigs.

Ian Edward Fraser could well have been born in Johore - an irony he himself observed as he was making his submerged way up the Johore Straits in XE.3. He was actually born at 79 Uxbridge Road, Ealing, in Middlesex on 18th December 1920, the son of Sydney Fraser, marine engineer, and Florence Irene (née McKenzie), but within six months he was in Kuala Lumpur where his father was employed as an engineer. He went to school in Wallasey, Wirral, Cheshire, and to High Wycombe Royal Grammar School in Buckinghamshire and then to HMS *Conway*, the Merchant Navy training ship in the Mersey. In 1938 he joined the Blue Funnel Line as a cadet and went to sea in *Tuscan Star* and *Sydney Star*. In June 1939 he joined the battleship *Royal Oak* as a Midshipman RNR for what he thought was to be four months' training and was on board her for the July 1939 Review of the Fleet in Weymouth Bay, Dorset. After war broke out, he served in the destroyer *Keith* and then went on to as eventful a war as many men had, setting his VC aside. He was in the destroyer *Montrose* at Dunkirk, and in another destroyer, *Malcolm*, when she and other escorts sank U.651 in the Atlantic on 29th June 1941. Then, 'for no valid reason which I can now recall', he volunteered for submarines.

He served in P.35 and H.43 and then, on 1st April 1942, joined *Sahib* in the 10th S/M Squadron in the Mediterranean, winning the DSC. In one depot ship party after a patrol, somebody threw a heavy brass ashtray which landed on Frasers foot and broke a bone. He was unable to go on *Sahib's* next patrol, in which she was lost and all but one of her crew became prisoners-of-war. Fraser, the survivor, was appointed First Lieutenant of the old submarine H.44, refitting at Sheerness.

In 1943, while standing by for H.44's refit, Fraser married his 'childhood sweetheart' or at least a girl he had known from their teens, Miss Melba Estelle Hughes, of Wallasey. His bride was a Wren, then serving at Pwllheli on the North Wales coast. They eventually had six children, four boys and two girls.

H.44 went to Londonderry, 'ping running' for escorts working up. It was a boring life and, more from boredom than anything else, Fraser volunteered for X-craft in March 1944. He trained in X.20 in Loch Cairnbawn before, on 27th November 1944, XE.3 was launched at Rothesay by Mrs Fraser. XE.3 was unofficially named *Sigyn*, after the ever-loving wife of Loki in Norse mythology, and had the unofficial motto 'Softly, softly, catchee monkey'.

Fraser was made officer of the US Legion of Merit in 1945. He kept his RNR rank until he finally retired as a Lieutenant Commander in 1966. The Borough of Wallasey raised just over £300 by public subscription for Lieutenant Fraser, and presented him with a Sword Of Honour.

James Joseph Magennis was at the Palace with Fraser on 11th December 1945, and he was discharged from the Navy on 24th November 1949, but for him post-war life was rather different. He was born at 4 Majorca Street, Belfast on 27th October 1919, the son of William Magennis and Mary (née Murphy). As the only Ulster VC winner of the Second World War, Magennis was obviously a huge celebrity in Belfast. The citizens of Belfast, through a 'Shilling Fund', raised £3,066 for their VC, which was soon spent by Mr and Mrs Magennis. 'We are simple people,' Magennis's wife Edna explained, 'we were forced into the limelight. We lived beyond our means because it seemed the only thing to do.' Fraser explained Magennis's problem better than anybody - from personal experience:

A man is trained for the task that might win him the VC. He is not trained to cope with what follows. He is not told how to avoid going under in a flood of public adulation. Three months after I received my VC I refused all further invitations to functions in my honour. All this flattery was becoming dangerous.

Magennis was a regular RN sailor, who joined as a boy seaman *Ganges* on 3rd June 1935. He served in the battleship *Royal Sovereign*, the cruiser *Dauntless* trooping to China, the cruiser *Enterprise* on the East Indies Station, and the aircraft carrier *Hermes* with the Home Fleet. After torpedo courses at *Defiance*, the torpedo school at Devonport, he joined the destroyer *Kandahar* and was one of her survivors when she was mined off Tripoli in December 1941. He then volunteered for submarines and after that for midget submarines. He was one of the passage crew in Place's X.7 for the attack on *Tirpitz* in September 1943. He was, as Fraser said, 'the first frogman to work against an enemy from a midget submarine in the manner designed; he was the first and only frogman during the whole X-craft operations ever to leave a boat under an enemy ship and to attach limpet mines; in fact, he was the only frogman to operate from an X-craft in harbour against enemy shipping'.

As a torpedoman and an electrician's mate in the Navy, Magennis worked as an electrician at Harland & Wolff's after the war. In 1952 he was in the news, because he had sold his VC for £75. 'I'm ashamed at having to sell the VC,' he was quoted as saying. 'The medal meant a lot to me. But what is the use of a medal when you need money for your family to live? The £75 has almost gone too, but we're economising and saving all we can.' After the publicity that followed the sale, Magennis's VC was bought and given back to him by a well-wisher on condition he never sold it again. In 1962, Magennis was once again news; because he was on the dole. He, his wife and his two sons were living on a council estate in Bradford, when he lost his job as a television and radio engineer. Few knew he was a VC, 'and I don't expect them to care,' he said. 'That was all a long time ago. No one should live on his past exploits. All I want is a steady job so that I can get out from under my wife's feet.' Magennis found that, to be a VC, meant public interest in all his misfortunes.

Captain W.R. Fell RN, *The Sea our Shield* (London: Cassell 1966).
Ian Fraser, *Frogman VC* (London: Angus & Robertson, 1957).
C.E.T. Warren and James Benson, *Above Us the Waves* (London: Harrap, 1953).

Robert Hampton Gray:
Onagawa Wan, Honshu, Japan, August 1945

Gray's posthumous VC was the last of the Second World War and in a sense the saddest. The war was so nearly over. The cause for which Gray gave his life was already won.

After the Battle of Leyte Gulf in October 1944, Japan lay almost prostrate as a naval power. In the later campaigns to secure the Philippines and in the operations off Iwo Jima and Okinawa in 1945, the Japanese used *kamikaze* suicide aircraft against Allied ships as a substitute for a fleet at sea; the last voyage of the giant battleship *Yamato* in April 1945 was itself a *kamikaze* sortie on a Homeric scale. By July and August 1945 the US Third Fleet, with ten aircraft carriers, and the British Pacific Fleet, with four, were able to operate off the Japanese mainland with virtual impunity, carrying out air strikes on airfields and the remnants of the immobilised Japanese Navy, as well as surface bombardments, submarine operations and air minelaying in Japanese waters.

Lieutenant R.H. Gray RCNVR was Senior Pilot of 1841 Squadron, flying Corsair Mark IVs from the aircraft carrier *Formidable* (Captain P. Ruck-Keene). She had relieved *Illustrious* in the British Pacific Fleet at Leyte in April 1945 and, surviving two serious *kamikaze* attacks in May, served with the fleet until the Japanese surrender. Gray joined 1841 in June 1944, replacing a pilot who had been shot down over the *Tirpitz* in Kaafjord. Gray himself took part in later attacks on *Tirpitz* in July and August, when his squadron acted as escort for the Barracuda bomber force and broke off to strafe targets of opportunity in the fjord. Gray was mentioned in despatches for his own attack on three *Narvik* class German destroyers, anchored at the end of the fjord, where they could add to the flak barrage over *Tirpitz*. Part of Gray's Corsair's tail-plane was shot away and the aircraft itself damaged.

Camera guns were mounted and their developed film later told the story. Gray's squadron CO Lieutenant-Commander Richard Bigg-Wither RNVR, later wrote that he

...would never forget Hammy's comments when his first film came up to show him opening fire at the bridge at fairly long range - then a series of black flashes (it was a negative film, of course) appeared from the AA guns fore and aft and his aim shifted aft and held until at point-blank range flying right down the barrels only the after guns and a huge black flash filled the screen. Hammy turned round to the operator and said, 'Hey, are you sure you haven't got my film mixed up with someone else's? This is really giving me the twitch - I shall have to have a very serious talk with that pilot,' and when assured that it really was his, 'Well, all I can say is they make them mighty dumb in Nelson BC.' I think this story exactly illustrates his character and of course he went up next day and did exactly the same.

'Perhaps', Bigg-Wither added significantly, 'this is where he acquired his dislike for enemy destroyers which ended so tragically in Onagawa Wan a year later.'

A year later, Gray had flown in innumerable fighter-bomber strikes - RAMRODS, as they were named - against airfields in the Sakishima Gunto and in Japan. On the 24th, 25th and 28th July, he took part in strafing and bombing attacks against Japanese shipping, including a destroyer, and his DSC for his 'determination and address' was gazetted on 21st August, after his death.

On 9th August, it was clear the war was nearly over. The first atomic bomb had been dropped on Hiroshima on the 6th and the second was actually dropped on Nagasaki that day. Bigg-Wither led the first RAMROD of twelve Corsairs that morning and 'Hammy' Gray the second, with eight Corsairs. Ruck-Keene had asked his squadron COs to 'take it easy' and not to take undue risks.

Bigg-Wither passed the caution on to Gray and the other pilots. They were to 'do the rounds of the airfields, making one pass only at each, keep the kamikazes grounded, and do what damage we could'.

Gray did not let the caution affect his flying. The fleets that day were about 150 miles east of the northern end of the island of Honshu, and the targets for the day were airfields around the coastal towns of Matsushima, Maizuru, Shiogama, and shipping in Onagawa Wan (Bay). The Corsairs often carried two 500-lb bombs which the pilots naturally wished to find targets for as soon as possible, to leave their aircraft freer for manoeuvring and strafing. As Gray's RAMROD flew over the bay, they were fired on by a destroyer, camouflaged and close inshore, and the batteries surrounding it. Gray decided this was a most suitable target. He flew down to within fifty feet of the destroyer's masts and dropped both bombs. The destroyer sank, but Gray's Corsair caught fire and crashed. It was a magnificent feat of agressive flying, what Rear-Admiral Vian, commanding the carriers, called 'his brilliant fighting spirit and inspired leadership, an unforgettable example of selfless and sustained devotion to duty without regard to safety of life and limb'. But Bigg-Wither and the others in the Squadron had mixed feelings: 'It has always seemed such a terrible shame to me that this quite unexpected chance should have occurred when the war was virtually over.' While Gray's RAMROD were landing on *Formidable* without him, another pilot crashed on deck and was killed; the following day, one of 1841 Squadron's best pilots was shot down making a second strafing run on an airfield. 'It was a very sad end of the war for us.'

Gray's posthumous VC was gazetted on 13th November 1945 (so long after the war ended that, twenty years later, many men in the British Pacific Fleet were quite unaware that one of them had won a VC). The Cross was presented to Gray's parents by the Earl of Athlone, the Governor-General of Canada, at Ottawa in February 1946.

Robert Hampton Gray was born on 2nd November 1917 in Trail, British Columbia, the eldest son of John Balfour and Wilhelmina Gray. The family moved to Nelson, British Columbia, where Mr Gray had a jewellery business. Gray went to Nelson High School and to the University of Alberta for a year from 1937 to 1938, and then spent two years as a medical student at the University of British Columbia.

'Hammy' was a universally likeable fellow. At school he was 'a good student, always pleasant and courteous, quiet-spoken, and with a fine spirit of co-operation.' 'At university,' 'wherever "Hammy" went he made friends, not only because of his high good fellowship and his wonderful sense of humour but because he was unselfish and honest and was never known to do anyone a bad turn'.

246

In 1940, Gray and two of his closest friends decided to enlist. He joined on 3rd August 1940 reporting at HMCS *Stadacona*, Halifax, and was sent with a draft of seventy-five men across the Atlantic to *St Vincent* in Gosport for training. He volunteered for the Fleet Air Arm and did six months' flying training at Colliers Bay, Kingston, Ontario. He was promoted Sub-Lieutenant RNCVR on 6th October 1941, and came back to England to join 757 Squadron at Winchester. He went out to Kenya, served with 795, 803 and 877 Squadrons and was in the carrier *Illustrious* for a time in 1943. He was promoted Lieutenant on 31st December 1942.

Gray's younger brother, John Balfour ('Jack') Gray, joined the RCAF and served as an air gunner. In December 1941 he joined 144 Squadron Bomber Command and completed one tour of operations. He was killed when his aircraft crash-landed at Doncaster, after returning from a mine-laying mission on the Elbe estuary.

Joseph Schull, *The Far Distant Ships* (Ottawa: Queen's Printer, 1961).
J. Swettenham, *Valiant Men: Canada's VC and GC Winners* (London: Seeley Service & Cooper).
John Winton, *The Forgotten Fleet* (London: Michael Joseph, 1969).
The Wardroom Officers of HMS *Formidable, A Formidable Commission* (London: Seeley Service & Co., 1945).
Nelson Daily News, Nelson, British Columbia, 14th November 1945.

Bibliography

AIR MINISTRY, *VCs of the Royal Air Force* (a calendar) (London: HMSO 1949).

BARNETT, G., *VCs of the Air: The glorious record of men of the British Empire Air Force awarded the Victoria Cross for valour. With an additional chapter on heroes of America* (London: Burrow, 1919).

BEETON, S.O., *Our Soldiers and the Victoria Cross* (London: Ward Lock, 1967).

BENSON, A.C., and Viscount ESHER (editors), *The Letters of Queen Victoria, 1837–61, Volume III* (London: John Murray, 1907)

BOYLE, W.H.D., *Gallant Deeds: A record of the circumstances under which the Victoria Cross, Conspicuous Gallantry Medal, or Albert Medal, were won by petty officers, non-commissioned officers and men of the Royal Navy, Royal Marines and the reserve forces during the war of 1914-1918* (London: Gieves, 1919)

BRANCH, N., *The Boy's Book of VC Heroes* (London: Publicity Products, 1953)

BURKE, Peter, 'Behind the Cross' (Lloyd's Log, Vol.45, No.11, November 1974)

CREAGH, General Sir O'Moore, and HUMPHRIS, H.M., *The VC and DSO Volume I, The Victoria Cross from its institution in 1856 to date; Volumes II and III, The DSO, 1886 to date* (Standard Art Book Co., 1924)

CROOK, M.J., *The Evolution of the Victoria Cross* (Tunbridge Wells, Kent: Midas Books, 1975, in association with the Ogilby Trusts)

DAVIES, Glanville J. 'The Wreck of the SS *Sarah Sands*: The Victoria Cross Warrant of 1858', *Mariner's Mirror*, Vol.61, No.1, February 1975

DORLING, Captain H.T., and GUILE, L.F., *Ribbons and Medals*, 2nd Impression with enlarged Supplement (London: George Philip & Son Ltd., 1963)

HARE-SCOTT, Kenneth, *For Valour* (London: Peter Garnett, 1949)

HAYDON, A.L., *The Book of the VC* (London:Andrew Melrose, 1906)

IMPERIAL WAR MUSEUM, *Illustrated Handbook of the VC and GC* Cox and Wyman (printers) 1970

IRWIN, D. Hastings, *War Medals and Decorations* (London: Upcott Gill, 1890)

JAMESON, Sir William, *Submariners VC* (London: Peter Davies, 1962)

JOCELYN, Captain A., *The Orders, Decorations and Medals of the World – The British Empire* (London: Nicholson & Watson, 1934)

JOHNS, Captain William Earl, *The Air VCs* (London: Hamilton, 1935)

JOHNSON, Stanley C., *The Medals of our Flying Men* (London: A. & C. Black, 1917)

The Medal Collector. A Guide to Naval, Military, Air Force and Civil Medals and Ribbons (London: Herbert Jenkins, 1921)

KNOLLYS, Lieutenant-Colonel W.W. *The Victoria Cross in the Crimea* (Deeds of Daring Library) (London: Dean, 1877)

LEASK, George A., *VC Heroes of the War* (London: Harrap, 1917)

LEE, P.H., *The Victoria Cross* 2nd Edition Huddersfield, Preston, 1912

LEYLAND, E., *For Valour: The Story of the Victoria Cross* (London: Edmund Wald, 1960)

LONG, W.H., *Medals of the British Navy, and How They Were Won* (London: Norie & Wilson, 1895)

LUCAS-PHILLIPS, C.E., *Victoria Cross Battles of the Second World War* (London: Heinemann, 1973)

LUMMIS, Canon W.M., *The Roll of the Victoria Cross*, privately printed in Belgaum, India, 1925.

The Victoria Cross, List showing number of Crosses won by branches of His Majesty's forces, corps, regiments and units. Held in Imperial War Museum (1950).

The LUMMIS FILES. Held in Imperial War Museum.

MACHUM, Colonel George C., *Canada's VCs* (Toronto: McClelland & Stewart, 1956)

MAYO, John Horsley, *Medals and Decorations of the British Army and Navy* (London: Constable, 1897)

MINISTRY OF INFORMATION, *VC, Stories of Victoria Cross awards during the Second World War up to June 1943*, Robinson (printers) 1943

MUDDOCK, J.E., *For Valour* (London: Hutchinson, 1895)

Orders, Decorations and Medals Research Society of Great Britain, *Orders and Medals Bulletin* (mineographed) 1958

Orders, Decorations and Medals, A select bibliography edited by A.A. Purvis (London: Spink, 1958)

PARRY, D.H., *Britain's Roll of Glory* (new and revised edition) (London: Cassells, 1898)

The RANKEN FILES. Held in Imperial War Museum.

ROBERTS, T.G. (Editor), *Thirty Canadian VCs, 23rd April 1915 to 30th March 1918*, compiled by the Canadian War Records Office, Skeffington, 1918

ROBERTSON, B. (Editor), *Air Aces of the 1914-1918 War* (Letchworth: Barleyford Publications, 1959)

ROBSON, J.O., 'The First Presentation of the Victoria Cross', *Journal of the Royal United Service Institution*, Vol. LXXXVII (1942)

ROE, F. Gordon, *The Bronze Cross* (London: P.R. Cawthorn, 1945)

SMYTH, Brigadier The Rt.Hon.Sir John, Bt., VC, MC, *The Story of the Victoria Cross 1856-1963* (London: Muller, 1963)

Great Stories of the Victoria Cross (London: Arthur Barker, 1977)

STANAWAY, Kate, *Britain's Calendar of Heroes* (London: Allen & Unwin, 1914)

STEWART, Lieutenant-Colonel Rupert MVO, *The Victoria Cross: The Empire's Roll of Valour* (London: Hutchinson, 1928)

Strand Magazine, 'Sailor VCs', Vol. XII, July-December 1896 (London: Newnes)

SWETTENHAM, J., *Valiant Men; Canada's VC and GC Winners* (London: Seeley Service & Cooper, 1975)

The Times, 29th July 1959, 'Unconditional Award of £100 Tax-Free Annuity for VCs'

TOOMEY, Colour-Sgt. T.E., *Victoria Cross and How Won* (London: Alfred Boot, 1890)

Heroes of the Victoria Cross (London: Newnes, 1895)

TURNER, John Frayn, *VCs of the Royal Navy* (London: Harrap, 1956)

UYS, Ian, *For Valour: The History of South Africa's VC Heroes* (London: Seeley Service & Cooper, 1970)

Victoria Cross. An official chronicle of deeds of personal valour achieved in the presence of the enemy during the Crimea and Baltic Campaigns, the Indian Mutinies and the Persia, China and New Zealand Wars, Third Edition (London: O'Byrne Bros., 1866)

VICTORIA CROSS CENTENARY EXHIBITION CATALOGUE, Marlborough House 15th June-7th July 1956, Stories of the winning of the Victoria Cross which are represented in the Exhibition, Hazell Watson & Viney (printers) 1965

VULLIEZ, A. *Victoria Cross, Trois heros de la Marine Anglaise* (Paris: Bonne, 1949)

WAR OFFICE, Alphabetical list of recipients of the Victoria Cross during the campaign from August 1914 to 30th April 1920; list of recipients of the Victoria Cross (mimeographed) 1953.

WIGMORE. L., and HARDING. B., *They Dared Mightily* (Canberra: Australian War Memorial ACT, 1963)

WILKINS, Philip Aveling, *The History of the Victoria Cross* (London: Constable, 1904)

WILSON, Sir Arnold, and McEWEN, J.H.F., *Gallantry* (Oxford: OUP, 1939)

Battles and Campaigns

ALEXANDER, Colonel Sir James, *History of the Maori War*

BONNER-SMITH, David (ed.), 'The Russian War 1855', Baltic Official Correspondence; Navy Records Society, vol.LXXXIV (1944)

BONNER-SMITH, David, and DEWAR, Captain A.C., RN (eds), 'The Russian War 1854, Baltic and Black Sea', Official Correspondence; Navy Records Society, vol LXXXIII (1943)

BUSH, Captain Eric W., DSO, DSC, RN, *Gallipoli* (London: Allen & Unwin, 1975)

CORBETT, Sir Julian, and NEWBOLT, Henry, *Naval Operations*; the official history of the war, July 1914 to November 1918, five volumes, 1920-31

CHURCHILL, Sir Winston, *The Second World War*, six volumes (London: Cassell, 1949-54)

DEWAR, Captain A.C., RN (ed.), 'The Russian War 1855, Black Sea', Official Correspondence; Navy Records Society, Vol. LXXXV (1945)

GRAY, Edwin, *A Damned Un-English Weapon*: the story of submarine warfare 1914-1918 (London: Seeley, Service & Co., 1971)

JELLICOE of SCAPA, Admiral Viscount, GCB, OM, GCVO, *The Grand Fleet 1914-16: Its Creation, Development and Work* (London: Cassell, 1919)

JERROLD, Douglas, *The Royal Naval Division* (London: Hutchinson, 1923)

KINGLAKE, Alexander W., *The Invasion of the Crimea*, 8 volumes, (Edinburgh and London: Blackwood & Sons, 1863)

LAIRD CLOWES, Sir William, *The Royal Navy, A History from the Earliest Times to the Present*, seven volumes (London: Sampson Low, Marston, vol. VI [1901] and vol. VII [1903]

LOW, Charles Rathbone, *History of the Indian Navy (1613-1863)* (London: Richard Bentley & Son, 1877)

MACINTYRE, Captain Donald, DSO, DSC, RN *Jutland* (London: Evans Bros., 1957)

MARS, Commander Alastair,DSO, DSC, RN, *Submarines at War 1939-1945*, (London: William Kimber, 1971)

MOOREHEAD, Alan, *Gallipoli* (London: Hamish Hamilton, 1956)

MURRAY, Joseph, *Gallipoli 1915* (London: William Kimber, 1965)

ROSKILL, Captain Stephen, DSC, RN, *The War at Sea 1939-45*, three volumes (London: HMSO, 1954-1961)

ROWBOTHAM, Commander W.B., RN, 'Naval Brigades in the Indian Mutiny 1857-58', *Navy Records Society*, vol LXXXVII (1947)

RUSSELL, Sir William Howard, *Russell's Dispatches from the Crimea 1854-1856*, ed. Nicolas Bentley (London: Andre Deutsch, 1966)

Index

253

256